WORK AND UNEMPLOYMENT
1834–1911

WORK AND UNEMPLOYMENT 1834–1911

Edited by
Marjorie Levine-Clark

Volume I

The Meanings of Work

Routledge
Taylor & Francis Group
LONDON AND NEW YORK

First published 2022
by Routledge
2 Park Square, Milton Park, Abingdon, Oxon OX14 4RN

and by Routledge
52 Vanderbilt Avenue, New York, NY 10017

Routledge is an imprint of the Taylor & Francis Group, an informa business

British Library Cataloguing-in-Publication Data
A catalogue record for this book is available from the British Library

Library of Congress Cataloging-in-Publication Data
A catalog record for this book has been requested

ISBN: 978-0-367-33510-6 (set)
eISBN: 978-0-429-32033-0 (set)
ISBN: 978-0-367-33515-1 (volume I)
eISBN: 978-0-429-32032-3 (volume I)

DOI: 10.4324/9780429320323

Typeset in Times New Roman
by Apex CoVantage, LLC

CONTENTS

Acknowledgments *ix*
Bibliography *xii*

General introduction **1**

Volume 1 Introduction **20**

PART 1
The respectability of honest toil **33**

1 W. Cobbett, 'To the Labourers of England, on Their Duties and Their Rights' (1831) **35**

2 J. Livesey, 'An Address to Working Men' (1838) **41**

3 J. F. Bray, *Labour's Wrongs and Labour's Remedy* (1839) **48**

4 Anon., 'The Production and Distribution of Wealth' (1840) **51**

5 J. Adshead, *Distress in Manchester: Evidence (Tabular and Otherwise) of the State of the Labouring Classes in 1840–42* (1842) **58**

6 The *British Workman* on the nobility of labour **65**

6.1 M. Howitt, 'Labourer's Thanksgiving Hymn', British Workman *(1856)* 67

6.2 Rev N. Hall, 'The Dignity of Labour', British Workman *(1856)* 68

6.3 'No. I. – The Working Man', British Workman *(1859)* 72

7 **Rev. A. Oxenden, 'The Labourer at His Work', in *The Labouring Man's Book* (1860)** **75**

8 **Dr J. C. Hall, *The Trades of Sheffield . . . Read before the National Association for the Promotion of Social Science*, 2nd ed. (1865)** **82**

9 **J. B. Glasier, 'Honest Toil' (c. 1890)** **100**

10 **G. Milligan, 'A Man and His Work', 'Only a Working Man', and 'The Toiler's Toast', in *Life Through Labour's Eyes* (1911)** **106**

PART 2
Men and machines **115**

11 **Society for the Diffusion of Useful Knowledge, *The Working Man's Companion: The Results of Machinery . . . An Address to Working Men* (1831)** **117**

12 **Anon., *The Petition of the Undersigned Operative Spinners and Others Employed in the Spinning of Cotton Wool into Yarn, in Ashton-under-Lyne and Its Neighbourhood* (1832)** **129**

13 **G. C. Burrows, 'Introduction', 'Letter I', 'Letter VI', and 'Appendix' in *A Word to Electors. Letters to the Present Generation on the Unrestrained Use of Modern Machinery Particularly Addressed to my Countrymen and Fellow Citizens* (1832)** **133**

14 **Debating political economy and the condition of the handloom weavers** **144**

14.1 G. P. Scrope, The Letter of George Poulett Scrope, Esq., M.P., to the Chairman of the Central Committee of the Hand Loom Worsted Weavers, of the West-Riding of York: With Their Answer to the Same *(1835)* 146

14.2 J. Dewhirst, 'To George Poulett Scrope, Esq., M.P.', Poor Man's Guardian, *1 August 1835* 148

15 **J. Maxwell, *Manual Labour versus Machinery* (1834)** **157**

16 Anon., 'The Present Condition of British Workmen' (1834) 174

17 H. Leggeth and S. Cowle, 'The Address of the Female Chartists of Manchester to Their Sisters of England, Ireland, Scotland, and Wales' (24 July 1841) 176

18 W. Carpenter, 'The Question of Machinery Fairly Stated', 'Machinery Creates a Demand for Manual Labour', and 'Condition of the Hand-Loom Weavers', in *Machinery as It Affects the Industrial Classes and the Employment of Children in Factories* (1844) 181

19 Literary depictions of mechanization 193

19.1 C. Dickens, chapter 5 'The Key-Note', Hard Times *(1854)* 195
19.2 B. Brierley, 'Out of Work', in Tales and Sketches of Lancashire Life *(1885)* 197

20 J. Samuelson, 'Introductory', 'The Displacement of Hand-Labour in Agriculture', 'Displacement of General Labourers by Machinery', and 'Inferences – The General Question of Labour – Conclusion', in *Labour-Saving Machinery* (1893) 201

PART 3
Women's work: productive and reproductive 221

21 J. Livesey, 'To the Females Employed in Factories and All Our Large Manufacturing Establishments' (1 February 1832) 223

22 Chartist women 233

22.1 Anon., 'Miss Mary Anne Walker on the People's Charter', Northern Star *(1842)* 235
22.2 S. Price, 'Address of the Female National Charter Association of Upper Honley and Smallthorn' (1842) 237

23 *Reports of Special Assistant Poor Law Commissioners on the Employment of Women and Children in Agriculture* (1843) 240

24 **E. Copley, 'Introduction' to *The Young Women of the Factory, or Friendly Hints on Their Duties and Dangers* (c. 1840)** **254**

25 **Anon., 'Female Education and Female Labour' (1845)** **258**

26 **M. F. Tupper, 'The Workwoman', in *A Dozen Ballads for the Times about White Slavery* (1854)** **263**

27 **Sentimental Depictions of Working-class Women in the *British Workman*** **267**

27.1 Anon., 'A Few Words to the Wives of Working Men', British Workman *(1856)* 268
27.2 Anon., 'Finery and Freedom, or "Lucy's Choice"', British Workman *(1858)* 269

28 **A. Munro, 'Our Unemployed Females, and What May Best Be Done for Them' in *Transactions of the Manchester Statistical Society* (1863)** **276**

29 **T. Wright, 'Working Men's Homes and Wives', in *The Great Unwashed* (1868)** **287**

30 **J. B. Kinnear, 'The Social Position of Women in the Present Age', in *The Right of Women to Labour* (1873)** **294**

31 **M. Harkness, 'Palm-Workers', in *Toilers in London; or Inquiries Concerning Female Labour in the Metropolis* (1889)** **304**

32 **G. Reid et al., 'Legal Restraint upon the Employment of Women in Factories before and after Childbirth' (30 July 1892)** **311**

33 **Anon., 'Health of Lead Workers' (December 1893)** **321**

34 **E. Dilke, 'Preface', in A. Bulley and M. Whitley, *Women's Work* (1894)** **327**

35 **H. Bosanquet, *Economics of Women's Work and Wages* (1907)** **334**

Index *343*

ACKNOWLEDGMENTS

This collection became a project of the coronavirus pandemic. Who knew – in June 2019, when I spent a month in London doing research – that I would not be able to return to do additional work? This made the excellent assistance I received from librarians and archivists at the Senate House Library, University of London; the Reading Room at the London School of Economics and Political Science; the National Archives; the London Metropolitan Archives; and the British Library all the more important. I want to give a special appreciation to the staff at Senate House, who pulled documents they were in the process of digitizing so that I could use them. I was able to spend that month in London thanks to a University of Colorado Denver Office of Research Services Large Research Grant. While at home, the fantastic digital collections at the University of Denver allowed me to continue my research during the lockdown without being terribly frustrated. I have my husband, Michael Levine-Clark, dean of libraries at the University of Denver, to thank for access to those materials.

The pandemic lockdowns and remote work provided me with unanticipated extra time for this project, but the time was often anxious and unproductive due to the circumstances. I am extremely grateful to Rachel Douglas, the editor for Routledge Historical Resources, for being incredibly understanding of the erratic nature of completing a project during a pandemic and for her overall support and enthusiasm. Her interest in the direction I wanted to take with the collection was encouraging from the outset. Many thanks also to Simon Alexander, senior development editor, for answering many questions (sometimes the same one more than once, I imagine) and for his kind assistance throughout. Marie Roberts patiently took me through the production process, and I deeply appreciated her cheerful emails during a stressful time.

My colleagues in the College of Liberal Arts and Sciences' Dean's Office at the University of Colorado at Denver received more updates about this collection than they probably wanted. Dean Pam Jansma and associate deans Rich Allen, Laura Argys, Kathleen Bollard, Stephanie Santorico, and David Tracer took on more than their fair share of work as I buried myself in writing. I cannot begin to convey my thanks to all of them for their patience, good spirits, and friendship as I received multiple extensions that made me less present as an associate dean. They were all rock stars in helping get CU Denver through the worst of the pandemic.

Chris Agee, friend and chair of the History Department, celebrated this collection from its early days; that mattered a lot. Historian friends in Denver and elsewhere listened (enthusiastically?) as I worked through the phases of this project. Many thanks to Phil Harling (over a pint during that first and only research trip to London), Pete Kopp, Pam Laird, Rachel Gross, Dale Stahl, Andy August, Nadja Durbach, Susie Steinbach, Dani Picard, Greg Smith, Chris Frank, Tim Jenks, Paul Deslandes, Jamie Bronstein, Philippa Levine, Lara Kriegel, Jim Rosenheim, and many others my pandemic brain is blocking out. Thanks to Lia Paradis, host of 'Historians Happy Hour' on Zoom, which brought together colleagues and friends old and new on Sunday evenings. Thanks to the Facebook historian community who jumped in whenever I posted a query about some random question I was unable to answer without access to the research materials. Thanks to the North American Conference on British Studies for creating an intellectual and collegial community so needed during stressful times.

Historians are obviously not immune from our own historical contexts. The pain of the world around me – the pandemic, the economic insecurity enhanced by COVID, the murder of George Floyd, the needed reckoning with systemic racism – sometimes made it hard to concentrate but also informed my thinking as I put this collection together. I work with some amazing people who helped me process the sadness and anger, learn how to be a better listener, and find ways to take action: deep gratitude to the College of Liberal Arts and Sciences Council on Diversity, Equity, and Inclusion; the Social Justice Teach-In Leadership; the Restorative Justice working group; CU Denver Antiracist Advocacy and Action, especially Katy Mohrman, Katherine Miller, Amy Ferrell, Sarah Hagelin, Sarah Tyson, and Jacob McWilliams; the Inclusive Pedagogy Academy Team; and Soyon Bueno, Faye Caronan, and Brenda J. Allen.

For much of the lockdown, on Saturday evenings, Michael and I Zoomed with Beth Allen, Rich Allen, David Hildebrand, Margaret Woodhull, Gillian Silverman, and Philip Joseph. These dear, dear friends lifted me in hard times and generally sustained me through the months when it felt like all I did was work on this collection. I am always grateful for having them in my life. Laura Argys continually inspired me during our regular conversations over drinks, virtual and in-person, about our simultaneous research projects and other not-so-serious subjects. Although we didn't connect as often, I drew tremendous strength from the friendship of Jill Cooper, Maren Stephenson, Bridget Rosenberg, Jeff Schweinfest, Natalie Schaefer, Tess Jones, and Catherine Rymph. Kolby Morris-Dahary, Caryn Aviv, and the rest of the Shabbat aLive crew gave me something I didn't know I needed, but I needed it a lot. Thanks go to them for providing such a warm and welcoming community. I am also deeply indebted to the fantastic women – Sania Killion, Jenny Ettinger, Dana Dreifus, and Chantal O'Brien – who worked at keeping my neck, back, and migraines healthy enough that I could continue to write.

A collection of this size has to be a team effort. Mine was only a team of three. I can't heap enough praise on my research assistant, Matt Fulford, history MA student at CU Denver (and full-time high school teacher). He brilliantly organized thousands of pages of digitized materials, offered valuable feedback on drafts of introductions and headnotes, and provided a ready Zoom screen when I needed to sort through ideas. Matt worked overtime on this project, and I deeply appreciate his commitment. My daughter, Isabel Levine-Clark, was the unexpected third member of the team. The pandemic led Isabel to take a fall 2020 leave from Wesleyan University, where she is an interdisciplinary social sciences major. She became my second research assistant, gathering background on people, places, and things (her skill at finding obscure information online is truly impressive); reading multiple drafts of headnotes; doing painstaking citation work; and keeping me grounded. We spent months together in our den-turned-office devoted to this collection, developing a truly special working partnership that enriched our mother-daughter relationship. She was the glue that held this project together, and it sounds trite to say it, but I never would have finished without her. She is my star. As I write, Matt and Isabel are already drawing on sources from the collection as starting points for their theses – an excellent kick-off for the volumes.

My mom, Ann Friedman; my dad, Robert Levine; my stepmom, Anne Levine; my brother, Matt Levine, and his wife, Laurice Levine; and my in-laws, Andrea Schieckel and Jon Clark, all cheered me on from the coasts. Their love and support kept me energized in difficult times, but, boy, did I miss them during the lockdown. At home in Denver, my old pup Theo shared my writing space, with his soft snores providing constant comfort. My remarkable husband, Michael, cooked, cleaned, did laundry, and shopped, nurturing me with the work of the everyday that gave me the gift of time and more time. I cherished this, and him, beyond what I can communicate.

Jeff Cox, my graduate advisor at the University of Iowa, died suddenly in February 2020. I was fortunate to have been able to spend time with him at a conference just a few months before. Jeff introduced me to classic British labour history and then challenged me to reinterpret it. I am the historian I am today because of him. His warm support over the years meant the world to me. As I told his wife, Lois, at his memorial service, I think Jeff may have been my biggest fan. I miss him dearly. I dedicate this project to his memory.

BIBLIOGRAPHY

Secondary sources

Abel, E. K., 'Toynbee Hall, 1884–1914', *Social Service Review*, 53:4 (December 1979), pp. 606–632.

Allett, J., *New Liberalism: The Political Economy of J.A. Hobson* (Toronto: University of Toronto Press, 1981).

Auerbach, J., *The Great Exhibition of 1851: A Nation on Display* (New Haven, CT: Yale University Press, 1999).

August, A., *Poor Women's Lives: Gender, Work, and Poverty in Late Victorian London* (Madison, NJ: Fairleigh Dickinson University Press, 1999).

August, A., *The British Working Class 1832–1940* (New York: Pearson Education Limited, 2007).

Bailey, V., '"In Darkest England and the Way Out": The Salvation Army, Social Reform and the Labour Movement, 1895–1910', *International Review of Social History*, 29: 2 (1984), pp. 133–171.

Baines, D., *Migration in a Mature Economy: Emigration and Internal Migration in England and Wales, 1861–1900* (Cambridge: Cambridge University Press, 1985).

Bales, K., 'Popular Reactions to Sociological Research: The Case of Charles Booth', *Sociology*, 33:1 (February 1999), pp. 153–168.

Ballhatchet, J., 'The Police and the London Dock Strike of 1889', *History Workshop*, 32 (1991), pp. 54–68.

Bartrip, P. W. J., *The Home Office and the Dangerous Trades: Regulating Occupational Disease in Victorian and Edwardian Britain* (New York: Rodopi, 2002).

Belich, J., 'The Rise of the Angloworld: Settlement in North America and Australasia, 1784–1918,' in P. A. Buckner (ed), *Rediscovering the British World* (University of Calgary Press, 2005).

Berg, M. and P. Hudson, 'Rehabilitating the Industrial Revolution', *Economic History Review'*, New Series 45:1 (Feb. 1992), pp. 24–50.

Bernstein, G. L., 'Liberals, the Irish Famine, and the Role of the State', *Irish Historical Studies*, 29:116 (Nov. 1995), pp. 513–536.

Bevir, M. *The Making of British Socialism* (Princeton: Princeton University Press, 2011), pp. 97–114.

Blackburn, S., '"No necessary connection with homework": Gender and sweated labour, 1840–1909', *Social History*, 22:3 (1997), pp. 269–285.

Blackburn, S., *A Fair Day's Wage for a Fair Day's Work? Sweated Labour and the Origins of Minimum Wage Legislation in Britain* (Burlington, VT: Ashgate, 2006).

Bland, L., *Banishing the Beast: English Feminism and Sexual Morality, 1885–1914* (London: Penguin, 1995).

Bland, L. and L. Hall, 'Eugenics in Britain: The View from the Metropole', in A. Bashford and P. Levine (eds), *The Oxford Handbook of the History of Eugenics* (Oxford: Oxford University Press, 2012), pp. 214–223.

Blaug, M., 'The Myth of the Old Poor Law and the Making of the New', *Journal of Economic History*, 23:2 (1963), pp. 151–184.

Boss, H., *Theories of Surplus and Transfer: Parasites and Producers in Economic Thought* (London: Unwin Hyman, 1989).

Boyer, G. R., *An Economic History of the English Poor Law, 1750–1850* (Cambridge: Cambridge University Press, 1990).

Boyer, G. R. 'Poor Relief, Informal Assistance, and Short Time during the Lancashire Cotton Famine', *Explorations in Economic History*, 34:1 (1997), pp. 56–76.

Boyer, G. R., 'The Evolution of Unemployment Relief in Great Britain', *Journal of Interdisciplinary History*, 34:3 (2004), pp. 393–433.

Boyer, G. R., *The Winding Road to the Welfare State: Economic Insecurity and Social Policy in Britain* (Princeton, NJ: Princeton University Press, 2018).

Bradshaw, D. J. and S. Ozment (eds), *The Voice of Toil: Nineteenth-century British Writings about Work* (Athens, Ohio: Ohio University Press, 2000).

Briar, C., *Working for Women?: Gendered Work and Welfare Policies in Twentieth-century Britain* (London: UCL Press, 1997).

Briggs, A., 'Samuel Smiles and the Gospel of Work', in *Victorian People: A Reassessment of Persons and Themes, 1851–1867* (Chicago: University of Chicago Press, 1975, orig. 1955).

Brodie, M., 'Artisans and Dossers: The 1886 West End Riots and the East End Casual Poor', *The London Journal*, 24:2 (1999), pp. 34–50.

Bronstein, J., *Caught in the Machinery: Workplace Accidents and Injured Workers in Nineteenth-Century Britain* (Stanford, CA: Stanford University Press, 2008).

Brown, J., 'Charles Booth and Labour Colonies', *Economic History Review*, 21:2 New Series (Aug. 1968), pp. 349–360.

Brown, K. D., 'Conflict in Early British Welfare Policy: The Case of the Unemployed Workmen's Bill of 1905', *Journal of Modern History* 43:4 (Dec. 1971), pp. 615–629.

Brundage, A., *The Making of the New Poor Law: The Politics of Inquiry, Enactment, and Implementation, 1832–1839* (New Brunswick, NJ: Rutgers University Press, 1978).

Brundage, A., 'Private Charity and the 1834 Poor Law', in D. T. Critchlow and C. H. Parker (eds.), *With Us Always: A History of Private Charity and Public Welfare* (Oxford: Rowman and Littlefield, 1998), pp. 99–119.

Brundage, A., *The English Poor Laws, 1700–1930* (New York: Palgrave Macmillan, 2001).

Burnett, J., *Idle Hands: The Experience of Unemployment, 1790–1990* (New York: Routledge, 1994).

Burton, A., *At the Heart of Empire: Indians and the Colonial Encounter in Late Victorian Britain* (Berkeley: University of California Press, 1998).

Bush, J., '"Special Strengths for Their Own Special Duties": Women, Higher Education and Gender Conservatism in Late Victorian Britain', *History of Education*, 34:4 (2005), pp. 387–405.

Caine, B., *Victorian Feminists* (Oxford: Oxford University Press, 1992).

Carey, J. and C. McLisky (eds.), *Creating White Australia* (Syndey: Syndey University Press, 2009).

Chase, M., 'Chartism and the Land: "The Mighty People's Question"', in M. Cragoe and P. Readman (eds), *The Land Question in Britain, 1750–1950* (New York: Palgrave Macmillan, 2010).

Childs, M. J., 'Boy Labour in Late Victorian and Edwardian England and the Remaking of the Working Class', *Journal of Social History*, 23:4 (Summer 1990), pp. 783–802.

Clark, A., *The Struggle for the Breeches: Gender and the Making of the British Working Class* (Berkeley: University of California Press, 1997).

Clark, A., 'The New Poor Law and the Breadwinner Wage: Contrasting Assumptions', *Journal of Social History*, 34:2 (Winter 2000), pp. 261–281.

Cohen, M., and M. Hanagan, 'Politics, Industrialization and Citizenship: Unemployment Policy in England, France and the United States, 1890–1950', *International Review of Social History*, 40: Supplement 3 (1995), pp. 91–129.

Constantine, S., 'British Emigration to the Empire-Commonwealth since 1880: From Overseas Settlement to Diaspora?', *Journal of Imperial and Commonwealth History*, 31:2 (2003), pp. 16–35.

Cooper, J., *The British Welfare Revolution, 1906–1914* (London: Bloomsbury Academic, 2017).

Cordery, S., *British Friendly Societies, 1750–1914* (New York: Palgrave Macmillan, 2003).

Cott, N., 'Passionlessness: An Interpretation of Victorian Sexual Ideology, 1790–1850', *Signs*, 4:2 (1978), pp. 219–236.

Cowherd, R., *Political Economists and the English Poor Laws: A Historical Study of the Influence of Classical Economics on the Formation of Social Welfare Policy* (Athens, OH: Ohio University Press, 1978).

Cragoe M., and P. Readman (eds), *The Land Question in Britain, 1750–1950* (New York: Palgrave Macmillan, 2010).

Crick, M., '"A Call to Arms": The Struggle for Socialist Unity in Britain, 1883–1914', in D. James, T. Jowitt, and K. Laybourn (eds), *The Centennial History of the Independent Labour Party* (Edinburgh: Edinburgh University Press, 1992), pp. 181–204.

Crick, M., *History of the Social Democratic Federation* (Keele: Edinburgh University Press, 1994).

Critchlow, D. T., and C. H. Parker (eds), *With Us Always: A History of Private Charity and Public Welfare* (Lanham, MD: Rowman and Littlefield, 1998).

Croley, L. S., 'A Working Distinction: Vagrants, Beggars, and the Laboring Poor in Mid-Victorian England', *Prose Studies*, 18:1 (1995), pp. 74–104.

Cronin, J. E., 'Strikes and Power in Britain', *International Review of Social History*, 32:2 (1987), pp. 144–167.

Crossick, G. (ed), *The Lower Middle Class in Britain, 1870–1914* (Croom Helm Ltd, 1977).

Crowther, M. A., *The Workhouse System, 1834–1929: The History of an English Social Institution* (London: Batsford, 1981).

Crowther, M. A., 'Family Responsibility and State Responsibility in Britain before the Welfare State', *Historical Journal*, 25:1 (1982), pp. 131–145.

Cunliffe, M., *Chattel Slavery and Wage Slavery: The Anglo-American Context, 1830–1860* (Athens: University of Georgia Press, 1979).

Darwen L. et al., '"Unhappy and Wretched Creatures": Charity, Poor Relief and Pauper Removal in Britain and Ireland during the Great Famine', *English Historical Review*, 134:568 (2019), pp. 589–619.

Daunton, M. (ed), *Charity, Self-Interest, and Welfare in the English Past* (London: UCL Press, 1996).

Daunton, M. J., *Progress and Poverty: An Economic and Social History of Britain, 1700–1850* (Oxford: Oxford University Press, 1995).

Davidoff, L., and C. Hall, *Family Fortunes: Men and Women of the English Middle Class, 1780–1850*, 3rd ed. (New York: Routledge, 2018).

Davidson, R., 'The Board of Trade and Industrial Relations, 1896–1914', *Historical Journal* 21:3 (September 1978), pp. 571–591.

Davidson, R., 'Thatcher's Legacy and Social Security', in A. Mullen, S. Farrall, and D. Jeffrey (eds), *Thatcherism in the 21st Century: The Social and Cultural Legacy* (Switzerland: Palgrave Macmillan, 2020), pp. 209–227.

Davis, G., 'The Irish in Nineteenth-Century Britain', *Saothar*, 16 (1991), pp. 130–135.

de Nie, M., *The Eternal Paddy: Irish Identity and the British Press, 1798–1882* (Madison: University of Wisconsin Press, 2004).

Digby, A., *Pauper Palaces* (London: Routledge and Kegan Paul, 1978).

Doolittle, M., 'Fatherhood and Family Shame: Masculinity, Welfare, and the Workhouse in Late Nineteenth-Century England', in L. Delap, B. Griffin, and A. Wills (eds), *The Politics of Domestic Authority in Britain since 1800* (New York: Palgrave Macmillan, 2009), pp. 84–108.

Driver, F., *Power and Pauperism: The Workhouse System, 1834–1884* (Cambridge: Cambridge University Press).

Duffy, A. E. P., 'Differing Policies and Personal Rivalries in the Origins of the Independent Labour Party', *Victorian Studies*, 6:1 (September 1962), pp. 43–65.

Dunkley, P., *The Crisis of the Old Poor Law in England, 1795–1834* (New York: Garland Publishing, 1982).

Dunn, D. S., and E. E. Andrews, 'Person-First and Identity-First Language: Developing Psychologists' Cultural Competence Using Disability Language', *American Psychologist*, 70:3 (2015), pp. 255–264.

Edsall, N. C., *The Anti-Poor Law Movement, 1834–44* (Manchester: Manchester University Press, 1971).

Ellis, H., 'Thomas Arnold, Christian Manliness and the Problem of Boyhood', *Journal of Victorian Culture*, 19 (2014), pp. 425–441.

Elliott, D. W., 'Servants and Hands: Representing the Working Classes in Victorian Factory Novels', *Victorian Literature and Culture*, 28:2 (2000), pp. 377–390.

Evans, E., *The Great Reform Act of 1832*, 2nd ed. (New York: Routledge, 2016).

Feldman, D., *Immigrants and Workers, Englishmen and Jews: Jewish Immigration to the East End of London, 1880–1906* (Cambridge: Cambridge University Press, 1985).

Feldman, D., and M. P. Baldwin. 'Emigration and British State, Ca. 1815–1925.' in N. Green and F. Reil (eds), *Citizenship and Those Who Leave: The Politics of Emigration and Expatriation* (University of Illinois Press, 2007), pp. 135–155.

Feurer, R., 'The Meaning of "Sisterhood": The British Women's Movement and Protective Labor Legislation, 1870–1900', *Victorian Studies*, 31:2 (1988), pp. 233–260.

Field, J., *Working Men's Bodies: Work Camps in Britain, 1880–1940* (Manchester University Press, 2013).

Finlayson, G., *Citizen, State, and Social Welfare in Britain, 1830–1990* (New York: Oxford University Press, 1994).

Flew, S., 'Unveiling the Anonymous Philanthropist: Charity in the Nineteenth Century', *Journal of Victorian Culture*, 20:1 (March 2015), pp. 20–33.

Frankel, O., 'Blue Books and the Victorian Reader', *Victorian Studies*, 46:2 (Winter 2004), pp. 308–318.

Fraser, D., *The Evolution of the British Welfare State: A History of Social Policy since the Industrial Revolution* (London: Macmillan, 1973).

Fraser, D. (ed), *The New Poor Law in the Nineteenth Century* (New York: St. Martin's Press, 1976).

Freeden, M., 'Eugenics and Progressive Thought: A Study in Ideological Affinity', *Historical Journal*, 22:3 (September 1979), pp. 645–671.

Freeden, M., *The New Liberalism: An Ideology of Social Reform* (Oxford: Oxford University Press, 1986).

Freeman, M., 'The Agricultural Labourer and the "Hodge" Stereotype, c. 1850–1914', *Agricultural History Review*, 49:2 (2001), pp. 172–186.

Fuchs, R., *Gender and Poverty in Nineteenth-Century Europe* (New York: Cambridge University Press, 2005).

Gagnier, R. and J. Dupré, 'On Work and Idleness', *Feminist Economics*, 1:3 (1995), pp. 96–109.

Gibson-Brydon, T. R. C., *The Moral Mapping of Victorian and Edwardian London: Charles Booth, Christian Charity, and the Poor-But-Respectable* (Quebec: McGill-Queen's University Press, 2016).

Gilbert, B. B., 'David Lloyd George: Land, the Budget, and Social Reform', *American Historical Review*, 81:5 (1976), pp. 1058–1066.

Glynn, D., '"Exporting Outcast London": Assisted Emigration to Canada, 1886–1914', *Histoire Sociale/Social History*, 15:29 (1982), pp. 209–238.

Goldman, L., 'Octavia Hill, Beatrice Webb and the Royal Commission on the Poor Laws, 1905–9: A Mid Victorian in an Edwardian World' in E. Baigent and B. Cowell (eds), *Octavia Hill, Social Activism and the Remaking of British Society* (London: University of London Press, 2016), pp. 255–274.

Gough, I., 'Marx's Theory of Productive and Unproductive Labour', *New Left Review*, 76 (1972), pp. 47–72.

Grada, C. O., *The Great Irish Famine* (Cambridge: Cambridge University Press, 2012).

Gray, R., *The Factory Question and Industrial England, 1830–1860* (Cambridge: Cambridge University Press, 2002).

Green, D., *From Artisans to Paupers: Economic Change and Poverty in London, 1790–1870* (Brookfield, VT: Ashgate Publishing, 1995).

Green, D., *Pauper Capital: London and the Poor Law, 1790–1870* (Burlington, VT: Ashgate, 2010).

Griffin, E., *Bread Winner: An Intimate History of the Victorian Economy* (New Haven: Yale University Press, 2020).

Gunn, S., 'The Ministry, the Middle Class, and the "Civilizing Mission" in Manchester, 1850–80', *Social History*, 21:1 (1996), pp. 22–36.

Haines, R. F., *Emigration and the Labouring Poor: Australian Recruitment in Britain and Ireland, 1831–1960* (New York: St. Martin's Press, 1997).

Haines, R., '"The Idle and the Drunken Won't Do There": Poverty, the New Poor Law and Nineteenth-Century Government-Assisted Emigration to Australia from the United Kingdom', *Australian Historical Studies*, 27:108 (1997), pp. 1–21.

Hall, C., 'The Early Formation of Victorian Domestic Ideology', in *White, Male and Middle Class: Explorations in Feminism and History* (Cambridge: Polity Press, 1993), pp. 75–93.
Hall, C., K. McClelland, and J. Rendall, *Defining the Victorian Nation: Class, Race, Gender and the British Reform Act of 1867* (New York: Cambridge University Press, 2000).
Hall, C., *Civilising Subjects: Metropole and Colony in the English Imagination, 1830–1867* (Chicago: University of Chicago Press, 2002).
Hammerton, A. J., *Cruelty and Companionship: Conflict in Nineteenth-Century Married Life* (New York: Routledge, 2002).
Hanagan, M., 'Citizenship, Claim-Making, and the Right to Work: Britain, 1884–1911', *Theory and Society*, 26:4 (1997), pp. 449–474.
Harper, M., 'Rhetoric and Reality: British Migration to Canada, 1867–1967', in P. A. Buckner (ed), *Canada and the British Empire* (Oxford; New York: Oxford University Press, 2010).
Harris, B., *The Origins of the British Welfare State: Social Welfare in England and Wales, 1800–1945* (New York: Palgrave Macmillan, 2004).
Harris, B., 'Parsimony and Pauperism: Poor Relief in England, Scotland and Wales in the Nineteenth and Early Twentieth Centuries', *Journal of Scottish Historical Studies*, 39:1 (2019), pp. 40–74.
Harris, B., *Famine and Fashion: Needlewomen in the Nineteenth Century* (London: Routledge, 2016).
Harris, J., *Unemployment and Politics: A Study in English Social Policy 1886–1914* (Oxford: Clarendon Press, 1972).
Harris, J., 'Between Civic Virtue and Social Darwinism: The Concept of the Residuum', in David Englander and Rosemary O'Day (eds), *Retrieved Riches: Social Investigation in Britain 1840–1914* (Brookfield, VT: Ashgate, 1995), pp. 67–87.
Harrison, B., *Not Only the Dangerous Trades: Women's Work and Health in Britain, 1880–1914* (London: Taylor and Francis, 1996).
Harrison, B. H., *Drink and the Victorians: the Temperance Question in England, 1815–1872* (Staffordshire: Keele University Press, 1994).
Harrison, J. F. C., 'The Victorian Gospel of Success', *Victorian Studies*, 1:2 (1957), pp. 155–164.
Harrison, R. J., *The Life and Times of Sidney and Beatrice Webb, 1858–1905: The Formative Years* (New York: Palgrave 2000).
Harzallah, M. S., 'The Great Irish Famine: Public Works Relief During the Liberal Administration', *Nordic Irish Studies*, 8 (2009), pp. 83–96.
Hatton, T. J., 'Emigration from the U.K., 1870–1913 and 1950–1998', *European Review of Economic History*, 8 (2004), pp. 149–169.
Hay, J. R., *The Origins of the Liberal Welfare Reforms, 1906–1914* (New York: Palgrave, 1983).
Henderson, W. O., *The Lancashire Cotton Famine, 1861–1865* (Manchester: Manchester University Press, 1934).
Hennock, E. P., 'Poverty and Social Theory in England: The Experience of the Eighteen-Eighties', *Social History*, 1:1 (1976), pp. 67–91.
Hennock, E. P., 'The Measurement of Urban Poverty: From the Metropolis to the Nation, 1880–1920', *Economic History Review*, 40:2 (May 1997), pp. 208–227.
Hewitt, M., 'The Travails of Domestic Visiting: Manchester, 1830–70', *Historical Research*, 71:175 (June 1998), pp. 196–227.
Higgs, E., 'Domestic Servants and Households', *Social History*, 8:2 (May 1983), pp. 201–210.

Hills, J., *Good Times, Bad Times: The Welfare Myth of Them and Us* (Bristol: The Policy Press, 2015).

Hilton, B., *The Age of Atonement: The Influence of Evangelicalism on Social and Economic Thought* (Oxford: Clarendon Press, 1992).

Hobsbawm, E. J., 'The Machine Breakers', *Past & Present*, 1 (1952), pp. 57–70.

Hobsbawm, E. J., 'The Labour Aristocracy in Nineteenth-Century Britain', in E. Hobsbawm, *Labouring Men: Studies in the History of Labour* (London: Weidenfield and Nicolson, 1964), pp. 272–315.

Hobsbawm, E. J., 'The "New Unionism" Reconsidered', in W. J. Mommsen and H. G. Husung (eds), *The Development of Trade Unionism in Great Britain and Germany, 1880–1914* (London: George Allen and Unwin, 1985).

Hobsbawm, E. J., *Industry and Empire: 1750 to the Present Day* (London: Penguin Books, 1990).

Hollis, P., *The Pauper Press: A Study in Working-Class Radicalism of the 1830s* (London: Oxford University Press, 1970).

Honeyman, K., *Women, Gender and Industrialisation in England, 1700–1870* (New York: St. Martin's Press, 2000).

Honeyman, K., and J. Goodman, 'Women's Work, Gender Conflict, and Labour Markets in Europe, 1500–1900', *Economic History Review*, 44:4 (1991), pp. 608–628.

Hopkins, E., *Working-Class Self-Help in Nineteenth-Century England: Responses to Industrialisation* (London: UCL Press, 1995).

Hopkins, E., *Industrialisation and Society: A Social History, 1830–1951* (London and New York: Routledge, 2000).

Horn, J., 'Machine Breaking in England and France during the Age of Revolution', *Labour*, 55 (Spring 2005), pp. 143–166.

Horn, P., *The Rise and Fall of the Victorian Servant* (New York: St. Martin's Press, 1975).

Horrell S., and J. Humphries, 'Women's Labour Force Participation and the Transition to the Male Breadwinner Family, 1790–1865', *Economic History Review*, 48:1 (Feb. 1995): 89–117.

Horrell, S., and J. Humphries, 'The Origins and Expansion of the Male Breadwinner Family: The Case of Nineteenth Century Britain', *International Review of Social History*, 42: Supplement S5 (1997), pp. 25–64.

Houghton, W. E., *The Victorian Frame of Mind, 1830–1870* (New Haven: Yale University Press, 1985).

Howell, D., *British Workers and the Independent Labour Party*, 1888–1906 (Manchester: Manchester University Press, 1906).

Howells, G., '"On Account of Their Disreputable Characters": Parish-Assisted Emigration from Rural England, 1834–1860', *History*, 88:4 (2003), pp. 587–605.

Howkins, A., 'The Discovery of Rural England' in R. Colls and P. Dodd (eds), *Englishness: Politics and Culture, 1880–1920* (London: Croom Helm, 1986), pp. 62–88.

Hulme, A. *A Brief History of Thrift* (Manchester: Manchester University Press, 2019).

Humphreys, R., *Sin, Organized Charity, and the Poor Law in Victorian England* (London: Macmillan, 1995).

Humphreys, R., *Poor Relief and Charity 1869–1945: The London Charity Organisation Society* (Basingstoke: Palgrave Macmillan UK, 2001).

Hurren, E., *Protesting About Pauperism: Poverty, Politics, and Poor Relief in Late-Victorian England, c. 1870–1914* (Rochester, NY: Boydell and Brewer, 2007).

Janssens, A., 'The Rise and Decline of the Male Breadwinner Family? An Overview of the Debate', *International Review of Social History*, 42, Supplement S5 (1997), pp. 1–23.

Johnson, G., 'Social Democracy and Labour Politics in Britain, 1892–1911', *History*, 85:277 (2000), pp. 67–87.

Johnston, H. J. M., *British Emigration Policy 1815–30: Shovelling Out Paupers'* (Oxford: Clarendon Press, 1972).

Johnston, R., 'Charity That Heals: The Scottish Labour Colony Association and Attitudes to the Able-Bodied Unemployed in Glasgow, 1890–1914', *The Scottish Historical Review*, 77:203 (April 1998), pp. 77–95.

Jones, P., and S. King, 'From Resistance to Reform: Changing Attitudes to the New Poor Law Workhouse in England and Wales' in *Pauper Voices, Public Opinion and Workhouse Reform in Mid-Victorian England* (Palgrave Macmillan, 2020) https://doi.org/10.1007/978-3-030-47839-1 [accessed 14 June 2021].

Jordan, E., 'The Exclusion of Women from Industry in Nineteenth-Century Britain', *Comparative Studies in Society and History*, 31:2 (April 1989), pp. 273–296.

Joyce, P. *Visions of the People: Industrial England and the Question of Class, 1840–1914* (New York: Cambridge University Press, 1990).

Kale, M., '"Capital Spectacles in British Frames": Capital, Empire and Indian Indentured Migration to the British Caribbean', *International Review of Social History*, 41 (1996), pp. 109–133.

Kerber, L., 'Separate Spheres, Female Worlds, Woman's Place: The Rhetoric of Women's History', *The Journal of American History*, 75 (1988), pp. 9–39.

Kidd, A., *State, Society and the Poor in Nineteenth-Century England* (Basingstoke and London: Macmillan Press Ltd, 1999).

Kidd, A., 'Philanthropy and the "Social History Paradigm"', *Social History*, 21:2 (May 1996), pp. 180–92.

Kinealy, C., *This Great Calamity: The Irish Famine, 1845–52* (Dublin: Gill and Macmillan, 1994).

King, J. E., 'Utopian or Scientific? A Reconsideration of the Utopian Socialists', *History of Political Economy*, 15:3 (1983), pp. 345–373.

King, S., and A. Tompkins (eds), *The Poor in England, 1700–1850: An Economy of Makeshifts* (New York: Palgrave, 2003).

Kirk, N., 'Fifty Years of Labour History: Challenge, Crisis, Renewal? Themes in the Labour History of Britain, 1960–2010', *Labour History Review*, 75:2 (August 2010), pp. 162–180.

Kohli, M., and J. A. D. Lorente, *The Golden Bridge: Young Immigrants to Canada, 1833–1939* (Dundurn Press, 2003).

Koven, S., *The Match Girl and the Heiress* (Princeton: Princeton University Press, 2014).

Kumar, K., 'Unemployment as a Problem in the Development of Industrial Societies: The English Experience', *Sociological Review* 32:2 (1984), pp. 185–233.

Kurz, H. D., 'Technical Progress, Capital Accumulation and Income Distribution in Classical Economics: Adam Smith, David Ricardo, and Karl Marx', *European Journal of the History of Economic Thought*, 17:5 (2010), pp. 1183–1222.

Lagneau-Ymonet, P., and B. Reynaud, 'The Making of a Category of Economic Understanding in Great Britain (1880–1931): The Unemployed', *Cambridge Journal of Economics*, 44:6 (2020), pp. 1–17.

Laite, J., *Common Prostitutes and Ordinary Citizens: Commercial Sex in London: 1885–1960* (New York: Palgrave Macmillan, 2012).

Laybourn, K., *Unemployment and Employment Policies Concerning Women in Britain, 1900–1951* (Lewiston, NY: Edwin Mellen Press, 2002).

Laybourn, K., '"Waking up to the Fact that there are any Unemployed": Women, Unemployment, and the Domestic Solution in Britain, 1918–1939', *History*, 88:4 (292) (October 2003), pp. 606–623.

Laybourn, K., *The Independent Labour Party, 1914–1939: The Political and Cultural History of a Socialist Party* (New York: Routledge, 2020).

Lees, L. H., *The Solidarities of Strangers: The English Poor Laws and the People, 1700–1948* (New York: Cambridge University Press, 1998).

Levine-Clark, M., 'Engendering Relief: Women, Ablebodiedness, and the New Poor Law in Early Victorian England', *Journal of Women's History*, 11:4 (2000), pp. 107–130.

Levine-Clark, M., *Beyond the Reproductive Body: The Politics of Women's Health and Work in Early Victorian England* (Columbus: Ohio State University Press, 2004).

Levine-Clark, M., *Unemployment, Welfare, and Masculine Citizenship: "So Much Honest Poverty" in Britain, 1870–1930* (New York: Palgrave Macmillan, 2015).

Lewis, J., *Women and Social Action in Victorian and Edwardian England* (Palo Alto, CA: Stanford University Press, 1991).

Lewis, J., *The Voluntary Sector, the State, & Social Work in Britain: The Charity Organization Society/Family Welfare Association since 1869* (Aldershot, UK: Edward Elgar, 1995).

Long, J., 'The Colour of Disorder: Women's Employment and "Protective" Intervention in the Lead Industry in Victorian England', *Women's History Review* 7:4 (1998), pp. 531–546.

Lovell, J. C., and B. C. Roberts, *A Short History of the T.U.C* (London: Macmillan, 1968).

Lowe, R., *The Welfare State in Britain since 1945*, 3rd ed. (New York: Palgrave Macmillan, 2005).

Luckin, B., 'Revisiting the Idea of Degeneration in Urban Britain, 1830–1900', *Urban History*, 33:2 (August 2006), pp. 234–253.

MacKinnon, M., 'English Poor Law Policy and the Crusade against Outrelief', *Journal of Economic History*, 47:3 (1987), pp. 603–625.

MacRaild, D.M., 'Irish Immigration and the "Condition of England" Question: The Roots of an Historiographical Tradition', *Immigrants and Minorities*, 14:1 (1995), pp. 67–85.

Mahase, R. '"Plenty a Dem Run Away" - Resistance by Indian Indentured Labourers in Trinidad, 1870–1920,' *Labor History*, 49:4 (November 2008), pp. 465–80.

Malchow, H. L., 'Trade Unions and Emigration in Late Victorian England: A National Lobby for State Aid', *Journal of British Studies*, 15:2 (Spring 1976), pp. 92–116.

Malchow, H., *Population Pressures: Emigration and Government in Late-Nineteenth-Century Britain* (Palo Alto, CA: Society for the Promotion of Science and Scholarship, 1979).

Malone, C., 'The Gendering of Dangerous Trades: Government Regulation of Women's Work in the White Lead Trade in England, 1892–1899', *Journal of Women's History*, 8:1 (Spring 1996), pp. 15–35.

Mandler, P., 'Poverty and Charity in the Nineteenth-Century Metropolis: An Introduction', in P. Mandler (ed), *The Uses of Charity: The Poor on Relief in the Nineteenth-Century Metropolis* (Philadelphia: University of Pennsylvania Press, 1990), pp. 1–37.

Mandler, P. (ed), *The Uses of Charity: The Poor on Relief in the Nineteenth-Century Metropolis* (Philadelphia: University of Pennsylvania Press, 1990).

Mansfield, M., 'Putting Moral Standards on the Map: The Construction of Unemployment and the Housing Problem in Turn-of-the-Century London', *Journal of Historical Sociology*, 21:2/3 (June 2008), pp. 166–182.

Matthews, D., '1889 and All That: New Views on the New Unionism', *International Review of Social History*, 36:1 (June 1991), pp. 24–58.

McBriar, A. M., *Fabian Socialism and English Politics, 1884–1918* (Cambridge: Cambridge University Press, 1966).

McClelland, K., 'England's Greatness, the Working Man', in C. Hall, K. McClelland, and J. Rendall (eds), *Defining the Victorian Nation: Class, Race, Gender and the Reform Act of 1867* (Cambridge and New York: Cambridge University Press, 2000), pp. 71–118.

McClelland, K., 'Masculinity and the "Representative Artisan"', in M. Roper and J. Tosh (eds), *Manful Assertions: Masculinities in Britain since 1800* (New York: Routledge, 1991), pp. 74–91.

McIvor, A., *A History of Work in Britain, 1880–1950* (New York: Palgrave, 2001).

Meacham, S., '"The Sense of an Impending Clash": English Working-Class Unrest before the First World War', *The American Historical Review*, 77:5 (1972), pp. 1343–1364.

Meacham, S., *Toynbee Hall and Social Reform, 1880–1914. The Search for Community* (New Haven, CT: Yale University Press, 1987).

Milne-Smith, A., 'Work and Madness: Overworked Men and Fears of Degeneration, 1860s – 1910s', *Journal of Victorian Culture*, 24:2 (2019), pp. 159–178.

Moorhouse, H. F., 'The Marxist Theory of the Labour Aristocracy', *Social History (London)*, 3:1 (1978), pp. 61–82.

Mort, F., *Dangerous Sexualities: Medico-Moral Politics in England since 1830*. 2nd ed. (New York: Routledge, 2000).

Murkens, J., 'Unintended Democracy' in K. Grotke and M. Prutsch, *Constitutionalism, Legitimacy, and Power* (Oxford: Oxford University Press), pp. 351–370.

Owen, D., *English Philanthropy: 1660–1960* (Cambridge, MA: Belknap Press, 1964).

Owens, J., 'Dissident Missionaries? Re-Narrating the Political Strategy of the Social-Democratic Federation, 1884–1887', *Labour History Review*, 73:2 (2008), pp. 187–207.

Outram, Q., and K. Laybourn (eds), *Secular Martyrdom in Britain and Ireland: From Peterloo to the Present* (New York: Palgrave Macmillan, 2018).

Packer, I., 'Unemployment, Taxation and Housing: The Urban Land Question in Late Nineteenth- and Early Twentieth-Century Britain', in M. Cragoe and P. Readman (eds), *The Land Question in Britain, 1750–1950* (New York: Palgrave Macmillan, 2010), pp. 201–218.

Paterson, A., 'The Poor Law in Nineteenth-Century Scotland', in D. Fraser (ed), *The New Poor Law in the Nineteenth Century* (New York: St. Martin's Press, 1976), pp. 171–193.

Peck, G., 'White Slavery and Whiteness: A Transnational View of the Sources of Working-Class Radicalism and Racism', *Labor*, 1:2 (Durham, NC: Duke University Press, 2004), pp. 41–64.

Perkin, H., *The Origins of Modern English Society*, 2nd ed. (London: Routledge, 2002).

Perry, A., *On the Edge of Empire* (Toronto: University of Toronto Press, 2001).

Pick, D., *Faces of Degeneration: A European Disorder, c. 1848–c. 1918* (Cambridge: Cambridge University Press, 1989).

Pickering, P., 'Loyalty and Rebellion in Colonial Politics: The Campaign Against Convict Transportation in Australia', in Phillip Alfred Buckner (ed), *Rediscovering the British World* (University of Calgary Press, 2005), pp. 87–107.

Pinker, R., 'New Liberalism and the Middle Way', in R.M. Page and R. Silburn (eds), *British Social Welfare in the Twentieth Century* (New York: St. Martin's Press, 1999), pp. 80–104.

Powell, D., 'The New Liberalism and the Rise of Labour, 1886–1906', *The Historical Journal*, 29:2 (1986), pp. 369–393.

Prochaska, F., *Women and Philanthropy in Nineteenth-Century England* (Oxford: Clarendon Press, 1980).

Prochaska, F., *The Voluntary Impulse: Philanthropy in Modern Britain* (London: Faber, and Faber, 1988).

Prochaska, F., *Christianity and Social Service in Modern Britain: The Disinherited Spirit* (Oxford: Oxford University Press, 2008).

Reisman, D., *The Economics of Alfred Marshall*, Routledge Revivals (New York: Routledge, 2011, orig. St. Martin's Press, 1986).

Richards, P., 'The State and Early Industrial Capitalism: The Case of the Handloom Weavers', *Past & Present*, 83:1 (1979), pp. 91–115.

Riley, J. C., *Sick, Not Dead: The Health of British Workingmen during the Mortality Decline* (Baltimore, MD: Johns Hopkins University Press, 1997).

Roberts, D., 'How Cruel Was the Victorian Poor Law?' *Historical Journal*, 6:1 (1963), pp. 97–107.

Roberts, F. D., *The Social Conscience of the Early Victorians* (Stanford, CA: Stanford University Press, 2002).

Roddy, S., J. Strange, and B. Taithe, 'Franchise Fundraising: Mansion House Appeals', in *The Charity Market and Humanitarianism in Britain, 1870–1912* (London: Bloomsbury Academic, 2019), pp. 121–142.

Roopnarine, L., 'Indian Migration during Indentured Servitude in British Guiana and Trinidad, 1850–1920', *Labor History*, 52:2 (May 2011), pp. 173–91.

Rose, M. E., 'Settlement, Removal, and the New Poor Law', in Derek Fraser (ed), *The New Poor Law in the Nineteenth Century* (London: Macmillan, 1976), pp. 25–44.

Rose, S. O., 'Gender Segregation in the Transition to the Factory: The English Hosiery Industry, 1850–1910', *Feminist Studies*, 13:1 (Spring 1987), pp. 163–184.

Rose, S. O., *Limited Livelihoods: Gender and Class in Nineteenth-Century England* (Berkeley: University of California Press, 1992).

Rose, S. O., 'Respectable Men, Disorderly Others: The Language of Gender and the Lancashire Weavers' Strike of 1878 in Britain', *Gender and History*, 5:3 (1993), pp. 382–397.

Rose, S. O., 'Protective Labour Legislation in Nineteenth Century Britain: Gender, Class, and the Liberal State', in L. L. Frader and S. O. Rose (eds) *Gender and Class in Modern Europe* (Ithaca, NY: Cornell University Press, 1996), pp. 193–210.

Ross, E., *Love and Toil: Motherhood in Outcast London, 1870–1918* (New York: Oxford University Press, 1993).

Ruiz, M., *British Female Emigration Societies and the New World, 1860–1914* (New York: Palgrave Macmillan, 2017).

Ryan, P. A., '"Poplarism" 1894–1930', in P. Thane (ed), *The Origins of British Social Policy* (London: Croom Helm, 1978), pp. 56–83.

Sanders, V. R., '"Is There No Work in Hand": The Idle Son Theme at Midcentury', *Studies in the Literary Imagination*, 43:1 (2010), pp. 49–67.

Sayer, K., *Women of the Fields: Representations of Rural Women in the Nineteenth Century* (Manchester: Manchester University Press, 1995).

Schneider, M., *J. A. Hobson* (London: Macmillan, 1996).

Scott, E. A., '"The Ill-name of the Old Country": London's Assisted Emigrants, British Unemployment Policy, and Canadian Immigration Restriction, 1905–1910', *Journal of the Canadian Historical Association/Revue de la Société historique du Canada*, 26:1 (2015), pp. 99–130.

Scott, E. A., '"Unite Idle Men with Idle Land': The Evolution of the Hollesley Bay Training Farm Experiment for the London Unemployed', in B. Althammer, L. Raphael, and

T. Stazic-Wendt (eds), *Rescuing the Vulnerable: Poverty, Welfare and Social Ties in Modern Europe* (New York: Berghan Books, 2016), pp. 237–258.

Searle, G. R., *Morality and the Market in Victorian Britain* (New York: Oxford University Press, 1998).

Seccombe, W., 'Patriarchy Stabilized: The Construction of the Male Breadwinner Norm in Nineteenth Century Britain', *Social History*, 11:1 (1986), pp. 53–76.

Shave, S., *Pauper Policies: Poor Law Practice in England, 1780–1850* (Oxford: Manchester University Press, 2017).

Simonton, D., *A History of European Women's Work: 1700 to the Present* (New York: Routledge, 1998).

Slack, P., *The English Poor Law, 1531–1782* (Basingstoke: Macmillan, 1990).

Stedman Jones, G., *Outcast London: A Study in the Relationship Between Classes in Victorian Society* (Oxford: Clarendon Press, 1971).

Stedman Jones, G., *Languages of Class: Studies in Working-Class Radicalism and Culture, 1832–1982* (New York: Cambridge University Press, 1983).

Strong, R., 'Pilgrims, Paupers or Progenitors: Religious Constructions of British Emigration from the 1840s to the 1870s', *History*, 100:341 (July 2015), pp. 392–411.

Summers, A., 'A Home From Home—Women's Philanthropic Work in the Nineteenth Century', in A. Digby (ed.), *Fit Work for Women* (London: Croom Helm, 1979), pp. 33–63.

Taylor, M., 'Rethinking the Chartists: Searching for Synthesis in the Historiography of Chartism', *The Historical Journal*, 39:2 (1996), pp. 479–495.

Thackeray, D. A., 'The Crisis of the Tariff Reform League and the Division of "Radical Conservatism", c.1913–1922', *History*, 91:1 (301) (January 2006), pp. 45–61.

Thane, P., 'Women and the Poor Law in Victorian and Edwardian England', *History Workshop Journal*, 6 (Autumn 1978), pp. 29–51.

Thane, P., 'The Working Class and State "Welfare" in Britain, 1880–1914', *Historical Journal*, 27:4 (1984), pp. 877–900.

Thane, P. 'Old People and Their Families in the English Past', in M. Daunton (ed), *Charity, Self-Interest and Welfare in the English Past* (New York: Routledge, 1996), pp. 113–138.

Thompson, A. S., 'Tariff Reform: An Imperial Strategy, 1903–1913', *Historical Journal*, 40:4 (December 1997), pp. 1033–1054.

Thompson, A. S., *Imperial Britain: The Empire in British Politics, 1880–1932* (New York: Routledge, 2000).

Thompson, D., *The Chartists: Popular Politics in the Industrial Revolution*, (New York: Pantheon Books, 1984).

Thompson, E. P., *The Making of the English Working Class* (New York: Vintage Books, 1963).

Thompson, E. P., 'Time, Work-Discipline, and Industrial Capitalism', *Past and Present*, 38:1 (1967), pp. 56–97.

Thompson, E. P., 'The Moral Economy of the English Crowd in the Eighteenth Century', *Past and Present*, 50:1 (1971), pp. 76–136.

Tomes, N., 'A "Torrent of Abuse": Crimes of Violence between Working-Class Men and Women in London, 1840–1875', *Journal of Social History*, 11:3 (Spring 1978), pp. 328–345.

Tompkins, A., and S. King, *The Poor in England, 1700–1850: An Economy of Makeshifts* (Manchester: Manchester University Press, 2003).

Tosh, J., 'Hegemonic Masculinity and the History of Gender', in S. Dudink, K. Hagemann, and J. Tosh (eds), *Masculinities in Politics and War: Gendering Modern History* (Manchester: Manchester University Press, 2004).

Tosh, J., *Manliness and Masculinities in Nineteenth-Century Britain: Essays on Gender, Family, and Empire* (New York: Pearson Longman, 2005).

Tosh, J., 'Masculinities in Industrializing Society: Britain, 1800–1914', *Journal of British Studies* 44:2 (April 2005), pp. 330–342.

Tosh, J., *A Man's Place: Masculinity and the Middle-Class Home in Victorian England* (New Haven, CT: Yale University Press, 2007).

Travers, T., *Samuel Smiles and the Victorian Work Ethic* (New York: Routledge, 1987).

Twells, A., *The Civilising Mission and the English Middle Class, 1792–1850* (New York: Palgrave Macmillan, 2009).

Valenze, D., *The First Industrial Woman* (New York: Oxford University Press, 1995).

Valverde, M., '"Giving the Female a Domestic Turn": The Social, Legal, and Moral Regulation of Women's Work in British Cotton Mills, 1820–1850', *Journal of Social History* 21:4 (Summer 1998), pp. 619–634.

Vernon, J., *Hunger: A Modern History* (Cambridge, MA: Harvard University Press, 2007).

Vickery, A., 'Golden Age to Separate Spheres? A Review of the Categories and Chronology of English Women's History', *The Historical Journal* 36:2 (1993), pp. 383–414.

Vincent, A., 'Classical Liberalism and Its Crisis of Identity', *History of Political Thought*, 11:1 (Spring 1990), 143–161.

Walker, M., '"Encouragement of Sound Education amongst the Industrial Classes": Mechanics' Institutes and Working-Class Membership, 1838–1881', *Educational Studies*, 39:2 (2013), pp. 142–155.

Walkowitz, J., *Prostitution and Victorian Society: Women, Class, and the State* (Cambridge: Cambridge University Press, 1980).

Walters, W., 'The Discovery of "Unemployment": New Forms for the Government of Poverty', *Economy and Society*, 23:3 (1994), pp. 274–275.

Welshman, J., 'The Concept of the Unemployable', *Economic History Review*, 59:3 (August 2006), pp. 578–606.

Welshman, J., *Underclass: A History of the Excluded Since 1880*, 2nd ed (London: Bloomsbury Academic, 2013).

'Who was Charles Booth?', *London School of Economics: Charles Booth's London*, at https://booth.lse.ac.uk/learn-more/who-was-charles-booth [accessed 8 June 2021].

Whiteside, N., 'Constructing Unemployment: Britain and France in Historical Perspective', *Social Policy and Administration*, 48:1 (2014), pp. 67–85.

Whiteside, N., 'Transforming the Unemployed: Trade Union Benefits and the Advent of State Policy,' in K. Laybourn and J. Shepherd (eds), *Labour and Working-Class Lives: Essays to Celebrate the Life and Work of Chris Wrigley* (Manchester: University of Manchester Press, 2017), pp. 68–86.

Wiener, M., *English Culture and the Decline of the Industrial Spirit, 1850–1980* (New York: Cambridge University Press, 1981).

Williams, K., *From Pauperism to Poverty* (London: Routledge and Kegan Paul, 1981).

Williams, R., *The Country and the City* (Oxford: Oxford University Press, 1975).

Williams, S., *Poverty, Gender, and the Life-Cycle under the English Poor Law, 1760–1834* (Rochester, NY: Boydell and Brewer, 2011.

Wood, P., *Poverty and the Workhouse in Victorian Britain* (Wolfboro Falls, NH: Alan Sutton Pub., 1991).

Woodroofe, K., 'The Royal Commission on the Poor Laws, 1905–09', *International Review of Social History*, 22:2 (1977), pp. 137–164.

Wright, S., D. R. Fletcher, and A. B. R. Stewart, 'Punitive Benefit Sanctions, Welfare Conditionality, and the Social Abuse of Unemployed People in Britain: Transforming Claimants into Offenders?' *Social Policy and Administration*, 54:2 (February 2020), pp. 278–294.

Primary sources

Beveridge, W., *Unemployment: A Problem of Industry* (London: Longmans, Green and Co., 1909).

Booth, C., *Life and Labour of the People in London*, 17 vols. (London: Macmillan, 1902–1903).

Booth, W., *In Darkest England and the Way Out* (London: Salvation Army, 1890).

Carlyle, T., *Past and Present: Thomas Carlyle's Collected Works, Vol. XIII* (Project Gutenberg ebook, 2008) www.gutenberg.org/cache/epub/13534/pg13534.html [accessed 8 November 2021].

Chadwick, E., *Report on the Sanitary Condition of the Labouring Population of Great Britain* (London: HMSO, 1843, orig. 1842).

Engels, F., *The Condition of the Working Class in England* (London: Penguin Books, 2005, orig. 1845).

Green, T. H., 'Lecture on Liberal Legislation and Freedom of Contract', in R.L. Nettleship (ed), *Works of Thomas Hill Green*, Vol. III (London: Longmans, Green, and Co., 1900), pp. 365–386.

Hobson, J. A., and A. F. Mummery, *The Physiology of Industry: Being an Exposure of Certain Fallacies in Existing Theories in Economics* (London: John Murray, 1889).

Keynes, J. M., *The General Theory of Employment, Interest and Money* (London: Palgrave Macmillan 1936).

Local Government Board, *Sixteenth Annual Report*, 1886–1887, Appendix 1: 'Pauperism and Distress: Circular Letter to Boards of Guardians', 15 March 1886.

Locke, J., *Two Treatises on Government* (Project Gutenberg ebook) www.gutenberg.org/files/7370/7370-h/7370-h.htm [accessed 20 June 2021].

Malthus, T., *An Essay on the Principle of Population* (Oxford: Oxford University Press, 1993, orig. 1798).

Marshall, A., *Principles of Economics*, Eighth Edition (London: Palgrave Macmillan UK, 2013, orig. 1890).

Mayhew, H., *London Labour and the London Poor* (London: Griffin, Bohn, and Company, 1861).

Mearns, A., and W. C. Preston, *The Bitter Cry of Outcast London: An Inquiry into the Condition of the Abject Poor* (London: James Clarke and Co., 1883).

Morris, W., *Useless Work versus Useful Toil* (London: Socialist League Office, 1886).

Morris, W., 'Art and Socialism', in M. Morris (ed), *The Works of William Morris*, Vol. 23, (London: Longman Green and Co., 1915), pp. 192–214.

Oastler, R., *Slavery in Yorkshire: Monstrous Barbarity* (Bradford: J. Atkinson, 1835).

Ricardo, D., *The Principles of Political Economy and Taxation* (London: J.M. Dent & Sons, 1911).

Rowntree, B. S., *Poverty: A Study of Town Life* (London: Macmillan and Co., 1901).

Ruskin, J., *The Stones of Venice*, Vols. 1–3 (London: Smith, Elder, and Co. 1851).

Say, J. B., *A Treatise on Political Economy: Or the Production, Distribution, and Consumption of Wealth*, 6th American ed. (Philadelphia: Grigg & Elliott, 1834, orig. 1803).

Smith, A., *An Inquiry into the Nature and Causes of the Wealth of Nations* (London: Penguin, 1970, orig. 1776).

Smiles, S., *Self Help: with Illustrations of Conduct and Perseverance*, Popular ed. (London: John Murray, 1897, orig. 1859).

Smiles, S., *Character*, Popular ed. (London: John Murray, 1917, orig. 1871).

Weber, M., *The Protestant Ethic and the Spirit of Capitalism* (New York: Dover Publications, 2003, orig. 1905).

GENERAL INTRODUCTION

That one great object of all governments ought to be the welfare of the productive classes of the society; that the object will be materially promoted by a well regulated system of poor laws, and that the wisdom and justice of our ancestors have given to the labourer in distress as great a right to relief as the landowner has to the profit of his estate.

'New Poor Law – Great Yorkshire Meeting',
Preston Chronicle, 1837 (Volume 2, Part 1, Chapter 2)

The honest, industrious, sober, pious working-man has a right to magnify his office, for the world is his debtor. The curse of labour bore with it a blessing. It is man's noble benefaction to his fellow-man, and his grateful oblation to God.

'The Working Man', *British Workman*, 1859
(Volume 1, Part 1, Chapter 6)

No man who has to work for his livelihood is ever esteemed a 'gentleman' . . . A working man is never made knight or a peer, the chairman of a missionary society, or the president of a football club. . . . The fact that a man has to do 'honest toil' utterly unfits him, apparently, from occupying any honourable position in Church, State, or Society.

John Bruce Glasier, 'Honest Toil', Penny Pamphlet, Socialist
League, c. 1890 (Volume 1, Part 1, Chapter 9)

'Unemployment' is perhaps the most illusive term which confronts the student of modern industrial society.

J. A. Hobson, 'The Meaning and Measure of "Unemployment"',
Contemporary Review, 1895 (Volume 4, Part 1, Chapter 1)

The 1834 Poor Law Amendment Act made it much harder for an able-bodied, unemployed man to receive assistance from the state – assistance to which he had been entitled since Elizabethan times. Under most conditions, the law stated, a man without work would be forced into a humiliating workhouse to break stone

DOI: 10.4324/9780429320323-1

for his relief.[1] This reflected the widespread attitude among the newly enfranchised industrial and commercial middle classes who supported the New Poor Law that work – in the marketplace, to earn one's living – was an expression of godliness and industriousness.[2] The honest toil of the labouring poor was blessed because of its exertion, not in spite of it. Work in this moral discourse signaled virtue and respectability; a lack of work indicated the opposite: immorality and corruption.[3] But the upright middle classes also regarded work through the lens of political economy as a mark of the liberal individual's independence.[4] Classical economists believed that the labour market always tended towards full employment, so being unemployed was a voluntary status for those unwilling to work at the going wage rates.[5] These views shaped the New Poor Law's harsh approach to those without work and the stance that if a man was only more hardworking, surely he could find a job. Resistance to these views came from poor men, who argued that their joblessness did not signify the absence of morality or conscientiousness so much as an absence of available employment. Along with their wives and well-to-do allies, they fought back against economists' emphasis on the equilibrium of markets and the state's *laissez-faire* approach to the economy.[6] Yet moralists, economists, and working men themselves all believed in what I call the 'work imperative', the expectation that 'honest' working-class men desired and were committed to 'work' – paid employment in the wage-labour market. The working classes, however, saw the work imperative from a very different angle than those who looked to define working men's experiences for them.[7]

The passage of the Poor Law Amendment Act signified a shift in the welfare culture of Great Britain.[8] It provides a fitting starting point for this collection, with its almost obsessive attention to the plight of the unemployed, able-bodied man. The sources in these volumes emphasize that, for Victorians and Edwardians, the meanings attached to work and the meanings attached to being without work were always dependent upon each other, knotted together by the imperative for a man to desire employment and be willing to work. Many scholars have written about the mid-Victorian middle-class fixation on work, and many have written about the late nineteenth-century 'discovery of unemployment'. These have, for the most part, been separate stories, featuring very different players. This collection demonstrates that the chronology 1834 to 1911 was a distinct period in British history in which these stories connected, united by the struggles to come to terms with the meanings of work and unemployment and the insecurity of poor people's lives in new and rapidly changing economic circumstances. Mechanization and the decline of old trades, the creation of single-industry cities and towns, the migration of agricultural labourers from the countryside to these cities and to London, the intensification of the sweated industries, and the displacement of the labour of adult men by the labour of women and adolescent boys all contributed to urgent conversations about the relationships between work and unemployment.

The story of 'work' has focused on the early to mid-Victorian industrial middle classes, with their emphases on self-reliance and thrift. They associated virtue with the accumulation of capital through intense spiritual devotion to work.[9] Jeremy

Bentham's utilitarianism assigned work the value of 'the most "useful" thing' in a man's life.[10] In *The Protestant Ethic and the Spirit of Capitalism*, Max Weber sought to explain the religious calling that supported the strengthening of the capitalist system.[11] While the writer Thomas Carlyle praised work as ennobling for all, especially when separated from 'mammonism' (the pursuit of wealth), Samuel Smiles's call to self-help through diligent work as the path to both financial and social improvement is more familiar.[12] The working classes in this story often appear as objects of middle-class reformers' efforts to cure them of idleness and apathy, which supposedly led them to stray from work.[13] According to these reformers, individual moral failings caused people's poverty and produced their dependence on charity and the Poor Law. Smiles, representing a common belief, saw great danger in the aversion to work: 'It is idleness that is the curse of man – not labor. Idleness eats the heart out of men as of nations, and consumes them as rust does iron'.[14] Other reformers, critical of the harshness of the industrial system, tried to make the story of work more inclusive of workers themselves by improving conditions of labour and living.[15] The grand mid-Victorian celebration of work was the 1851 Great Exhibition, designed to showcase the progress of Britain as the 'workshop of the world', which rested on the success of the industrial and commercial classes.[16]

The story of the 'discovery of unemployment' is less well known and certainly less celebrated. It looks at the ideas of a group of 'new liberal' thinkers at the end of the Victorian era who recognized that most unemployed individuals did not, in fact, choose 'idleness'; it was foisted upon them by economic forces over which they had no control. Rather than focusing on unemployed workers and their problems of character, 'unemployment' pointed to something inherent to the economic system. 'Unemployment' was meant to indicate a structural problem as opposed to a moral failing, challenging the easy equation of virtue with work and viciousness with the lack of it. For the new liberal J. A. Hobson, unemployment was 'the total quantity of human labour-power not employed in the production of social wealth'.[17] It was waste, or surplus, labour. Meanwhile, William Beveridge, the social welfare pioneer, named unemployment 'a problem of industry'.[18] Addressing unemployment became the purview of economists and politicians, not philanthropists and Boards of Guardians. Charity and the Poor Law had no power in a world of structural unemployment; rather, the state needed to act to formulate national unemployment policies that would impact the economy through features such as wages and labour markets, as well as develop more sophisticated means of protecting unemployed workers, such as national insurance.[19] Although this narrative focuses on economists and new liberal social theory, the development of a mature labour movement and socialist critiques of industrial capitalism also play a significant role in this story of unemployment. Working-class activism helped push the state to recognize 'unemployment' as a problem requiring national attention.[20]

Some of the sources in this collection contain elements of these oversimplified narratives, and some highlight their oversimplification. For example, critics of the sermon on work always existed, as did those who recognized the structural underpinnings of trade depressions in the early and mid-nineteenth century (think Karl Marx in both cases).[21] The sources show that problems of casual labour, or underemployment, as much as actual joblessness, led thinkers to adopt the economic approach to unemployment.[22] And efforts to solve the structural problem of unemployment, which in theory should have left questions of morality behind, continued to pose questions about individual character.[23]

Additionally, these stories are predominantly about men – the development of men's moral and economic success, on the one hand, and the concern about men's loss of employment, on the other. Women are present in these stories, but primarily as signs of men's status. The male breadwinner norm came to matter for both middle- and working-class families in the nineteenth century, promoting a socio-economic order where men would earn enough (a family wage) to be able to support their wives and children, who could be removed from the labour force. Scholars have framed this development as an attachment to an ideal of 'separate spheres' for the middle class, where men worked in the political and economic public sphere to provide for their families, while wives tended to the private domestic sphere of social reproduction. While we know that these spheres were far less separate in practice than in prescription, the story of 'work' is very much about a prosperous middle-class man whose wife at home was a symbol of his success. John Tosh, in his history of masculinities, notes that the struggle of skilled artisans to maintain their masculine work identities as breadwinners in the face of mechanization can be seen as a parallel to the middle-class story of work as a calling.[24] For working-class families more generally, the male breadwinner norm broke down on many levels, most commonly because men could not earn a sufficient wage to support wives and children without their income contributions. The story of 'unemployment' features starving wives and children as signs of men's failures to provide. Women who had to maintain their husbands also revealed men's inability to participate in the story of 'work'.[25] Historian Keith McClelland points to the connections between work and unemployment identities:

> Given the centrality of paid work to the construction of men's identities in capitalism, the loss of earnings and employment probably led to a sense of 'incompleteness' and shame as men and to a loss of dignity which could not be contemplated.[26]

Women worked and became unemployed, but both stories have marginalized their experiences.

One reason the stories of 'work' and 'unemployment' traditionally have been separate is that their narrators have been in different fields. The middle-class obsession with work has been a story of mid-nineteenth-century Victorianists – mostly historians and literary scholars.[27] They have relied on sources like advice literature, personal writings, business records, fiction, and literary essays. The 'discovery of unemployment', on the other hand, has been written by economists, economic and policy historians, and political scientists.[28] Their sources tend to be the more theoretical writings of the economists and social thinkers of the late nineteenth and early twentieth centuries. Of course, I am setting up a somewhat artificial divide, and many scholars have crossed this conceptual and chronological boundary between 'work' and 'unemployment' in studies that have encompassed elements of both. The social and cultural historian Lynn Hollen Lees's study of the Poor Law, for example, stretches from 1700 to 1948 and examines the ways middle-class reformers attached their notions of work and respectability to relief of the poor as well as how new ideas of unemployment in the 1890s changed approaches to poverty.[29] In *The Winding Road to the Welfare State*, George Boyer, an economist and economic historian, looks explicitly at the change from a welfare culture rooted in the Poor Law to one based in an economic understanding of 'unemployment'.[30]

In 1834, when large numbers of people were out of work, newspapers and government publications reported on 'distress', 'extreme destitution', and 'starvation'. They wrote about 'the unemployed', while workers suffered from 'want of employment' and being 'out of employ'. Although this language was still in use at the end of the nineteenth century, it was joined by references to 'unemployment', the new concept created by economists in the 1880s. 'Unemployment' did not become fully part of public discourse until the early part of the twentieth century.[31] Boyer, in an important 2004 article, wrote of the need to 'fill the gap' in the historiography of 'unemployment relief' that existed for the period 1834 to 1911,[32] the dates between the New Poor Law and the introduction of unemployment insurance, which also frame this collection. While Boyer uses the term 'unemployment' to describe the loss of employment from cyclical downturns throughout this period, my assumption in compiling these sources is that 'unemployment relief' was conceptually possible only after unemployment was part of people's vocabulary. I try to use 'unemployment' carefully to reflect this historical specificity. Volume 3, Part 1 looks at the development of this idea in detail.

I organized this collection's four volumes to illustrate the unevenness of working-class men's and women's experiences of work and unemployment and the attempts of a variety of groups and individuals to frame those experiences. Some sources describe material practices such as relief efforts and political demonstrations that aimed to manage relationships between work and unemployment. Other sources represent desired norms in texts such as government reports and journal essays. The documents express experiences, but they also helped shape knowledge about work and unemployment that voluntary and government bodies used to form policies and practices. Some sources are purposefully prescriptive, telling charitable organizations what types of men they should assist or arguing that women should avoid certain types of work. Some inform men how to respond when they were without work, and others set up appropriate judgments to make when seeking to assist someone without employment. Some of the documents are more descriptive, providing depictions of work conditions or accounts of being unemployed.

Volume 1 introduces 'The Meanings of Work', examining the ideals and experiences of work, where they intersected and diverged. The meanings attached to work had resonance in multiple aspects of people's lives, and the sources consider this breadth. Part 1 examines the association of work with respectability, which was a foundational expression of the middle-class story of work.[33] The sources, however, address the ways 'The Respectability of Honest Toil' registered with lives of men and women performing difficult labour in unpleasant conditions and the relative value attached to manual labour compared to other kinds of work. They consider the work imperative, the belief in the commitment to work, from radically different perspectives. 'Men and Machines' explores the challenges industrialization posed to men's traditional labour and identities. The documents illustrate a variety of viewpoints on the introduction of machines into skilled men's work, which had implications not only for their work relations but their positions as breadwinners for families.[34] The final section, 'Women's Work – Productive and Reproductive', looks at the pressures placed on working women by the increasingly normative domestic ideal.[35] While men worried about their ability to maintain jobs to support families, the sources show that women's paid labour tested the expectation that women should remain at home learning domestic skills. Each part suggests how ideas about the meaning of work shaped perceptions about how people became unemployed and why they remained unemployed.

Volume 2, 'Unemployed before Unemployment', explores questions surrounding what types of assistance were available to people out of work and who should receive that assistance. As the political sociologist William Walters noted, before the 'discovery of unemployment', managing 'the unemployed' was a social problem, not an economic one.[36] This management fell predominantly to local bodies: Poor Law Guardians, charitable organizations, and local government authorities. The sources reveal not only how this 'mixed economy of welfare'[37] operated for people out of work but how the spheres of this economy constructed moral categories of deservedness that would stay with unemployed people to the end of the nineteenth century and beyond. Documents on the Poor Law, voluntary organizations, and work relief schemes all demonstrate how absolutely central the work imperative was in the ways officials decided which applicants for assistance were deserving and which were not. While the sources in Part 1, 'The Poor Law', address many of the significant issues surrounding local relief to the unemployed, above all they show the authorized fixation on the performance of work by unemployed able-bodied men in exchange for relief and the difficulties this posed in practice. The sources in 'Charities' demonstrate the growing influence of methodical approaches to charitable giving, in order to curb 'indiscriminate' charity to 'undeserving' people. Part 3, 'Work Relief', reveals that even projects that tried to avoid the 'pauperizing' and disenfranchising elements of Poor Law relief still used measures of character embedded in the work imperative to choose worthy men to relieve. While the documents throughout the volume show the extent of real destitution, one of the main messages of the sources is that providers of assistance feared that any form of relief took away unemployed men's motivation to look for work independently.

Volume 3 sets up 'The Meanings of Unemployment', as economists constructed the category 'unemployment', referring to a structural problem that caused 'genuine workmen' to be temporarily unemployed through no fault of their own.[38] The sources in Part 1, 'The "Discovery of Unemployment"', indicate how social thinkers and politicians put forward a range of arguments about the reasons for unemployment, which suggested particular roles for the state in addressing the problem. Part 2, 'Classification of the Out-of-Works', reveals that the 'discovery of unemployment' was accompanied by increasingly detailed categorization of people without work. While sources in Volumes 1 and 2 clearly show the importance for relief providers of sorting the deserving unemployed from the undeserving 'idlers', reformers and policy makers in the second half of the century drew on the new pseudo sciences of eugenics and social Darwinism to refine their classifications to assure themselves they could clearly identify the 'genuine unemployed', based on people's relationships to work.[39] The sources in Part 3, 'The Politics of Unemployment', illustrate the growing movement to represent 'labour' both inside and outside Parliament, in large part to address the problem of unemployment. The section examines the development and politics of a variety of socialist parties in the late nineteenth and early twentieth centuries and their relationships to men and women out of work. Sources also look at strikes, marches, demonstrations, and deputations of unemployed men and women.[40] The problem of unemployment and concerns about the categories of men who were marching in the streets made headlines in this era and kept the conversation about unemployment alive in government.

Volume 4, 'Working for Unemployment', explores primarily late nineteenth- and early twentieth-century efforts to solve the problem of unemployment in the context of the new understandings of 'unemployment'. The sources show the continuing power of discovering men's commitment to employment by finding ways to make them work. Part 1, 'Emigration and Empire', focuses on emigration to put unemployed men to work in the British colonies, which people suggested as a solution to dealing with fears about overpopulation and overstocked labour markets in Britain.[41] While some sources argue that emigration would benefit both the British nation and the colonies, others reveal concerns that it would drain Britain of its best workers. Part 2, 'Domestic Labour Colonies', examines various projects to employ urban men without work on the land as a means to restore them morally and prepare them for lives as agricultural labourers at home and abroad.[42] In Part 3, the sources consider the increasing 'Intervention of the State' in efforts like emigration and labour colonies. The documents demonstrate that some reformers called for more government interference as a means to help 'genuine workmen' and others rejected state intervention as a danger to working men's independence. This section examines, in particular, the functioning of the 1905 Unemployed Workmen Act, an endeavour to empower local authorities to provide unemployed men and, for the first time, women with work.[43] The sources in this volume show the not-very-successful ideal that putting people to work at so-called productive labour in controlled environments would alter their attitudes towards work and permanently change their lives.

In addition to the broad themes of the volumes and their parts, I want to highlight six assumptions that shape the whole collection. First, throughout the nineteenth century and into the twentieth, moral and economic understandings of work were always in tension with each other but coalesced around the work imperative, the obligation of the able-bodied man to engage in paid employment. Second, although reformers and policy makers increasingly attributed being out of work to structural as opposed to individual causes, economic causes never replaced the rhetoric of moral, individual fault. Third, while Victorians praised work, and particularly manual labour, for working-class men as a means to develop self-respect, independence, and virtue, authorities also saw manual labour as a punishment to deter men from seeking relief and as a test of their willingness to work. Fourth, reformers believed that classifications of the poor and unemployed, which grew more and more complex over the course of the nineteenth century, would benefit social relations and the distribution of welfare and charity. Fifth, the gendered contexts and conventions of the times informed the policies, practices, and representations of work and the lack of work. Finally, men and women without work did not passively accept reformers' interpretations of being unemployed or their ideas regarding how best to address unemployment.

Furthermore, place is an important category in these volumes. The collection expands Britain's geographic story of work and unemployment by bringing together sources from England, Wales, Scotland, Ireland, Canada, Australia, New Zealand, and the West Indies. These intersecting geographies demonstrate the ways that histories of London's problems with casual labour and unemployment cannot be separated from histories of labour markets in England's agricultural districts or conditions for emigrants in Canada and Australia. The new imperial history has emphasized the importance of situating the metropole and colonies in one, mutually shaping, imperial framework, rather than seeing London – and, more broadly, Britain – as determining imperial histories.[44] The sources indeed show that Australia and Canada, in particular, held a lot of agency in the linked stories of emigration, work, and unemployment. Perhaps even more notably, conditions in the West Indian colonies forced government bureaucrats to address unanticipated issues of joblessness.[45] Similarly, London has often been the focal point for late nineteenth-century histories of unemployment and social crisis, because so many Victorian and Edwardian reformers wrote about London themselves.[46] Yet there is a larger story to be told of the ways other places contributed to London's narratives of work and unemployment and different stories about these other places on their own; sometimes the sources show remarkable continuity across localities, but sometimes they demonstrate interesting differences. The intersecting narratives of place appear across the volumes, but perspectives about London are still heavily represented, because the problem of unemployment did grow out of attention to conditions in London.

The sources in this collection come from a variety of locations. I included archival documents from the National Archives, the London Metropolitan Archives, the London School of Economics and Political Science (LSE), and the Senate House Library of the University of London (UCL). The collection also benefits from online archival material from archive.org and the National Library of Scotland. I drew upon the rich resources of the Family Welfare Association (founded in 1869 as the Charity Organisation Society) at UCL, as well as other pamphlet collections at UCL and the LSE. The British Library provided a wide range of documents, including newspapers from the online British Newspaper Archive. One goal in selecting sources was to make available less well-known materials, although even as I was scanning documents, UCL was in the process of digitizing the same sources I was adopting for what turned out to be another collection.[47] In addition, I have incorporated some documents from previously digitized sets, ProQuest's *British Periodicals* and Gale's *The Making of the Modern World*, both of which have fantastic sources that fit extremely well in this collection. Finally, Google Books has digitized so many texts that are easily available now, but they are not contextualized historically. In general, many documents that were once only accessible in physical archives are now digitized and easily found online. We might ask why it is useful to produce compilations such as this one in this new world of accessible digital texts. Situating the documents in their historical context and in conversation with each other gives them a different meaning than if they were simply located in a digital archive. The digitized archive is, of course, of tremendous value, but collections such as this one give shape to particular documents that the archive alone does not provide.

In a collection on nineteenth- and early twentieth-century 'Work and Unemployment', it may seem surprising not to find texts by Thomas Carlyle, William Morris, John Ruskin, Charles Booth, or the classic *Unemployment: A Problem of Industry*, by William Beveridge.[48] While I have selected a number of documents by well-known figures, I have tried to foreground material that broadens the historical thinking on connections between work and unemployment in some less familiar sources. Volume introductions and document headnotes put the sources in dialogue with some of the more recognizable texts. In collecting these materials together, the more well-known and the newly discovered, I hope to give them fresh meaning and significance read alongside each other.

Many of the documents included in the volumes are selections from larger texts, selections which I chose in order to focus on the particular theme of a volume section. For example, the documents in Volume 3, Part 2, 'Classification of the Out-of-Works', concentrate specifically on sections of texts that discuss classificatory schemes related to people without work. For some of the selections, I chose continuous segments, and for others, I used portions from various parts of a text. Some longer texts have been cut down in the interests of space.

Each document is accompanied by a headnote, which provides an introduction to the text. These headnotes differ in a variety of ways: for example, details on the author or the journal in which a document was published, the context necessary to understand the source, or clarification of historical events and terms. I have opted to include all explanatory information in the headnotes themselves, rather than in annotations of the documents, so that readers can approach the sources with needed background up front and read the sources cleanly. I also provide my own summary and brief analysis of the documents, helping to put them in conversation with other documents in the collection and with significant historiographical themes.

A word on language and the problematic effects of calling a group of people 'the unemployed'. In disability studies, scholars and activists debate using people-first language (person with a disability) and identity-first language (disabled person). Based on the work of disability rights advocates in the U.S., the Americans with Disabilities Act of 1990 emphasized the use of people-first language.[49] At the time activists argued that saying 'disabled person' or 'blind person' was dehumanizing, defining the person by their disability instead of recognizing the person first. Others, however, especially within the deaf and autistic communities, have claimed disability as part of their identities and prefer identity-first language.[50] I thought about this debate as I was writing about 'unemployed people' and 'men without work'. I do not have the space in this introduction to address the ways men (and women) without work might have adopted an identity as 'unemployed', especially as their unemployment became chronic.[51] I also thought about how using the terms 'the unemployed' and 'the poor' reproduced the dehumanizing language of the sources by reducing a group of people to a condition. In the end, I chose to write flexibly, using both person-first and identity-first constructions and sometimes mimicking the language of the time when discussing the sources directly.

These language issues seem particularly important to consider as I close out the writing of this project after almost eighteen months of the COVID-19 pandemic, which raised pressing new concerns about the meanings of work and unemployment. For example, in the U.S., where I live, and in the U.K., the pandemic drew extensive attention to 'frontline', 'essential', or 'key' workers, workers whose jobs were newly defined as critical to the functioning of the country. These included jobs in health care and security but also in groceries, food production and transportation, the postal service, public transit, teaching, cleaning, janitorial services, and waste disposal. The majority of these jobs are low-waged and frequently staffed by workers who come from socioeconomically disadvantaged and often minority and immigrant populations. They are also occupations that were made dangerous because of the virus.[52] The celebration of essential workers' labour as heroic during the pandemic pointed out the hypocrisy of companies and governments praising their work while simultaneously being reluctant to pay them living wages,[53] revealing a gap between the value attached to their work materially and ideologically and the value given to their work economically. This same story existed in nineteenth-century Britain regarding manual labour, as the sources show in Volume 1. Because the pandemic gap was exposed so publicly, activists put pressure on governments and executives to find ways to close it, most immediately by raising minimum wages and offering regular hazard pay.[54]

As was the case with the industrial transformations of the nineteenth century, the pandemic created a historical moment that unsettled meanings of work that were already undergoing 'disruptions'.[55] Companies that were able shifted their employees from in-person workplaces to remote working from home, which challenged ideas about where work happens and for whom. Surveys show that the percentage of workers who will permanently switch to some amount of remote work will rise dramatically as we move forward.[56] In some industries, executives want their employees back in-person, while workers desire to maintain the flexibility of working from home,[57] creating divisions between employers and employees surrounding the balance between efficiencies and job satisfaction. These kinds of questions were central throughout the nineteenth century, as workers adjusted to new patterns and processes of labour associated with mechanization.

In another example, the pandemic has drawn attention to the ways that, in the gig economy, 'the other side of the "flexibility coin" is chronic job insecurity'.[58] Gig workers, like ride-hailing drivers and food-delivery drivers, have been treated as self-employed, independent contractors, rather than as employees of the companies whose technology platforms they rely on.[59] Like frontline workers, gig workers, too, disproportionately come from immigrant communities and communities of colour.[60] Their dependence on the platform and the demand for service is reminiscent of the on-demand casual workers in the nineteenth century, whose economic insecurity wound up playing a large part in shaping new understandings of the economy (see Volume 3). In April 2021, a U.K. Supreme Court decision and the U.S. labor secretary's announcement both moved to recognize gig workers as 'workers' or 'employees' rather than as casual on-demand contractors, pointing the way forward to better wages, benefits, and job security.[61] The impact of technology in creating the possibilities of remote employment and the gig economy have forced these conversations about new meanings of work.

The meaning of unemployment was also very much at the centre of public debate as I was working on this project. In the U.S., the COVID-19 pandemic caused twenty million people to lose their jobs in March and April 2020 alone, and unemployment in April was the highest of any month since the Great Depression.[62] The U.K. provided a furlough program, the Coronavirus Job Retention Scheme (CJRS), which covered 3.9 million people by the end of April 2020, protecting them from lay-offs. Even so, the numbers claiming unemployment benefit doubled between March and May 2020, increasing by about 1.4 million. As of mid-May 2021, 11.5 million jobs had been furloughed through CJRS.[63] People employed in leisure and service industries like hotels and restaurants were disproportionately hard-hit in both countries.[64] In many ways they have been the face of pandemic unemployment because of the visibility of closed restaurants and the unusual nature of their loss of work. Voluntary relief funds have been established in the U.S. to supplement the federal government's stimulus checks, to show 'the nation just how important restaurant workers are to our industry and the communities where we work and live'.[65] In the U.K., the government, after pressure, instituted multiple programs to keep restaurants and pubs in business.[66] Less unusual, pandemic unemployment has affected workers of colour and immigrant workers more severely than other racial/ethnic groups.[67] They have not received outsized attention from the public, and they have also been at higher risk of contracting the virus. Already existing systemic racism and economic inequities produced these particular meanings of unemployment.[68]

As in the nineteenth century, moral and economic concerns continue to intersect in discussions of unemployment. COVID-19 forced workers to lose their jobs for structural reasons: primarily lack of demand for goods and services. In the parlance of the Victorians, they became unemployed through no fault of their own. Yet in debates about government support for unemployed workers, questions about individual character have played a role. As I write, many U.S. states have withdrawn from the congressional COVID-19 unemployment insurance agreements because their governors believe that, among other things, the benefit had 'turned into a dangerous federal entitlement, incentivizing and paying workers to stay at home rather than encouraging them to return to the workplace'.[69] This criticism, like those in the late nineteenth and early twentieth centuries, sees state support robbing independence from unemployed individual workers, who, if given the chance, would prefer to become dependent on benefits or relief schemes rather than return to regular employment. Such attitudes imply that these workers are not really deserving of continuing assistance, which raises implicit questions about the reality of their economic insecurity.[70] While the U.S. is experiencing a labour shortage, many of the workers who are not returning to work are those in what the economist Daniel Alpert identifies as 'low-quality jobs', job that pay less than $500 per week – jobs with 'spectacularly low incomes'.[71] Many of these workers are casual workers, worried about their health status and the health of those in their families. Fears of being unemployed are being outweighed by fears of going back to work. Other people are using the pandemic as an opportunity to try to find better work opportunities.[72] The media, however, presents a story that blames workers' laziness for unfilled positions.[73] Interestingly, this has been less the case in Britain, where government support for pandemic unemployed workers – even mediated through businesses – has been forthcoming with much less moralizing.

Here I come back to the importance of telling the often-separated stories of work and unemployment together. While the issues highlighted by the sources in this collection are historically specific to the period 1834 to 1911, they point to meaningful patterns and continuities. Understandings of skill and the value attached to particular types of work, for example, have and have had policy implications for unemployed workers. The casual workers of the nineteenth century and the gig workers of today both have suffered from being labeled not 'genuine workers'. Even though it is now almost 130 years since J. A. Hobson explained that unemployment was a structural problem of capitalist economies that should not be blamed on workers' choices, moral commentary on unemployment and individual workers has been a resilient feature of neoliberal politics and the press in Britain since Thatcher.[74] While women's employment is certainly normalized today in a way it was not in the nineteenth century, women continue to dominate the low-paid, part-time labour market and take on the majority of domestic household tasks and child-rearing. Because of domestic care pressures, women also persistently drop out of the labour market (become economically inactive) and therefore become ineligible for benefits.[75]

This collection ends in 1911 with the promise of insurance for unemployed men that was not based on character investigations that measured their deservedness. Britain's post-1945 Labour government certainly took this promise and implemented a welfare state, with unemployment benefits, in a way that would have surprised Lloyd George, but not its architect, William Beveridge, in 1911.[76] Over the last fifty years, the erosion of Britain's welfare state has importantly included the reintroduction of work tests as a way to ascertain people's commitment to a work imperative before they are deemed deserving of benefits. This demonstrates the heavy investment of (neo)liberal societies in work as a/the preeminent measure of a person's worth and the inextricable stories of work and unemployment.

Notes

1 For general analyses of the Poor Law, see A. Brundage, *The English Poor Laws, 1700–1930* (New York: Palgrave Macmillan, 2001) and L. H. Lees, *The Solidarities of Strangers: The English Poor Laws and the People, 1700–1948* (New York: Cambridge University Press, 1998).

2 In 1832, the Representation of the People Act enfranchised all men who paid ten pounds or more annually on their homes. It also, for the first time, defined a voter as a male person, disenfranchising the few women who had been able to vote. See E. Evans, *The Great Reform Act of 1832*, 2nd ed. (New York: Routledge, 2016). On the development of the middle class, see, for example, L. Davidoff and C. Hall, *Family Fortunes: Men and Women of the English Middle Class, 1780–1850*, 3rd ed. (New York: Routledge, 2018). Catherine Hall's *Civilising Subjects: Metropole and Colony in the English Imagination, 1830–1867* (Chicago: University of Chicago Press, 2002) demonstrates how the gospel of work became part of the colonial project.

3 W. E. Houghton, *The Victorian Frame of Mind, 1830–1870* (New Haven, CT: Yale University Press, 1985, orig. 1957), pp. 242–243.

4 H. Perkin provides a classic description of the shift from the 'old society' to the society of the political economists in *The Origins of Modern English Society*, 2nd ed. (London: Routledge, 2002), pp. 182–190.

5 J. M. Keynes in *The General Theory of Employment, Interest and Money* (London: Palgrave Macmillan, 1936) challenged the ideas of David Ricardo, Jean-Baptiste Say, and others that free markets would result in full employment.

6 N. C. Edsall, *The Anti-Poor Law Movement, 1834–44* (Manchester, UK: Manchester University Press, 1971); Lees discusses poor people's sense of entitlement to assistance in *Solidarities*, pp. 153–169.

7 I purposely write of working 'men' here. The work imperative and ideas about work and unemployment were understood in the gendered context of their times. See M. Levine-Clark, *Unemployment, Welfare, and Masculine Citizenship: 'So Much Honest Poverty' in Britain, 1870–1930* (New York: Palgrave Macmillan, 2015), chap. 1, where I first used the phrase 'work imperative'.

8 See, for example, G. Boyer, *The Winding Road to the Welfare State: Economic Insecurity and Social Policy in Britain* (Princeton, NJ: Princeton University Press, 2018), pp. 37–41.

9 Here, I am presenting a very particular narrative about work that I think is the dominant discursive construction of the Victorian ethos of work. Other narratives of work in nineteenth-century Britain certainly exist – for example, Marxist and socialist narratives, which sources in the collection represent. A. J. McIvor, *A History of Work in Britain, 1880–1950* (New York: Palgrave, 2001), pp. 5–25, examines this Marxist story of work and other narratives that have departed from it. D. J. Bradshaw and S. Ozment, (eds), in the compilation *The Voice of Toil: Nineteenth-Century British Writings about Work* (Athens: Ohio University Press, 2000), have included texts addressing 'Work as Mission', 'Work as Opportunity', 'Work as Oppression', and '(Separate) Spheres of Work'. They emphasize that 'work – the distinctive expression of earnestness – came to define the [Victorian] era' (xvii).

10 D. Fraser, *The Evolution of the British Welfare State: A History of Social Policy since the Industrial Revolution* (London: Macmillan, 1973), 113.

11 M. Weber, *The Protestant Ethic and the Spirit of Capitalism* (New York: Dover Publications, 2003, orig. 1905).

12 T. Carlyle, *Past and Present, Thomas Carlyle's Collected Works*, vol. 13 (Project Gutenberg, 2008), 244, at https://www.gutenberg.org/cache/epub/13534/pg13534.html [accessed 8 November 2021]; S. Smiles, *Self Help: With Illustrations of Conduct and Perseverance*, popular ed. (London: John Murray, 1897, orig. 1859). In 'Samuel Smiles and the Gospel of Work', in *Victorian People: A Reassessment of Persons and Themes, 1851–1867* (Chicago: University of Chicago Press, 1975, orig. 1955), Asa Briggs shows the influence of Carlyle's 'gospel of work' on Smiles's thinking.

13 See, for example, Robert Humphreys, *Sin, Organized Charity and the Poor Law in Victorian England* (New York: St. Martin's Press, 1995).

14 S. Smiles, *Character*, popular ed. (London: John Murray, 1917, orig. 1871), p. 99.

15 G. R. Searle has explored the tensions between Victorian moral and spiritual positions and their economic theories and practices: *Morality and the Market in Victorian Britain* (New York: Oxford University Press, 1998).

16 J. Auerbach, *The Great Exhibition of 1851: A Nation on Display* (New Haven, CT: Yale University Press, 1999). In *English Culture and the Decline of the Industrial Spirit, 1850–1980* (New York: Cambridge University Press, 1981), Martin Wiener argues that the Great Exhibition signaled the high point of Britain's commitment to 'work'. The second half of the century and beyond saw the very people who so successfully built the entrepreneurial culture turn their backs on the devotion to work in favour of gentility, which, Wiener contends, contributed in large part to Britain's loss of global economic competitiveness.

17 J. A. Hobson, 'The Meaning and Measure of "Unemployment"', *Contemporary Review* 67 (March 1895), pp. 419–420.

18 W. Beveridge, *Unemployment: A Problem of Industry* (London: Longmans, Green and Co., 1909).

19 W. Walters, 'The Discovery of "Unemployment": New Forms for the Government of Poverty', *Economy and Society* 23:3 (1994), pp. 265–290, on pp. 274–275.

20 See, for example, D. Powell, 'The New Liberalism and the Rise of Labour, 1886–1906', *The Historical Journal* 29:2 (1986), pp. 369–393; N. Whiteside, 'Transforming the Unemployed: Trade Union Benefits and the Advent of State Policy', in K. Laybourn and J. Shepherd (eds), *Labour and Working-Class Lives: Essays to Celebrate the Life and Work of Chris Wrigley* (Manchester, UK: University of Manchester Press, 2017), pp. 68–86; K. D. Brown, 'Conflict in Early British Welfare Policy: The Case of the Unemployed Workmen's Bill of 1905', *Journal of Modern History* 43:4 (December 1971), pp. 615–629; P. Thane, 'The Working Class and State "Welfare" in Britain, 1880–1914', *Historical Journal* 27:4 (1984), pp. 877–900; and J. Burnett, *Idle Hands: The Experience of Unemployment, 1790–1990* (New York: Routledge, 1994), p. 191.

For an opposing view, see J. Harris, *Unemployment and Politics: A Study in English Social Policy, 1886–1914* (Oxford: Clarendon Press), pp. 56 and 83.

21 See Volume 1.

22 See Volume 3.

23 See Volume 3.

24 J. Tosh, 'Masculinities in Industrializing Society: Britain, 1800–1914', *Journal of British Studies* 44:2 (April 2005), pp. 330–342, on p. 332.

25 For a summary of early literature on the breadwinner norm, see A. Janssens, 'The Rise and Decline of the Male Breadwinner Family? An Overview of the Debate', Supplement, *International Review of Social History* 42: S5 (September 1997), pp. 1–23. For Britain specifically, see W. Seccomb, 'Patriarchy Stabilized: The Construction of the Male Breadwinner Wage Norm in Nineteenth-Century Britain', *Social History* 11:1 (January 1986), pp. 53–75; S. Horrell and J. Humphries, 'Women's Labour Force Participation and the Transition to the Male Breadwinner Family, 1790–1865', *Economic History Review* 48:1 (February 1995), pp. 89–117; S. Horrell and J. Humphries, 'The Origins and Expansion of the Male Breadwinner Family: The Case of Nineteenth-Century Britain', Supplement, *International Review of Social History* 42:S5 (1997), pp. 25–64. On separate spheres and 'public' and 'private', see L. Kerber, 'Separate Spheres, Female Worlds, Woman's Place: The Rhetoric of Women's History', *Journal of American History*, 75 (1988), pp. 9–39; A. Vickery, 'Golden Age to Separate Spheres? A Review of the Categories and Chronology of English Women's History', *Historical Journal* 36:2 (1993), pp. 383–414; Davidoff and Hall, *Family Fortunes*; J. Tosh, *A Man's Place: Masculinity and the Middle-Class Home in Victorian England* (New Haven, CT: Yale University Press, 2007). On the working class and the breadwinner norm, see also, E. Griffin, *Bread Winner: An Intimate History of the Victorian Economy* (New Haven, CT: Yale University Press, 2020); S. O. Rose, *Limited Livelihoods: Gender and Class in Nineteenth-Century England* (Berkeley: University of California Press, 1992); A. Clark, *Struggle for the Breeches: Gender and the Making of the British Working Class* (Berkeley: University of California Press, 1995); and Levine-Clark, *Unemployment, Welfare, and Masculine Citizenship.*

26 Keith McClelland, 'Masculinity and the "Representative Artisan" in Britain, 1850–80', in Michael Roper and John Tosh (eds), *Manful Assertions: Masculinities in Britain since 1800* (New York: Routledge, 1991), pp. 74–91, on p. 79.

27 See, for example, Briggs, 'Samuel Smiles'; J.F.C. Harrison, 'The Victorian Gospel of Success', *Victorian Studies* 1:2 (1957), pp. 155–164; Houghton, *The Victorian Frame of Mind*; B. Hilton, *The Age of Atonement: The Influence of Evangelicalism on Social and Economic Thought* (Oxford: Clarendon Press, 1992); J. Tosh, 'Hegemonic Masculinity and the History of Gender', in S. Dudink, K. Hagemann, and J. Tosh (eds), *Masculinities in Politics and War: Gendering Modern History* (Manchester, UK: Manchester University Press, 2004), pp. 41–60; Heather Ellis, 'Thomas Arnold, Christian Manliness and the Problem of Boyhood', *Journal of Victorian Culture*, 19 (2014), pp. 425–441; Amy Milne-Smith argues that later in the century, people were concerned that the devotion to work could lead to overwork, which could result in madness: 'Work and Madness: Overworked Men and Fears of Degeneration, 1860s–1910s', *Journal of Victorian Culture* 24:2 (2019), pp. 159–178; Valerie R. Sanders reveals some of the tensions in the performance of the masculine ideal of work in '"Is There No Work in Hand": The Idle Son Theme at Midcentury', *Studies in the Literary Imagination* 43:1 (2010), pp. 49–67.

28 See, for example, Harris, *Unemployment and Politics*; K. Kumar, 'Unemployment as a Problem in the Development of Industrial Societies: The English Experience', *Sociological Review* 32:2 (1984), pp. 185–233; N. Whiteside, 'Constructing Unemployment: Britain and France in Historical Perspective', *Social Policy Administration* 48:1

(2014), pp. 67–85; Walters, 'Discovery of "Unemployment"'; P. Lagneau-Ymonet and B. Reynaud, 'The Making of a Category of Economic Understanding in Great Britain (1880–1931): "The Unemployed"', *Cambridge Journal of Economics* 44:6 (2020), pp. 1–17; M. Freeden, *The New Liberalism: An Ideology of Social Reform* (Oxford: Oxford University Press, 1986); A. Vincent, 'Classical Liberalism and Its Crisis of Identity', *History of Political Thought* 11:1 (Spring 1990), pp. 143–161; and J. Allett, *New Liberalism: The Political Economy of J.A. Hobson* (Toronto: University of Toronto Press, 1981).

29 Lees, *Solidarities*.

30 Boyer, *The Winding Road*.

31 For a discussion of the public usage of 'unemployment', see Burnett, *Idle Hands*, p. 149.

32 G. R. Boyer, 'The Evolution of Unemployment Relief in Great Britain', *Journal of Interdisciplinary History* 34:3 (2004), pp. 393–433, on p. 394. Boyer also uses the term 'unemployment' for the earlier period in his book *The Winding Road to the Welfare State*.

33 See n. 27.

34 See n. 24.

35 On the impact of the domestic ideal, or the ideology of domesticity, on working-class women, see, for example, Clark, *Struggle for the Breeches*.

36 Walters, 'Discovery of "Unemployment"', pp. 273–274.

37 J. Lewis, *The Voluntary Sector, the State, & Social Work in Britain: The Charity Organisation Society/Family Welfare Association since 1869* (Aldershot, UK: Edward Elgar, 1995), p. 3.

38 See n. 28.

39 See, for example, J. Welshman, 'The Concept of the Unemployable', *Economic History Review* 59:3 (2006), pp. 578–606; G. Stedman Jones, *Outcast London: A Study in the Relationship Between Classes in Victorian Society* (Oxford: Clarendon Press, 1971), pp. 127–129, 286–287; J. Harris, 'Between Civic Virtue and Social Darwinism: The Concept of the Residuum', in David Englander and Rosemary O'Day (eds), *Retrieved Riches: Social Investigation in Britain 1840–1914* (Brookfield, VT: Ashgate, 1995), pp. 67–87, on pp. 76–78.

40 See n. 20.

41 See, for example, D. Feldman and M. P. Baldwin, 'Emigration and the British State, Ca. 1815–1925', in N. Green and F. Reil (eds), *Citizenship and Those Who Leave: The Politics of Emigration and Expatriation* (Champaign, IL: University of Illinois Press, 2007), pp. 135–155, on p. 136; H.J.M. Johnston, *British Emigration Policy 1815–30: 'Shovelling Out Paupers'* (Oxford: Clarendon Press, 1972); H. Malchow, *Population Pressures: Emigration and Government in Late-Nineteenth-Century Britain* (Palo Alto, CA: Society for the Promotion of Science and Scholarship, 1979).

42 See, for example, J. Field, *Working Men's Bodies: Work Camps in Britain, 1880–1940* (Manchester, UK: Manchester University Press, 2013); J. Brown, 'Charles Booth and Labour Colonies', *Economic History Review*, new series, 21:2 (August 1968), pp. 349–360; Harris, *Unemployment and Politics*, pp. 115–144; Welshman, 'Concept of the Unemployable'.

43 Harris, *Unemployment and Politics*, pp. 157–210; Boyer, *The Winding Road*, pp. 128–132; on women, see K. Laybourn, *Unemployment and Employment Policies Concerning Women in Britain, 1900–1951* (Lewiston, NY: Edwin Mellen Press, 1997), pp. 32–34.

44 See, for example, Hall, *Civilising Subjects*; A. Burton, *At the Heart of Empire: Indians and the Colonial Encounter in Late Victorian Britain* (Berkeley: University of California Press, 1998); and A. Thompson, *Imperial Britain: The Empire in British Politics, 1880–1932* (New York: Routledge, 2000).

45 See Volume 4 Introduction and Volume 4, Part 1.
46 The three with the greatest impact were A. Mearns and W. C. Preston, *The Bitter Cry of Outcast London: An Inquiry into the Condition of the Abject Poor* (London: James Clarke and Co., 1883); W. Booth, *In Darkest England and the Way Out* (London: Salvation Army, 1890); and C. Booth, *Life and Labour of the People in London*, 17 vols. (London: Macmillan, 1902–1903).
47 The publisher Adam Matthew came out in May 2021 with *Poverty, Philanthropy and Social Conditions in Victorian Britain.* This contains the entire Family Welfare Association Library, correspondence between Poor Law Inspectors and the Poor Law Commission, and scholarly introductions. At www.povertyinvictorianbritain.amdigital.co.uk/ [accessed 12 June 2021].
48 Carlyle, *Past and Present*; W. Morris, *Useless Work versus Useful Toil* (London: Socialist League Office, 1886); J. Ruskin, *The Stones of Venice*, vols. 1–3 (London: Smith, Elder, and Co., 1851); Booth, *Life and Labour*; and Beveridge, *Problem of Industry*.
49 The 2010 Equality Act in the United Kingdom uses the language 'disabled people'.
50 See, for example, 'Identity-First Language', Autistic Self-Advocacy Network, at https://autisticadvocacy.org/about-asan/identity-first-language/ [accessed 4 June 2021]; D. S. Dunn and E. E. Andrews, 'Person-First and Identity-First Language: Developing Psychologists' Cultural Competence Using Disability Language', *American Psychologist* 70:3 (2015), pp. 255–264.
51 Sources throughout the collection suggest that unemployed men did indeed develop these identities, especially political identities and gendered identities. They identified as unemployed in political actions, and they identified as unemployed in family contexts where they failed as breadwinners, issues I am exploring in other work.
52 F. Blau, J. Koebe, and P. Meyerhofer, 'Who Are the Essential and Frontline Workers?', *NBER Working Paper Series*, National Bureau of Economic Research, Working Paper 27791, September 2020, revised March 2021, at www.nber.org/papers/w27791 [accessed 14 June 2021]; B. Butcher, 'Coronavirus: Key Workers are Clapped and Cheered, but What Are They Paid?', BBC News, 7 January 2021, at www.bbc.com/news/uk-52312038 [accessed 22 June 2021]. In the U.K., 'key workers' are named by the government as 'people whose jobs are vital to public health and safety' during the pandemic. J. White and C. Hope, 'Who Is on the List of Key Workers?', *Telegraph*, 22 February 2021, at www.telegraph.co.uk/news/0/key-workers-essential-list-who-uk-new-lockdown-2021/ [accessed 23 June 2021].
53 M. Kinder and L. Stateler, 'Essential Workers Comprise about Half of All Workers in Low-Paid Occupations', Brookings Institution, at www.brookings.edu/blog/the-avenue/2021/02/05/essential-workers-deserve-minimum-wage-increase/ [accessed 16 June 2021]; I. Ivanova, 'Most Companies Haven't Given Essential Workers Pandemic "Hazard Pay". One City Is Changing That', CBS News, updated 9 June 2021, at www.cbsnews.com/news/oxnard-california-hazard-pay-stimulus-american-rescue-plan/ [accessed 17 June 2021]. On opposition to hazard pay, S. P. Raymond, 'The Hazards of Hazard Pay', U.S. Chamber of Commerce, 4 February 2021, at www.uschamber.com/article/the-hazards-of-hazard-pay [accessed 17 June 2021].
54 M. Kinder, L. Stateler, and J. Du, 'The COVID-19 Hazard Continues, But the Hazard Pay Does Not: Why America's Essential Workers Need a Raise', Brookings Institution, 29 October 2020, at www.brookings.edu/research/the-covid-19-hazard-continues-but-the-hazard-pay-does-not-why-americas-frontline-workers-need-a-raise/ [accessed 17 June 2021]; 'Minimum Wage of at least £10 and an End to Rip-Off Youth Rates – Usdaw Gives Evidence to the Low Pay Commission', USDAW, 18 June 2021, at www.usdaw.org.uk/About-Us/News/2021/Jun/Minimum-wage-of-at-least-10-and-an-end-to-ripoff-y [accessed 22 June 2021]; Ivanova, 'Most Companies'.

55 A. W., '*The Economist* Explains: What Disruptive Innovation Means', *Economist*, 15 January 2015, at www.economist.com/the-economist-explains/2015/01/25/what-disruptive-innovation-means [accessed 22 June 2021].
56 C. Castrillon, 'This Is the Future of Remote Work in 2021', *Forbes*, 27 December 2020, at www.forbes.com/sites/carolinecastrillon/2021/12/27/this-is-the-future-of-remote-work-in-2021/?sh=69ebc3e51e1d [accessed 16 June 2021]; S. Taneja, P. Mizen, and N. Bloom, 'Working from Home Is Revolutionising the UK Labour Market', *VoxEU*, 15 March 2021, at https://voxeu.org/article/working-home-revolutionising-uk-labour-market [accessed 22 June 2021].
57 M. M. Carino, 'Executives, Workers See Future of Remote Work Differently', *Marketplace*, 10 May 2021, at www.marketplace.org/2021/05/10/executives-workers-see-future-of-remote-work-differently/ [accessed 16 June 2021].
58 A. Cefaliello, 'Addressing the Impact of the Precarious Working Conditions of On-Demand Gig Workers' Health and Safety in Europe Needs Regulatory Action', A-id, Agenda for International Development, 10 March 2021, at www.a-id.org/2021/03/10/addressing-the-impact-of-the-precarious-working-conditions-of-on-demand-gig-workers-health-and-safety-in-europe-needs-regulatory-action/ [accessed 23 June 2021].
59 Cefaliello, 'Addressing the Impact'; E. Yerby and R. Page-Tickell, 'Where Next for the Gig Economy and Precarious Work Post COVID-19?', *London School of Economics and Political Science Blog*, 1 May 2020, at https://blogs.lse.ac.uk/management/2020/05/01/where-next-for-the-gig-economy-and-precarious-work-post-covid-19/ [accessed 23 June 2021]; A. Gaskell, 'Gig Workers in Times of Covid', *Forbes*, 20 April 2021, at www.forbes.com/sites/adigaskell/2021/04/20/gig-workers-in-times-of-covid/?sh=38e4cfa448e1 [accessed 23 June 2021].
60 J. Schor, 'How the Gig Economy Promotes Inequality', *Milken Institute Review*, 18 September 2020, at www.milkenreview.org/articles/how-the-gig-economy-promotes-inequality [accessed 23 June 2021]; 'BME Workers on Zero-Hours Contracts: A Joint Report by the Trades Union Congress and Race on the Agenda', Trades Union Congress, June 2021, at www.tuc.org.uk/sites/default/files/2021-06/RotAreport.pdf [accessed 23 June 2021].
61 B.C.L. Paisner, 'UK Supreme Court's Decision on Status of Uber Drivers and Its Significance on Gig Economy', *JDSupra*, 26 April 2021, at https://www.jdsupra.com/legalnews/uk-supreme-court-s-decision-on-status-3871977/; N. Bose, 'EXCLUSIVE: U.S. Labor Secretary Supports Classifying Gig Workers as Employees', *Reuters*, 29 April 2021, at https://www.reuters.com/world/us/exclusive-us-labor-secretary-says-most-gig-workers-should-be-classified-2021-04-29/ [accessed 8 November 2021].
62 N. Petrosky-Nadeau and R. G. Valletta, 'An Unemployment Crisis after the Onset of COVID-19', *FRBSF Economic Letter*, 18 May 2020, at www.frbsf.org/economic-research/files/el2020-12.pdf [accessed 16 June 2021].
63 A. Powell and B. Francis-Devine, 'Coronavirus: Impact on the Labour Market', House of Commons Library, at https://researchbriefings.files.parliament.uk/documents/CBP-8898/CBP-8898.pdf [accessed 23 June 2021]. The CJRS was originally supposed to have had two phases, which would have ended in October 2020, but it stayed in place until September 2021, furloughing a total of 11.7 million workers. A. Powell, B. Francis-Devine, and H. Clark, 'Coronavirus Jobs Retention Scheme', *House of Commons Library*, at https://commonslibrary.parliament.uk/research-briefings/cbp-9152/ [accessed 22 November 2021].
64 Congressional Research Service, 'Unemployment Rates during the COVID-19 Pandemic', updated 20 May 2021, at https://fas.org/sgp/crs/misc/R46554.pdf [accessed 16 June 2021], p. 2; Powell and Francis-Devine, 'Coronavirus', p. 5.
65 National Restaurant Association Educational Foundation, Restaurant Employee Relief Fund, at https://rerf.us/ [accessed 16 June 2021]. See also, Restaurant Workers'

Community Foundation, 'Frequently Asked Questions about Our COVID-19 Relief Fund', at www.restaurantworkerscf.org/covid19faq [accessed 16 June 2021].

66 A. Coghlan and J. Hansen, 'The Government Banks on £4,000–£9,000 Grants to Keep Restaurants Afloat Until Spring', *Eater London*, at https://london.eater.com/22214754/coronavirus-lockdown-uk-new-business-grants-2021 [accessed 23 June 2021]; A. Coghlan, 'What the Budget Means for Restaurants', *Eater London*, at https://london.eater.com/22309948/uk-budget-2021-rishi-sunak-announcement-coronavirus-grants-vat-cut-restaurants [accessed 23 June 2021].

67 Congressional Research Service, 'Unemployment Rates', p. 2.

68 E. Gould and V. Wilson, 'Black Workers Face Two of the Most Lethal Preexisting Conditions for Coronavirus – Racism and Economic Inequality', Economic Policy Institute, 1 June 2020, at www.epi.org/publication/black-workers-covid/ [accessed 16 June 2021].

69 Gov. McMaster to Dir. Ellzey re: federal UI benefit termination, 6 May 2021, at https://governor.sc.gov/sites/default/files/Documents/5-6-21%20Gov%20McMaster%20to%20Dir%20Ellzey%20re%20Federal%20UI%20benefit%20termination.pdf [accessed 16 June 2021]; Congressional Research Service, 'States Opting Out of COVID-19 Unemployment Insurance (UI) Agreements', 24 May 2021, at https://crsreports.congress.gov/product/pdf/IN/IN11679 [accessed 16 June 2021].

70 A. Holpuch, '"No One Wants to Work Anymore", The Truth Behind this Unemployment Benefits Myth', *Guardian*, 7 May 2021, at www.theguardian.com/business/2021/may/07/truth-behind-unemployment-benefits-myth [accessed 11 July 2021].

71 D. Alpert, 'Americans Don't Want to Return to Low-Wage Jobs', *New York Times*, 1 June 2021, at www.nytimes.com/2021/06/01/opinion/labor-shortage-jobs-biden-covid.html [accessed 16 June 2021].

72 Holpuch, '"No One Want to Work Anymore"'.

73 A. North, 'Bosses Are Acting Like the Pandemic Never Happened', *Vox*, 28 May 2021, at www.vox.com/22455058/jobs-restaurants-office-employers-covid-pandemic-work [accessed 17 June 2021].

74 See, for example, S. Wright, D. R. Fletcher, and A.B.R. Stewart, 'Punitive Benefit Sanctions, Welfare Conditionality, and the Social Abuse of Unemployed People in Britain: Transforming Claimants into Offenders?', *Social Policy and Administration* 54:2 (February 2020), pp. 278–294; R. Davidson, 'Thatcher's Legacy and Social Security', in A. Mullen, S. Farrall, and D. Jeffrey (eds), *Thatcherism in the 21st Century: The Social and Cultural Legacy* (Switzerland: Palgrave Macmillan, 2020), pp. 209–227; B. B. Geiger, 'Benefit "Myths"? The Accuracy and Inaccuracy of Public Beliefs about the Benefits System', LSE, CASE Paper 199 (2016), at http://sticerd.lse.ac.uk/dps/case/cp/casepaper199.pdf [accessed 23 June 2021]; J. Hills, *Good Times, Bad Times: The Welfare Myth of Them and Us* (Bristol, UK: Policy Press, 2015).

75 B. Francis Devine, N. Foley, and M. Ward, 'Women and the Economy', Briefing Paper Number CBP06838, *House of Commons Library*, 2 March 2021, at https://researchbriefings.files.parliament.uk/documents/SN06838/SN06838.pdf [accessed 23 June 2021].

76 See, among many others, R. Lowe, *The Welfare State in Britain since 1945*, 3rd ed. (New York: Palgrave Macmillan, 2005).

VOLUME 1 INTRODUCTION

The meanings of work

Nineteenth-century Britons experienced several major transformations that led them to ponder the meanings of work with new urgency. The most material was, of course, the change in the means of production in which machines were introduced into labour processes that had always been done by hand: what historians have called the industrial revolution.[1] As Britain industrialized, the meanings of work changed as many men and women of the labouring classes adapted themselves to the industrial order by learning new forms of 'work-discipline' measured by factory time, as historian E. P. Thompson has famously argued.[2] Others in non-mechanized industries found their labour intensified to match the needs of factory production.[3] The introduction of machines occurred irregularly, with the use of steam power in textiles leading the way, although mechanized cotton outpaced wool, for example, and the use of machines across the industry was not universal even at the middle of the nineteenth century.[4]

Accompanying these material changes were ideological shifts. Beginning with the Methodist movement in the mid-eighteenth century, a religious transformation – a revival of serious Christianity – took place, which saw work as the centre of the spiritual and material self and wealth accumulation as the sign of God's reward.[5] The public world of work, however, was a man's world. Evangelicalism helped spread a doctrine of 'separate spheres' that praised women's role as the moral keepers of the private, domestic world of the home, while men served the family by earning to support the household.[6] The spiritual value of work was complemented by the new political economy. In this period, a business society's interest in free markets and free trade overtook the protectionist impulses of landowners. The economic ethos coming into the 1830s fostered competition in open markets, which was thought to naturally balance individuals' self-interests.[7] The utilitarian thinking of Jeremy Bentham, which influenced state development, bolstered the free market doctrines of political economy.[8] Evangelical religion and political economy both reinforced a work imperative, leaving no room for idleness.[9] These material and ideological transformations created fodder for substantial conversations about work and workers.

DOI: 10.4324/9780429320323-2

The respectability of honest toil

While industrialization brought on changes in the structure of work, increasing numbers of men and women became urban dwellers who had less control over the nature, pace, and stability of their work.[10] It is not surprising, then, that many writers felt compelled to say something about the status of labourers and the value of manual labour. If, accepting the controversial argument of the cultural Marxist historian E. P. Thompson, the working class had solidified in the early 1830s in response to their exclusion from parliamentary reform in 1832, then labourers and those observing them wrote from newly evolving class perspectives.[11] While some held onto paternalistic stances about social relations, many envisioned a struggle between those who toiled to benefit human needs and those who lived on the bounty of that toil. In this part, I have chosen sources that, from very different viewpoints, proclaim the value of labour and the potential threats to that value in Britain's industrial capitalist society.

These sources were situated in a time when the meaning of work was often framed in the language of the classical economists. The dominant economic view of work was David Ricardo's labour theory of value. This stressed that the value of all goods was based on the labour it took to produce them, which helped determine prices in the market.[12] Ricardo, however, was not concerned with how much workers got paid; indeed, like other political economists, he thought the free market would determine wages.[13] Many thinkers believed Thomas Malthus's theory that population growth would leave labourers without work, drive wages down, and increase poverty.[14] Some came to blame the poor for their own condition, especially for having too many children. Political economists also emphasized property as a right to be protected but did not go so far as to argue for the protection of labour, which for most working men was their only property.[15] The doctrines of political economy did not present a positive outlook on the potential improvement of workers' circumstances.

Some reformers, however, took these ideas in more progressive directions to provide workers themselves with a sense of their worth in processes of production and in their respectability as men. The much-published radical journalist William Cobbett in 1831 addressed himself 'To the Labourers of England' in order to tell them of their 'rights and duties' (Volume 1, Part 1, Chapter 1). Workers had a duty to labour, but Cobbett argued that the wealthy, who benefited from that labour, had a duty to maintain them in times of need. J. F. Bray (Volume 1, Part 1, Chapter 3) was what came to be known as a Ricardian socialist.[16] In his 1839 *Labour's Wrongs and Labour's Remedy*, he challenged the capitalist organization of society where labourers – the producers – worked for the benefit of the few – the idlers. Bray believed in the possibility of an equal society where wealth was redistributed to recognize the value of the productive class. Similarly, in 1842, the *Chartist Circular* (Volume 1, Part 1, Chapter 4; see below for discussion of Chartism) from a radical perspective used the language of producers and idlers to critique working-class disenfranchisement. The only way that workers themselves would be valued, the article argued, would be through the representation of the productive classes in Parliament.

While the language of political economy was one way in which the respectability of work was articulated, it was not necessarily the dominant one. Victorians assigned tremendous moral and religious significance to work. Novels, sermons, advice manuals, journal articles, and more were devoted to the virtues of work. Protestantism imbued capitalism with moral purpose and justified the accumulation of wealth, supporting the political economists' vision of the free market.[17] The flipside to the moral project of labour was idleness, which reformers regarded as sinful and wasteful. While idleness was used to censure poor labourers, the reproach could also be turned on its head. For example, when Bray and the *Chartist Circular* (Volume 1, Part 1, Chapters 3 and 4) critiqued upper-class idlers for living off the labour of the poor, they had this moral as well as an economic framework in mind. The Scottish writer Thomas Carlyle, who in 1843 proclaimed work to be the new gospel of the Victorians, assured the working class that even the simplest labour participated in this project of virtue: 'All work, even cotton-spinning, is noble; work is alone noble: be that here said and asserted once more'.[18]

Ideas about the respectability and spirituality of labour could provide solace for workers in menial and dangerous occupations, although moralists more often used their pens hoping to keep workers in their place. Joseph Livesey, the founder of the temperance movement in England, in 1838 published 'An Address to Working Men' in his *Moral Reformer* (Volume 1, Part 1, Chapter 2). As part of his free-market message on improving employment opportunities, Livesey argued that workers needed to cultivate higher moral practices, such as temperance and thrift. Thomas Bywater Smithies's *British Workman* had as its goal the moral uplift of manual labourers. The three selections (Volume 1, Part 1, Chapter 6) from the paper all emphasize the dignity of manual labour and labourers, thanking God for providing ennobling hard work. Whereas Livesey's vision was of a class society that needed a shared morality to tie it together, the articles in the *British Workman* idealize rural society and more vertical relationships. Nostalgia for the rural was common across the nineteenth century, as an antidote for the supposed corruption of urban, industrial society.[19] In *The Labouring Man's Book*, the Reverend Ashton Oxenden (Volume 1, Part 1, Chapter 7) wrote to assure workers that even if their labour was difficult, it had been ordained by God, so it was holy. Livesey, Oxenden, and the articles in the *British Workman* all took a paternalistic attitude towards workers, assuming that men (and women) needed their advice to recognize the value of their work and understand how to behave morally.

The messages of the economic and moral uplift of work as a good in itself often conflicted with material realities of labourers' experiences. It was one thing for the *British Workman* to proclaim the 'dignity of labour' and another for a worker to be suffering from illness and hunger due to poor working conditions or lack of regular employment. Joseph Adshead, in his 1842 *Distress in Manchester* (Volume 1, Part 1, Chapter 5), collected case histories of men, women, and children enduring severe privation because of a trade depression in the city. Their narratives revealed their attachment to work, particularly for men, and a challenge to men's identities in being unemployed. Perhaps this can be read as an internalization of the messages about the centrality of work. In 1865, Dr J. C. Hall (Volume 1, Part 1, Chapter 8) reported on *The Trades of Sheffield* to the National Association for the Promotion of Social Science. He demonstrated the dangers their trades posed to file cutters and grinders, who suffered diseases from the dust produced when metal hit stone.[20] The workers themselves were fatalistic regarding the illnesses they experienced, knowing that they had jobs they could not afford to leave.

Claims about the respectability of labour also seemed politically problematic to some social thinkers and workers themselves who were critical of the system in which they laboured. John Ruskin, the art critic, and William Morris, the socialist designer, both damned industrial society for fostering the division of labour through machinery and taking away the labourer's joy in imaginative production.[21] John Bruce Glasier, who was a regular contributor to Morris's *Commonweal*, the journal of the Socialist League, published 'Honest Toil' in 1890 (Volume 1, Part 1, Chapter 9) to challenge visions of 'honest toil' promoted by publications such as the *British Workman*.[22] Labour, according to Glasier, could never be dignified under the conditions of industrial capitalism, which operated by a wage system that degraded working men. By contrast, in *Life through Labour's Eyes* (Volume 1, Part 1, Chapter 10), George Milligan, a Liverpool dock worker, in 1911 emphasized the respectability of manual labour in order to stress the value of physical work, which he believed society did not sufficiently recognize. Honest toil did indeed exist, in Milligan's perspective, but the men who performed it were not receiving their worth in wages, and this tested their masculine identities.[23]

Men and machines

The challenge industrial society posed to men's identities as workers was strongest in labouring men's relationship to machines. Proponents of machines wrote of their promise for Britain's economy, the positive impact of mechanization on the creation of jobs, and the proliferation of consumer goods at lower prices. Machines' opponents depicted starving artisans, with suffering wives and children, who could no longer compete in the new industrial economy. In this section, I have included sources that explore this debate about mechanization and the relative value of the cheapness of goods and a man's livelihood.

Many men's identities were tested by machines, as their sense of themselves as workers was transformed by the new pace and requirements of their labour, and some men were indeed pushed out as their hand-worked jobs became obsolete. The traditional historical narrative regarding the loss of work with industrialization has focused on adult, skilled, able-bodied men being replaced by machines or displaced by women and children who could work machines that called for less skill and lower wages.[24] The political economist Ricardo originally thought that machinery would have little effect on employment, but in the third edition of his *Principles of Political Economy*, he wrote, 'I am convinced, that the substitution of machinery for human labour, is often very injurious to the interests of the class of labourers'.[25] E. P. Thompson famously described the trials of the handloom weavers in his monumental *The Making of the English Working Class*, arguing that the first phase of their decline started with an overstocked labour market and wage cuts even before the introduction of the power loom. By the 1830s, as machines began more rapidly to displace hand labour, Thompson says, 'the great majority of weavers were living on the edge – and sometimes beyond the edge – of the borders of starvation'.[26] Men, who were meant to provide for their families, now faced a world where their wives found work, while they found none. Historian Anna Clark, in *The Struggle for the Breeches: Gender and the Making of the British Working Class*, argues that artisans blamed women as much as machines for undercutting skilled men's labour both in mechanized and unmechanized industries.[27]

The handloom weavers' story is certainly iconic, and sources reveal contests over the meaning of their condition. Sir John Maxwell (Volume 1, Part 2, Chapter 15), a Scottish member of Parliament, put forward the case of the handloom weavers against power looms to the public in 1834 after failing to convince the government to intervene with protectionist legislation. By contrast, the young member of Parliament for Stroud, George Poulett Scrope (Volume 1, Part 2, Chapter 14), in 1835 called the handloom weavers 'delusional' in asking for government regulation of machines, since this interference would be a violation of the doctrine of *laissez-faire*. The Handloom Weavers' Central Committee responded to Scrope (Volume 1, Part 2, Chapter 14) by emphasizing that free trade and mechanization were the very causes of their distress. In 1844, the radical journalist William Carpenter (Volume 1, Part 2, Chapter 18) argued that machinery was not the reason for the desperate condition of the handloom weavers. Rather, they suffered in Manchester, the city on which he focused, because their industry was dominated by the unwelcome Irish: individual, not structural, issues were to blame.

Political economists regarded mechanization as the means to achieve perfection in industry, and many reformers and politicians, such as Scrope, adopted this viewpoint. According to historian John Burnett in *Idle Hands*, 'Most political economists saw the machine as a benign wealth-creator in which, ultimately, all would share'.[28] The Society for the Diffusion of Useful Knowledge (SDUK) (Volume 1, Part 2, Chapter 11) addressed working men in 1831 as rational beings, hoping to demonstrate the multiple benefits of machinery, including cheaper goods and higher wages. Directly countering the SDUK in 1832, the radical G. C. Burrows (Volume 1, Part 2, Chapter 13) accused the society of putting machines before the lives of workers. Cheapness, Burrows argued, was not worth the price of unemployed and destitute men. Sixty years later, James Samuelson (Volume 1, Part 2, Chapter 20), a factory owner but ally of trade unionists, offered a cautious analysis of the trade-off between mechanization and the displacement of workers caused by machines. From the 'economic' perspective, he praised the benefits of labour-saving machinery, but from a human perspective, he recognized the pain of the transition for manual labourers.

The 1830s saw workers, radicals, and paternalist Tories come together in a movement against what they saw as the brutality of the new factory system.[29] As E. P. Thompson argued, the 'moral economy' of the pre-industrial world was structured by 'social norms and obligations' by which the poor expected certain protections from their betters, and their betters agreed.[30] The *laissez-faire* political economy of the factory system shattered this structure. Led by the abolitionist Evangelical Tory Richard Oastler, who called what he witnessed in factories 'Yorkshire slavery', the factory movement focused on achieving a ten-hour day.[31] Workers set up 'Short Time' committees for factory reform, and their cause became a 'mass movement'.[32] A petition (Volume 1, Part 2, Chapter 12) from the spinners of the busy mill town of Ashton-on-Lyne, for example, asked Parliament to enact the ten-hour day. One claim of the short-timers was that fewer hours would produce more jobs, which would help unemployed workers. The factory movement continued to gain momentum, focusing especially on regulating the work of women and children. Both paternalist reformers and working men themselves regarded women and children as lacking the agency to make decisions about their work that belonged to adult men.[33] Important acts limited the hours of children's and young persons' (thirteen to eighteen) work in 1833 and of women's and children's work in 1842, 1844, and 1847. In 1853, a ten-and-a-half-hour day was established for women and young persons, which effectively limited adult men's hours as well.[34] The politics of the factory movement, including Oastler's anti-slavery rhetoric, became entwined with the anti–Poor Law movement from 1834 on (see Volume 2 Introduction). The ballad, 'The Present Condition of British Workmen' (Volume 1, Part 2, Chapter 16), brings all these themes together, explicitly connecting criticisms of mechanization with loss of employment, starvation, and attacks on the cruelty of the New Poor Law.

The factory movement and the anti–Poor Law movement also fed Chartism, the great radical working-class political movement that was most active between 1838 and 1848.[35] Chartism was a national movement, which, historian Dorothy Thompson argues,

> came about because the people in the different manufacturing districts found themselves agreed on the need for a movement to protect their existing institutions and achievements, to resist the attacks being mounted on them by the newly-enfranchised employing class, and to press forward for more freedoms and a more equitable system of taxation, employment, and citizenship than the society of the 1830s offered them.[36]

Chartists believed that political rights would solve economic problems and therefore situated questions of work within the political sphere. The six demands of the People's Charter were universal male suffrage, secret ballots, the abolition of the property qualification to sit in Parliament, salaries for members of Parliament, constituencies of equal size, and annual parliamentary elections.[37] Chartists organized three separate petitions demanding the points of the Charter. Each time they gathered millions of signatures, and each time they were rejected by Parliament.[38] The source in Volume 1, Part 2, Chapter 17 is a newspaper article covering a meeting of female Chartists, who argued that their unemployed husbands had been displaced by machines because working-class men lacked the franchise. Women, they claimed, had a role in supporting the Charter: to help empower their husbands politically so that families would no longer starve with men out of work.

Fiction helped Victorians contemplate the changes that the mechanization of key industries brought to their world. The 'condition of England' novels of the mid-nineteenth century, such as *Mary Barton* and *North and South* by Elizabeth Gaskell, *Shirley* by Charlotte Bronte, and *Sybil* by Benjamin Disraeli, wrestled with the social consequences of industrialization and sought to draw the attention of middle-class readers to the plight of poor workers. Charles Dickens's *Hard Times* (1854) (Volume 1, Part 2, Chapter 19), one of the most well-known texts in this collection, combined a critique of political economy, utilitarianism, and the culture of factory life, in which workers were reduced to 'hands' and individuals were ruled by 'fact' and allowed no time for 'fancy'. Benjamin Brierley's *Tales and Sketches of Lancashire Life* (Volume 1, Part 2, Chapter 19), published in 1885, still spoke to issues that were relevant earlier in the century: in the selection here, the displacement of handloom weavers by machines. Brierley focuses on the moral and environmental corruption caused by the new factory economy and, like Dickens, criticizes political economy for its lack of feeling. Mechanization and the laws of economics made work meaningless, taking away the dignity identified by the sources in Volume 1, Part 1.

Women's labour: Productive and reproductive

It is not surprising that so many of the 'condition of England' texts had female protagonists or focused on the plight of working women in industrial society. The meaning of work for women in the new economy centred on three interconnected narratives that also encompassed labouring men in significant ways. The first was that employers used women either to displace men with the use of machines, putting men out of work and causing destitution, or to compete with men, de-skill working processes, and lower wages. This narrative also related to fears about the emasculation of working men.[39] In sources in Part 2, both labouring men and anti-mechanization advocates made this argument. The second narrative was that industrialization, and, more specifically, women working in factories, destroyed the working-class family.[40] The third held that female factory workers, by virtue of working in a factory environment, became corrupted and lost the ability to serve as good wives and mothers.[41] The final two narratives were for the most part constructed by moralists and social reformers, who saw working women through the lens of the male breadwinner norm, which positioned women as wives dependent on working husbands, although working men adopted these narratives for their own purposes as well.[42] According to historian John Tosh,

> Notwithstanding the prevalence of women's employment in the working class, the cultural weight attached to the *male* bread-winner was overwhelming. It was reflected positively in the demand for a 'family wage', and negatively in the humiliation of the unemployed man obliged to depend on his wife's earning, and in the anger of the skilled artisan displaced by female labour.[43]

The reality was that many women, including married women, had to work to contribute income to their households; many of these women, though, were not employed in factories but in sweated occupations in workshops or in their homes or in domestic service.[44] Theirs was a secondary labour market, marginalized by an economy that privileged the paid work of men.[45] The sources in this section examine anxieties about women's work in industrial society and how, later in the nineteenth century, women sought to change the narratives.

When steam power came to the textile industry in the late eighteenth century, women who were involved in domestic weaving and spinning were among the first to enter factories. As their visibility increased, they drew an outsized amount of attention in relation to their numbers. By the 1830s, an entire literature existed on 'factory girls'.[46] Joseph Livesey (Volume 1, Part 3, Chapter 21; see Volume 1, Part 1, Chapter 2), the temperance reformer, wrote directly 'To the Females Employed in Factories', with the aim of improving their morality. Livesey believed factories produced immodest women, who damaged their opportunity to be successful wives and mothers. One of the sources in Volume 1, Part 3, Chapter 22 is a newspaper article from 1842 recounting a female Chartist meeting at which Sarah Price condemned a nation where an 'inverted' gender arrangement existed: men went unemployed, dependent on their wives who were forced to work in factories, which degraded everyone. Livesey and Price, from very different perspectives, agreed that factories tarnished women's respectability. The writer Esther Copley (Volume 1, Part 3, Chapter 24) in the 1840s challenged this prevalent narrative through a text also providing advice to 'young women of the factory'. Although Copley agreed with the other two sources that women's ultimate role was domestic, she acknowledged that young working-class women would need to work before marriage and that some of them would work in factories. Copley accepted that factory work posed dangers for women's morality but saw value in women's work and believed that women could triumph over moral challenges with proper instruction

While female factory workers took the brunt of the blame for the 'immoral' state of the industrial working class in the 1830s and 1840s, reformers throughout the century also focused on women in sweated trades, where they performed unmechanized piecework. Parliament passed legislation to regulate the health and safety of factories over the course of the nineteenth century, but 'outwork' remained unregulated and was characterized by long hours, poor wages, and usually horrible working conditions.[47] The image of the pitiful seamstress, barely surviving, always on the edge of falling into prostitution, haunted Victorian literature and reform societies.[48] Mary Anne Walker, who became a well-known Chartist speaker, used the plight of the seamstress (Volume 1, Part 3, Chapter 22) to point to the injustice of wealth distribution in the country and the need for working-class parliamentary representation to fix it. While Richard Oastler famously equated factory workers with slaves on British plantations, others, like the ballad in Volume 1, Part 3, Chapter 26, accused wealthy women, who supported the luxury fashion piecework trades, of underpinning 'white slavery'. Margaret Harkness's description of the 'palm' needlewomen (Volume 1, Part 3, Chapter 31) provided evidence of harsh working conditions and the dangers of the trade with the aim of publicizing the conditions of home industries. In 'Finery and Freedom, or Lucy's Choice' (Volume 1, Part 3, Chapter 27), the *British Workman*'s moral tale cautioned women to be content as domestic servants and not to seek out the temptations of the city, where they would find themselves degraded as seamstresses.

All of the alarmist narratives about women's industrial work came down to the fact that women's work outside the home competed with their 'natural' domestic roles. This was based on the middle-class separate spheres ideal, which positioned men in the public realm earning a 'family wage' to support wives and children in the private realm.[49] The *British Workman*'s 'A Few Words to the Wives of Working Men' (1858) (Volume 1, Part 3, Chapter 27) provides advice to wives about how to please their husbands, locating women in the home waiting for their husbands' return from work. Advice literature, such as that in Volume 1, Part 3, Chapters 21 and 24, tried to convince working women of what they lost in their time away from home but admitted that if women had to work, they should choose domestic service. Yet some, like Thomas Wright, author of *The Great Unwashed* (1868) (Volume 1, Part 3, Chapter 29), believed servants made terrible wives because they did not receive broad domestic training but focused on one aspect of the domestic sphere, such as cooking. The Reverend Alexander Munro (Volume 1, Part 3, Chapter 28) also thought that women received insufficient training for their domestic roles, proposing during the Lancashire cotton famine (see Volume 2, Part 3, Chapters 33 and 34) that unemployed factory women should take classes in domestic skills. Both Munro and Wright, in the end, considered the best solution was for young women to stay out of the labour force and learn domestic skills from their mothers or in their new husbands' homes. An interesting tension exists in these sources between understanding women's domestic skills as innate and acknowledging that women needed training to become adept in the home.

These understandings of working-class women's capabilities, and indeed their embodied natures, were investigated and shaped by some of the many inquiries into the conditions of work in the nineteenth century.[50] The selection from the 1843 Royal Commission into Women and Children in Agriculture (Volume 1, Part 3, Chapter 23), for example, portrayed agricultural labour for women as generally healthy and female agricultural workers as usually respectable, a contrast with the image of the 'factory girl'. This fits with the overall assumption that agricultural labour and the countryside produced healthier workers altogether.[51] A study by Dr George Reid in 1892 (Volume 1, Part 3, Chapter 32) found that infant mortality rates were much higher in industrial areas where married women worked; he presented this information to the British Medical Association's Public Medicine Section hoping to bring it before Parliament to control married women's work. Various factory acts restricted women's work throughout the nineteenth century, but none specifically regulated married women's work. White lead was made a dangerous trade in 1892, and an 1893 summary report of a Committee into White Lead (Volume 1, Part 3, Chapter 33) detailed why the industry was considered more dangerous for women, whose labour was restricted.[52] Women's reproductive bodies shaped the types of work officials believed that women could undertake.

Still, even in the realm of production, women and men tended to work in different occupations and, when their occupations overlapped, at different tasks. Historian Sonya Rose has demonstrated how certain jobs became de-skilled as women took them over; indeed, skill itself was gendered so that women would always be considered less skilled than men.[53] In an unusually progressive article for its time, the *Artizan* in 1845 (Volume 1, Part 3, Chapter 25) argued that in order to improve women's position in the labour market, men should abandon occupations that women were capable of performing, such as printing. Then men and women would not compete for the same jobs, and women could become skilled. The journalist John Boyd Kinnear (Volume 1, Part 3, Chapter 30) made basically the same argument in 1873, insisting that women would never be competitive with men, so occupations should be redistributed. More occupations needed to be open to women, and this shift would happen as men left jobs that did not require strength to women.

Activists for the rights of women's labour often adhered to some vision of separate spheres that informed their arguments about women's work.[54] Emilia Dilke (Volume 1, Part 3, Chapter 34), who became president of the Women's Trade Union League in 1886, believed in the natural differences between the sexes and thought this should be reflected in the work they undertook. She assumed married women's work should be regulated in order to support the male breadwinner family and that men and women should work in separate occupations. In 1907, the Charity Organisation Society (see Volume 2, Part 2, Chapter 20) leader Helen Bosanquet, a great supporter of women's rights but believer in women's 'difference', spoke to the National Liberal Club Political and Economic Circle (Volume 1, Part 3, Chapter 35) about factors that disadvantaged women in the labour market. While she made the unusual argument that industrial occupations provided good training for the discipline and organization required of domestic life, like Dilke, she supported restrictions on married women's work. Thus, even advocates for improving the opportunities for working-class women's work situated their recommendations within the boundaries of assumptions about proper occupations for men and women and the capabilities of women's bodies.

Throughout the nineteenth century and into the twentieth, work meant different things for men and women of the labouring classes, and people asked questions to probe how the changes mechanization brought affected working men and women differently. There is no doubt that industrialization, factory work, and the intensification of non-mechanized industries, along with increasing trade depressions and deprivation, drew attention to labouring people in new and penetrating ways. Reformers and workers themselves struggled over the meaning of honest toil and what types of and attitudes towards work associated a labourer with respectability. As economic and moral frameworks developed over the course of the century, the ways they intersected and diverged shaped the variety of conversations about industrial capitalism, economic insecurity, and unemployed workers.

Notes

1 On debates about using the term 'industrial revolution' and a perspective that adopts 'radical change', see M. Berg and P. Hudson, 'Rehabilitating the Industrial Revolution', *Economic History Review*, new series, 45:1 (February 1992), pp. 24–50.
2 E. P. Thompson, 'Time, Work-Discipline, and Industrial Capitalism', *Past and Present* 38:1 (1967), pp. 56–97.
3 Berg and Hudson, 'Rehabilitating', pp. 31–32.
4 E. Hopkins, *Industrialisation and Society: A Social History, 1830–1851* (London: Routledge, 2000), p. 10.
5 W. E. Houghton, *The Victorian Frame of Mind, 1830–1870* (New Haven, CT: Yale University Press, 1985), pp. 189, 249.
6 For a classic articulation of this domestic ideal, see C. Hall, 'The Early Formation of Victorian Domestic Ideology', in *White, Male and Middle Class: Explorations in Feminism and History* (Cambridge: Polity Press, 1993), pp. 75–93.
7 G. R. Searle, *Morality and the Market in Victorian Britain* (New York: Oxford University Press, 1998), p. 27.
8 D. Fraser, *The Evolution of the British Welfare State: A History of Social Policy since the Industrial Revolution* (London: Macmillan, 1973), p. 111.
9 For more on the work imperative, see M. Levine-Clark, *Unemployment, Welfare, and Masculine Citizenship: 'So Much Honest Poverty' in Britain, 1870–1930* (New York: Palgrave Macmillan, 2015), chaps. 1 and 2.
10 M. J. Daunton, *Progress and Poverty: An Economic and Social History of Britain, 1700–1850* (Oxford: Oxford University Press, 1995), pp. 141–142.
11 E. P. Thompson, *The Making of the English Working Class* (New York: Vintage Books, 1963). This argument is highly contested – for its chronology, its privileging of skilled men, and its lack of attention to gender and ethnicity. For an overview of how positions on 'class' have developed, see A. August, *The British Working Class, 1832–1940* (Harlow, UK: Pearson Longman, 2007), pp. 1–4. See also, N. Kirk, 'Fifty Years of Labour History: Challenge, Crisis, Renewal? Themes in the Labour History of Britain, 1960–2010', *Labour History Review* 75:2 (August 2010), pp. 162–180.
12 D. Ricardo, 'On Value', in *The Principles of Political Economy and Taxation* (London: J. M. Dent & Sons, 1911), pp. 5–32.
13 Searle, *Morality and the Market*, p. 37.
14 G. Stedman Jones, *Outcast London: A Study in the Relationship between Classes in Victorian Society* (Oxford: Clarendon Press, 1971), p. 2; T. Malthus, *An Essay on the Principle of Population* (Oxford: Oxford University Press, 1993, orig. 1798), p. 13.
15 D. Thompson, *The Chartists: Popular Politics in the Industrial Revolution* (New York: Pantheon Books, 1984), p. 275.
16 For more on Ricardian socialism, see J. E. King, 'Utopian or Scientific?' A Reconsideration of the Utopian Socialists', *History of Political Economy* 15:3 (1983), pp. 345–373.
17 J. Tosh, *Manliness and Masculinities in Nineteenth-Century Britain: Essays on Gender, Family, and Empire* (New York: Pearson Longman, 2005), pp. 74–75; and Volume 1 introduction prior.

18 T. Carlyle, *Past and Present: Thomas Carlyle's Collected Works*, vol. 13 (Project Gutenberg, 2008, orig. 1843), p. 192, at https://www.gutenberg.org/cache/epub/13534/pg13534.html [accessed 8 November 2021].
19 For an analysis of the rural ideal, see R. Williams, *The Country and the City* (Oxford: Oxford University Press, 1975).
20 On workplace health dangers, see, for example, J. Bronstein, *Caught in the Machinery: Workplace Accidents and Injured Workers in Nineteenth-Century Britain* (Stanford, CA: Stanford University Press, 2008); P.W.J. Bartrip, *The Home Office and the Dangerous Trades: Regulating Occupational Disease in Victorian and Edwardian Britain* (New York: Rodopi, 2002); B. Harrison, *Not Only the Dangerous Trades: Women's Work and Health in Britain, 1880–1914* (London: Taylor and Francis, 1996).
21 W. Morris, 'Art and Socialism', in M. Morris (ed), *The Works of William Morris*, vol. 23 (London: Longman Green and Co., 1915), pp. 192–214; J. Ruskin, *The Stones of Venice*, vols. 1–3 (London: Smith, Elder, and Co. 1851).
22 For more on William Morris and the Socialist League, see Volume 3, Part 3, Chapter 24.
23 On challenges to working-class masculinity, see, for example, A. Clark, *The Struggle for the Breeches: Gender and the Making of the British Working Class* (Berkeley: University of California Press, 1995); S. O. Rose, *Limited Livelihoods: Gender and Class in Nineteenth Century England* (Berkeley: University of California Press, 1992); Levine-Clark, *Unemployment, Welfare, and Masculine Citizenship.*
24 See, for example, Clark, *Struggle for the Breeches*, 3, 5–6.
25 D. Ricardo, quoted in H. D. Kurz, 'Technical Progress, Capital Accumulation and Income Distribution in Classical Economics: Adam Smith, David Ricardo, and Karl Marx', *European Journal of the History of Economic Thought* 17:5 (2010), pp. 1183–1222, on p. 1197.
26 Thompson, *The Making of the English Working Class*, p. 286.
27 Clark, *Struggle for the Breeches.*
28 J. Burnett, *Idle Hands: The Experience of Unemployment, 1790–1990* (New York: Routledge, 1994), p. 61.
29 R. Gray, *The Factory Question and Industrial England, 1830–1860* (New York: Cambridge University Press, 1996).
30 E. P. Thompson, 'The Moral Economy of the English Crowd in the Eighteenth Century', *Past and Present* 50:1 (1971), pp. 76–136, on pp. 78–79.
31 R. Oastler, *Slavery in Yorkshire: Monstrous Barbarity* (Bradford: J. Atkinson, 1835). On the use of the slavery metaphor in factory politics, see G. Peck, 'White Slavery and Whiteness: A Transnational View of the Sources of Working-Class Radicalism and Racism', *Labor* 1:2 (2004), pp. 41–64; M. Cunliffe, *Chattel Slavery and Wage Slavery: The Anglo-American Context, 1830–1860* (Athens: University of Georgia Press, 1979).
32 Fraser, *Evolution of the British Welfare State*, pp. 16–17.
33 M. Levine-Clark, *Beyond the Reproductive Body: The Politics of Women's Health and Work in Early Victorian England* (Columbus: Ohio State University Press, 2004), pp. 48–54; S. O. Rose, 'Protective Labour Legislation in Nineteenth Century Britain: Gender, Class, and the Liberal State', in L. L. Frader and S. O. Rose (eds), *Gender and Class in Modern Europe* (Ithaca, NY: Cornell University Press, 1996), pp. 193–210.
34 Fraser, *Evolution of the British Welfare State*, p. 29.
35 See, for example, Thompson, *The Chartists*; G. Stedman Jones, 'Rethinking Chartism', in *Languages of Class*: *Studies in Working-Class Radicalism and Culture, 1832–1982* (New York: Cambridge University Press, 1983), pp. 90–178; M. Taylor, 'Rethinking the Chartists: Searching for Synthesis in the Historiography of Chartism', *The Historical Journal* 39:2 (1996), pp. 479–495.
36 Thompson, *The Chartists*, p. 37. The 'newly enfranchised employing class' refers to the Reform Act of 1832, which enfranchised ten-pound householders.

37 Thompson, *The Chartists*, p. ix.
38 Thompson, *The Chartists*.
39 See, for example, Clark, *Struggle for the Breeches*; S. O. Rose, *Limited Livelihoods: Gender and Class in Nineteenth-Century England* (Berkeley: University of California Press, 1992); M. Valverde, '"Giving the Female a Domestic Turn": The Social, Legal, and Moral Regulation of Women's Work in British Cotton Mills, 1820–1850', *Journal of Social History* 21:4 (Summer 1998), pp. 619–634.
40 Friedrich Engels famously made this argument in *The Condition of the Working Class in England* (London: Penguin Books, 2005, orig. 1844).
41 See, for example, D. W. Elliott, 'Servants and Hands: Representing the Working Classes in Victorian Factory Novels', *Victorian Literature and Culture* 28:2 (2000), pp. 377–390; Levine-Clark, *Beyond the Reproductive Body*, chap. 2.
42 See, for example, S. Horrell and J. Humphries, 'The Origins and Expansion of the Male Breadwinner Family: The Case of Nineteenth-Century Britain', Supplement, *International Review of Social History* 42:S5 (1997), pp. 25–64; W. Seccomb, 'Patriarchy Stabilized: The Construction of the Male Breadwinner Wage Norm in Nineteenth-Century Britain', *Social History* 11:1 (1986), pp. 53–76; Clark, *Struggle for the Breeches*, p. 199; R. Fuchs, *Gender and Poverty in Nineteenth-Century Europe* (New York: Cambridge University Press, 2005), p. 11; Engels, *Condition of the Working Class*, pp. 165–167. E. Griffin, *Bread Winner: An Intimate History of the Victorian Economy* (New Haven, CT: Yale University Press, 2020) shows the struggles of families trying to survive in the context of a male breadwinner economy. E. Ross, *Love and Toil: Motherhood in Outcast London, 1870–1918* (Oxford: Oxford University Press, 1993) focuses on mothers as a way to understand women's identities and survival strategies in this context.
43 Tosh, *Manliness and Masculinities*, p. 36.
44 See, for example, S. Blackburn, *A Fair Day's Wage for a Fair Day's Work? Sweated Labour and the Origins of Minimum Wage Legislation in Britain* (Burlington, VT: Ashgate, 2006), part 1; P. Horn, *The Rise and Fall of the Victorian Servant* (New York: St. Martin's Press, 1975); E. Higgs, 'Domestic Servants and Households', *Social History* 8:2 (May 1983), pp. 201–210.
45 See, for example, K. Honeyman and J. Goodman, 'Women's Work, Gender Conflict, and Labour Markets in Europe, 1500–1900', *Economic History Review*, new series, 44:4 (November 1991), pp. 608–628.
46 See, for example, Elliott, 'Servants and Hands'.
47 Blackburn, *A Fair Day's Wage*, part 1; Fuchs, *Gender and Poverty*, p. 126.
48 B. Harris, (ed), *Famine and Fashion: Needlewomen in the Nineteenth Century* (London: Routledge, 2016).
49 See n. 6.
50 On parliamentary investigations, see, for example, O. Frankel, 'Blue Books and the Victorian Reader', *Victorian Studies* 46:2 (Winter 2004), pp. 308–318.
51 Levine-Clark, *Beyond the Reproductive Body*, pp. 23–24.
52 On the restriction of women in the lead industry, see J. Long, 'The Colour of Disorder: Women's Employment and "Protective" Intervention in the Lead Industry in Victorian England', *Women's History Review* 7:4 (1998), pp. 531–546.
53 Rose, *Limited Livelihoods*; Valverde, '"Giving the Female a Domestic Turn"'.
54 Women in many parts of the women's movement adopted a 'difference feminism'. See, for example, B. Caine, *Victorian Feminists* (Oxford: Oxford University Press, 1992); L. Bland, *Banishing the Beast: English Feminism and Sexual Morality, 1885–1914* (London: Penguin, 1995); J. Bush, '"Special Strengths for Their Own Special Duties": Women, Higher Education and Gender Conservatism in Late Victorian Britain', *History of Education* 34:4 (2005), pp. 387–405.

Part 1

THE RESPECTABILITY OF HONEST TOIL

1

W. COBBETT, 'TO THE LABOURERS OF ENGLAND, ON THEIR DUTIES AND THEIR RIGHTS'

Cobbett's Weekly Register 71:5 (1831), pp. 285–290

William Cobbett (1763–1835), according to one of his editors, 'was one of the most influential and singular English writers of the past three centuries'.[1] A farmer and radical political commentator, he issued the *Political Register* almost continuously from 1802 until his death in 1835. He is said to have published about thirty million words over the course of his life. His writings were influential at all levels of the class hierarchy, and he became dangerous as he turned to issues of political corruption, resulting in his imprisonment and temporary exile. In 1832, Cobbett was elected to the 'reformed' Parliament, for which he had campaigned (see Volume 1 Introduction). Although he maintained radical political stances, they were mostly in the interests of improving life for agricultural labourers and promoting a nostalgic programme of rural life to contrast with the industrial changes he witnessed.[2] Cobbett's vision of a bucolic rural England opposed to the dirt and dangers of industrial urban decay would be repeated throughout the nineteenth century in critiques of industrial society from the likes of Charles Dickens, John Ruskin, and William Morris.[3] Cobbett is perhaps most famous for his 'rural rides' in the 1820s, about which he published his reflections in the *Register*.[4] From his observations of the countryside, he became familiar with the general economic distress, lack of employment, and low wages of the rural labouring population. He argued that workers, and rural workers in particular, had a right to fair employment opportunities and living wages. In the piece included here from the *Register*, Cobbett lays out his principles on the rights and duties of the labouring classes. In order to claim rights, he argues, working men had to follow their duties. According to Cobbett, the duty to labour was the primary duty; men needed to work or demonstrate their willingness to do so if unable to find a position. Attending to these duties allowed labourers to demand rights to good wages and better working conditions. Articulating John Locke's theory of property, Cobbett states that all men have a right to property, but the worker's property

DOI: 10.4324/9780429320323-4

is first of all in his labour, which should be protected. A man gains a right to property through the labour he invests in any object he works: 'Whatsoever . . . he removes out of the state that nature hath provided, and left it in, he hath mixed his labour with, and joined to it something that is his own, and thereby makes it his property'.[5] The individual's right to property was central to the origins of nineteenth-century liberalism, but the focus on property in labour itself aligned Cobbett with radical politics.[6] Cobbett also believed that humans entered into civil society for the collective good, which meant that those who benefited from the labour of the poor had a duty to support them when they suffered from economic need. Or, put another way, because labour was the 'sole foundation' of the property from which the wealthy benefited, labourers had the right to demand the preservation of 'life, health, and vigor' in times of crisis.[7] In being willing to work, labourers earned the right to have themselves and their families maintained by taxes ('superfluities') on the rich when times were hard. Cobbett believed in a natural hierarchy, where rich and poor would always exist. While articulated in radical language, Cobbett's vision was at heart paternalistic; he expected the well-to-do to look after the poor, whose labour rendered them deserving. This fits with his nostalgia for a vertical rural society where the haves were responsible for the have-nots, as opposed to a horizontal class society, where classes were in opposition to each other.

'To the Labourers of England, on their Duties and their Rights'

Kensington, 24*th January*, 1831.

DEAR FELLOW-COUNTRYMEN,

YOU have always been dear to me, whose greatest pride it is that I was born and bred amongst you; who has, in his travels about the world, never seen any people so industrious, so sincere, so virtuous, parents so tender, children so affectionate, servants so willingly obedient, friends so steady and so true. Your character and your conduct have always made you dear to me; no time, no distance, has weakened my regard for, or my anxiety for, your welfare; from across the seas I addressed you; through the walls of a prison you heard my voice; my heart has always been gladdened by your happiness, and saddened by your calamities; but, if you have always been dear to me, you are *doubly dear to me now*, when your afflictions are so great and so various, and when I am cheered with the hope of seeing you once more the happy people that our grandfathers and grandmothers were.

In this important crisis, *pray hear me patiently*, while I speak to you of your *duties* as well as of your *rights:* for, in demanding the latter, you ought not to forget the former; duties and rights go together; and he who refuses to perform the first, tacitly abandons his right to the last. Good food, raiment, and all the necessaries of life, the labourer has a *right* to; but that right is founded on his performing *the duty* of labouring; or on his being *willing to perform it*. It is of great importance that you understand this matter *clearly;* and I will now endeavour to enable you to do it.

There was a time when, in every country in the world, there were no laws, and no such thing as property. The people used the earth and all its produce as they pleased; that is to say, each man took whatever he wanted, if his strength or cunning would allow him to do it. No one acknowledged the superiority of any other: might gave right: strength and wisdom were superior to weakness and folly: and there was no other superiority or inferiority acknowledged amongst men. This was called living under the law of nature. When God put it into the hearts of men to change this state of things, and to make rules and laws for the observance of the whole, they agreed that the whole of the community or body of people should enforce these laws, against any one or more that broke them. The great law of all was this; that, in future, every man should keep to himself; should call *his own:* should be able to apply to his own use solely; that which he had got by his labour. For instance, John Stiles, when living under the law of nature, might take a piece of land, and cultivate it, and have a crop of wheat growing on it; but, when fit for the sickle Tom Nokes, a great deal stronger man than Stiles, might come and cut the wheat and carry it away and let Stiles have none of it. It is not likely that men would be so villanously unjust as this, or that the rest of the people would be so base as to stand by and to see Stiles thus bereft of his wheat, and have nothing left to exist upon, perhaps, but a few wheel-barrows full of damned potatoes; this is not likely; but it might happen, and sometimes did happen, perhaps, and therefore all the people agreed to enter into a society, to make rules that should give Stiles an exclusive right to his crop, and that should punish such a fellow as Nokes as a robber, if he came to take the crop away.

Here, my friends, you see the origin of *property*, which word means a thing which belongs to a person's self, and a thing that nobody else has any right to. But, observe, Stiles had no property in the crop till he created it by his *labour;* and that, therefore, labour, and labour only, is the sole foundation of any property whatsoever. Man's first duty, then, is to labour in some way or other in order to raise his means of living. If his father, for instance, have laboured before him, and has given or left him the fruit of his labour, he has as good a right to that as if it were the fruit of his own labour; a man's next duty is, to refrain from taking by force or by fraud the property of another man; for, to protect men in the enjoyment of their property was the great end in forming civil society. Perhaps it would not be difficult to prove, that men who are compelled to work for their bread, are, provided they earn a sufficiency of food and of raiment and other necessaries of life, as happy and even happier than those who are not compelled to work for their bread; but at any rate, such is the nature of things, such is the order of the world, that there always have been and always must be some very rich and some very poor, and great multitudes not rich; but in a just state of things, there never will be great multitudes steeped in poverty. The order of the world demands that some shall think, while others work; that some shall make and execute the laws to which all are to yield obedience. Poverty, therefore, even in its extreme state, gives no man a right to view his rich neighbour with an evil eye, much less to do him mischief on account of his riches. If the laws be impartial in themselves, and be executed with impartiality, every man's conscience will tell him, that it is his bounden duty to yield them a cheerful obedience, and further, to yield respect and honour to those who are charged with the execution of the laws.

Such are the great duties of all men in civil society; and God forbid that these principles should ever be rooted out of the hearts of the very best and most virtuous of all mankind, the agricultural labourers of this land, so favoured by God Almighty, and for so many ages the freest and happiest country in the world! But, my friends, men did not enter into civil society for the purpose of bringing upon themselves *duties only:* they had another object; namely, that of creating and enjoying *rights*. Just, indeed, as we have seen in the case of John Stiles, who had his crop of wheat taken away by the stronger man Nokes, who left him nothing but a few wheel-barrows full of accursed potatoes, and all their natural consequences, poverty of blood, leprosy, scrofula, pottle-belly, and swelled heels! Now, whenever civil society produces such a state of things, when a laborious man like John Stiles is treated in the same way that Nokes treated him, that civil society has not answered its purpose. Labour, as we have seen, was the foundation of all property, and must always be the foundation of property. The labourer, therefore, has a property in his labour; and, as St. James says in his Epistle, and as Moses and Jesus Christ himself say, to rob the labourer of his hire, that is to say, to take from him or to withhold from him the due reward of his labour, is the greatest crime that man can commit against God.

The *rights* of the labourer are, first, to have food, raiment, fuel lodging, medical and spiritual comfort, in return for his labour, and all these, too, in quantity and quality sufficient for the preservation of his life, health, and vigour. Next, if he be unable to work, unable to earn a sufficiency for his family, or unable to obtain work so as to obtain that sufficiency; in either of these cases, he and his family have a right to have a sufficiency supplied out of the superfluities of those to whom the law of civil society has secured more than they want. This claim of the poor man is, as Judge Blackstone states, founded in the very first principle of civil society; for it cannot be believed that men can have assented to enter civil society for any purpose other than that of the benefit of the whole; it cannot be believed that a million of men, for instance, entered into civil society in order that a couple of thousand should have all the meat and all the bread and all the good clothing, and that all the rest should live upon potatoes and go covered with miserable rags. No man upon earth, unless he be one who lives upon the labour of others, will pretend to believe that men entered into civil society, in order that those who did no work, that led idle lives, that created nothing, should have bread and flour and beer and clothing and all sorts of good things, a hundred times more than they wanted; while those that laboured and made all these things, were compelled to live upon a miserable watery root, or die with starvation.

Such are the *duties* and such the *rights* of labouring men. Our forefathers, who well understood those duties and those rights, cheerfully performed the one and amply enjoyed the other. They had an abundance of meat, of bread, and of all the fruits of the earth; they were clothed throughout in good woollen and linen; they had great store of household goods and of every-thing to make life easy and pleasant; and when old age or widowhood, or the orphan state, or accident, or any circumstance producing indigence, befel them, the priest of the parish maintained them out of the tithes, administering to their wants as the law enjoined, "with his own hands in charity, humility, and mercy." And this, observe, was a RIGHT which they enjoyed, and that, too, a right as perfect as that of any man to his house or his land. When our country was bereft, by means which I have not now the room to describe, of that species of protection for the poor, the poor-law was passed to supply the place of that protection; to parochial relief, therefore, the aged, the widow, the orphan, the infirm, amongst the labouring people, have just the *same* right as their forefathers had to that which was administered to them in so just and kind and Christian-like a manner.

That the ministers and the Parliament may be pleased to listen to the advice which I have so respectfully tendered to them in the forgoing letter; that you may live as happy lives as our forefathers lived, and that we may all see harmony once more restored in England, is the sincere prayer of

Your faithful Friend,
Wm. COBBETT.

Notes

1 J. Grande and J. Stevenson, *The Opinions of William Cobbett* (Farnham, Surrey, UK: Routledge, 2013), p. 1.

2 I. Dyck, 'Cobbett, William', *Oxford Dictionary of National Biography*, 23 September 2004, at https://doi-org.du.idm.oclc.org/10.1093/ref:odnb/5734 [accessed 13 June 2021].

3 For an analysis of this critique, see M. Wiener, *English Culture and the Decline of the Industrial Spirit, 1850–1980*, 2nd ed. (New York: Cambridge University Press, 2004).

4 Dyck, 'Cobbett'.

5 J. Locke, *Two Treatises on Government*, book 2, chap. 5, sec. 27 (Project Gutenberg ebook), at www.gutenberg.org/files/7370/7370-h/7370-h.htm [accessed 20 June 2021].

6 On Cobbett's rural radicalism and rocky relationship with urban radicals, see I. Dyck, 'W. Cobbett and the Rural Radical Platform', *Social History* 18:2 (May 1993), pp. 185–204.

7 W. Cobbett, 'To the Labourers of England, on Their Duties and Their Rights', *Cobbett's Weekly Register* 71:5 (1831), pp. 285–290, on pp. 287–288.

2

J. LIVESEY, 'AN ADDRESS TO WORKING MEN'

J Livesey's Moral Reformer 13 (1838), pp. 97–98

Joseph Livesey (1794–1884) was a successful cheese merchant based in Preston, Lancashire. He helped start the temperance movement in Britain and was an active temperance reformer during his lifetime, emphasizing respectability and responsibility for both the middle and working classes.[1] He was also committed to anti–Corn Law politics, an effort to abolish controversial tariffs that supported the landed class and increased the cost of grain by interfering with free markets. The anti–Corn Law campaign was central to liberal ideas about *laissez-faire* economics in this era.[2] Livesey published the *Moral Reformer* monthly from 1831 to 1883, with a four-year hiatus from 1834 to 1838 when it became the *Preston Temperance Advocate*, the first temperance publication in England.[3] This source, from the *Moral Reformer*, written after a hard winter that had caused many working men to lose their jobs, illustrates Livesey's belief that economics and morality were interconnected spheres. Livesey expected that attention to higher moral practices among workers, employers, and investors alike would contribute to better relationships between capital and labour and create more employment opportunities for the poor. He composed this document as a letter to working men and takes a paternalistic tone, assuming both ignorance and purposeful bad behaviour in his readers, who need to be instructed by his expertise. Admonishing working men to save money during the summer when they have good wages, Livesey also tells them to stay away from alcohol and not to abuse their wives and children. Historians have demonstrated the connections between domestic violence and alcohol among the nineteenth-century working poor, so this temperance message would have resonated with working-class women.[4] Livesey urges workers to avoid politics and trade unions, since be believed unions curtailed free markets. As a paternalist, Livesey would have thought that workers' needs should have been taken care of by those with more knowledge and experience, meaning the wealthier classes. The letter also stresses, however, that employers should steer clear of 'combinations', where they could collude on price-setting, presenting a consistent free-market message.[5] Livesey cautions the middle and upper classes,

DOI: 10.4324/9780429320323-5

telling them to invest more of their capital at home rather than in foreign markets in order to increase employment for the working classes. If working men would focus on purchasing British-made goods and landlords and employers would stay in Britain, hire British men, and invest their money at home, the demand for British labour would increase and fewer men would be unemployed.

'An Address to Working Men'

DEAR FRIENDS,

The weather is now becoming fine; the winter is nearly over, and we are entering upon the interesting season of spring. Seldom have you experienced so hard a winter, as the one which is past. Owing to the severe frost, outdoor work in particular, has been almost at a stand; but having with much difficulty encountered the storm, and having now brighter prospects before you, I venture, as a friend, to offer you a few words of advice.

From correct information I can affirm, that by foresight and prudence much of this suffering endured by many of your class might have been prevented. During the last summer, when you were earning from 20*s*. to 30*s*. per week, you ought to have kept out of debt, replenished your clothing and bedding, and been able to reserve something against winter, when work is usually scarce. Like the bees, remembering that winter was sure to come, you should have laid by a stock in reserve. However, I am not anxious to dwell more than necessary upon that which is past; but would rather beg your candid attention to a little advice, in reference to the future.

Begin this season with a determination to avoid past errors, and to do your duty both to yourselves and families. Instead of dragging out a miserable existence, punishing your wives and children, and disappointing those who depend upon you, try this year, by uniting prudence and sobriety to industry, to diffuse that happiness through every part of your family, which good conduct and steady habits are sure to produce. Unite cordially with your wives in endeavouring to manage your household concerns, and turn every halfpenny of your wages to the best account. Cultivate self respect, and while you see others do well, whose wages are no more than your own, in the spirit of honest emulation, instead of grovelling in obscurity, be determined to be equal to any of your neighbours.

To effect any good change it is essential that you abandon the habit of frequenting public houses, and drinking intoxicating liquor. Whatever other changes you make, be your wages *ever so large*, while you lose your time at these places in agitating about political reform, or trades' unions, neglecting at the same time *self-reform*, you are sure to be disappointed. "Ah" says a bricksetter, "if I had all the money I spent with the landlords last summer, I should not now be starving in the house, or seeking a ticket for charity."

Do not join in dangerous combinations against *the freedom of industry*. But as much ignorance exists upon this subject, frequently leading well meaning workmen into error, I will claim your indulgence while I enter into this subject at some length. Trade should be left *perfectly free*, for all monopolies in the long run tend to its ruin. Demand and supply, *if not interfered with* will regulate the labour market as it does all other markets, upon the most equitable principles. When the demand *exceeds* the supply wages will rise, when it comes short they will necessarily fall. Fictitious prices, either below or above the real value may be created, and for some time maintained, by chartered companies, legal interference, or combinations, all tending to embarrass if not to annihilate trade, and at any rate to do a positive injustice to the public. Let wages be bolstered up, so that capital will yield no profit, or let its safe investment be endangered by combinations, and *its removal is certain;* and although you have often been taught to look upon capital and labour as *antagonists*, the very reverse is the fact: joined together they are favourable to each other's welfare, but separation is fatal to both. Without capital to provide machinery for the labourer and to support him till his work is disposed of, what could he do? and without labour the greatest extent of capital would be inoperative and could yield no profit. Like food and the stomach they are made for each other. *Peace* and *freedom* are the guardians of capital, and consequently of employment and wages.

These remarks are worthy [of] the attention, and intended to apply both to yourselves and your employers. It is equally an act of injustice and oppression, for masters to combine against men, as for men against their masters. Every man has the same right to sell his labour at the highest price, as the master has to dispose of his goods at the best market. But while you may refuse to part with your labour on terms which you disapprove, you have clearly *no right* to forbid any other individual disposing of his labour as he may think proper. The labour market ought to be as open as any other; and the farmers who attend Preston market might as well say, for the purpose of keeping up their own prices, "we will allow no strangers to bring their samples in here," as any set of men attempt to prevent others, who want employment, accepting it on such terms as they may choose. Every attempt, therefore, to contend for wages, ought to be made upon the acknowledgment of this principle, and keeping this in view, it will always be your policy to calculate, in all disputes with your masters, its probable bearing upon your own interests.

As I may pursue this subject further in a future paper, I will now draw your attention to the means of *increasing employment*, which is the *only* sure method of *keeping up wages* and preventing injurious competition among workmen; and I feel astonished that this, by far the most important question, should have received so little attention. The quantity of employment depends upon the amount of capital in the country, the nature of its investment, and the spirit of enterprize with which its owners are actuated; and if we come to examine the subject closely, we shall find that legislative interference, can do little beyond securing *freedom of exchange*, and preserving the tranquillity of the country, both of which are favourable to the investment of capital, and consequently to an increased amount of employment. With our present resources, as *we advance in morals* there will be *an increase of employment*. If the united capital of all the artizans in England, or, in other words, the wages of the working men, had been divided among the shoemakers, tailors, hatters, joiners, cabinet makers, upholsterers, &c., &c., and through them among every branch of useful industry, instead of being placed in the landlord's hands as an instrument for evil, what an immense change would have been produced! If every ragged mechanic had two suits of clothes; every empty house were well furnished, and the bed rooms supplied with beds, the increase to the trade of this country would have been beyond conception, in favour of all classes of useful artizans. Home consumption is most to be depended upon; and if the working men studied their own interest, they would purchase those articles which their fellow-labourers produce. And as to others spending the money which they receive from you for liquor, I maintain, on the one hand, that they spend no more now with the public than they would do if their time and capital were employed in some honourable trade; while, on the other hand, they are now furnished with the means of destroying the produce of the earth, paralysing man's intellect, destroying his ingenuity, and loosing all the moral and social ties of society. I am confident if the working men were sober and virtuous, they might themselves produce an immense increase to the demand for labour.

But it is also on the morality and correct habits of the middle and higher classes that the contraction and extention of employment depends, for they are the principal owners of capital. If those who have made their fortunes, or are deriving their incomes from the country, would consider the condition of the people, they would remain at home, and spend their wealth by employing the people. Every man who takes up his residence abroad, whether from extravagance or a love of pleasure, still deriving from this country his supplies, virtually takes away the bread of the poor. It is stated that there are seven thousand residences within twelve miles of London, consisting of mansions with parks, pleasure grounds, &c., whose owners are spending millions among foreigners. – Let these and all the nobility and gentry, amounting to an immense number, settle in the country whence they draw their incomes, and the demand upon the labour market would be immense. Instead of thus drawing around them a great number of workmen, many people are impoverished for want of employment, by their deserting the country, and must either flee into the towns for a chance of work, or fall into the merciless hands of the overseer. I think it is worthy of enquiry, how far this cause has operated in producing the excessive pauperism of the south. And what is even worse, while poor men are deprived of employment, and their wages consequently reduced by this system of *absenteeism*, their provisions are enhanced in price by a restriction on the importation of corn principally for the benefit of this same class. It is certainly a double cruelty upon the workmen of this country, both to *tax their bread* and lessen the amount of employment, with the wages of which they have to pay this tax.

It may also be mentioned, that low wages necessarily throw more labour into the market, and consequently produce a still greater depreciation. The quantity of work performed is very much regulated by the relation which wages bear to the necessaries of life. Men must *live*, – and rather than starve, they will work sixteen hours a day, which excessive labour has a tendency to throw others out of work; but let employment be plentiful, wages will advance, the hours of labour will become contracted, and consequently a glut in the market sooner relieved.

I contend therefore that those who remain at home, and sink their capital in factories and public works, though they do nothing more than their duty, are not deserving of the calumny which is often heaped upon them; for supposing *they* were to leave the country, as a vast number of the aristocracy and landed gentlemen do, where could employment be found for our rapidly increasing population? When you bear in mind the immense wealth which is carried away and spent abroad, I am quite sure you will think more favourably than you have been wont to do, of those who remain at home and employ their capital, and their skill, and their incessant attention, in furnishing the means of employment for the people. Do we pity to see so many exhibiting so much vice and wretchedness and want, in connection with our factory system? We should endeavour to ascertain the real cause. These people flock from the country to the factories because their proper guardians have forsaken them, and left them to fend for themselves. You might as well blame the Mendicity Institution, at Dublin, for producing the wretchedness of the people who come daily for relief, as the factories for producing all the poverty which we are compelled to witness. It is not the *factory*, but the *causes which are in operation to drive the people to the factory*, upon which the blame ought to be cast. It is possible to charge our best friends with producing our calamities, whilst the unobserved conduct of others, and even our own, may be the real cause.

Politics, in my opinions, have much less to do with the prosperity of the working class, than most of you seem to think. A great number of what are called national questions, have been settled during the last dozen years, but where are the benefits conferred upon the working class? Supposing there was a change in the ministry to morrow, how would that add to the stock of employment? No; your greatest source of relief is, *an increase of employment;* added to a reduction in the price of the first necessaries of life. The former may be brought about by the working people appropriating the wages of drunkenness to the purchase of their own industry, and by the rich absentees being induced to spend their wealth among the people who produce it. To me, therefore, it is self-evident that a high tone of morals in all classes, a deeper conviction of our duty to our countrymen, which I *maintain to be incompatible with absenteeism*, or with *home combinations*, are what we ought to look to as the likeliest means of increasing employment, and consequently preventing a reduction in wages.

In conclude with observing, *let industry be free;* let no man encroach upon the liberty of his fellow-workman, by interfering with his right to enter into any employment he pleases, and at such wages as he may think proper to accept. And instead of keeping up the value of labour, by unions and combinations, or instead of foolishly expecting government to fix a rate of wages, let us, by all the means in our power, endeavour to increase the supply of employment, so that every labourer may obtain an equitable and a remunerating price for his work. Instead of petitioning parliament to fix a minimum of wages, which, were it attempted, would certainly be evaded, I would prefer petitioning all the *English* and *Irish absentees* to *come home*, and, engaging the capital, enterprise, and sobriety of the country, to find work for every unemployed man in the kingdom.

The home investment and expenditure of British wealth; the dissolution of all trades' combinations; and the universal spread of temperance, involve in them some of the greatest measures for promoting the prosperity and happiness of the working classes.

Hoping that these plain, and I may add, faithful remarks will be received in the same spirit of kindness in which they are given, I remain your sincere friend,

J. LIVESEY.

Notes

1 'Death of Mr. Livesey', *Manchester Evening News*, 2 September 1884, p. 3; 'Death of Mr. Livesey', *Preston Herald*, 3 September 1884, p. 4. The classic account of the temperance movement in Britain is B. Harrison, *Drink and the Victorians: The Temperance Question in England, 1815–1872* (Edinburgh, UK: Edinburgh University Press, 1997, orig. 1971).

2 See, for example, N. McCord, *The Anti-Corn Law League, 1838–1846* (London: Routledge, 2013, orig. 1968).

3 B. Harrison, 'Livesey, Joseph', *Oxford Dictionary of National Biography*, 21 May 2009, at https://doi-org.du.idm.oclc.org/10.1093/ref:odnb/16796 [accessed 13 June 2021].

4 See, for example, N. Tomes, 'A "Torrent of Abuse": Crimes of Violence between Working-Class Men and Women in London, 1840–1875', *Journal of Social History* 11:3 (Spring 1978), pp. 328–345; and A. J. Hammerton, *Cruelty and Companionship: Conflict in Nineteenth-Century Married Life* (New York: Routledge, 2002), part 1, 'Working-Class Marriage', pp. 10–55.

5 J. Livesey, 'An Address to Working Men', *J Livesey's Moral Reformer* 13 (1838), pp. 97–98, on p. 97.

3

J. F. BRAY, *LABOUR'S WRONGS AND LABOUR'S REMEDY*

(Birmingham: David Green, Briggate: 1839), pp. 22–24

John Francis Bray (1809–1897) moved with his family from the United States to England in his teens and trained as a printer in Yorkshire. He began writing about issues of working-class poverty in industrial society and became a Chartist (see Volume 1 Introduction). Bray's Ricardian socialist development of the labour theory of value led him to advocate for the ownership of the means of production by society through a model of worker-controlled joint-stock companies, or cooperatives.[1] In this short selection from *Labour's Wrongs and Labour's Remedy*, Bray, like Cobbett (see Volume 1, Part 1, Chapter 1), associates workers' rights with their duties.[2] Unlike Cobbett, however, Bray did not believe in a natural social hierarchy, where a certain number of rich and poor would always exist. Rather, he stresses that an equality of rights and duties should be present among all classes. All men (and women, perhaps) should have the duty to labour and the right to the rewards of their labour. Yet as society existed, many men laboured for the benefit of the few: there were producers and idlers. Men who worked maintained those who did not, and until this unjust distribution of labour and reward was transformed, society would could not achieve equality. Bray challenges the inevitability of a socio-economic organization made up of productive and unproductive classes. This language of the productive and unproductive classes originated from the classical economists, who wrote about the need to minimize the parts of the economy that consumed parts of the national wealth without adding to it and to maximize labour that increased the national wealth.[3] Radicals appropriated this language to position the productive middle and working classes against the parasitic aristocracy and financiers. Chartists and socialists – significantly, Karl Marx – would take it further by suggesting that only the working class was productive in a capitalist system.[4] Bray adopts this position, arguing that equality could never be realized when the many worked for the few.

 DOI: 10.4324/9780429320323-6

Labour's Wrongs and Labour's Remedy

. . . Equality of rights is the very soul of society; but equality of rights cannot exist unallied with equality of duties. This is the sum and substance of equality. Thus, if three men be placed upon a desart island, and they each give an equal portion of labour for the common good, and receive an equal reward, the communion is *equally* beneficial to all the three. But if one of the party, by force or fraud, obtain *double* allowance of produce for only *single* work, the union cannot longer be *equally* beneficial to all the three. If, again, the same man compel his fellows to give him double allowance of produce for *no labour whatever*, every shadow of equality and justice vanishes at once; and no law nor regulation can restore the equilibrium of right, unless it compel this receiver of an unearned share to give his labour for such share; for the very essence of the inequality and the wrong consists in the inequality of the duties rendered and the rewards received by the several parties. There is no exponent of equal rights but that which also stands for equal duties; and if duties be unequal, or equal duties be unequally rewarded, the very principle of justice is at once invaded, and equality of rights destroyed.

In all civilised countries, as they are called, society is thus divided into idlers and producers – into those who obtain double allowance for doing nothing, and those who receive only half-allowance for doing double work; and so long as this difference of position and inequality of condition is suffered to exist, inequality of rights and laws and enjoyments will also exist. It matters not how society came to be in its present state. It is sufficient that it is found thus, and that it may be altered and amended. Why *should* some men receive double allowance for doing only single work, or quadruple allowance for rendering no service whatever? All the excessive toil, and poverty, and misery of the working classes of all countries arise solely from this most unjust and iniquitous manner of apportioning the labour and the reward; and never, until we alter the social arrangements which produce and perpetuate this injustice, can we obtain relief. What arguments are needed to prove to common sense, that, if ten men have to maintain twenty, the ten must work harder or longer than if they had only themselves to keep? What kind of *equality of rights* can there possibly be between the keepers and the kept? There is neither equality of service rendered nor received; for the one party *gives all*, and the other party *takes all* – and herein lies the essence and spirit of all inequality.

It does not follow, merely because society is now divided into productive and unproductive classes, that the division is either natural or inevitable, as the political economists have asserted. A very cursory examination of the causes which render men rich and poor, and maintain the inequality of condition after it has been created, will shew us that this inequality, so far from being dependent on inequality of bodily and mental powers in individuals, exists in *defiance* of any such inequality of powers, and is in no way connected with these powers – that it arises from causes which no individual can properly command or control, whatever may be the superiority or inferiority of his mental and corporeal faculties.

Notes

1 N. Thompson, 'Bray, John Francis', *Oxford Dictionary of National Biography*, 23 September 2004, at https://doi-org.du.idm.oclc.org/10.1093/ref:odnb/47330 [accessed 13 June 2021]. On Ricardian socialism, see J. E. King, 'Utopian or Scientific? A Reconsideration of the Utopian Socialists', *History of Political Economy* 15:3 (1983), pp. 345–373.

2 J. F. Bray, *Labour's Wrongs and Labour's Remedy* (Birmingham: David Green, Briggate, 1839), Google Books, pp. 22–24.

3 See, for example, A. Smith, *An Inquiry into the Nature and Causes of the Wealth of Nations* (London: Penguin, 1970, orig. 1776), pp. 429–430.

4 See, for example, I. Gough, 'Marx's Theory of Productive and Unproductive Labour', *New Left Review*, 76 (November 1972), pp. 47–72; H. Boss, *Theories of Surplus and Transfer: Parasites and Producers in Economic Thought* (London: Unwin Hyman, 1989).

4

ANON., 'THE PRODUCTION AND DISTRIBUTION OF WEALTH'

Chartist Circular 38 (13 June 1840), pp. 153–154

Published from September 1839 to July 1842, the *Chartist Circular* was an unstamped (untaxed) and therefore illegal newspaper addressed to the working classes. It originated in Scotland, when the Chartist William Pattison suggested the need for a publication to circulate Chartist ideas (on Chartism, see Volume 1 Introduction). George Ross, another active Scottish Chartist, funded the paper.[1] This article focuses on the inequality in British society, based on the unfair distribution of wealth among producers and idlers. While adopting the language of producers and idlers, like Bray (see Volume 1, Part 1, Chapter 3), the author complicates the binary by not simply focusing on class. For this writer, not all in the working classes were productive: half were 'females', some of whom did not work at all and others who forced able-bodied men to be idle because they took their jobs.[2] The unproductive also included the elderly, the young, the disabled, the 'lazy', and the unemployed, who did not produce anything.[3] The wealthy non-producers were not only idle, they were wasteful. Their consumption was excessive, and the profits they received from rents was theft of the labour of the working classes. In these arguments, the Chartists declaimed against the classical economists, who believed in the necessity of the capital of landowners and capitalists to reinvest in the economy; their spending and saving kept the economy flowing. In such a system, the author insists, it was not surprising that the workers were unhappy. Their toil went to support the idle, while the idlers dismissed them. The author raises a theme that would be relevant throughout the century: the challenge posed to men's identity as men when they were positioned in negative ways with regard to work – whether in poor conditions, through lack of employment, in overwork, or in the inability to support a family.[4] In the end, the writer argues, the existing system caused criminality and prostitution. Families ended up in 'pauper prisons'.[5] The system as it existed would never sustain the labouring classes, and the unwritten solution in the article was the Charter. The language in which the Chartists articulated their demands, according to historian Gareth Stedman Jones and others, was that of radicalism, which attributed 'unemployment, low wages,

DOI: 10.4324/9780429320323-7

[and] economic security' to a 'political cause', which would be remedied by the enfranchisement of working-class men.[6] In this interpretation, Chartism was not a politics of class that was a precursor to socialism but rather a continuation of a radical tradition that critiqued the idle and celebrated the productive members of society.

'The Production and Distribution of Wealth'

THAT we may ascertain as nearly as possible the amount of wealth created yearly by our national industry, we will suppose the population of the United Kingdom of Great Britain and Ireland to be, in round numbers, 26,000,000 of human beings. All these individuals must be fed, clothed, and housed in some way or other – they all make a perpetual call upon the material of subsistence, whether they labour or not, and whether much or little is produced by those who perform the labour. Some of them, perhaps, consume and waste their thousands of pounds sterling a year, while others starve upon as many thousand pennies. But if we take every thing into consideration – the comparative numbers of rich and poor, the price of food and clothing, and the number of children – we may safely, for the sake of data, estimate the entire maintenance of the twenty-six millions of people to be worth, on the average, at least £15 per head annually. This gives £390,000,000 as the yearly value of the maintenance of the whole people of the United Kingdom. We do not, however, employ ourselves merely in producing articles of subsistence, for our labour creates, likewise, many inconsumable articles. We every year add to our stock of accumulations, or capital, by increasing the number of our houses, ships, implements, machines, roads, and other assistants to further production, besides making good all wear and tear. Thus, although our subsistence may be worth but three hundred and ninety millions sterling a year, the total annual value of the wealth created by the people of the United Kingdom will not be less than five hundred millions sterling. A near approximation to this result has been given at various times, and by different persons; and, in the present state of statistics, it is perhaps as near the truth as we can arrive.

This vast amount of wealth, let it be borne in mind, is not created by the labour of every individual comprised in the twenty-six millions of inhabitants. The half of this number are females; and of the remaining half, some are too old to work, some too young, some too lazy, and some cannot get work; so that we cannot calculate upon having above one-fourth of our population, or about six millions of men – that is, those between the ages of fourteen and fifty – as effective producers. Of this number, however, scarcely five millions can be said, under the present arrangements of society, to assist in production; for thousands of able-bodied men in Great Britain are compelled to stand idle while the work which they ought to do is being performed by women and children; and hundreds of thousands of men in Ireland can obtain no employment whatever. Thus less than five millions of men, assisted by a few thousands of women and children, have not only to create produce for the consumption of themselves and families, but likewise for the whole mass of willing and unwilling idlers, and unprofitable labourers of every description, amounting in the aggregate to twenty-six millions of human beings.

The five millions of men already enumerated as assisting in production, will include all who labour little or much – the actual distributers as well as the producers – all those who can be said to yield society any equivalent for the benefits they receive. Some of these persons do not work five hours a day, while others, again, toil on for fifteen hours; and when to this is added the time lost by the compulsory idleness of great numbers in times of depression in trade, it will be found that our annual production is created and distributed by less than one-fifth of the community, working, on the average, ten hours a day.

Thus it appears that there are nearly one million of able-bodied men who do nothing towards the production or proper distribution of wealth – comprising landed proprietors, large capitalists, soldiers, &c. But if we suppose that the wealthy non-producers of every description, with their families and dependents, amount only to two millions of persons, yet this number alone would cost the working classes £30,000,000 annually, if their maintenance were averaged, like that of the latter, at £15 per head. But it so happens, that the great body of these non-producers belong to what is termed the "independent order" – that they waste, or consume unprofitably, a great part of the conveniencies, and nearly all the luxuries which the toils of the working classes produce: therefore, upon the most moderate computation, their maintenance will cost not less than £50 per head. This gives a total of £100,000,000 as the annual cost of the mere drones of society – the utterly unproductive, and worthless, either in respect to ornament or use!

It has been laid down as a principle, recommended by reason, and sanctified by justice, that all those who perform equal labour should receive an equal reward. It is only by acting upon this principle that the present order of things can be done away with, and equality of rights established and enjoyed. Under present arrangements, however, the reward is greatest where the labour is least; and of the five millions of men engaged in production and distribution in the United Kingdom, the remuneration is as unequally and as unjustly bestowed as it is possible for it to be. Thus, in estimating their losses under the present system, the working class must put into the account, not only the expense of the general and local government, amounting to at least the annual sum of £60,000,000 – not only the cost of the wealthy drones, and idlers, and unproductive labourers, amounting to the annual sum of £100,000,000 – but likewise the double and quadruple allowance received by the various classes of small proprietors, manufacturers, and tradesmen, in the shape of profit and interest. Upon the most modern computation, the share of wealth enjoyed by this extensive portion of the community will amount to not less than £140,000,000 annually, *above the average of what is received by an equal number of the best paid of the working classes*. Thus, along with *their* government, the two classes of idlers and livers on profit – comprising, perhaps, one-fourth of the entire population – absorb about £300,000,000 annually, or above one-half of the entire wealth produced!

In the various sums and numbers here mentioned, none are supposed to be precisely correct, for we have few data, except those furnished by observation and experience, from which calculations can be made. As a whole, they may be greater or less; but, as parts, they will bear about the same mutual relation as is here assigned them. The present arrangements of society, therefore, cost the working classes, in taxes to government and in rent and profit to proprietors and capitalists, the enormous annual sum of £300,000,000 sterling, which is an average loss of above £50 per head to every working man in the empire. This leaves no more than an average of about £11 per head per annum, to be divided amongst the remaining three-fourths of the nation. From calculations made in 1815, it appears that the annual income of the whole people of the United Kingdom amounted to about £430,000,000; of which the working class received £99,742,547, and the rent, pension, and profit class £330,778,825! The whole property in the country was at the same time calculated to be worth nearly three thousand millions of pounds sterling.

There is, perhaps, scarcely one man in the United Kingdom who is ignorant of the fact, that there are many hundred idlers in the country who receive £10,000 or £20,000 a year in what are called rents and profits. It has, however, been perceived by these idlers, that the present fraudulent system could not always go on unexamined – that the insufferable burthens sustained by the working class would be certain, sooner or later, to incite them to inquire what became of the vast amount of wealth annually drawn from them – and that they would set about devising remedies. The capitalist, therefore, and the livers on rent and profit – ever ready to excuse their rapacity, and maintain themselves in wealth and idleness at the expense of the working class – have endeavoured to render to the latter an account of their stewardship, that the plundered might not trouble themselves by inquiring into the subject. To this end they tell us that it is utterly impossible for any individual to consume £10,000 or £20,000 a year; and that of the sum so received by any idler, a very small portion only is consumed by himself and family – the remainder being employed in setting labour in motion, and thus assisting in further production; so that, in reality, the rich and idle capitalist and proprietor are of great benefit to society, because they fulfil the duties of distributors! Thus, the advocates for exorbitant individual wealth and inequality of condition endeavour to make it appear, that the actual loss to the working part of the community, by these rich idlers, is only just so much as the individuals themselves consume – not the whole of £20,000 which they yearly receive and spend. Admitting this to be the case, the loss to the working class will still amount annually to the £100,000,000 before stated; for the loss is occasioned by the unprofitable employment and the waste of labour which these idlers cause, as well as by their mere maintenance. The man of £20,000 a-year will keep his servants, horses, dogs, and other incumbrances, none of which – although all of them may work – yield any actual service to the community at large: they are not engaged in the business of production, nor are they advancing, in any way, the interests of society: they give no profitable labour in exchange for the maintenance they receive; and therefore their consumption, as well as that of their employer, the idler, is a dead loss to the producing community.

There are many, even amongst the working classes, who still think, as they have been taught to think, that these "independent" idlers are a great blessing to the community. "Look," cry these benighted men, "how Lord So-and-so spends his money! See what numbers of servants, and horses, and dogs he keeps, and how good it makes trade! Were it not for such as him, poor folks like us would starve!"

It is sickening and pitiable to hear such exclamations as these come from the very same despised and oppressed beings from whom the money was originally taken! – who thus manifest an almost idiotic joy at beholding a wholesale plunderer squander away *their* money! – money produced by *their* toil and deprivation!

It is well that we are no longer ignorant that labour is the creator of all wealth, or we might suppose that the vast sums annually received by capitalists and landed proprietors were paid by their tenants, because the money comes directly from them. But these tenants do not in reality pay the rent, for they lay the whole of it upon their produce. The consumers of the produce then appear to pay it; but all those consumers who belong to the trading classes cover themselves by placing a certain profit upon the articles in which they deal. Thus the charge is perpetually shifted from one class to the class immediately below it, until, at length, its whole accumulated weight rests solely upon the working class. Without labour there can be no production – no rent – and the rent or profit received by any proprietor or capitalist, is but the representative of so much produce and so much labour.

Having thus probed the evil to its core, who can be surprized at the discontentment of the toiling millions? Who will start at their fierce and deep-breathed imprecations on a system which yearly plunders them of wealth of the value of three hundred millions of pounds sterling – a system which compels them to produce this vast amount for the enjoyment of those who treat them with derison and contempt? Shall the working man everlastingly toil and sweat, and be for ever thus plundered, and degraded, and trampled upon? Is it to pamper the unholy pride of those who thus abuse him, that the infancy of his little ones is seared and blighted amid the foul and steamy air of cotton mills and factories? – that his own manhood is bowed down with the premature age produced by excessive toil? Shall his complaints be always hushed by the roaring of artillery – his indignant heart stilled by the thrust of the bayonet – his upbraidings stifled in dungeons? If he would have things to continue thus, let him still go on, as he has heretofore done, drivelling and dreaming of relief from classes and castes, who, deriving their wealth and their supremacy from his toil and abasement, know him only as a bondman or an inferior.

"He who hath wife and child, hath given hostages to fortune;" and ought not fortune, likewise, to give him hostages? The toils of the past and the present should always secure to the working man and his family the enjoyment of the future. But the present system offers the worn-out workman no enjoyment – and no alleviation of unmerited distress and poverty, except in connection with degradation and hardship. And, again, what kind of a welcome and a shelter does society at large now offer to the wife and the children of the expiring working man – to those for whom he has worn out his strength in unremitting toil? None. They wander over the earth as poor and penniless beggars, or, like criminals, they are confined in pauper prisons. The mother becomes separated from the children, and the children are parted from each other – the chords which bound their young hearts together are snapped asunder for ever – and they wander over the face of the earth homeless and friendless, despised and enslaved because they are ignorant, and disregarded and ill-treated because they are poor. Is it to be wondered at that these unfavourable circumstances should do their work – that misery and prostitution is the portion of the one sex, and the transport-ship or the gallows the fate of the other! Even the small and miserable pittance which grinding capital permits tired labour and unprotected childhood still to enjoy, by means of what are termed "poor-laws," will shortly be withheld. These miserable substitutes for justice, inefficient and almost worthless as they are, will soon exist only in name; for it has been acknowledged by those who drink up the very life-blood of the working class, and who are now experimenting as to the length which human endurance of oppression can go, that "poor-laws" are a great and growing evil, which must by some means be got rid of.

Look at the present social system on whatever side and in whatever light we may, we behold but one compact mass of deformity and depravity. If tyranny would revel in the wealth of one people and the blood of another, then is this the proper system for tyranny; if priestcraft would enslave and stultify the human mind, and manufacture soulless tools for despotism, then is this the proper system for priestcraft: if the commission of crime, and the practice of vice, and the waste of labour, be the chief ends for which men unite in society, then is this a proper social system?

Notes

1 'Chartist Circular', *British Newspaper Archive*, at www.britishnewspaperarchive.co.uk/titles/chartist-circular [accessed 15 May 2021]. On the unstamped press, see P. Hollis, *The Pauper Press: A Study in Working-Class Radicalism of the 1830s* (London: Oxford University Press, 1970).
2 Anon., 'The Production and Distribution of Wealth', *Chartist Circular* 38 (13 June 1840), Google Books, pp. 153–154, on p. 153.
3 Anon., 'Production and Distribution', p. 153.
4 On challenges to working-class masculinity, see, for example, A. Clark, *The Struggle for the Breeches: Gender and the Making of the British Working Class* (Berkeley: University of California Press, 1997); S. O. Rose, *Limited Livelihoods: Gender and Class in Nineteenth Century England* (Berkeley: University of California Press, 1992); M. Levine-Clark, *Unemployment, Welfare, and Masculine Citizenship: 'So Much Honest Poverty' in Britain, 1870–1930* (New York: Palgrave Macmillan, 2015).
5 Anon., 'Production and Distribution', p 154. On Poor Law workhouses, see Volume 2 Introduction.
6 G. Stedman Jones, *Languages of Class: Studies in English Working-Class History, 1832–1982* (Cambridge: Cambridge University Press, 1984), p. 106.

5

J. ADSHEAD, *DISTRESS IN MANCHESTER: EVIDENCE (TABULAR AND OTHERWISE) OF THE STATE OF THE LABOURING CLASSES IN 1840–42*

(London: Henry Hooper, Pall Mall East, 1842), pp. 25–30

Joseph Adshead (1800–1861) was an estate agent in Manchester, well known locally for his many reform commitments. He wrote and published on prison reform and helped establish and manage free ragged and industrial schools for the poor.[1] He also founded the Night Asylum for the Destitute Poor and was actively involved with the Manchester Royal Infirmary.[2] From November 1846 until his death, Adshead was a member of the Manchester City Council.[3] In *Distress in Manchester*, Adshead followed up on previous investigations with which he was involved into the extent of poverty in Manchester. His aim was to present the 'exact truth'[4] of destitution in 'tabular form',[5] not to appeal to the reader's emotions, but to try to engender some systemic change. In his words, it was time that 'the axe must be laid at the root of the evil'.[6] In this selection from the study, 'Narratives of Suffering', Adshead turns from tables to stories and certainly must have known he would provoke emotional responses from his readers. The 'Narratives of Suffering' are case histories gathered by the Town Mission about the condition of the working classes in Manchester.[7] These case histories detail accounts of individuals and families experiencing lack of work or low wages, which resulted in poor living conditions, illness, and hunger. They are certainly poignant, as the missionaries themselves and Adshead comment throughout the chapter, calling them 'heart-rending' and 'lamentable'.[8] The missionaries' descriptions indeed make for difficult reading, listing case after case of severe hunger and privation – men, women, and children near to death because they had no work.[9] The narratives reveal that these men living in severe poverty maintained strong work identities. Women, on the other hand, were usually identified as wives who sometimes did a little paid work. The stories also reveal the close association between health and employment, since those out of work and their families suffered many illnesses, often caused by lack of food.[10] The document suggests that the people

DOI: 10.4324/9780429320323-8

were familiar with missionaries in their streets, for example, asking them to visit in their houses, assuming that a visit might result in some form of charity.[11] Much of the information we have about the working classes, especially in the first half of the nineteenth century, comes from sources such as these, where middle-class visitors narrate the conditions of poor people's lives. These are mediated sources, and we need to read them as such, paying attention to the perspectives of the authors.

Distress in Manchester. Evidence (Tabular and Otherwise) of the State of the Labouring Classes in 1840-42

"The relief of human suffering is a sacred duty, written from the beginning on the hearts of men, enforced by the positive precepts of the Gospel, and which no nation can violate or neglect with impunity."

Dr. W. P. Alison.

LONDON:
HENRY HOOPER, PALL MALL EAST. 1842.

Narratives of Suffering

I now propose to avail myself of the labours of the agents of the Town Mission, than whom no persons are better qualified to speak of the condition of the labouring classes of this populous neighbourhood. And here I would gladly bear testimony to the efforts of the Ministers of all denominations – Church, Catholic, and Dissenters, – whose ministrations to the temporal and spiritual wants of the poor have indeed been most exemplary.

It may be proper to observe, in this place, that more than three-fourths of Manchester and Salford, with their immediate vicinities, are occupied by the missionaries of this society, who are employed during the whole of their time in communicating religious instruction, chiefly by visiting from house to house. At present they occupy 47 districts, each containing about 750 families of the class usually visited, so that at least 35,000 families come directly under their influence; and in daily labouring among this large portion of the population, they are necessarily brought to an acquaintance with their real character and condition.

Missionary A. C. reports –

> I have met with many who have not had a meal for two days, and many have pawned almost everything they had for want of food.

Missionary J. E. reports –

> In one house in my district there is a family four in number. The man has been out of work for several months, and for want of food was taken ill, and has been in the Infirmary for a length of time. Now he is out, but he has no work; and if he had, he has not strength to do it.
>
> A family in the same district I found in a deplorable condition. The man has been long out of work; is a spinner by trade, and has a wife and three children. On Saturday morning he obtained work, went off at five o'clock in the morning, and wrought all day without taking bite or sup. When I was there he came in, threw himself in an old chair, and looked as if he was fainting. His wife burst into tears, and said, "I know what's the matter; you want something to eat, but there's not a morsel to give you." This was at five o'clock in the evening. I gave them a few pence to get a little bread, and when it came in and was divided, it was a sorry sight to see how ravenous the little ones were. They prayed that the Lord would preserve me from hunger.

While I was on one side of the street a child came to me, and said, "Mother wants you to call in our house, please." I went, and found seven in family – five children – they were sitting round some embers, for the fire was nearly out. The man, a spinner, was out of work, and had been for some months: his wife had used to get a few shillings by reeling, but had nothing to do for a long while. It was Saturday night, and they had neither fire nor food under their walls; nor had they a farthing to get them with. Although I had nothing to spare from my own family, I gave them a little to help to pass through Sunday. I could mention several cases equally as bad as this. It is needless to multiply cases, for distress is all the cry.

J. G. lives in a cellar. This man has a sick wife. I believe her sickness originated, and is protracted, by starvation. They have been many years in the same cellar, and have always paid their rent until lately, but now expect to be turned out destitute of every thing but the rags they stand in.

H., also living in the same district, has been nearly thirty years in Manchester; has always paid his rent till lately; has a wife and six children, all out of work, everything in pledge, and are daily expecting to be turned out of doors in a state of starvation.

Missionary T. A. reports –

—— Crawford, Brooks-street, a painter by trade. In this cellar there is not so much as a seat, bricks being used for that purpose; no bed; a few shavings, scarcely sufficient for a child to lie upon, is all that four of a family have to keep them off the cold flags.

A widow, with two children, living in Brooks-court; clothes in pawn, no bed, and in want of food; had nothing for three days till I gave her a soup ticket.

Margaret Hinnesy, with one child, Brooks-court; clothes in pawn; had nothing for several days till I gave her a ticket.

Buck Wamby, Brooks-street; out of work; when I called was in bed, having nothing to eat – clothes in pawn.

M'Farlan, with three children, Brooks-street; clothing in pawn. The husband is a painter by trade; has been out of work a long time. The last day that I called she told me, "We have had nothing to eat to-day. (It was then four o'clock.) I am going to pawn these things to get a little bread for my starving children." Another day she had pawned her little boy's trowsers, which I enabled her to redeem. He cannot go to school for want of clothes, having a very decent suit in pawn.

Another Missionary reports –

R. Cann, five in family, three children; all out of work, man sick, and one child sick. The child was laying down on a few shavings of wood in the corner of a damp cellar, without a rag to cover it. Nothing whatever in the cellar. The man said he had been out of work for sixteen weeks.

The Missionary adds – “I might have given many more cases, and will do, if required.”

Missionary G. S. reports –

> Robert O’Brien, Jersey-street, a dyer, with four children; has had no work for many months; his wife has been lately confined; they have been whole days without any food; they have sold or pledged all that they could for food, or rent for the cellar they occupy.
>
> Mary Gorman, a widow, with three children. She has been turned out of a room in Gun-street, her few goods taken for the rent for a few weeks. After having been out for three nights, A. M‘Conville allowed her to sit by their fire at night with her children.

The Missionary says in conclusion – “The above cases, though very briefly stated, may serve to show in some measure the poverty and distress prevailing to a lamentable extent in this district. I have only produced a few cases out of the many (in not one-third of the district), fearing to be too tedious in my details of poverty and wretchedness.” [. . .]

Mr. Buckland, a Missionary to the Poor, gives some heart-rending narratives of cases which he had visited. Here is an extract from a report of his made in the early part of the year 1840: –

> I will here narrate as briefly as possible a few particulars of an appalling case of destitution, which happened in the immediate vicinity of our institution. In a house almost destitute of any thing in the shape of furniture or things of domestic convenience, lived a man and wife and three small children. The husband had been ill for a long time, so that the family was supported by the labour of the woman and what little the eldest child, not ten years of age, could do. For the last twelve months their whole income has not, I believe, exceeded six or seven shillings a week; I have occasionally relieved them with food and clothing, for they were almost literally naked. Indeed they must have perished but for the assistance of their poor neighbours. Last Sunday fortnight the husband died. The little boy was weaving till past eleven o’clock on Saturday night, and the woman was washing the children’s few bits of clothes. Soon after midnight the poor man, who was lying on what was intended for a bed in the same room, was suddenly taken worse; it was evident that he was struggling with death: the little boy was despatched to a relative, a short distance off, almost in a state of nudity, having only an old cloak over him. This was about one o’clock on Sabbath morning, and the poor man was a few minutes afterwards released from his poverty and his sufferings by the friendly hand of death. I cannot attempt to describe the scene which I witnessed next day, or rather the same day. No words can represent it. The simple facts which I have stated will speak for themselves.

The heart bleeds at the recital of such a case of human suffering. Here is a parallel case, – a fit companion picture of want and its awful consequences: –

> This is another case in which death was, I have every reason to believe, induced by gradual starvation. It was that of a young man only twenty-six years of age, with a wife and one child, the woman being at the point of confinement. He had been for a long time without work, except at short and uncertain intervals, and hence got into a poor, weakly state of health. The night before the day on which he died he was working, but not having had food for a considerable time, he actually dropped from his loom, became delirious, and in a short time death put an end to his poverty and his sufferings.

And this is Mr. Buckland's summary of the state of the poor – the result of an extensive personal examination which he undertook in pursuance of the inquiry to which I have already referred: –

> At the request of the Mayor, (the late Mayor, Sir Thomas Potter,) whose sympathy for the suffering poor, and anxiety for their improvement and welfare, need no testimony of mine, I undertook to assist in a statistical inquiry through the No. 1 District, with a view to ascertain from personal observation, carried on from house to house, the exact condition of the working classes. I was engaged in this investigation upwards of a fortnight. The visiting the abodes of distress and poverty was no novelty to me; but I must confess that within no period like that which was devoted to this inquiry have I ever seen a tithe of the suffering and misery which was then brought under observation. I cannot attempt to sketch even the outlines of that frightfully-distressing picture; nothing short of the evidence of the senses can afford an adequate conception of the length and breadth of its deformity. We found vast numbers either totally unemployed, or only having work at short and uncertain intervals. It was no uncommon thing to hear men and women say, one after another, we have had no work for several weeks, and sometimes months. Indeed, it was a rare thing among the numerous families we visited to find one that it could be strictly said was fully employed. As to domestic comforts – alas! in very many cases there were none. Of clothing and bedding we found large numbers quite destitute. Several families were almost in a state of absolute nudity. A few shavings, or a little straw, not unfrequently on the floor or bare flags, with scarcely a bit of covering, constituted the hard pillow on which some half-dozen of a family were compelled to rest their weary heads. In these comfortless, destitute homes, we found that the best and most necessary articles were at the pawn-shop. And as a proof that distress had increased with an accelerated force within the last few months, it is only necessary to mention the

> fact which I ascertained in a large number of instances, namely, that the people had pawned the best part of their bedding after the winter had set in. Indeed, in a very great number of cases we found that all the most useful articles of bedding and wearing apparel had been pawned; the natural consequence of which must be, as was painfully brought under our notice, utter discomfort and destitution.

I can to a great extent confirm the statements of Mr. Buckland, as I accompanied him in the early part of his inquiry.

Notes

1 The ragged school movement emerged in the mid-nineteenth century. These schools provided education to poor students who could not afford the fees at existing schools and were often turned away from Sunday schools because of their 'dirty appearance'. The movement grew rapidly: by 1860, the most prominent organization of the movement, the London Ragged School Union (LRSU), oversaw 560 schools with nearly 50,000 students. L. M. Mair, 'A "Transcript of Their Mind"?: Ragged School Literacy in the Mid Nineteenth Century', *Journal of Victorian Culture* 24:1 (January 2019), pp. 18–32, on pp. 21–22.

2 'Local and District', *Manchester Times*, 23 February 1861, p. 6.

3 'County and District News', *Manchester Guardian*, quoted in *Ulverston Mirror and Furness Reflector*, 23 February 1861, p. 7.

4 J. Adshead, *Distress in Manchester-Evidence (Tabular and Otherwise) of the State of the Labouring Classes in 1840–42* (London: Henry Hooper, Pall Mall East, 1842), British Library, p. v.

5 Adshead, *Distress in Manchester*, p. vii.

6 Adshead, *Distress in Manchester*, p. viii.

7 On 'domestic missions' and the context of middle-class religion in Manchester, see S. Gunn, 'The Ministry, the Middle Class, and the 'Civilizing Mission' in Manchester, 1850–80', *Social History* 21:1 (1996), pp. 22–36.

8 Adshead, *Distress in Manchester*, pp. 28, 27.

9 On the representation of hunger in this era, see J. Vernon, *Hunger: A Modern History* (Cambridge, MA: Harvard University Press, 2007), pp. 18–20; C. Boyce, 'Representing the "Hungry Forties" in Image and Verse: The Politics of Hunger in Early-Victorian Illustrated Periodicals', *Victorian Literature and Culture* 20:2 (2012), pp. 421–449.

10 On gender and work identities, see, for example, A. Clark, *The Struggle for the Breeches: Gender and the Making of the British Working Class* (Berkeley: University of California Press, 1995); S. O. Rose, *Limited Livelihoods: Gender and Class in Nineteenth-Century England* (Berkeley: University of California Press, 1992).

11 On 'domestic missions' broadly, see A. Twells, *The Civilising Mission and the English Middle Class, 1792–1850* (New York: Palgrave Macmillan, 2009).

6

THE *BRITISH WORKMAN* ON THE NOBILITY OF LABOUR

The following three selections are from the early years of the *British Workman*, a paper whose goal was to improve the working classes and spread the gospel of temperance.[1] Founded by Thomas Bywater Smithies (1817–1883), the *British Workman* ran from 1855 to 1921, with the publishing company continuing its run after Smithies's death.[2] By the late 1850s, the paper had achieved great success, with a circulation of over 200,000 copies a month.[3] Smithies believed that the best way to convey messages about respectability to the working classes was through images, so the *British Workman*, a penny monthly, is filled with detailed and dramatic illustrations.[4] The central message Smithies aimed to communicate in almost all items in the paper was that labour was dignified and godly, as long as the worker was temperate and honest. The *British Workman* offers an idealized portrait of rural life and work, sometimes presenting an outright critique of industrial labour but more often simply praising the qualities of agricultural pursuits.[5] All three selections included here reflect a celebration of labour and the labouring classes, trying to convince workers of the value of their work.

The first selection (6.1) is by Mary Howitt (1824–1884), who was best known as a painter connected to the pre-Raphaelite circle, and who also wrote to support herself.[6] Writing from the perspective of a labouring man, Howitt thanks God for making him a labourer and giving him hard work to do because it ennobles him. This is Thomas Carlyle's famous perspective in *Past and Present*.[7] According to Howitt, rather than being trapped in lineage like the wealthy, the labouring man is free to be a man. The 'hardships' of toil, not wealth or rank, create the virtues that make a man, and labourers should learn self-respect.[8]

The second piece (6.2), 'The Dignity of Labour', is a reprint of an extract from a lecture delivered by the Rev. Newman Hall (1816–1902)[9] at the Young Men's Christian Association, Exeter Hall, in January 1856. Hall presents the accomplishments of many different realms of labour, identifying 'Labour' itself as an actor. It is Labour that creates 'human happiness' in feeding, clothing, and housing the people. Labour produces commerce and foreign trade and allows other nations to appreciate 'British industry and British skill'.[10] Labour can control nature, construct beauty, and envision civilization out of a wasteland. In sum, Labour reconstructs the world so that humanity can inhabit it. Essentially, Hall reproduces the labour theory of value within a religious framework.

DOI: 10.4324/9780429320323-9

The final item (6.3), without a byline, is the first in a series, probably by Smithies himself as editor of the paper. The author emphasizes a broad definition of hard work that encompasses the brain-work of men like judges, lawyers, doctors, and clergymen. He wants to assure the reader that these men 'are worthy of their manhood'[11] and that not only manual labour makes a man.[12] Nevertheless, the article stresses the special, godly nature of the work of the labouring classes and urges working men to live up to their inheritance by taking care of their minds, bodies, and souls. All three articles have in common the goal of convincing the reader of his noble place as a labourer in a valuable social hierarchy.

6.1 'Labour's Thanksgiving Hymn'

THAT I must work I thank thee, God!
I know that hardship, toil, and pain,
Like rigorous winter in the sod,
Which doth mature the hardy grain,
Call forth in man his noblest powers;
Therefore I hold my head erect,
And amid life's severest hours,
Stand stedfast in my self-respect.

I thank thee, God, that I must toil!
Yon ermined slave, of lineage high,
The game-law lord, who owns the soil,
Is not a man so free as I!
He wears the fetter of his clan;
Wealth, birth, and rank, have hedged him in;
I heed but this – that I am man,
And to the great of mind akin.

Thank God, that, like the mountain oak,
My lot is with the storms of life;
Strength grows from out the tempest's shock,
And patience in the daily strife.
The hardened hand, the furrowed brow,
Degrade not, howe'er sloth may deem;
'Tis this degrades – to cringe and bow,
And ape the vice we disesteem.

Thank God for toil, for hardships, whence
Come courage, patience, hardihood;
And for that sad experience
Which leaves our bosoms flesh and blood;
Which leaves us tears for others' woe.
Brother in toil, respect thyself,
And let thy stedfast virtues show
That man is nobler far than pelf.

Thank God for toil! nor fear the face
Of wealth nor rank – fear only sin;
That blight which mars all outward grace,
And dims the light of peace within.
Give me thy hand, my brother give
The hard yet honest hand to me;
We are not dreamers – we shall live
A brighter, better day to see.

MARY HOWITT.

THE DIGNITY OF LABOUR.

6.2 'The Dignity of Labour'

THE DIGNITY OF LABOUR – consider its achievements! Dismayed by no difficulty, shrinking from no exertion, exhausted by no struggle, ever eager for renewed efforts in its persevering promotion of human happiness, – "clamorous labour knocks, with its hundred hands, at the golden gate of the morning," obtaining each day, through succeeding centuries, fresh benefactions for the world.

Labour drives the plough, and scatters the seed, and reaps the harvest, and grinds the corn, and converts it into bread, the staff of life.

Labour, tending the pastures, and sweeping the waters as well as cultivating the soil, provides with daily sustenance the 900 millions of the family of man.

Labour gathers the gossamer web of the caterpillar, the cotton from the field, and the fleece from the flock, and weaves it into raiment soft, and warm, and beautiful; the purple robe of the prince, and the grey gown of the peasant, being alike its handy work.

Labour moulds the brick, and splits the slate, and quarries the stone, and shapes the column, and rears not only the humble cottage, but the gorgeous palace, and the tapering spire and the stately dome.

Labour, diving deep into the solid earth, brings up its long-hidden stores of coal, to feed ten thousand furnaces, and in millions of habitations to defy the winter's cold.

Labour explores the rich veins of deeply-buried rocks, extracting from them the gold, the silver, the copper, and the tin.

Labour smelts the iron, and moulds it into a thousand shapes for use and ornament, from the massive pillar to the tiniest needle, from the ponderous anchor to the wire gauze, from the mighty fly-wheel of the steam-engine to the polished purse-ring or the glittering bead.

Labour hews down the gnarled oak, and shapes the timber, and builds the ship, and guides it over the deep; plunging through the billows and wrestling with the tempest, to bear to our shores the produce of every clime.

Labour brings us Indian rice and American cotton, African ivory, and Greenland oil; fruits from the sunny South, and furs from the frozen North; tea from the East, and sugar from the West, carrying in exchange to every land the products of British industry and British skill.

Labour, by the universally spread ramifications of trade, distributes its own treasures from country to country, from city to city, from house to house, conveying to the doors of all, the necessaries and luxuries of life, and by the steady pulsation of an untrammelled commerce, maintaining healthy life in the great social system.

Labour, fusing the opaque particles of rock, produces transparent glass, which it moulds and polishes, and combines so wondrously that sight is restored to the blind, while worlds, before invisible from distance, are brought so near as to be

weighed and measured with an unerring exactness; and atoms, which had escaped all detection from minuteness, reveal a world of wonder and beauty in themselves.

Labour, possessing a secret far more important than the philosopher's stone, transmutes the most worthless substances into the most precious, and placing in the crucible of its potent chemistry, the putrid refuse of the sea and land, extracts fragrant essences and healing medicines, and materials of priceless importance in the arts.

Labour, laughing at difficulties, spans majestic rivers, carries viaducts over marshy swamps, suspends aërial bridges above deep ravines, pierces the solid mountain with its dark, undeviating tunnel, blasting rocks, and filling hollows, and while linking together with its iron but loving grasp all nations of the earth, verifying in a literal sense the ancient prophecy, "Every valley shall be exalted, and every mountain and hill shall be brought low."

Labour draws forth its delicate iron thread, and stretching it from city to city, from province to province, through mountains, and beneath the sea, realises

more than fancy ever fabled, while it constructs a chariot on which speech may outstrip the wind, compete with the lightning, and fly as rapidly as thought itself.

Labour seizes the thoughts of genius – the discoveries of science – the counsels of experience – the admonitions of piety; and with its magic types impressing the vacant page, renders it pregnant with life and power, perpetuating truth to distant ages, and diffusing it to all mankind.

Labour sits enthroned in palaces of crystal, whose high arched roofs proudly sparkle in the sunshine which delighteth to honour it, and whose ample courts are crowded with the trophies of its victories, in every country and in every age.

Labour, a mighty magician, walks forth into a region uninhabited and waste: he looks earnestly on the scene, so quiet in its desolation; then waving his wonder-working wand, those dreary valleys smile with golden harvests, – those barren mountain slopes are clothed with foliage, – the furnace blazes – the anvil rings – the busy wheels whirl round – the town appears, the mart of commerce, the hall of science, the temple of religion, rear high their lofty fronts, – a forest of masts, gay with varied pennons, rises from the harbour, – the quays are crowded with commercial spoils, the peaceful spoils which enrich both him who receives and him who yields, – representatives of far-off regions make it their resort, – science enlists the elements of earth and heaven in its service, – art, awaking, clothes its strength with beauty, – literature new born, redoubles and perpetuates its praise, – civilization smiles – liberty is glad – humanity rejoices – piety exults, for the voice of industry and gladness is heard on every hand; and who, contemplating such results, will deny that there is *Dignity in Labour?*

Extract from a lecture by the Rev. Newman Hall, B.A., delivered in Exeter Hall, in January last, to the Young Men's Christian Association. The entire lecture is published by J. Nisbet, Berners Street, price fourpence.

6.3 'No. I. – The Working-Man'

A VERY mistaken notion prevails in some men's minds about work and workers. They think that the rich man gets all the play, and the poor man all the work; and they murmur that this world's good is so unequally shared. Now as to work, there is by no means the inequality that some hastily suppose. There are nearly as many kinds of work as of workers. Some work with the brain, some with the hand, and some with both. It is generally believed that brainwork wears the body, and taxes the health more than any other kind of toil. Think of the judge who sits from ten in the morning until eight or ten at night, with only a short interval of rest, in a crowded court – not only listening to endless, and often most painful and weary talking, but making a written abstract of tedious, perplexing evidence, and then closely thinking it all over – so as to give a clear summary to the jury, and doing this for days and weeks together, amid the infirmities of old age, for our judges are rarely young or even middle-aged men. Surely that learned judge is a worker – a very hard worker. Think of the lawyer – whether counsellor, barrister, or attorney – years of study and toil are theirs, to fit them for their profession; and then if they get a good practice, what nights of toil – what days of exhaustion – hard-thinking and arguing, until mind and body must both be tried to the utmost.

Think of the doctor – called up at all hours, to scenes of suffering and pestilence, however ill or tired he himself may be, go he must, or he forfeits his good name, and ruins his prospects. He has noteven [sic] the rest of the Sabbath, for sickness comes at all times – and this is one reason why medical men as a class are not long-lived. These men, in the midst of peculiar peril, are surely hard-workers. Think of the teacher of God's Word – the preacher of righteousness! if he is in earnest to win souls, how his laborious days of visitation, alternate with frequent public teaching, followed by nights of careful study; instant in season and out of season; he sows the good seed beside all waters, and is a hard-worker. Yes! men at the desk – men who go down to the sea in ships, whatever their rank – men who travel in distant lands – to say nothing of the men in every land who make the laws that govern their fellowman, are all, if worthy of their manhood, workers!

It is perfectly absurd to say that idleness is gentility. No real true-hearted gentleman ever lived or believed that maxim. All work is noble – and all good men, according to their degree, find their work, and do it manfully.

But we all understand the special meaning of the terms, "working-man," "working-class." Those who are born to toil, who have nothing but their strong or skilful hands to depend on for the bread that perisheth. Well, these, whose inheritance is labour, are among the best benefactors of the world. God gives the coal, and iron, and stone, and clay and wood – but He gives the world a better gift still in the active hands that delve, and hew, and smelt, and fashion these into forms of elegance, usefulness and comfort. The honest, industrious, sober, pious, working-man has a right to magnify his office, for the world is his debtor. The curse of labour bore within it a blessing. It is man's noble benefaction to his fellow-man, and his grateful oblation to his God.

Oh working man! live up to your privileges. Be careful of your body – it is fearfully and wonderfully made – let no intemperance mar its health – no uncleanness destroy its purity. Fresh air, pure water, plain wholesome food, regular hours, these, in most cases, are within the means of the humblest working-man to procure, and these with the rest of the Sabbath, are the likeliest means of preserving the health.

"But man does not live by bread alone," He has a mind! whether fustian or broad cloth clothe the outward frame, the inner man must not be neglected. What good food is to the body, good books are to the mind. We live in an age when some of the best books that were ever written are so cheap as to come within the means of most working-men. A single half-hour every evening, regularly given to reading would be a great improvement and a great refreshment. Working-men should practise reading aloud; it is worth any trouble it may cost to acquire a clear, distinct, intelligent way of reading aloud. Often the meaning of a book or paper is far more clearly understood if read aloud. And if working-men practised this more, they would improve and entertain one another, and would be much pleasanter companions. A love of reading makes lonely hours cheerful, and social hours instructive.

But important as body and mind are, "That the soul be without knowledge is not good." A well-trained body and an active mind with a darkened soul, is like a good house with large windows, whose shutters are never opened to receive the light, and that is damp and dark, where it might be airy and light. Let in the Heavenly light! God's Word is a sun, in its light you shall see light shining more and more unto the perfect day. If the working-men of England had their souls open to the light of truth, if the Sun of Righteousness had arisen upon them, – would they suffer any one for money or for pleasure to lay a profane or grasping-hand upon their Sabbath, that seventh of their time which they need for the body's repose, the mind's refreshment, and the soul's enlightenment? No! They would guard the Sabbath as their sacred right, their dearest privilege. They would see that the Sabbaths of a man's life are the shining rundles in the ladder that reaches from earth to heaven. God blessed and rested on it, and hallowed it in paradise. Christ renewed the blessing in old Judea, and wrote the charter of man's Sabbath-rights in His blood, and sealed it in the rest of the sepulchre, – rising on that first day of the week, which all Christendom has since commemorated as "The Lord's-day."

Working-man be true to yourself, labour diligently six days of the week for the bread that perisheth, and enjoy on the Divine holyday the bread of life sent down from Heaven: so shall your life here be noble, your life hereafter triumphant.

Notes

1 On the temperance movement, see B. H. Harrison, *Drink and the Victorians: The Temperance Question in England, 1815–1872* (Edinburgh, UK: Edinburgh University Press, 1997, orig. 1971).

2 F. Murray, 'Smithies, Thomas Bywater', *Oxford Dictionary of National Biography* [hereafter ODNB], 29 May 2014, at https://doi-org.du.idm.oclc.org/10.1093/ref:odnb/74113 [accessed 13 June 2021].

3 'British Workman Magazine: Administrative/Biographical History', Jisc Archives Hub, at https://archiveshub.jisc.ac.uk/search/archives/a0b0c8e6-3658-39dc-95d9-fc11583d921f [accessed 15 May 2021].
4 '*British Workman*', Nineteenth-Century Business, Labour, Temperance & Trade Periodicals, at www.blt19.co.uk/periodicals/british-workman/ [accessed 15 May 2021].
5 For an analysis of the rural ideal, see R. Williams, *The Country and the City* (Oxford: Oxford University Press, 1975).
6 P. Hirsch, 'Howitt [*married name* Watts], Anna Mary', *ODNB*, 6 January 2011, at https://doi-org.du.idm.oclc.org/10.1093/ref:odnb/63040 [accessed 13 June 2021]. On the pre-Raphaelites, see, for example, T. Barringer, *Reading the Pre-Raphaelites* (New Haven, CT: Yale University Press, 2012).
7 T. Carlyle, *Past and Present, Thomas Carlyle's Collected Works*, vol. 13 (Project Gutenberg, 2008), 244, at https://www.gutenberg.org/cache/epub/13534/pg13534.html [accessed 8 November 2021].
8 M. Howitt, 'The Labourer's Thanksgiving Hymn', *British Workman* (1856), British Library General Reference Collection, 1856–1861: LOU.LON 71, p. 91.
9 'Death of Dr. Newman Hall', *Aberdeen Press and Journal*, 19 February 1902, p. 6.
10 Rev. N. Hall, 'The Dignity of Labour', *British Workman* (1856), British Library General Reference Collection, 1856–1861: LOU.LON 71, p. 9.
11 'The Working Man', *British Workman* (1859), British Library General Reference Collection, 1856–1861: LOU.LON 71, p. 215.
12 On nineteenth-century masculinity, see J. Tosh, *Manliness and Masculinities in Nineteenth-Century Britain: Essays on Gender, Family, and Empire* (New York: Pearson Longman, 2005).

7

REV. A. OXENDEN, 'THE LABOURER AT HIS WORK', IN *THE LABOURING MAN'S BOOK*

(London: Wertheim, Mackintosh, and Hunt, 1860), pp. 47–61

The Reverend Ashton Oxenden (1808–1892) was the rector of Pluckley with Pevington in Kent when *The Labouring Man's Book* was published. He was known for his very popular weekly lectures designed for family religious education, which were published as the *Barham Tracts* (1852–1857). He went on to become the Anglican Bishop of Montreal (1869).[1] In the preface to *The Labouring Man's Book*, Oxenden presents himself as a 'friend' to the working man who will provide guidance on good and godly living.[2] The chapter selected here, 'The Labourer at His Work', aims to assure the working classes that they were valued, since their labour was needed to feed society. Even if their labour was 'lowly, toilsome, [and] irksome',[3] it was ordained by God, so the worker should feel blessed. Oxenden mentions men in the Bible who performed hard work as proof of the value of labour. As in Volume 1, Part 1, Chapters 3 and 4, Oxenden juxtaposes the productive labourer with the idler, but here it is for conservative rather than radical purposes as Oxenden's idler is the unemployed working man rather than the aristocrat. Much of the chapter is taken up with Oxenden's 'hints' to workers on how to choose their employments and employers, if they have a choice, and how to maintain a positive attitude toward their labour.[4] His assumption seems to be that workers need this advice; otherwise, they might wind up as idlers. Oxenden warns his readers not to simply take on easy work or work that offers good wages, since either of these situations may present other discomforts that outweigh the benefits. Regarding employers, Oxenden 'rejoices' that in England most workers were 'treated more as a Friend than a Servant',[5] so men for the most part did not have to worry about choosing bad employers. Still, Oxenden is clearly concerned that employers be attentive to their role in developing good relationships with their workers and regards the master-servant bond as central to the functioning of society.[6] He tells workers to be patient about the 'little roughnesses' that will come up in a working relationship and that they should remain with an employer once they had found a good job.[7] However, he warns his readers never to perform work

DOI: 10.4324/9780429320323-10

that went against Christian conduct, providing labouring men with a reason to challenge their employers. We can see Oxenden's assumption that 'the labourer' is a married man, as he expects him to 'hasten home' to a waiting wife.[8] He does acknowledge, however, that his 'reader [might] chance to be a female' and that his messages would apply 'almost as much to Mistresses and Maid-servants, as to Masters and Men',[9] limiting his idea of women's work to domestic service.

'The Labourer at His Work'

Doubtless God might have so ordered it, that the earth should of its own accord have produced its fruits. The soil might have needed no tilling, and the corn might have sprung up like the grass, without the yearly sowing of seed. God *could* have given us food without our labour, just as well as with it. But such is not His will. He has ordained that man should labour for the bread he eats, that it should not be obtained without the cost of toil – either his own toil, or that of others.

Hence it is that in this and other countries the Labouring Class is a large and important one. Without it there would be a general stagnation; there would be a famine in the land. Bread could not be purchased even with silver and gold, if the Labourer did not cause it to grow. Shillings and sovereigns, however plentiful, would never of themselves satisfy the cravings of hunger; nor would banknotes shield the back from cold, and ward off the pelting storm.

Think not then that your work is to be despised. Oh, no; far otherwise. The post you fill is an honourable one; and, if God blesses it, it may be a very happy one. You may have the great comfort of feeling that in serving your earthly Master, you are serving God; and that even in your ordinary work you are pleasing Him. Lowly, toilsome, irksome that work may be; but still, if it is performed from Christian motives, it becomes (as has been well said) a consecrated offering of obedience to God, and of goodwill to men.

Far, far better is it to be a hardworking Labourer than a lazy Idler. The one is a useful member of society; the other a mere cumberer of the ground. "Of all tasks the most irksome is the task of doing nothing. Then the chief object of every day's existence is to hasten to its close; the only occupation is to chide the leaden-footed hours for the weary pace at which they creep along. Life itself is to the unemployed an intolerable burden."

"Ho! ye who at the anvil toil
And strike the sounding blow,
Where from the burning iron's breast
The sparks fly to and fro,
While answering to the hammer's ring,
And fire's intenser glow –
Oh, while ye feel 'tis hard to toil
And sweat the long day through,
Remember, it is harder still
To have no work to do.

"Ho! ye who till the stubborn soil,
Whose hard hands guide the plough,
Who bend beneath the summer sun,
With burning cheek and brow –
Ye deem the curse still clings to earth
From olden times till now;

But while ye feel 'tis hard to toil
And labour all day through,
Remember, it is harder still
To have no work to do."

Yes, labour is honourable to all. Adam worked till the sweat fell from his brow. Jacob was a Shepherd to Laban. Joseph was at one time in service. St. Peter and the Sons of Zebedee were Sailors. St. Paul was a Tent-maker; and we find him exhorting his Thessalonian Brethren "to do their own business, and to work with their own hands." Even the Saviour of the world, when He came among us, "took upon Him the form of a servant;" and "though He was rich, yet for our sakes He became poor." And no doubt He actually worked in the shop at Nazareth, and thereby put an honour on labour by His own bright example.

But the English Labourer does not usually work for himself, but for another. He has a Master who employs him, and an appointed task which is allotted to him.

Sometimes a man has no choice as to where his work lies, or what it is to be. He must undertake a certain employment, or be thrown out of work altogether. If this is the case, he should take his portion cheerfully, and do his best. But, generally speaking, a choice *is* open to him. He has the opportunity of placing himself under this or that Master, as he may like best. Now, since much depends upon *the kind of service* you engage in, I will throw out a few hints, which may be worth your considering.

First, you will be wrong in taking a place, merely because *the work seems to be light*. A wise Traveller does not always choose the road that appears smoothest; for there may be many reasons why that road may be the worst in the end. And so too a Labourer may undertake a situation which is easy enough, but there may be many disadvantages belonging to it. The *lightness* of the place is not everything. There is more to be looked at than merely this – as, for instance, the kind of Master you are to work for, the sort of men you are likely to be thrown in with, and other matters which might be mentioned.

Secondly, do not think too much about *the amount of pay*. You may have high wages, but a very uncomfortable place. More shillings may be coming in to you, than to your neighbour; but you may have to earn them amidst much discomfort, and even suffering. It is true, at the close of the week you must look to your earnings. You need money for your daily wants; and the Poor Man has at best but little. Still, money alone will not make up for other things. It will not give you happiness. Much misery may come along with it.

For instance, suppose you have a good place as far as pay goes, still if it so happens that you are kept from home comforts – that you cannot spend a reasonable time with your family in the evening – that you are forced to neglect your wife and children – or that you are unable to get to church – then, what a poor make up for all this will a few extra shillings be at the week's end!

Thirdly, try and place yourself under one who has the character of being *a good and kind Master*. Some care but little for their men, so that they perform the work for which they are hired. But I rejoice to think there are but few such in this country, and in these our days. The time is gone by, when the Employer used to look upon his Labourer as a mere machine. In "the olden time," a few hundred years ago, he was little better than a slave. He was sure of meat and drink, it is true, at his Master's table He was kept in good fighting trim for his Master's battles. But he was cared for only for the same reason that his owner's cattle were cared for – that he might be fit for use when he was wanted. But now, thank God, the Labourer is admitted into the great brotherhood of man, and is often treated more as a Friend than a Servant.

Still, even in these days, some Masters are kinder, more just, and more considerate than others; they look after the welfare of those whom they employ. Now, try to get into the service of such: it will, I am sure, add no little to your comfort.

Happy that Employer, who has a kindly feeling for his workmen; who bears in mind that he must answer to God for his conduct towards them; and who, instead of having always before him a selfish desire for his own advantage, does all he can for the real good of those whom God has placed under him! It is well when a feeling of confidence grows up on both sides – the Master respecting his Servant, and treating him with kindness; and the Servant looking upon the Master as his Friend, having a constant eye to his interests, and cheerfully and willingly doing the work allotted to him!

Fourthly, never engage in any work which will *expose you to what is wrong*. For instance, if it should be proposed to you to undertake some unnecessary labour on Sunday – or if you should be set to do anything which is clearly contrary to the commands of God – pause before you engage yourself for such a work; for it cannot be right for a Christian to do that which God's word condemns. You can never prosper, *if you knowingly do anything which is opposed to His will.*

John Bentley, of whom you may have read, was a poor man, but one who feared God. He worked for a millwright who was a worldly man. On one occasion his Master wished him to do some work on Sunday. John Bentley positively refused. "I told him," said he, "that I would die first. Nothing should induce me thus to treat God's day. Ask me no more about it. I'm willing to work as early as you like on the Monday morning, and till I drop at night; but on God's day I will do nothing." He stood firm, for his conscience whispered to him that he was right, and he gained his point. So much so, that his Master, who had thus tried to persuade him to do what was clearly wrong, and whom he so nobly refused, proved afterwards a real friend to him, and honoured him for his Christian conduct.

This man's rule was *to do the thing that is right;* and it answered in his case. Such too should be our great rule, cost us what it may. And I am sure, if we act upon it, we shall be carried over most of the difficulties of life.

Fifthly, having a fair place, and a good Master, *continue in his service*. In these days there is a spirit of change come over many of us – a restless feeling which runs through all classes. Beware of it. Few things add more to our peace than a fixed, settled, and contented frame of mind. Besides, one who is always changing will soon lose his character for steadiness.

One reason, why so few keep their places long, is that too much is expected both by the Servant and the Master. We are unwilling to put up with *little difficulties*. We are not forbearing enough. We do not make allowance for one another. And therefore, if everything does not go on quite smoothly, we get restless and impatient. Is it not so?

For example, your Master gives what seems to you an unreasonable order; and you instantly take offence. Or you return a short and sharp answer to some question which is put to you; and immediately he becomes angry. Or, it may be, you have a job set you which is not quite to your taste; and this puts you into a grumbling and dissatisfied humour. Or another Labourer appears to be more in favour than yourself; and a nasty jealous spirit comes over you.

Now, we should be prepared for all these little roughnesses; and we should try and take them patiently and good-humouredly. If there was more of the "give and take" principle on both sides, there would be more of that lengthened service which we do now and then hear of even in these days, and which is such a credit to both Master and Men.

Lastly, always endeavour to *do justice to your Employer*. Deal fairly with him. Act honestly and faithfully towards him. Serve him as heartily and cheerfully, as if you were labouring for yourself. Do the very best you can for him. Work just as hard when his back is turned, as when his eye is upon you.

Labour is but a toil indeed, when it is taken up unwillingly. Every stroke of work done is an effort, when it is done grudgingly. But one who labours with a contented and cheerful mind, taking a real interest in his Master's concerns, labour to him becomes a pleasure, and he feels happy at his work.

Then too there is another thought which cheers the Labourer as he toils. He feels, whilst he earns his bread by the sweat of his brow, that he is not labouring for himself only, but for others who are dear to him. This sweetens his toil, and makes many a rough task smooth. And, when his work is over, he hastens home with a light heart; for he feels sure there is one there, whose bright look tells him that his return is welcome.

But now I must be closing my chapter. As you have been reading it, the thought very likely may have come across you, "Ah, he who writes all this never was a Servant himself, and therefore does not know half our difficulties." No, perhaps not. But this I know – that we, all of us, are apt to increase our own difficulties; but where there is a little watchful care, and patience, and forbearance, we may often wonderfully lighten them; and perhaps one-half of them may be entirely got rid of. Try to do this with God's help, and you will be blest in the effort.

If my reader chance to be a Female, let her remember that what I have said refers almost as much to Mistresses and Maid-servants, as to Masters and Men.

Notes

1 G. C. Boase, 'Oxenden, Ashton', *Oxford Dictionary of National Biography*, 23 September 2004, at https://doi-org.du.idm.oclc.org/10.1093/ref:odnb/21049 [accessed 13 June 2021]; *Morning Post*, 25 February 1892, p. 5.

2 Rev. A. Oxenden, *The Labouring Man's Book* (London: Wertheim, Mackintosh, and Hunt, 1860), Google Books, p. vi.

3 Oxenden, *The Labouring Man's Book*, p. 48.

4 Oxenden, *The Labouring Man's Book*, p. 52.

5 Oxenden, *The Labouring Man's Book*, p. 55.
6 This is a vision of a vertical, paternalistic society, rather than a horizontal, class society.
7 Oxenden, *The Labouring Man's Book*, p. 59.
8 Oxenden, *The Labouring Man's Book*, p. 61.
9 Oxenden, *The Labouring Man's Book*, p. 61.

8

DR J. C. HALL, *THE TRADES OF SHEFFIELD . . . READ BEFORE THE NATIONAL ASSOCIATION FOR THE PROMOTION OF SOCIAL SCIENCE*, 2ND ED

(London: Longmans, Green and Co, 1865), pp. 7–21

Dr John Charles Hall (1816–1876) worked at Sheffield Public Hospital and Dispensary, where he had many opportunities to observe the impact of local industries on the health of the labouring population. He served as president of the Sheffield Medico-Chirugical Society in 1871–1872 and was vice president of the Medicine Section of the British Medical Association.[1] The lecture included here, originally read before the National Association for the Promotion of Social Science, was also printed in the *Illustrated London News*, with multiple images detailing the trades he discusses.[2] Hall's expertise was called on throughout his career, including to provide evidence to a Royal Commission on the special diseases about which he wrote.[3] While the source in Volume 1, Part 1, Chapter 7 discusses the nobility of labour and expresses the ways God glorifies work, this selection focuses on the negative material consequences of work on the well-being of men. Many nineteenth-century industries were extremely dangerous; with a lack of safety and health regulations, workers suffered from frequent accidents and illnesses resulting from their conditions of work.[4] As new industries developed or old industries became overcrowded, many individuals and organizations – parliamentary, municipal, private, and public – undertook investigations to try to understand working conditions. These conditions of work in many ways contributed to the meanings assigned to that work. Agricultural work, because it was predominantly performed outdoors, was understood to be healthy, while workshops with little light and ventilation were viewed as unhealthy. Investigators saw factories, where men and women worked together, as both unhealthy and immoral, especially for young women. Many of these conclusions rested on the testimony of physicians and surgeons.[5] The testimony of doctors became particularly important as Parliament considered protective legislation and acts limiting the hours of work,

DOI: 10.4324/9780429320323-11

predominantly for women and children, but increasingly for men as well.[6] Hall's paper is typical of the investigations undertaken to understand the conditions of various industries. Hall here describes the labour of file cutters and grinders, offering details of their work processes, work spaces, materials, and the diseases associated with them. In the source, we can see the hierarchy of labour in the industry, with union men being paid the highest wages and women, children, and unskilled workers at the bottom. The work of file cutters, according to Hall, included shaping steel on a bed of lead, producing fine lead dust, which resulted in lead poisoning, especially because the workers put their fingers in their mouths and ate without handwashing. Hall offers suggestions to prevent 'File Cutters' Disease',[7] many of which depended on changing the habits of the workers. The other industry Hall examines is grinding, in which men sharpened metal items, such as razors and knives, on a wheel, causing steel bits to fly off the wheel. According to Hall, this process caused damage to the eyes, even when industrial glasses were used. Additionally, the workers suffered severely from dust, with fork grinders having a life expectancy under forty. Hall notes that grinders who worked in rural areas were healthier than those who worked in towns, which was consistent with all the public health reporting of the time.[8] He recommends limiting the grinders' hours of work and making sure that owners provided fans in grinding halls. In developing his recommendations, Hall spoke with file cutters and grinders, and their narratives reveal a fatalism about the danger of their work. Throughout the text, Hall uses his position at the Sheffield Public Hospital and Dispensary to offer specific examples of the diseases he has treated.

The Manufacture of Files

The forging, grinding, cutting, and hardening of files forms one of the most important branches of our local trades, and one in which the workmen suffer most severely, at any rate in one part of the manufacture of a file. This is one of the trades which is "*in Union,*" and consequently one, the numbers employed in which can more readily be ascertained. At the present time there are engaged in the File Trade: –

Forgers and Cutters	3,500
File Grinders	250
Hardeners	200
Females	300
Boys	1,000
Dressers, Strippers, and Coke Riddlers	300
Managers	200
	5,750

If to this number we add the Manufacturers, and those not connected with the Union, it will be seen that more than 6,000 of the inhabitants of Sheffield and its vicinity are engaged in the manufacture of files. The Filesmiths' Union is one of the most powerful in Sheffield. From 1854 to 1865 it has paid to its members when out of work, £51,044 17s. 2½d. From 1860 to the end of 1864, (five years,) this Union paid for 312 deaths, viz. 297 men and women and 15 boys, £1,156 6s. 0d. The wages of the better class of double-handed forgers will average about 40s. a week; single-handed forgers, 25s. to 30s. a week; cutters of a superior class of work, 30s.; boys, 6s. to 18s.; female cutters, 6s. to 18s. a week; scourers, &c., 9s. to 12s. a week.

Manufacture of a File

In speaking of the wages of File forgers, single and double-handed forgers were mentioned. Small Files – say all under ten inches are made single-handed: the larger files require a striker who using a very heavy double-headed hammer aids the skilled forger in moulding the steel into the requisite shape. The history of a file is simply this – as a rule horse rasps are forged from bar steel; other files from cast steel. When forged the file is sent to be annealed or softened in a furnace or baking oven, it then goes to the grinder, who placing it upon the wet stone grinds it until he makes it perfectly white and marked only by the grain of the stone. The best smooth files are then stripped and filed from heel to point; in which condition they are sent to the Cutter[1] who uses a hammer which varies in weight according to the size of the file – also a leather stirrup which is for the purpose of holding the file upon an anvil enclosed in a stone stock.[2]

The file while being cut, rests upon a bed of lead, and where many are cutting in the same shop, fine particles of lead dust abound in considerable quantity. In cutting files it is the custom of the men to wet the thumb and finger of the left hand by putting them to the mouth and so moistening them with their saliva. At every shifting, and when the file has to be turned, the lead is handled and thus in a variety of ways it is absorbed into the system. The next process the file undergoes is hardening, and were it not for the practice of some Houses of hardening files in lead it would not be necessary for my present purpose further to describe the manufacture of a file. I say the practice of some Houses to harden in lead, for out of 200 Firms manufacturing files I find as yet only about 15 that have adopted this system. After the file is cut it has to be hardened.

Hardening Files in a Coke Fire.

If the old process of hardening in a coke fire be adopted the file is brushed over with ale grounds and salt, a covering which protects it from the effects of the coke fire, in which it is thoroughly heated without being burnt; it is then set and straightened either with a hammer of wood or of lead. It is then dipped into salt and water, and afterwards taken out and "strained" by the hardener to the requisite form. The files are then scoured with water and fine sand and plunged into lime water, which imparts that peculiar grey colour which renders the Sheffield Files as beautiful to look at, as they are confessedly valuable to use. The *Tang* of the file is tempered in hot lead, after which the file is brushed, oiled, and wrapped up for market.

Hardening Files in Lead.

The file is covered with a composition of 1 part of wheaten flour, 2 parts of fine charcoal dust, and 3 parts of common salt. A small pan containing the lead, about ten inches in diameter, is surrounded by a coke fire, and stands in the centre of the furnace which presents a surface, more or less heated, of about four feet square. The lead is kept, or perhaps rather ought I to say, should be kept, covered with fine coke dust, or what is better still, with finely ground old steel pots, for this material is found to lie closer than any other to the surface and to prevent what the File Hardeners call waste *i.e.* oxidation of the lead. The metal is kept at a good red heat, but certainly below the temperature at which lead volatilizes.

Diseases of the Sheffield File Cutters.

What is the File Cutters' Disease? Poisoning by lead. I have already stated that the file rests on a bed of lead during the process of cutting, and that fine lead dust may be seen to rise every time the chisel is struck by the hammer. The men have a foolish habit of wetting the finger and thumb with which the chisel is held, by licking them – they frequently eat their meals without washing their hands – and often take dinner in the work-shop where the files are cut. As though fine lead dust, handling the lead at each shifting, and licking the fingers were not sufficiently poisonous. I saw in one of the file cutters' shops during the last few weeks a man, whose wife had just brought him his dinner, eating it with unwashed hands, and dipping his fingers blackened and covered with fine lead dust into a paper which contained the salt for seasoning his beef. I went this day (Sep. 25, 1865,) to a file shop in which several men were at work, cutting. These men all take their dinners in the shop – they never wash their hands until they get home at night – "sometimes not then." They do not change their clothes when they get home. One man made this statement. "*I have known a thousand file cutters, but I only know one who takes the trouble to wash his hands before he gets his dinner, he works at Cammells'. I never think of washing mine.*" With regard to the symptoms of lead poisoning I need not dwell on them at any length here. Lead as a poison first appears to act on the peripheral nerves of the body, and afterwards, on the nervous centres; its chief manifestations being on the nerves of the intestines, producing colic – and on those of the arms, producing paralysis. I know not why this substance should exert a special influence on these parts. The File Cutters after repeated attacks, have a peculiar dirty-white and sallow appearance; the dropped wrist is common, and the blue line round the teeth arising from the deposition of a sulphuret of lead very marked. The deposit of sulphuret of lead is due either to the sulphur furnished from animal matters received into the tartar on the teeth; or to the sulpho-cyanic acid in the saliva. The lead is from the salt of that metal which has entered the circulation. A boy was admitted into the Sheffield Public Hospital a few weeks ago. He had all the symptoms of lead poisoning exept the blue line; being a file cutter no doubt existed as to the nature of the disease. Iodide of Potassium was given to him, and in a week the blue line appeared. If formed, it is difficult to say when it will disappear. I once had a File Cutter under my care who had suffered in early life from lead colic; *he had not however cut files for eighteen years before I saw him, nor had he been in any way exposed to the influence of lead. The blue line was still present.*

With respect to hardening files in lead producing the File Cutters' disease. The men who work at it say, "that sometimes they feel ill," and they consider it injurious to health. My own experience leads me to say that it most certainly is not nearly so injurious as file-cutting. At the Sheffield Public Hospital and Dispensary, where we have had the last two years, 56,858 in and out patients, and to which the Filesmiths' Union annually subscribes £52 10s., to have the privilege of sending the poorer brethren of the trade, when sick, I do not remember to have seen the last ten years, a file hardener suffering from lead colic. I saw one with the blue line, but he had only hardened in lead for a short time, but he had been a cutter previously for many years, and had often been a sufferer from the file-cutters' disease. If this process prove a valuable one, and if it be found not open to the objection urged so strongly against it, "that it makes soft and dumb files," a moment's consideration of the process already described, will convince any one, that with very ordinary precautions, the operation may be rendered quite harmless to the workmen. But unfortunately, it is just those ordinary precautions which are so frequently omitted through ignorance or carelessness in many departments of life. If the workmen suffer at all from hardening files in lead, how does the lead affect them? Clearly from the fine particles of oxide of lead (dust) which are carried upwards by the current of air rising from so large an extent of heated surface. This takes place more especially when the file is plunged into the pan, and the covering of coke dust and dross of oxide of lead is disturbed. Nothing can be more simple and easy than to place a hood over the pan leading up to an opening in the chimney of the furnace. The current of air would then pass in a direction away from the person of the hardener. Mr. Baker, whose great practical experience as a chemist connected with our lead works, all will admit, was kind enough to visit some of these places with me. He fully confirms my opinion, that the prevalent idea that any vapour containing lead is given off is altogether erroneous. Even supposing any chloride of lead were formed from the salt in the composition used in covering the files, its vapour would be visible, if the temperature were high enough to render it volatile. We saw no such vapour.

Prevention of the File Cutters' Disease

a. *Children should not begin to cut files at so early an age as at present. It tends to make them feeble in body, and deprives them of the possibility of being properly educated.*
b. *Without the greatest care lead will enter the system through the skin. Common sense will therefore, point out the importance of washing the hands, arms, and face many times a day – of frequently combing and brushing the hair, and of having one set of clothes for the shop and another when out of it. The mouth ought also to be frequently rinsed with water.*
c. *The meals ought not to be taken in the workshop, and never taken without first washing the hands, arms, face, and lips, and changing the working jacket, or the poison will enter the system with the food.*
d. *On no account lick the fingers when at work.*
e. *An orinasal respirator worn when working would keep out much of the fine lead dust, and consequently keep the poison from entering the air passages.*
f. *The dress should be of coarse linen – a cap of the same material would keep the lead dust from the hair.*
g. *The working dress and shirt should be put on when entering the shop, and both should be changed for the ordinary dress before going home.*
h. *On no pretence neglect the use of the hot and cold bath.*
i. *Attached to every large manufactory where files are cut, there ought to be a large room, supplied with hot and cold water, where the men could wash themselves, and change their dress.*

Treatment of the File Cutters' Disease

The treatment of lead poisoning admits only of the passing remark, that purgatives, an enema, opium, and hot baths are among the most useful remedies, and that the dropped wrist requires to be supported on a splint; counter irritation and galvanism, will be required. M. Duchenne has pointed out the importance of applying galvanism, not generally to the arm but more especially to the muscles affected; which, in these cases, are most commonly the extensores digitorum, and not the lumbricales nor interossei; hence, why the first phalanges only cannot be extended, whilst when these are supported, the second and third phalanges can be voluntarily raised without difficulty.

I hope most sincerely that thousands of my fellow-townsmen when these remarks are made public by the press, will seriously consider what I have stated, and what I am certain every physician and surgeon of experience will confirm. The means of prevention may be considered too simple, or trifling; but by these, and a free use of soap and water, how much of pain, of sorrow, and of wretchedness to themselves and to their families, might the File Cutters of Sheffield avoid.

The Causes and Prevention of the Sheffield Grinders' Disease.

Grinders are divided into three classes: – 1. *Dry Grinders, using only the dry stone*. 2. *Mixed, or those who partly grind on the wet, and partly on the dry stone*. 3. *Wet Grinders*. The Grinder carries on his work in a building called a wheel. The first steam-grinding wheel was erected in 1786, when grinding became a separate branch of trade.

Wheels and Hulls.

At the present time there are about 164 Wheels in and near Sheffield. Of these 132 are steam and 32 water wheels. There are 8 water wheels on the Sheaf, 2 on the Don, 7 on the Porter, 6 on the Loxley, 8 on the Rivelin and 1 at Whirlow.[3] In each wheel are a number of rooms which vary in size and the number of grindstones they contain. In these the Grinders work. As a general rule wet grinding, and the heavier branches of the trade are carried on down stairs; and the lighter branches in the rooms on the upper stories. There are however many exceptions to this rule, and it is no uncommon circumstance to see wet and dry grinders working in the same room. The heavier branches of grinding include saws, scythes, table knives machine knives, edge tools, files, &c., &c. The lighter branches are spring knives, (pen and pocket knives,) razors, scissors, forks, spindles, needles, &c., &c. Needle grinding is principally carried on at Hathersage, a village some few miles from Sheffield. A considerable number of men are employed in grinding glass.

The rooms in which the grinders work in the various wheels are called "*hulls*," the literal meaning of which is a *stye*. A visit to many of these places would convince you, Sir, and every member of the National Association for the Promotion of Social Science, that a more happy or appropriate appellation could not possibly be selected. In each room are placed a number of "*trows*" (troughs), more or less in proportion to its length. Some rooms will have ten, some not more than two or three. The trough, which is made of cast metal, is received into the floor of the room and contains the water in which the grinding stone revolves. When the stone is run dry, the water is removed from the trough. Each trough has several divisions – one for the stone, one for the glazer, the lap, and the polisher.

The *Glazer* is a wooden wheel, which varies in size from four inches to four feet in diameter: it is covered with leather. This is "dressed" over with glue and emery, and when this application hast set the surface is rubbed with emery-cake, which is a composition of emery, suet, and bees'-wax.

The *Lap* is a wooden tool faced with lead, on which the sides of penknives, the sides of razors, and the flat sides of the better finished scissors are rubbed to give them a flat surface. The effect of this will at once be evident to any one who has a first-class Sheffield knife, on comparing the pen with the pocket blade, or a razor with a table knife.

The *Polisher* is placed at the back part of the hull. It is smaller in size than the wooden wheel already described. It is covered with leather, and made to revolve much more slowly than either the grinding stone or the glazer. If it revolved rapidly the blades either of the knives or the razors that were undergoing the process of polishing, would become heated, and the fine temper of the steel destroyed. Although the glazer revolves with no little rapidity the paste with which it is covered prevents this effect. A dry powder, called by the workmen "*crocus*" (an oxide of iron), is used for polishing. Boys, who are apprenticed but too frequently to the lighter branches of the grinding trade at from nine to twelve years of age, are first put to polishing the different articles. *I found a boy at work in a wheel last week, engaged in polishing, aged only seven.* In my visits to wheels, I have frequently met with young boys with coughs, shortness of breath, and lungs extensively diseased, *who have never ground*, but who have been injured by this process of polishing, about which I shall presently have some remarks to make.

The *Drum*. In the back part of each room is a drum or wheel of large dimensions, which is set in motion by the steam-engine, and to it the grinding stones, glazers, and polishers are attached by the "wheel-bands," which are broad leather straps. The connection between the different wheels and the drum can be effected or discontinued in a moment with the utmost facility by putting the bands on or off. Every drum ought to be protected by a rail.

Grinding Stones. – A large portion of the grinding stones are brought from the neighbourhood of Wickersley and Dalton, a few miles from Sheffield. The whitening stones, used for smoothing articles before glazing, are brought from the Brincliffe-edge quarries, about a mile from the town. In grinding a razor both the dry and wet stones are employed. I will therefore, describe the process of making a razor, in order to show the effect this trade has on the health and lives of those employed.

Making a Razor.

The razor is first forged out of a bar of steel. It is then sent whilst in the soft state to the grinder, who shapes it *on the dry stone* into the required pattern. After the razor has been "*shaped*," it is returned to the forge to be "file cut" and "marked;" the mark stamped upon it is very frequently that of some distant firm, it may be in Glasgow, London, or some other town. The razor next undergoes the process of hardening and tempering, after which it is once more brought to the wheel and ground to an edge on a wet stone. It is then "lapped," on a tool the exact size of the stone on which it has been ground. The back and end of the tang is glazed. The whole blade is then wiped very clean, and highly polished with crocus. It is now sent to the hafter who places it in the scales (*handle*). The razor is then made ready for use by being "set" or sharpened.

In order to find out the exact quantity of steel dust of necessity created in the first process a razor undergoes on the dry stone, Mr. John Wilson, (a very well-educated and most intelligent pen-blade grinder – and for whom I have personally the highest respect,) – in himself a living example of what a grinder ought to be, and what he might be if he would, and who has worked for many years for the celebrated firm of J. Rodgers and Sons, Cutlers to Her Majesty, made, at my request, the following experiment, the result of which is shown in the annexed table.

Table showing the Weight of a Dozen Razors in the different stages of their Manufacture.

Shape of Razor. – Quill Backs.			*Shape of Razor – Swaged Backs.*		
	Weight.			*Weight.*	
	lbs.	*oz.*		*lbs.*	*oz.*
12 Razor Blades forged in the rough	2	4	12 Razor Blades, forged in the rough	2	0
12 Razor Blades, shaped	1	15	12 Razor Blades, shaped	1	15
12 Razor Blades, finished	1	10	12 Razor Blades, finished	1	8
Loss in shaping 5 ounces per dozen, principally on the dry stone.			Loss in shaping, 6 ounces per dozen (dry.)		
Loss in grinding on the wet stone, 5 ounces per dozen.			Loss in grinding, 2 ounces per doz. (wet).		
In shaping a dozen large razors on a stone seven inches in diameter, the stone would be reduced nearly one inch.					

To grind a razor to the proper shape great friction is required; razor backs are for the most part round and the pressure during the shaping is so great that no wet stone could sustain the rolling friction; the stone would soon become uneven like a hammer-stone, and so pulverised, that after shaping four or five blades, the workman would be unable to hold the blade on the stone. *Forks, razors, table knife-bolsters, scissors, shanks, and needles*, undergo the rolling process and consequently, require the dry stone. Spring knives five and twenty years ago were ground on a dry stone.

This process has been superseded, and these knives are now I am happy to say, all ground on the wet stone, which is made to revolve with great rapidity. In shaping razor blades on the dry stone, a number of red hot particles of steel fly about in all directions. From these "*Motes*," as they are called by the grinders, the eyes were at one time constantly injured, and in some instances permanently lost. This danger is now obviated by wearing large spectacles of ordinary window glass. The protection they afford is obvious, for on examination after they have been a short time in use, the glasses are found spotted all over by the sparks of heated steel. But even this precaution is not taken by all – a razor grinder told me only last week, he did not use the "specs" because his eyes were so good.

Dry grinding, hanging, and racing stones.

It is in dry grinding that the workmen are exposed to by far the greatest danger. The dust which is created by the stone and steel fills the room in considerable quantities, and when grinding scissors or forks two or three deep without a fan, those who sit behind throw a large quantity of dust on those who sit in the front. But it is not only in grinding that dust ascends. Much of the evil resulting from the trade of a grinder, and this remark applies alike to dry and wet grinding, proceeds from "hanging" and "racing" the stones. The stones are received at the wheel from the quarry in a rough state.

The grinder first drills a hole through the centre, and fixing it on the axle places it in the trough. It is then made to revolve slowly in order that the steel which is used in the process of racing may bite.

With this bar of steel the asperities of the stones are removed and their surface rendered level and smooth. During the operation, which frequently lasts half an hour, the rooms are unavoidably filled with dust; the dust also arises in dense clouds when the sides of the "trow" are swept after the process of racing is over. It is easy to protect the nose and mouth with a light handkerchief during this process; but the precaution is seldom taken. On my asking a file grinder at the Union Wheel a week or two ago, when collecting materials for this paper, and who I found racing a stone and covered with dust, why he was thus exposing himself to causes certain to induce a disease that would quickly bring him to a miserable death, he replied, "*we know all about it Doctor, but we never give it a thought.*" Much dust also, arises in glazing and polishing; the amount will depend in some measure on the nature of the glaze used. The glazing of forks is the most injurious. Almost all the grinding stones are now fitted with plates and screws, instead of as formerly, only with wedges: the number of accidents from the breaking of the grinding stones are, at present, much less frequent than when the old plan was in operation. The saw grinders at one time were often very seriously injured from the breaking of the stones when they were at work. The large size of the stones, and the weight and length of many of the saws they have to grind, will easily account for this branch of the trade, being more dangerous from the breaking of the stones, than when the articles are smaller and lighter.

Different Classes of Grinders.

It has been intimated already that grinders may be divided into dry, wet, and mixed. Forks, needles, brace bits, and spindles are ground entirely on the dry stone, and in addition, table knife bolsters, shanks, shaping razors, "humping" scissors, &c., &c., all require the dry stone to be employed. Some trades never use the dry stone: for example, saws, files, sickles, table knife blades, edge tools, scythes, &c., are only ground and glazed. There is also a numerous class of grinders who work for the most part on the wet stone, and who are employed in grinding engineers' tools, engravers' steel plates, hammers, fenders, fire irons, stove grates, busks for stays, candlestick-bottoms, nippers, garden-shears, hoops, &c.

Fork Grinders work on a dry stone, and their calling is perhaps more destructive than any of the grinding trades. The present number of men employed is about 150. Personal inquiries at the various wheels induce me to conclude the present condition of these men is no better than when a fork grinder told me, some years ago, "I shall be 36 next month, and you know that is getting an old man at our trade;" and when I found the average age of the men only 28. Individual instances may be found of fork grinders much older than this man, but it is nevertheless an undoubted fact that many fork grinders miserably perish before the age of 30. Take for example a boy of *ten*, (and at that early age many of them go into the wheel,) at the age of 21 his expectation of life, supposing he continue to work at his trade without a fan, would certainly not exceed 14 years. Now at 21 the probable expectation of life is 39 years; so we see, that these unfortunate men are exposed to influences which rob them of 25 years of existence – to that extent deprive their wives and families of the benefit of their labour, and fill the union poors'-houses with widows and fatherless children. There is no more melancholy object than a fork grinder, looking prematurely old and dying from the dust inhaled in his trade – no object more deserving of our pity, as we see him often crawling to his hull to labour when altogether unfitted by the grinders' disease for his calling – "his poverty and not his will consents." In this condition, a day or two in a week, he grinds for a few hours; inhales additional dust, and in order to obtain bread, increases the disease which already is rapidly destroying him.

Razor Grinders. – From the statements published a few weeks ago by the Committee of the Razor Grinders' Union, it appears there are 290 workmen employed in grinding razors, and 81 boys under 21.

Ages.	*Persons.*
21 to 25	83
25 to 30	57
30 to 35	36
35 to 40	35
40 to 45	29
45 to 50	29
50 to 55	9
55 to 60	8
60 to 65	3
65 to 75	1
	290

The above table may be left without a word of comment, to tell its own tale.

Scissors Grinders. – These men work partly on a wet and partly on a dry stone. The most destructive part of the work of a scissors grinder is when giving the rounded form to the blade, and which is called humping.

There are at the present time about 250 men employed in this calling. Some years ago, I found the average age of all then living to be 32. A few weeks ago I visited 86 scissor grinders when at work in the different hulls. I took down the age of each man at work, and found the average to be only 31 years. I took the same day the average of 40 razor grinders and found it only 31 years and six months. These men were at work on the dry stone, and a majority of them either had no fan or a fan that was almost useless. Others had a fan, and were working with dry grinders who had no fan. One man with a good fan was humping scissors, but received the dust from a grinder on either side of him who was shaping razors.

File Grinders use only the wet stone. 250 men are at present employed.

Saw grinders employ the wet stone. There are at present 220 men and 60 boys.

Table Blade Grinders are not so numerous as a few years ago. Many have gone to America, and from the low prices obtained few boys have been apprenticed. At present there are 660 men and 170 boys.

[4]*Spring Knives*, 650 men and 200 boys have been returned to me by the Secretary of the Union, as the number at present engaged in this branch of grinding.

Saw Grinders (wet), 220 men, 60 boys.

Scythes (wet), men and boys 60.

Sickles (wet), 72 men, 30 boys.

Edge Tools and Wool Shears, 230 men and boys.

If to these we add the grinders of surgeons' instruments, engineers' tools, jobbing grinders, needle grinders, &c., it will be found that in and out of the different unions there are 3,090 men, and 1,073 boys – total, 4163 men and boys employed in grinding, dry, wet, and mixed. I have tested the accuracy of my former return sufficiently to say that still the average ages of all the fork grinders living does not exceed 29. Scissors grinders, 32; edge tool and wool shear grinders, 33; table knife grinders, 35. The ages of all the razor grinders have already been given. I regret to be obliged to say that there is but too much truth in the remark once made to me by a young man aged 26, a fork grinder, – "*he reckoned in about two more years at his trade he might begin to think of dropping off the perch,*" adding "*you know a fork grinder is an old cock at thirty.*" On taking down the ages of all the grinders, wet, mixed, and dry, at one of our largest wheels, I found the average 34; boys under 21 were excluded from this calculation. There can be no difference now; all the same adverse influences are still in operation, and sickness and premature deaths will continue until the causes producing them are removed. Taking the returns of the ages of the grinders who had died at some of the wheels, from their club books, I found it to be 43, 40, 40, 41, 38½. Taking the deaths at the wheel of the Messrs. J. Rodgers & Sons, for some years past (1850 to 1865, wet and dry grinders,) the average age was 49 – of the dry grinders only 43. At the Union Wheel, from 1859 to 1864, the return including both wet and dry grinders, shows the average age at death to be only 46. But even these death rates may mislead us, if we do not remember that both these wheels are *first-class*, and that as a rule it is only the more prudent and better class of grinders who belong to such provident societies.

Men who work in the country, as a rule, are more healthy than those who grind at the wheels in the town; and as a body they are more temperate. One of the most healthy branches is saw grinding. Many saws are ground at the water wheels on the picturesque streams around Sheffield; and, as a rule, the men have not to work so many hours a day as at some of the other branches. Again, the trade is too heavy to admit of boys coming into it at a very early age. No boy is recognised by the Saw Grinders' Union under the age of 14. The men stand at their work, and consequently the lungs are not so compressed as when the grinder, sitting on his horsing, bends forward for many hours each day, in other branches of the trade about to be described.

The Causes which Produce the Grinders' Disease.

The cause of this disease is first, the irritation produced by the metallic and gritty partices inhaled in grinding and also in "hanging" and "racing" the grinding stones; and next, the constrained position in which they labour, and which is unfavourable to the free action of the respiratory organs; to this must be added, the working for many hours in a badly ventilated room. When at work the grinder mounts what he calls his "horsing." This is a low narrow wooden seat. His elbows rest upon his knees, and his head, particularly when employed on very small articles, is bent over the stone. This position is a very injurious one, and when long continued is calculated, unquestionably, to induce pulmonary congestion. In many of the branches – table knife grinding for example, the men often work in the coldest weather very thinly clad – their handkerchiefs off; their shirts open and their chests fully exposed; and this too, in a room every bit of glass from the windows of which has been removed, that the light may not be obstructed by the splashing of the dirty water from the grinding stones. The floors of such hulls are generally of mud, and always wet, dirty and uncomfortable. The men perspire freely at their work and in this condition often leave the hull, and without putting on additional clothing, lounge about the yard in the open air, even when the weather is very cold. Inflammation of the lungs, pleurisy, rheumatic fever, and diseases of the heart are not unfrequent among them. I have seen many young boys suffering from grinders' disease arising from the dust inhaled in polishing; and in dry grinders very often before the age of twenty, evidence is present of the existence of this fearful affection. I had a patient at the Public Hospital last week, a grinder aged 22 – on enquiring what was matter with him he said "I grind razors and have got what I shall never get *shut on*" (rid of).

He began to work at 11 and never had used a fan. Both lungs were affected by the grinders' disease, but not nearly to the extent I have seen them, even in younger men than this poor fellow. At the commencement of the disease the breathing is difficult – more particularly when walking up a hill, going up stairs, or ascending the steps leading to the upper hulls in which they work. At this early stage, the shoulders are often elevated, in order to relieve the distress occasioned by shortness of breath. The disease quickly increases; and day by day, makes certain progress in all dry grinders, working without the protection of the fan. The digestive organs become impaired, the breathing is more and more short and oppressed – the face has a dirty white aspect – the countenance is indicative of much suffering – he stops to cough in the street as he crawls to his work – supporting himself against the walls. They all complain of a dry sensation in the throat and tell you "they feel screwed up" and that something is so tight across their chests they cannot breathe. The cough is at first dry but after a time there is a good deal of expectoration which at first is frothy, and indicative of irritation. If asked by my medical friends to give them a brief *resumé* of the physical signs of the Sheffield Grinders' disease – I would say – those of bronchitis and dilated bronchi in some cases – in others, of emphysema or of consolidation, and, lastly of excavation. I have had several photographs prepared by Mr. Caloe of some sections of the lungs of those who have died from Grinders' disease. Also some drawings of the sputa in wet and dry grinders under my care, as seen with the microscope, and which Mr. Tuffin West has made for me. (Some beautiful illustrations were here handed round for the inspection of those present.) And now, I come lastly to consider how this terrible disease may be prevented.

Prevention of the Sheffield Grinders' Disease.

This Disease was formerly almost unknown, and for this reason. Until the year 1786, when the first steam wheel was erected, grinding wheels were built upon the banks of rivers in and near Sheffield; and water being the power employed, it will at once be obvious that the grinder would have many interruptions to his trade and that to grind day after day as the grinders now do, was then impossible, and many of them were makers as well as grinders of Cutlery. Nor was this all. By the old regulations of the Cutlers' Company, passed in the reign of Elizabeth, it was provided, "*that no person engaged in the said manufacture, either as a master, servant, or apprentice, shall perform any work appertaining to the said science or mystery of Cutlers for eight and twenty days next ensuing the 8th day of August in each year; nor from Christmas to the 23rd day of January, upon pain and forfeiture, for every offence found and presented by twelve men of the said fellowship of the sum of Twenty Shillings. No person occupying any wheel for the grinding of knives to allow of any work being done during the holiday months: penalty as before*. When grinding became a separate branch of trade, the hours were no longer limited, and then, it would appear, that the fearful effects, on the animal economy, of constantly inhaling particles of steel and grit day after day, began to develope themselves. This then leads me to a first practical suggestion for alleviating the condition of the Grinders, viz., to *diminish the hours of labour*; and the most effectual way to do this is to abolish "Saint days," as the first days of the week are called by these men, and which are spent by but too many of them in drunkenness and intemperance. What is the result? They crowd into three or four days the labour that ought to be distributed over the whole week, and many soon find, to their cost, the folly of such proceeding. It is a notion in some of the hulls that a drunken grinder often lives the longest. This is a very great mistake. Intemperance has hurried hundreds of these men into their graves. I almost invariably find that, so soon as the liver becomes affected, the chest symptoms are aggravated: and that when the liver fails to discharge its functions, a comparatively slight amount of disease in the lungs of the grinder, will cause far more distress and difficulty in breathing, than even in lungs more extensively diseased, when this organ acts properly. By limiting the hours of labour, time would be afforded for out of doors pursuits, for exercises which would bring the different muscles of the body into play, and prevent, especially in the young, some of the effects which result from bending over the wheel when at work. I have had to day in my study, Mr. Samuel Sharpe, a razor grinder, at the union wheel: he is now 48, strong and healthy, he has never suffered from the grinders' disease, he began to work at eleven, and he justly expressed the opinion that "*grinding takes most hold of young boys*." Mr. Sharpe has always used a fan, and will not work in a hull with dry grinders who are not so protected. He does not believe in "Saint days," and works on an average about 38 hours a week. It would be well therefore, 1, *to limit the hours of labour both in boys and men*. 2, *wet and dry grinders ought on no pretence to be allowed to work in the same hull*. After what I have already said, the reason for this will be too obvious to require additional remark. 3, *to oblige the owners of all wheels to provide a fan for every dry grinder, and to see that this fan is always kept in proper working order*. On this point I wish to make a few observations, to which I invite the serious attention of all who may hear or read what I have to say in support of this – to my mind, absolutely necessary requirement. I propose that the *owner of the wheel and not the grinder*, should provide the fan and see that it works properly. If the grinders are left to provide it for themselves, so reckless of life, so careless and indifferent are many of the fork, scissors, and razor grinders, that I am certain they will never provide it for themselves. Let me give some evidence in proof of this. In one hull

I found a man shaping razors with a first class fan. There was much dust – the fan was not working, he had not taken the trouble to affix the band, and that necessary act would have taken perhaps half a minute. In another hull, a scissors grinder had a good fan, and spoke to me of its "wonderful advantages" – "if they cost a hundred times as much as they do, they are worth it – no dry grinder can live without them" – and yet this man permitted razor grinders to work without a fan on his right hand and on his left, and to cover him with their dust. In another hull, in which five dry grinders were at work the fans had not been used for three weeks – the wheel band was wrong – and yet these men went on destroying themselves, rather than do to the wheel band a quarter of an hour's work – all that was requisite to set the fan in motion. A most intelligent scissors grinder, Mr. Wreaks, who has now left the trade, at which he began to work when only *nine*, told me "he always used a fan." He once offered to five scissors grinders who worked in the same hull with him, to put up a fan at his own cost, and to take the price of it from each by instalments of one shilling a week. They one and all refused his kind offer. I found hull after hull, in which scissors, razor, and fork grinders, are now working (September, 1865) without fans, – some are working in a very confined space without them, two and three deep. One man, a scissors grinder, told me, "it was not worth while to get one for the bit of time he should have to live." I only found one fan in all the hulls I visited attached to the polishing machinery. I think that where polishing is carried on, a fan ought always to be in use. I visited one hull in which an intelligent man at one end had put up a fan for each "trow," and for which he charged each fellow-workman a penny a week; the man working next to him had paid his penny for the fan, but having been too idle to fix a box, it was useless. Others I found with a fan fixed but not at work, because *they did not like the noise;*" and I have many times been told by dry grinders "the trade was full enough as it was, and that if the men lived longer it would be so full there would be no getting a living at it." What can I say to such men? – to dry grinders working without a fan – why this – if ever there was a trade more poisonous than the fabled valley of the upas – more slow in its effects it is true, but equally deadly with the inhaling of the atmosphere of the celebrated Grotto del Cani, it is that of a fork, a razor, or a scissors grinder, who works without employing the effectual means for his preservation which the fan affords; if bent on destroying yourselves thus recklessly, have the honesty to prevent others, the poor little boys, many of them your own sons, from entering the trade without a warning – write therefore, over the doorway leading to your infernal hulls

"ALL HOPE ABANDON YE WHO ENTER HERE;"

we do not use the fan, and without this protection your destruction after a few years misery and suffering is certain. The entrance to a dry grinders' hull, without a fan, I say emphatically is unmistakably the gate that leads to certain death!

A good fan will cost from £1 10s. to £3, or £5, but after what I have stated, I think all present will agree with me, that the *owner* of the wheel must be by law compelled to provide a fan as an absolutely necessary portion of the machinery of a wheel where dry grinding is carried on; and that he *must be held responsible* for having this fan always at work and in proper order. A small additional sum could be added to the weekly rent of the hull; which would not exceed one penny.

The fan is on the principle of a winnowing machine, and with a flue properly constructed, leading from each of the different stones in each room, the dust can most effectually be driven out of it, and both the particles of grit and metal which arise in grinding, and the dust created in glazing and polishing removed. I went last week into one of the rooms used for razor grinding at the wheel of Messrs. J. Rodgers and Sons, where many men were at work shaping razors; there was no dust, nor was I inconvenienced in the slightest degree, during the half hour I remained. Had the fan not been at work, I know by experience that I should soon have felt most uncomfortable. One of the men told me the wheel had been "lame" for three weeks, (*i.e.* not at work,) and he had been working at another place without a fannie, and felt so bad at his chest that he was glad to get back to his own "trow" again. He never felt bad there.[5] At the Soho Wheel, and at the Union Wheel also, and I may add, at many other wheels, I have seen the fan at work with the happiest effects, and in the next room I have seen a set of reckless fools destroying themselves because they would not use it. Many years ago, the late Mr. Trickett, at the Union Wheel, showed me how the different processes could be gone through without injury to the grinder from the dust, and at the Soho wheel, I saw that shaping razors and even racing a stone, by adding a properly contrived box could be rendered perfectly innocuous by the use of the fan; almost all the dust being driven off by the fan, up a shaft on the outside of the building. The particles of dust and steel not carried away by the fan, in "racing" a stone, may be prevented from entering the air passages by tying, as all intelligent grinders do, when performing this work, a light handkerchief over their nose and mouth. That these fans, or "Fannies," answer perfectly well, I have convinced myself by repeated experiments, and by the testimony of every dry-grinder who uses them.

To prevent the Grinders, disease I am therefore of opinion, 1st. That the hours of labour should be reduced, 2nd. That wet and dry grinders should on no pretence be allowed to work in the same room. 3rd. That the owners of wheels should be compelled to provide a fan for all dry grinders. 4th. That all wheels should be placed under proper inspection – properly[6] Ventilated and kept clean – the rooms built of a sufficient height with enough space for each man, and every wheel properly provided with conveniences, the want of which at present – or the substitutes for which, at many wheels are a disgrace to the civilization of the 19th Century, and in a sanitary point of view a great evil. No floor should be of mud. Where wet grinding is carried on the floor should be flagged with a sufficient incline to let the water run off.

Editorial Endnotes

1 'Obituary: John Charles Hall, M.D.', *British Medical Journal* 2:607 (4 November 1876), p. 607.

2 'The Trades of Sheffield', *Illustrated London News*, 6 January 1866, p. 18.
3 'Obituary: John Charles Hall', p. 607.
4 J. Bronstein, *Caught in the Machinery: Workplace Accidents and Injured Workers in Nineteenth-Century Britain* (Palo Alto, CA: Stanford University Press, 2008).
5 M. Levine-Clark, *Beyond the Reproductive Body: The Politics of Women's Health and Work in Early Victorian England* (Columbus: Ohio State University Press, 2004), chap. 1.
6 S. O. Rose, 'Protective Labor Legislation in Nineteenth-Century Britain: Gender, Class, and the Liberal State', in L. L. Frader and S. O. Rose (eds), *Gender and Class in Modern Europe* (Ithaca, NY: Cornell University Press, 1996), pp. 193–210.
7 Dr J. C. Hall, *The Trades of Sheffield . . . Read before the National Association for the Promotion of Social Science*, 2nd ed. (London: Longmans, Green and Co, 1865), p. 8, Archive.org.
8 This distinction became foundational in Edwin Chadwick, *Report on the Sanitary Condition of the Labouring Population of Great Britain* (London: HMSO, 1843, orig. 1842).

Source Endnotes

1 A file with a thousand cuts on each side is made with a hammer and chisel, the hammer weighing 7½lbs.; it has 300 cuts on the edge, for which a 3lbs hammer is used. A man working 10 hours can cut about 20 such files in a day. Mr. J. E. White has calculated that a man to do this must lift about 140 tons in weight during a day. Files are not cut by the machine in Sheffield; machine-cut files being considered very inferior to files cut by hand.
2 Those who may wish to understand thoroughly this beautiful process of File Manufacture in all its branches, cannot do better than consult the very able pamphlet of Mr. Henry Turner.
3 This may not, possibly include every wheel – as many old houses have of late years been devoted to this purpose. It is hardly necessary to state that in sanitary and other requisite requirements many of such places are totally unfitted for grinding.
4 When my book was published in 1857, on the Grinders' Disease. I returned 685 men and 600 Boys, under Spring Knife Grinders. Mr. Broomhead the Secretary to the Union informs me that of late years only Grinders' Sons have been allowed to enter the trade, hence the diminution. The same remark will apply to others of the grinding trades.
5 The Messrs. Rodgers provide the fans free of charge, and will not permit dry grinders to work without them.
6 *Ventilation of the Wheels.* – The hulls cannot be constructed with windows before and behind the grinder as has been suggested. The light at his back would interfere with his work. Ventilation, however, could be provided by gratings at the back of the hull. The fan also, when at work, powerfully assists ventilation- Too commonly the grinders regard the hull as "only a place to work in," and take every care that it shall remain, as its name implies, a stye.

9

J. B. GLASIER, 'HONEST TOIL'

Commonweal: Official Journal of the Socialist League (c. 1890), pp. 9–16

John Bruce Glasier (1859–1920) of Glasgow was one of the founding members of the Social Democratic Federation (SDF) in 1884 (see Volume 3, Part 1, Chapter 23). Being a great fan of the well-known socialist designer William Morris, however, he left the SDF at the end of 1884 when Morris and others split with Henry Hyndman. This breakaway group formed the Socialist League, and Glasier became secretary of the league's Glasgow branch.[1] The Socialist League was committed to class equality and revolutionary change. The league began publication of the *Commonweal* in 1885, with Morris as its editor, and Glasier was a regular contributing writer. During the 1880s, the league was gradually overtaken by anarchists, with many true socialists returning to the SDF or forming new organizations. In 1889, Glasier left his position as a league secretary and went to work in a foundry. He joined the Independent Labour Party (see Volume 3, Part 3, Chapter 29) in 1893 and was one of its early leaders, along with Keir Hardie (see Volume 4, Part 3, Chapter 28) and Ramsay MacDonald (see Volume 4, Part 3, Chapter 34).[2] He was remembered as a great figure in the socialist movement in Scotland.[3] In this selection, Glasier deconstructs the phrase 'honest toil' in order to demonstrate the lack of value society allotted to working men. He argues that the poor were constantly reminded of the virtue of honest toil, by which was understood manual labour to earn a living and to support the wider community. Here Glasier speaks directly to sources such as the *British Workman* and *The Labouring Man's Book* (see Volume 1, Part 1, Chapters 6 and 7), which explicitly address the value of working men's labour in moral terms. Yet, in reality, Glasier asserts, this type of labour was regarded as degrading. A working man who performed honest toil would never be a gentleman because he worked for wages. A gentleman, however, could do all the manual labour he liked and still remain a gentleman because he did this labour for pleasure. Glasier claims that people wished to avoid manual labour because '*it is associated with slavery, with poverty, with social ugliness*'.[4] It was part of a capitalist system that treated workers as slaves, who did hard labour for meagre earnings and were prevented from tending to the improvement of their minds and bodies.[5] For Glasier, like William Morris and John Ruskin, the loss of art and beauty in workers' lives was one of the worst consequences of industrial capitalism.[6] He believed labour was something that should be enjoyed and not

DOI: 10.4324/9780429320323-12

simply a task to be endured. Accordingly, workers should loathe their labour in the conditions under which they must perform it under capitalism; indeed, Glasier argues that socialists condemned 'those who consent to their own degradation and serfdom'.[7] When socialism was realized, 'honest toil' would no longer exist, and all work would instead be 'honourable'.[8]

'Honest toil'

THE virtue of "honest toil" is a precept which has been universally commended. We were taught it in childhood, and have not been allowed to forget it in our after years. It was engraved as a headline in our copy-books, and was a favourite theme of our Sunday-school stories. It is always at hand as a peg whereon rich moralists may hang their speeches when addressing poor men's gatherings; and it is specially serviceable to newspaper editors when advising working-men not to strike or ask for an increase of wages.

By "honest toil" is meant physical toil for the physical needs of the community. The supposition is, that by engaging in "honest toil," the toiler earns his own and his family's livelihood without having to beg, borrow, or steal any portion of it from his neighbours. The actuality is, that he not only earns his own and his family's livelihood, but the livelihood of a privileged class, which is thus saved the necessity of doing any toil at all. The term "honest" has no doubt been tacked on to this species of toil from a perception of the fact that the toiler undoubtedly honestly earns by it whatever necessities or comforts of life he is permitted to retain to himself, and from a perception that there are other species of toil which men may engage in without honestly earning these things.

But although universally commended in precepts and speeches, "honest toil" is by no means universally practised. Indeed, none practise it who can avoid doing so; and instead of the practice of it conferring honour upon the individual, it invariably confers contempt. No "Noble" or "Honourable" or "Right Honourable" person ever performs it. No man who has to work for his livelihood is ever esteemed a "gentleman," and is never called such, except in courtesy or when he is being solicited for a vote or a subscription. A working-man is never made a knight or a peer, the chairman of a missionary society, or the president of a football club. The Queen will make "a belted knight, a marquis, duke, and a' that" out of any kind of an effigy of a human being but a working-man. The fact that a man has to do "honest toil" utterly unfits him, apparently, from occupying any honourable position in Church, State, or Society. He may be physically as strong as a Hercules and as beautiful as an Apollo; he may have all the intellectual gifts of a Crichton and the moral resolution of a St. Anthony: but so long as he has of necessity to win his bread by the labour of his own hands and the sweat of his own brow, the door of refined society is shut in his face. If he were suddenly to enter a West-end drawing-room in his working garb the ladies would faint as though he were a Mid-African savage, and the gentlemen would kick him downstairs as though he were a bundle of hospital rags. A dog may sprawl upon the floor, a cat curl upon the hearthrug, and a parrot screech at the window, but he or his children may not even stand upon the doorstep. On the other hand, anything born of a woman, though it be physically fit only for a gynecological museum, though it has the intelligence of a hen and the morals of a zoological gardens gorilla, yet if it belongs to the class that does no useful work, but lives on the plunder of the labour of others, it will be welcomed into the best society, courted by beautiful girls, flattered by statesmen, and fawned upon by university professors.

"Honest toil," therefore, which is in precept a virtue, is in practice a crime. Instead of being regarded as noble and honourable, it is regarded as dishonourable and degrading; *and it is just because it is "honest"* that it is so regarded. The more "honest" it is, the more it is shunned and the more ignoble it is reckoned. Toil that is not in the current sense "honest" – toil *per se* – is not shunned or reckoned ignoble. A man may work till he is black in the face and white in the hair at any sort of physical occupation he chooses, providing he does not do so for the merely "honest" purpose of earning his own livelihood, and yet be esteemed an "honourable" man and a gentleman. He may, like Lord Lonsdale, tramp with bag and baggage over hundreds of miles in frost and snow; he may go into his garden and plant cabbages, lay dung, and hunt caterpillars; he may row a boat, sail a yacht, or drive a carriage; he may fish, fell trees, shoot birds, stalk deer, or engage in any manual labour he pleases, and still be a gentleman – so long as he does so for recreation or pleasure, and not with the "honest" motive of providing the food he eats, the clothes he wears, or the house he inhabits. But if he is compelled to do these things so as to be dependent upon the toil of others for his livelihood, then he is outside the pale of rank, titles, office, and respectability. Just think of it! Lord Lonsdale boasts that during one of his journeys he made his servants carry only 40 lbs. of baggage, and that he himself carried 50 lbs.: while at that very time thousands of poor men in England were toiling their lives away to provide him with the money he was spending on his useless escapade. He considers it a noble thing that he, during a freak of pleasure, should have burdened himself a little to lessen the burden of others, while he esteems it an honourable thing to compel millions of men and women to bear all their lives a fourfold burden that he and his class may live without bearing any burden at all. And this sentiment of what is honourable is the prevailing one in civilised life to-day, and upon this sentiment rests the whole superstructure of modern religion, morals, and politics.

The precept, therefore, is a lie, and a most barefaced one, too. Nobody believes it, but everybody preaches it – especially those who would be horrified at the mere notion of their being expected to put it into practice. If a bishop – who would as soon think of preaching the Gospel as of staining his episcopal fingers with an hour's work at tent-making or carpentry – has occasion to address a meeting of working folk for the purpose of begging subscriptions, he rolls oily phrases about the dignity and holiness of "honest toil" in his mouth with as much sanctimonious satisfaction as he afterwards rolls their shilling pieces in his breeches pocket. If a duke or an earl condescends to decorate the platform of a working-men's political meeting, held for the purpose of returning an aristocratic stripling to Parliament, he extols the nobility of "honest toil" with such apparent sincerity that one expects him to conclude with a declaration that he will get out of bed next morning at five o'clock and apply for a job as a navvy or dock-labourer at twelve or fifteen shilling a-week.

Of course, the bishop and the earl do not mean what they say, and nobody believes that they do; but everybody applauds their sentiments and affects to feel much encouraged and comforted by them. It is the same with reference to most matters nowadays. People preach what they do not believe, and conceal or deny what they do believe; and most people appear to be quite satisfied and delighted with this way of going on. If it were not so, peers would be paupers, priests lodged in lunatic asylums, and politicians in prison.

Why, then, is "honest toil" regarded as degrading? Why do the rich shun it and the poor try to escape from it? It is not, as I have shown, because toil – even hard toil – is of itself considered an ignoble or criminal thing. No; "honest toil" is regarded as degrading and ignoble *because it is associated with slavery, with poverty, with social ugliness, and the lack of pleasure and recreation.* Only those who are slaves, who are the tools of landlords and capitalists, earn their own livelihood by the labour of their own hands; and their toil is necessarily very hard and their livelihood very scanty. They have not the means or the opportunity of making their bodies healthy, their minds happy, or their homes beautiful. Art, leisure, travel, and all that gives enchantment to life and love are denied them. No wonder, then, that, associated with such hateful conditions and penalties, "honest toil" is shunned by all who can avoid it. After all, it is a truer and manlier instinct that regards toiling for one's bread, in the way the working class now toils, as a thing to be dreaded and despised, than the instinct that is content to perform it without prospect of rebellion. And however much we, as Socialists, must condemn the hypocrisy of the rich who preach and praise what they do not, and would not willingly, perform, we must give tenfold condemnation to those who consent to their own degradation and serfdom, without strong and persistent effort to free themselves and abolish for ever the system under which they suffer. Nor need we wonder that the rich – who do not understand Socialism, but regard it as a system that would compel them to work as they see the workers working to-day – fear it and seek to prevent its coming.

But Socialism does not imply that either the present rich or the present poor will require to work as the poor work to-day. If to toil and live as miners, dock-labourers, tramway-men, seamstresses, factory-girls, or even skilled artizans have now to toil and live, were the ideal which Socialists propose to realise when asserting that everyone will require to work for his livelihood, then none but madmen indeed would be Socialists. Surely, however, rich and poor alike can perceive that so long as so many do no work, and so many do useless work, and so long as the reckless waste of wealth which our present competitive system entails goes on, those who, by "honest toil," have to produce all the wealth which they and all the others consume must of necessity work very hard and get very little. But when Socialism is achieved – when all do useful work and there is no waste of wealth – toil will no longer be hard and degrading, but healthful and pleasurable, and consequently honourable; and "honest toil," as we now understand it, will be as unknown to all the people then, as health, plenty, and pleasure are unknown to nine-tenths of the population to-day.

Notes

1 C. Wrigley, 'John Bruce Glasier', *Oxford Dictionary of National Biography* (hereafter *ODNB*), 25 May 2006, at https://doi-org.du.idm.oclc.org/10.1093/ref:odnb/38468 [accessed 13 June 2021].

On William Morris, see E. P. Thompson, *William Morris: From Romantic to Revolutionary*, rev. ed. (London: Merlin Press, 1977).

2 F. MacCarthy, 'Morris, William', *ODNB*, 8 October 2009, at https://doi-org.du.idm.oclc.org/10.1093/ref:odnb/19322 [accessed 13 June 2021].

3 Wrigley, 'John Bruce Glasier'; W. Stewart, 'John Bruce Glasier', *Forward*, 12 June 1920, p. 1.

4 J. B. Glasier, 'Honest Toil', *Commonweal: Official Journal of the Socialist League* (c. 1890), British Library, p. 14.

5 On the use of the slavery metaphor in nineteenth-century critiques of capitalism, see M. Cunliffe, *Chattel Slavery and Wage Slavery: The Anglo-American Context, 1830–1860* (Athens: University of Georgia Press, 1979).

6 W. Morris, 'Art and Socialism', in M. Morris (ed.), *The Works of William Morris*, vol. 23, (London: Longman Green and Co., 1915), pp. 192–214; W. Morris, *Useless Work versus Useful Toil* (London: Socialist League Office, 1886); J. Ruskin, *The Stones of Venice*, vols. 1–3 (London: Smith, Elder, and Co., 1851).

7 Glasier, 'Honest Toil', p. 15.

8 Glasier, 'Honest Toil', p. 16.

10

G. MILLIGAN, 'A MAN AND HIS WORK', 'ONLY A WORKING MAN', AND 'THE TOILER'S TOAST', IN *LIFE THROUGH LABOUR'S EYES*

(St. Louis: B. Herder, 1911), pp. 11–14, 92–97, and 167–169

George Milligan (1868–1925) began his working life as a barman and then became a dock worker in Liverpool, where he developed a strong identity as a docker. He was an active member of the National Union of Dock Labourers and founded the *Mersey Magazine*,[1] which 'was conceived written and distributed for seventeen months by a moneyless little band of dockers'.[2] He compiled some of the essays from the magazine into *Life through Labour's Eyes*. From the three selections presented here, it is clear that Milligan was concerned that manual labourers did not receive the respect and honour he believed was due to them. Of note in his writings is a particular bitterness towards lower-middle-class clerks and others who disdained physical labour. The lower middle class became the target of writers during the late Victorian period, in such texts as *Diary of a Nobody*, by George and Weedon Grossmith (1888–1889), which took aim at the affectations and pretentiousness of new office workers and shop assistants.[3] Milligan's critique comes from a different position but attacks much of the same posturing. In the first selection, 'A Man and His Work', Milligan, in contrast to Glasier (see Volume 1, Part 1, Chapter 9), asserts that 'manual work . . . degrades nobody'.[4] He writes that both men and women strove to achieve status in the lower middle class, often by putting on false airs, because they considered manual labour not respectable. While the first section of this piece critiques both men and women, Milligan goes on to focus on 'the lot of the working man' who 'has a right to manhood'.[5] In order to achieve true working-class masculinity and citizenship, Milligan asserts, working men should no longer have to struggle to survive. Capital and labour must come together to invest in making men men again. Milligan does not address what needs to happen to women.[6] In 'Only a Working Man', Milligan berates those – especially lower-middle-class workers – who denigrated manual labour. Indeed, he argues that physical labour was more valuable than 'wealth and influence'.[7] He

DOI: 10.4324/9780429320323-13

criticizes the 'spirit of the time' that had led working-class men to try to social climb,[8] leaving behind their humble roots. Physical labour was useful toil; work was a man's vocation. True working men were rewarded with a 'tender wife' and 'healthy children',[9] a vision that supported the patriarchal social structure.[10] The third selection, 'The Toiler's Toast', presents dockers, who were typically seen as some of the lowest workers, in a positive light, arguing for their dignity in labour. Milligan introduces a poem written by a 'comrade',[11] which also affirms the masculinity of the manual worker, who 'Is in all things, in all times, to all men – a Man'.[12] In all three selections, Milligan aims to give hope to men who do honest work and to restore their sense of respectability and masculinity.

'A Man and His Work'

If a man or a woman has a true grip of the meaning of life, they will never look down in scorn upon a manual worker, or upon manual work. Manual work – whether skilled or unskilled, whatever be its nature – degrades nobody. Useful honest labour should neither be a thing to be ashamed of nor to shun. While it is true that nearly all people like "soft jobs" and "pleasant billets," the conclusion to be drawn from the fact is not that these are true and worthy objectives, but that nearly all people are naturally lazy. There must always be leaders and guides: there must always be individuals with special gifts and adaptabilities who are immune from manual, or even certain kinds of other labour; but the majority of men and women must always be manual labourers – workers with the hands. We are sent into this world to work with our human bodies – bodies pregnant with great possibilities of skill and endurance, and in fulfilling that purpose of their physical being, a man or woman should be respected, however humble the work. To my mind, an honest street sweeper is more worthy of honour than a "star artiste," who is, after all, only an amuser of the real, useful, earnest units of the community, though the clever buffoon draw a hundred pounds a week.

But manual toil has become disrepectable. This is one of those false views of shallow-brained humanity that must make angels weep to see. It is pitiful to see a man breaking his neck to get a job where he can wear a collar, and pretend to be a clerk; lamentable to see a girl deck herself out, and use every subterfuge to secure an "appointment" where she can parade her frills and flounces from dawn till dusk; grotesque to see a labouring man and woman starve themselves to produce before an astonished world an imitation "gentleman" or "facsimile" lady. The thing is unnatural and ridiculous, but remarkably common. Give me a true and genuine working-man, who has recognised that his mission is to work, and who puts his mind and heart into it, while he is at it: who rears his family decently: who lays down in the clay after his life's work is done, unknown to the big sensation-loving world – but with the record of a man behind him, written in a life of useful toil. If such a man has, further, had the grace to have hallowed his toil, and to have understood whence his life came, why, and where it was to be consummated – even the kings and princes of this world might well envy that "poor" toiler. Beside him, many of them would be pigmies and paupers.

But the lot of the working-man – which should be no hard fate to bear – is hedged about with the artificial woes that human greed and callousness have raised. The rights of a man are oftentimes, in these days, utterly ignored by soulless employers. Every man has a right to his manhood; many men are reduced to a state little better than slavery itself by a grinding, bullying serfdom, when employed, that is an outrage upon both human and divine justice. Those responsible will, one day, answer for this. Every man has a right to a living wage when employed, but we find rich capitalists, in their organised power, beating down employment wage to starvation point. Again, we see a commercial system which demands a large half-employed surplus of labour. This is wrong, utterly, radically wrong.

Until the worker comes into his own again, until fair conditions are assured to him, men will find it hard to be true working-men and true citizens. The heart of a man is warped, and his soul is withered by the struggle for a casual existence. A recognition all round of the Christian obligation of duty with the possession of power, of responsibility with the claim of "rights," would revolutionise the relations of Capital and Labour. Then we might see the true ideal of labour more frequently in operation. When a manual worker may be, with dignity and freedom, a natural man, a respectable citizen, an honourable householder, and a practising Christian – then, and not till then, will we have come back to the normal. But the man and the master must co-operate to bring this about. Class hatreds must die out, and the motive power for a co-operation towards reform must spring from an appreciation of the common brotherhood of man, and the perpetual Fatherhood of God. [. . .]

'Only a Working Man'

"He's only a working man." How often have you heard the phrase used! Sometimes in a tone of wonder, sometimes in a tone of derision, sometimes in a tone of compassion, sometimes in a tone of disgust. And it is all taken quietly, as a rule, by the long-suffering son of toil. He accepts the wonder, the derision, the compassion, even the disgust, as a matter of course. He is used to it – to being looked down upon by everybody who is anybody. Anybody who may wear a decent coat and a clean collar at his business comes within the category of his critics. First, however, let it be declared that this effusion is not to be a diatribe against all men who are not manual workers. There are good and bad in every class – it is even possible that there are good millionaires; possible, however improbable. And so, worthy people may be found right down the long line of personal importance, from the currency-king to ourselves. Many of the writer's best friends wear decent coats and clean collars during business hours. Fanaticism is foolish. Yet, the object aimed at is the championship of the working man, and perhaps somebody's corns will be trodden on. The toiler particularly designated here is the manual worker who uses the physical strength or physical skill which God gave him to earn his daily bread with, and who, normally, when that day's work is done, bears the stains from his toil upon him.

Petty clerk and counter-jumper, comic-singer and flunkey – all the thousand and one people who follow unmanual occupations – lend us your ears. If the thought has ever penetrated your well-groomed skulls that toil is degrading, and that the toiler is an object of scorn – eradicate it. If there be a spark of manliness within your well-clad breast – respect a worker. If heretofore the limit of your horizon, as regards respect, has been bounded by the line of outward respectability, rise to a higher, truer, fuller point of view. The rock of respectability is the rock that many of us perish on in these days. "A good position." "Well-to-do." "A splendid business." These are some of the gods in the Pantheon of to-day, and they have countless worshippers. In vain you may look there for the shrine of Principle. Absent! Forgotten! The world doesn't want it.

See that old man there, bragging and boasting about his offspring; about his rich and influential son. He is a poor, unlettered old man; yet he has lived a long and useful life as a working-man. He himself is far more worthy of respect than the rich and influential son, but he has been tainted with the prevailing spirit of the time, and gloats over his son's wealth and influence. That boy was the show-boy at school, clever and brilliant, and the old man scraped and saved, and deprived himself and his helpmate of many a luxury, in order to send his brilliant boy to college. He has now a "high" position, and a "high opinion" of himself. He governs a mammoth establishment, and is noted for "keen" dealing and drastic methods. Is said to be unforgiving and unmerciful. Is ashamed of his humble parentage. Is, in short, a rogue, a tyrant, and a prig. And the old gentleman is proud of him. There is another son whom he never mentions, one who is something of a failure in the old father's eyes. This son never showed any aptitude for scholarship, but was always a steady plodder. He is now "only a working man," but a good one, an honest and honourable one, a dutiful servant, a true husband, son, and father, and a kindly-hearted man. The old man is one of the devotees at the shrine of Position.

Good clothing and a clean person look attractive, and are good in themselves, yet are only, after all, superfluities. Man was made for something more than looks, and it is not good to judge the contents of a book by the outside. So that beneath the coarse coat of the working man beats oftentimes many a noble, generous heart; under the surface of his rough, unrefined language lies oftentimes much solid human wisdom; behind his bluff, off-hand manner stands oftentimes stern, unswerving adherence to a sense of right which is – Principle. As for his work, and what is due to the worker, let all men understand his worth. Without labour the world could not go on. Of course, others, planners, architects, organisers, etc., are necessary also, but does the worker receive his due, considering his importance? Man was made to work. The countless powers with which the human creature has been endowed were not given to be ignored. Physical stamina, strength, agility, skill of ear and eye and hand, all these and other faculties were given for use. And what grander *earthly* use could they be put to than the service of mankind? Every working man – whatever be the nature of his work – is doing good to mankind. His life has not been lived in vain. Man is the steward of the talents which have been lent him, and it is his duty to spend those talents for the general good of humanity. All too soon his little term of usefulness will have expired. All too soon his talents will fade. It is for him to work while it is yet day, "for the night cometh when no man can work." It has been written, "an endless significance lies in Work; a man perfects himself by working. Foul jungles are cleared away; fair seed-fields rise instead, and stately cities, and withal the man himself first ceases to be a jungle and foul, unwholesome desert thereby. Consider how, even in the meanest sorts of labour, the whole soul of a man is composed into a kind of real harmony the instant he sets himself to work. Doubt, desire, sorrow, remorse, indignation, despair itself, all these like hell-dogs lie, beleaguering the soul of the poor day-worker, as of every man, but he bends himself with free valour against his task, and all those are stilled, all these shrink murmuring far off into their caves. The man is now a man. The blessed glow of labour is in him; is it not as purifying fire, wherein all poison is burnt up, and of sour smoke itself there is made bright, blessed flame?"

And what is mean work? What is useful toil? Many a man who has won a world-renown has done naught but mischief. At least our toiler works not uselessly. He is called to his vocation, to his life's mission, when very young. He begins his work. From the days of his bed-loving boyhood, day after day, week after week, month after month, year after year, he trudges forth in the early morn to his day's duty. He is not unhappy, unless this duty is impeded by sickness or some other abnormal cause. So he lives and grows older, and finally his strength fails and he dies – and the world and its improvement is the poorer by one man. Sneer at the pettiness of his job if you dare, poor little shallow-brain. He was called to do a work, and he has done it, and has gone back to the strange region whence he was called. The duty may not have been pleasant; it may have been what you would call a "low occupation." Let it be declared that, in the doing of it, lay a nobility that you never knew. Yes, the children of toil are nature's noblemen. Watch them at five in the evening, when their day's work is done. Stand for a few moments at the corner of any of the great avenues leading from the docks, and see them in their thousands. It is a goodly sight. Grimy faces, weary limbs, hands hardened with their toil. This is a procession which should inspire respect in any onlooker. Tramp, tramp, tramp. This is one regiment of the army of the world's workers. A hundred years hence not one of these thousands will be alive. The enemy Time will have silently mowed them all down. But others will have taken their places. It can be safely surmised that the same procession will still take place nightly, if the world lasts till then. Because of the world's great army, there are many regiments which are for show, or for amusement, but the regiment of workers is for *use*, and the world cannot do without it.

Only a working man. Labourer, artisan, what not! He that is "something in the city," perhaps, despises you, but you need care little. Your duty is in your work, and your pleasure is in your home. Where your hope and consolation lie depends upon yourself. And Nature, truer even than human mother, understands you and blesses you. None know the sweets of relaxation better than the toiler, none feel so keenly the joys of repose. And she blesses him in his home. The home of a good working man is a picture of contentment. Tender wife; rosy-cheeked, healthy children, and, as a rule, many of them.

Hang not down your head, then, brother, for the shame of your work. Much you may have to be ashamed of. The "faithfullest of us are unprofitable servants." The faithfullest of us may say, "Much of my life has been trifled away." But if you have read your life's lesson aright, if the clarity of your vision has not been dimmed by the prevailing false chimeras of position and place-worship, you will do your work conscientiously, for duty's sake, and in doing it will not find shame in, but take pride in, the fact of your being – only a working man. [. . .]

'The Toiler's Toast'

It has been our mission to put heart into the dock-workers, or any other workers; to show them that there is no degradation in honest toil; to give those who have been discouraged by calumny a new hope. The day will come – if it please God to allow it – when it will not be counted a calling of shame to toil at the docks. There is magnificent material there for the building up of a character for self-respect and industry and honourableness. The old order changeth for the new. Meanwhile, hear the words of a comrade –

Let the fine bard of loftier flight
His classic audience delight;
Let him, the cultured and refined,
Invoke the muses for his kind:
I envy not his gifts, nor long
For his deep words and tuneful tongue;
And, while for naught from him desiring,
His subtler talents still admiring,
I hope, if it be not too bold,
That he his censure will withhold.
In this big world where naught is narrow
There's room for nightingale and sparrow –
Let him forbear with scorn to brand me,
I speak to them that understand me.

To you, my friends, and you alone I say,
That wrestle with grim Labour day by day;
Who careless of the pangs or pains ye feel,
Turn with your sturdy arms the world's great wheel.
To you that delve the earth, that plough the soil,
That 'mid the dust in hives of labour toil,
That in all useless idle arts unlearned
Eat the sweet bread which honest sweat has earned –
To you, my mates, of all my friends the best,
For whom warm feelings glow within this breast,
These musings of a comrade are addrest:
One of yourselves, a brother of the band,
Here speaks with you and takes you by the hand.

Though wealth may feast on pleasure till it cloys,
May purchase Pomp's delights and Power's joys,
There is a dignity in labour, boys!
There's not a monarch seated on a throne,
There's not a statesman that the world has known,
There's not a warrior gory from the strife,

There's not a man that breathes the breath of life,
Wins greater credit from his fellow-man
Than does the humble, honest artisan,
If he but act the part which God assigned
With a clear conscience and a cheerful mind –
If he, through all a poor man's stress and strain,
The honour of an upright life maintain.

The pleasures of a working-man are few,
'Twixt work and home his sands of life run through.
The fruits of his hard toil are oft too small
To meet his helpmate's and his children's call,
And in their comfort lies his pleasure – all.
Seldom has he the chance of e'er revealing
Unto his mates his fellowship and feeling,
Can rare afford out of his weekly dole
"The feast of reason and the flow of soul";
But, if for once occasion give the power,
And he may snatch with comrades a brief hour,
May he remember, for 'twill please them most,
To give his friends, and mine, The Toiler's Toast:

"Here's to the man, Tom, Dick, or Dan,
Who without show or shout does the best that he can.
And, making the most of his life's little span,
Is upright in principle, practice, and plan.
No fair-weather, fly-away flash in the pan –
A true friend regardless of party or clan,
Who, though he have faults if we too closely scan,
Is in all things, at all times, to all men – a Man.
May vigour and health brave the powers that press him
And the thorns of existence but little distress him.
In his home may Love's kindnesses ever caress him,
And oft may we meet him and greet him – God bless him."

Notes

1 E. Taplin, 'Milligan, George Jardine', *Oxford Dictionary of National Biography*, 23 September 2004, at https://doi-org.du.idm.oclc.org/10.1093/ref:odnb/48764 [accessed 13 June 2021].
2 G. Milligan, *Life through Labour's Eyes* (St. Louis: B. Herder, 1911), p. vii.
3 G. Grossmith and W. Grossmith, *Diary of a Nobody* (London: J. W. Arrowsmith, 1892); G. Crossick, ed., *The Lower Middle Class in Britain, 1870–1914* (London: Croom Helm Ltd: 1977).
4 Milligan, *Life through Labour's Eyes*, p. 11.
5 Milligan, *Life through Labour's Eyes*, p. 13.

6 This focus on men is no surprise, since the labour market was organized around the assumption of a male breadwinner. See, for example, M. Levine-Clark, *Unemployment, Welfare, and Masculine Citizenship: 'So Much Honest Poverty' in Britain, 1870–1930* (New York: Palgrave Macmillan, 2015), especially chap. 3.
7 Milligan, *Life through Labour's Eyes*, p. 93.
8 Milligan, *Life through Labour's Eyes*, p. 93.
9 Milligan, *Life through Labour's Eyes*, p. 97.
10 See J. Tosh, *Manliness and Masculinities in Nineteenth-Century Britain: Essays on Gender, Family, and Empire* (New York: Pearson Longman, 2005).
11 Milligan, *Life through Labour's Eyes*, p. 167.
12 Milligan, *Life through Labour's Eyes*, p. 169.

Part 2

MEN AND MACHINES

11

SOCIETY FOR THE DIFFUSION OF USEFUL KNOWLEDGE, *THE WORKING MAN'S COMPANION: THE RESULTS OF MACHINERY . . . AN ADDRESS TO WORKING MEN*

(London: Charles Knight, 1831), pp. 5–8, 16–21, 24–26, 179–180, 182–190

The Society for the Diffusion of Useful Knowledge was a popular educational organization, based in London, which operated from 1826 to 1848. Its membership was middle class, including lawyers, scientists, and prominent businessmen, as well as prominent politicians like its founder, the Whig Henry Brougham. Steering clear of politics and religion, the society's goal was to spread cheap pamphlets and books to allow people without formal education to learn about what its members considered important topics for an informed person to know, such as science, history, and the questions of the day.[1] This source, *The Results of Machinery*, a book in the society's series the *Working Man's Companion*, is the first of several in this section to point to the difficulties suffered by handloom weavers as a result of the introduction of machinery into their industry.[2] The handloom weavers and other textile workers were the first to systematically rebel violently by breaking machines when employers brought in the power loom in the eighteenth century. What was called the Luddite Rebellion (1811–1816) covered much of northern England. The government response included transportation to Australia, as well as the enactment of an 1812 law that made machine-breaking a capital offence.[3] Machine-breaking associated with textile work would continue sporadically through mid-century. The document included here was written in the early 1830s, when agricultural labourers were destroying threshing machines in protest in the South of England.[4] The writer opens his text by introducing Joseph Foster, a handloom weaver, who gave evidence to a Select Committee in 1827 about the possibility of emigration for distressed workers. Foster testified that the power loom had contributed to the paltry wages and suffering of the handloom weavers but that he and other Glasgow weavers knew the growth of machinery

DOI: 10.4324/9780429320323-15

was inevitable. The author laments that most working men were not like Foster; instead of complying with the introduction of machinery, they acted to destroy it. The purpose of the book was to convince labourers to realize the benefits of machinery for their class. It addresses them as rational men who should understand the need to accept machinery and as thinking men who should be able to envision the huge negative consequences for labourers in a world in which machine-breaking was successful. This world, which the author conjures specifically for agricultural labourers, would leave them in the state of 'barbarous people, that were ignorant of the inventions that constitute the power of civilization'.[5] The writer recognizes that everyone should expect an adjustment period with the introduction of machines, when hand workers would indeed see first their wages and then their industry as a whole decline. In the end, however, he argues, mechanization will result in more employment, better wages, and cheaper goods that advantage labourers and their families. Machines will help make a larger range of products that workers would be able to afford, shaping new consumer desires. The author's argument that the creation of more supply would make goods cheaper, leading to more demand, which by implication would increase employment, was most famously laid out by the French economist Jean-Baptiste Say: 'A product is no sooner created, than it, from that instant, affords a market for other products to the full extent of its own value'.[6]

The Results of Machinery

Chapter I

In the year 1827, a Committee of the House of Commons was appointed to examine into the subject of Emigration – that is, to see whether it was desirable and practicable to remove distressed labourers from the United Kingdom to distant places, where their labour might be profitably employed to themselves and others. The first person examined before that Committee was Joseph Foster, a working weaver, of Glasgow. He told the Committee, that he and many others, who had formed themselves into a society, were in great distress; that numbers of them worked at the *hand-loom* from eighteen to nineteen hours a-day, and that their earnings, at the utmost, did not amount to more than seven shillings a-week, and that sometimes they were as low as four shillings. That twenty years before that time they could readily earn a pound a-week by the same industry; and that as *power-loom* weaving had increased, the distress of the hand-weavers also had increased in the same proportion. A power-loom is one worked by machinery, and not by the hand of man as most of our readers perhaps know. The Committee then put to Joseph Foster the following questions, and received the following answers: –

Q. "Are the Committee to understand that you attribute the insufficiency of your remuneration for your labour to the introduction of machinery?

A. Yes.

Q. Do you consider, therefore, that the introduction of machinery is objectionable?

A. We do not. The weavers in general, of Glasgow and its vicinity, do not consider that machinery can or ought to be stopped, or put down. They know perfectly well that machinery must go on, that it will go on, and that it is impossible to stop it. They are aware that every implement of agriculture or manufacture is a portion of machinery, and, indeed, everything that goes beyond the teeth and nails (if I may use the expression) is a machine. I am authorized, by the majority of our society, to say, that I speak their minds, as well as my own, in stating this."

If all, or if a large majority of the working-men of our country had come to the same sound opinions as Joseph Foster, we should not take the trouble, because it would be needless, now to address them. But when we hear on all sides that misguided men are violating the laws by which the rights of all are protected; that they are wickedly and ignorantly destroying the property of the farmer and the manufacturer, in the belief that machinery *can* be stopped or put down; that they do *not* know as the poor weavers of Glasgow *did* know, that machinery must go on, will go on, and that it is impossible to stop it; we think it our duty, having the means of appealing to their reason and to their regard for their own interest, to endeavour to bring their minds to the same conclusions as those of the respectable weaver, whose words we have repeated. He felt that, although he was in his own person a sufferer from the improvement of machinery, it was utterly out of his power, because it was contrary to his reason, and to the reason of all thinking people, whether working-men or not, to resist the progress of that improvement. There are many working-men who entertain the same sound opinions, which they have come to, probably, by an accurate and dispassionate observation of the facts which are within their own view. To such men we hope to offer many new facts to strengthen their opinions; and we rely greatly upon their influence to point out their errors either to those who are violating the laws, or to those who think the violators of the laws have justice on their side. For the benefit of you all, the informed as well as the uninformed, we address you as men capable of reasoning. We give you a great body of facts to reason upon. We offer nothing to your passions or your prejudices. We shall attempt to make you feel, by bringing before you the same sort of facts by which that sensible man, Joseph Foster, convinced his own mind, that although your individual labour may be partially displaced, or unsettled for a time, by the use of a cheaper and a better power, which power is machinery, you are great gainers by the general use of that power. We shall strive to show you, that through this power you possess, however poor you may be, many of the comforts which make the difference between man in a civilized and man in a savage state; and further that, in consequence of machinery having rendered productions of all sorts cheaper, and therefore caused them to be more universally purchased, it has really increased the demand for that manual labour, which it appears to some of you, reasoning only from a few instances, it has a tendency to diminish. If we make out these propositions, we think you will agree with Joseph Foster, that the introduction of machinery is not objectionable. [. . .]

Chapter II

Amongst the many accounts which the newspapers of December, 1830, give of the destruction of machinery by agricultural labourers, we read that in the neighbourhood of Aylesbury, a band of mistaken and unfortunate men destroyed all the machinery of many farms, *down even to the common drills*. The men conducted themselves, says the county newspaper, with civility; and such was their consideration, that they moved the machines out of the farm-yards, to prevent injury arising to the cattle from the nails and splinters that flew about while the machinery was being destroyed. They *could not make up their minds* as to the propriety of destroying a horse-churn, and therefore that machine was passed over.

We will suppose, by way of argument, that there were no laws to repress such outrages; that if the labourers in agriculture chose to believe that not only thrashing machines were injurious to them, but that every one of those ingenious implements which have aided in rendering British agriculture the most perfect in the world, was equally harmful, they might, without interruption, break them to pieces. We will further suppose, that while these proceedings go forward, the landowner looks on, the farmer looks on, the magistrate does not stir, there are no judges or juries in the land, the people in the towns leave the machine-breakers to their own devices. So they break on – thrashing machine, winnowing machine, chaff-cutting machine, drill, and every other newfangled invention, as they call these things. We will suppose, still further, that the farmer yields to all this violence; that the violence has the effect which it was meant to have upon him; and that he takes on all the hands which were out of employ, to thrash and winnow, to cut chaff, to plant with a dibber instead of with a drill, to do all the work, in fact, by the dearest mode instead of the cheapest. The destroyers of property have got the law, therefore, into their own hands, as far as their triumph over machinery is concerned. And how do they proceed in their career? The farmer, we have imagined, takes all this quietly; he pays the new labourers who have got into his barns and his fields, ready for hand-work, with their flails and their dibbers; but he employs *just as many people as are absolutely necessary*, and no more, for getting his corn ready for market, and for preparing, in a slovenly way, for the seed-time. In a month or two, the victorious destroyers find that not a single hand the more of them is really employed. And why not? There are no drainings going forward, the hedges and ditches are neglected, the dung-heap is not turned over, the chalk is not fetched from the pit; in fact, all those labours are neglected which belong to a state of agricultural industry which is brought to perfection. *The farmer has no funds to employ in such labours;* he is paying a great deal more than he paid before, because his labourers choose to do certain labours with rude tools instead of perfect ones. If he is a humane man, but not a firm one, and yields to the notion that it is a good thing to do work in the most round-about way, and, consequently, at the greatest expense, he does not regret the loss of the drill-plough, which, as well as many other agricultural tools, lessens labour, lessens the quantity of seed, and increases the crop. He spends all the saving which the drill-plough has caused upon the clamorous labourers, who insist that their arms are better for his work than the instrument which they have broken. But still some work must be neglected, and thus the actual amount of money paid for labour is just the same.

We will imagine that this state of things continues till the next spring. All this while the price of grain has been rising. Many farmers have ceased to employ capital at all upon the land. The neat inventions, which enabled them to make a living out of their business, being destroyed, they have abandoned the business altogether. Others, who have yielded to the uproar, go on as well as they can, neglecting a great many labours that unite to make a good crop, although they are more and more pressed upon by the demand for labour, in consequence of a deal of land going out of cultivation. They pay as long as they can; they pay much more for labour than they did before, some out of compassion and some out of fear. But the prices are steadily rising, and, therefore, although there is more money paid to a greater number of labourers, and although some receive higher wages, in the common sense of the word, than they did before they broke the machines, they are infinitely worse off, for the rate of wages is really lower. A day's work will then no longer purchase as much bread as before. It requires the work of a day and a half to procure the same quantity. Wages are, therefore, really lower, because a less crop is being produced at a greater cost, and the market-price is influenced accordingly.

The labourers now either begin to quarrel amongst themselves, and give up their unwise combinations; or they still combine with the determination to obtain employment by the destruction of every thing that appears to them to stand in the way of it, – every thing beyond the teeth and nails of the workmen, as Joseph Foster expressed himself – and on they go in the work of ruin. The horse, it may be probably found out, is as great an enemy as the drill-plough; so the horses are turned out to starve, or have their throats cut, the laws being still idle. This is, indeed, a great point gained, for as a horse will do the fieldwork of six men, there must be six men employed, without doubt, instead of one horse: so would conclude these most mistaken violators of the laws by which society is held together. But how would the fact turn out? If the farmer still went on, in spite of all these losses and crosses, he might employ men in the place of horses, but not a single man more than the number that would work at the price of the keep of one horse. To do the work of each horse destroyed he would require six men; but he would only have about a shilling a day to divide between these six, – the amount which the horse consumed.

In the mean time it would be perfectly evident, from all this convulsion amongst the labourers, from all this wanton and profitless ruin, that a great deal of the land would very quickly go out of cultivation altogether, if the laws were still idle. While the land was going out of cultivation, the stock of corn on hand would be much more quickly decreasing than in quiet times. One-tenth, it is said by some, would be lost of that stock by employing flails instead of thrashing machines. This is, probably, an extreme statement, grounded only upon a comparison between the regular produce of the thrashing-machine, and the most careless thrashing by the flail. But there is no doubt that the machine saves some corn. The destruction of drills, also, would cause a larger quantity of seed to be sown than would be otherwise necessary. Thrashing machines and drills, taken together in their savings, prevent therefore some thousand quarters of wheat alone from being wasted. Fifteen million quarters of wheat are annually consumed in Great Britain. If they save only a fiftieth of the wheat, as much, therefore, as would feed all the people of Great Britain for a week, or three hundred thousand of those people all the year, would be absolutely thrown away, trodden under foot, sent to the dunghill with the straw, wasted for ever, by one wrong act alone of the labourers; and all this while we should be preparing to grow a great deal less for the next harvest. We should have a famine, if foreign countries could not supply us with what the labourers had destroyed. And how do we know that foreign labourers would be wiser than English ones, and abstain from such acts, in the knowledge that whatever raises the price of produce lowers the rate of wages? Are foreign labourers better informed than English labourers? If so, let us all take shame to ourselves, that the means of acquiring knowledge which this country affords have been neglected; for upon sound knowledge must rest the safety and happiness of all. [. . .]

As the year advanced, and the harvest approached, it would be discovered that not one-tenth of the land was sown; for although the ploughs were gone, because the horses were turned out to starve, and there was plenty of *labour* for those who chose to labour for its own sake, or at the price of a horse, this amazing employment for human hands, somehow or other, would not quite answer the purpose. It has been calculated that the power of horses, oxen, &c. employed in husbandry in Great Britain is ten times the amount of human power. If the human power insisted upon doing all the work with the worst tools, the certainty is that not even one-tenth of the land could be cultivated. Where, then, would all this madness end? In the starvation of the labourers themselves. The people in the towns would probably use *their* machines, which are ships, and barges, and wagons, to bring them as much of the produce of foreign countries as they could get (and that would be little) in exchange for their manufactures; and the agricultural labourers, who had put themselves out of the sympathy and protection of society, if they were allowed to eat up all they had produced by such imperfect means, would be in an infinitely more wretched state than they could possibly be, if the demand for labour was many times less than it now is. They would be just in the condition of any other barbarous people, that were ignorant of the inventions that constitute the power of civilization. They would eat up the little corn which they raised themselves; and have nothing to give in exchange, for clothes, and coals, and candles, and soap, and tea, and sugar, and all the many comforts which those who are even the worst off are not wholly deprived of.

All this may appear as an extreme statement; and certainly we believe that no such evils could happen: for if the laws were passive, *which they will not be*, the most ignorant of the labourers themselves would, if they proceeded to carry their own principle much farther than they have done, see in their very excesses the real character of the folly and wickedness to which it has led, and would lead them. Why should the labourers of Aylesbury not destroy the harrows as well as the drills? Why leave a machine which separates the clods of the earth, and break one which puts seed into it? Why deliberate about a horse-churn, when they are resolved against a winnowing machine? The truth is, these poor men perceive, even in the midst of their excesses, the gross deception of the reasons which induce them to commit them. Their motive is a natural, and if lawfully expressed, a proper impatience, under a condition which has certainly many hardships, and those hardships in great part produced by the want of profitable labour. But in imputing those hardships to machinery, they are at once embarrassed when they come to draw distinctions between one sort of machine and another. This embarrassment decidedly shows that there are fearful mistakes at the bottom of their furious hostility to machinery. Some of these mistakes it is the object of this little book to clear up. We apply ourselves to the task with a confident hope of doing good, because in this very embarrassment we perceive the workings of a conscientious principle. There is much ignorance to be encountered; but there is a disposition for honest inquiry, which will, in time, produce the best effects. [. . .]

Chapter XVIII

THERE are great temporary inconveniences in the introduction of a new machine. Who can doubt it? Who can deny that it is a serious evil, when the honest industry of a working man is suddenly invaded by a power against which he cannot struggle; – when, in fact, such a man as Joseph Foster, laborious, intelligent, reflecting, and singularly honest in the expression of his opinions, says, that his condition has been declining ever since the introduction of power-loom weaving; – that he has not any hope that any possible improvement in the cotton trade would provide in future for the hand-weavers out of employment; – that the well-informed weavers have a general persuasion that the hand-weaving is a business which is nearly extinct altogether. The state of change is doubtless a state of suffering. The moment the machine comes into competition with human labour, the wages of that labour begin to adjust themselves to the lesser cost of production by the machine. [. . .]

In the consideration of the evils resulting from the introduction of a new machine, you must never forget the principle which we have sought to impress upon you throughout this book, – that the object for which machines are established, and the object which they do effect, is cheapness of production. Machines either save material, or diminish labour, or both. "Which is the cheapest," said the Committee to Joseph Foster, "a piece of goods made by a power-loom, or a piece of goods made by a hand-loom?" He answered, "a power-loom is the cheapest." What, then, is the effect of this reduced cost of production, ultimately, upon the employment of labour? That the manufacture is increased, – that more cloth is consumed, – that the consumer has more money to lay out in cloth, or more money to lay out in other things. We have shewn you, most distinctly, the effect of the spinning machinery in increasing twenty-fold the number of people engaged in that branch of manufacture. But let us put the circumstance before your eyes once more, in the words of a person old enough to recollect the precise facts connected with the first introduction of that machinery. The Committee that we have so often mentioned examined Mr. Fielden, a resident at Blackburn, upon this particular subject.

"*Q*. Do you remember what occurred in Lancashire when spinning factories were first established?

A. I recollect that period very well.

Q. Were not a very considerable number of persons thrown out of work, and was not there great distress, in consequence of the introduction of machinery, when spinning was done by machinery and not by hand labour?

A. Yes, there was a great deal of distress, and much rioting took place at the time.

Q. Persons who had formerly obtained a good living by spinning by hand-labour, were unable to obtain the same wages, and in the same manner, in consequence of the introduction of spinning machinery?

A. If the description of spinning that was carried on in the neighbourhood of Blackburn is alluded to, that which was done by the hand, the raw cotton was taken out by the weaver, and spun in his own house, and the change was productive of considerable inconvenience in the first instance; great alarm was created, and some spinning-mills were destroyed at the time; many persons were thrown out of employment; but at that time the manufacture of the kingdom was in a very limited state, compared with what it is at present.

Q. Was not the result of the introduction of that machinery an immense increase of the manufacture?

A. Very great.

Q. And more advantageous wages for a considerably increased number?

A. Yes, materially so."

It is, we think, self-evident, that if the temporary distress of the hand-spinners, which produced the rioting, and the destruction of spinning-mills here described, had gone on to prevent altogether the manufacture of cotton thread by the spinning machinery, the consumption of cotton cloth would have been little increased, and the number of persons engaged in the manufacture would have been twenty, thirty, or even forty times less than the present number. But there would have been another result. Think you that the great body of the people of Europe would have chosen to wear for many years *dear* cloth instead of *cheap* cloth, that a few thousand spinners might have been kept at their ancient wheels in Lancashire? Capital can easily shift its place, and invention follows where capital goes before. The people of France, and Germany, and America, would have employed the cheap machine instead of the dear one; and the people of England would have had cheap cloth instead of dear cloth from thence. We cannot build a wall of brass round our islands; and the thin walls of prohibitive duties are very easily broken through. A profit of from twenty to thirty per cent will pour in any given quantity of smuggled goods that a nation living under prohibitive laws can demand. Buonaparte, in the height of his power, passed the celebrated Berlin decree for the exclusion of all English produce from the continent of Europe. But our merchants laughed at him. The whole coast of France, and Holland, and Italy, became one immense receiving place for smuggled goods. If he had lined the whole coast with all the six hundred thousand soldiers that he marched to Russia, instead of a few custom-house officers, he could not have stopped the introduction of English produce. It was against the nature of things, that the people who had been accustomed to cheap goods should buy dear ones; or that they should go without any article, whether of necessity or luxury, whose use had become general. Mark, therefore, if the cotton-spinners of Lancashire had triumphed sixty years ago over Arkwright's machinery, there would not have been a single man, woman, or child of those spinners employed *at all*, within twenty years after that most fatal triumph. The manufacture of cotton would have gone to other countries; cotton spinning in England would have been at an end. The same thing would have happened if the power-loom, twenty years ago, had been put down by combination; that is, if the hand-loom weavers had not been as well-informed and as reasonable as we see they are. Mr. Fielden, whose evidence we have already quoted, says, "The introduction of the power-loom, I conceive, will be the cause of saving the manufactures to this kingdom; without the power-looms the manufactories must be annihilated entirely, for the Americans are making use of the power-loom."

Those who have taken a superficial view of the question of machinery say, that, whenever there is a greater demand than the existing means can supply, every new discovery in mechanics is a benefit to society, because it gives the means of satisfying the existing wants. They add, that, on the contrary, whenever the things produced are sufficient for the consumers, the discovery is a calamity, because it does not add to the enjoyments of the consumers; it only gives them a better market, which better market is bought at the price of the existence of the producers.

All such reasoning is false in principle, and unsupported by experience. There is no such thing, nor, if machines went on improving for five hundred years at the rate they have done for the last century, could there be any such thing, as a limit to the wants of the consumers. The great mass of facts which we have brought together in this book must have shewn you, that the cheaper an article of necessity becomes, the more of it is used; that when the most pressing wants are supplied, and supplied amply by cheapness, the consumer has money to lay out upon new wants; that when these new wants are supplied cheaply, he goes on again and again to other new wants; that there are no limits, in fact, to his wants as long as he has any capital to satisfy them. Bear in mind this; that the first great object of every invention and every improvement is to confer a benefit upon the consumers, – to make the commodity cheap and plentiful. The working man stands in a double character; he is both a producer and a consumer. But we will be bold to say that the question of cheapness of production is a much more important question to be decided in his favour as a consumer, than the question of dearness of production to be decided in his favour as a producer. The truth is, every man tries to get as much as he can for his own labour, and to pay as little as he can for the labour of others. If a mechanic, succeeding in stopping the machine used in his own trade, by any strange deviation from the natural course of things were to get higher wages for a time, he himself would be the most injured by the extension of the principle. When he found his loaf cost him two shillings instead of one; when he was obliged to go to the river with his bucket for his supply of water; when his coals cost a guinea a bushel instead of eighteen-pence; when he was told by the hosier that his worsted stockings were advanced from a shilling a pair to five shillings; when, in fact, the price of every article that he uses should be doubled, trebled, and, in nine cases out of ten, put beyond the possibility of attainment; – what, we ask, would be the use to him of his advance in wages? Let us never forget that it is not for the employment of labourers, but for the benefit of consumers, that labour is employed at all. The steam-engines are not working in the coal-pits of Northumberland, and the ships sailing from the Tyne to the Thames, to give employment to colliers and to sailors, but to make coals cheap in London. If the people of London could have the coals without the steam-engines and the ships, it would be better for them, and better for the rest of the world. If they could get coals for nothing, they would have more produce to exchange for money to spend upon other things; and the comforts, therefore, of every one of us would be increased.

This increase of comfort, some of you may say, is a question that more affects the rich than it affects us. This again is a mistake. The whole tendency of the improvements of the last four hundred years has not only been to lift the meanest of you, in regard to a great many comforts, far above the condition of the rich four hundred years ago, but absolutely to place you, in many things, upon a level with the rich of your own day. You are surrounded, as we have constantly shewn you throughout this book, with an infinite number of comforts and conveniences which had no existence two or three centuries ago; and those comforts and conveniences are not used only by a few, but are within the reach of almost all men. Every day is adding something to your comforts. Your houses are better built, – your clothes are cheaper, – you have an infinite number of domestic utensils, whose use even was unknown to your ancestors, – you can travel cheaply from place to place, and not only travel at less expense, but travel ten times quicker than the richest man could travel two hundred years ago. Above all, you are not only advancing steadily to the same level in point of many comforts with the rich, but you are gaining that knowledge, which was formerly their exclusive possession. Keep fast hold of that last and best power; and you will learn what your true individual interest is, in every situation in which you can be placed: you will learn now, that it is useless in any way to struggle against that progress of society, whose tendencies are to make all of us more comfortable, more instructed, more virtuous, and, therefore, more happy.

We have endeavoured to shew throughout this book that the one great result of machinery, and of every improvement in art, is to lessen the cost of production; to increase the benefit to the consumer. But it is a most fortunate arrangement of the social state, as we have also shewn you all along, that cheap production gives increased employment. The same class of false reasoners who consider that the wants of society are limited, cry out, it is better to have a population of men than of steam-engines. That might be true, if the steam-engines *did* put out the men; but inasmuch as they increase the productions by which men are maintained, they increase the men. What has increased the population of England nearly ten-fold during the last five hundred years, but the improvement of the arts of life, which has enabled more men to live within the land? There is no truth so clear, that as the productions of industry multiply, the means of acquiring those productions multiply also. The productions which are created by one producer furnish the means of purchasing the productions created by another producer; and, in consequence of this double production, the necessities of both the one and the other are better supplied. The multiplication of produce multiplies the consumers of produce. There are, probably, upon the average, no more hats made in the year than there are heads to wear them; but as there are fifteen millions of heads of the British subjects of King William IV. and there were only five millions of the British subjects of Queen Anne, it is self evident that the hat-makers have three times as much work as they had a century and a quarter ago. What has given the hat-makers three times as much work? The trebling of the population. And what has trebled the population? The trebling of produce, – the trebling of the means of maintaining that population.

Notes

1 T. P. Johansen, 'The World Wide Web of the Society for the Diffusion of Useful Knowledge: On the Global Circulation of Broughamite Educational Literature, 1826–1848', *Victorian Periodicals Review* 50:4 (2017), pp. 703–720.
2 On handloom weavers, see Volume 1 Introduction.
3 J. Horn, 'Machine Breaking in England and France during the Age of Revolution', *Labour* 55 (Spring 2005), pp. 143–166, on pp. 146–149.
4 Horn, 'Machine Breaking', pp. 147–148.
5 Society for the Diffusion of Useful Knowledge, *The Working Man's Companion-The Results of Machinery . . . An Address to Working Men* (London: Charles Knight, 1831), Google Books, p. 25.
6 J. B. Say, *A Treatise on Political Economy: Or the Production, Distribution, and Consumption of Wealth*, 6th American ed. (Philadelphia: Grigg & Elliott, 1834, orig. 1803), p. 138.

12

ANON., *THE PETITION OF THE UNDERSIGNED OPERATIVE SPINNERS AND OTHERS EMPLOYED IN THE SPINNING OF COTTON WOOL INTO YARN, IN ASHTON-UNDER-LYNE AND ITS NEIGHBOURHOOD*

(Ashton-under-Lyne: T. Cunningham, 1832)

The House of Commons regularly received petitions on a wide variety of issues, including, in the early 1830s, the abolition of slavery, the repeal of the union between Ireland and England, and requests for and against bills to reform conditions in factories.[1] The petition included here, from the wool and cotton spinners of Ashton-under-Lyne, is typical of those of factory workers in this era who pressured Parliament to legislate shorter working hours.[2] Ashton-under-Lyne, part of the Greater Manchester conurbation, had been a small market town that grew into one of the most important mill towns in the area. Handloom weavers and domestic spinners were displaced by power looms, with increasing numbers of factories operating in the region.[3] In this petition, the Operative Spinners of Ashton-under-Lyne called on Parliament to legislate ten-hour work days. The ten-hour or short-time movement of the 1830s, which was concerned with conditions as well as hours, was driven by a mix of factory workers, their allies, and Tory paternalists, such as Richard Oastler and Lord Ashley, critical of what they saw as the collapse of a 'moral economy' under the new free-market industrial order (see Volume 1 Introduction).[4] In the Ashton-under-Lyne petition, the workers clearly tie the demand for ten-hour days to the employment of labourers who had lost their jobs from the increase in machinery. Their text tries not to be critical of machines themselves, but rather condemns the over-use of machinery. Short-timers believed that reducing hours would lead to more jobs, assuming that factory owners would want to make up lost productivity by building new mills and hiring more labourers. It would also benefit distressed trades that would gain employment in the erection of new factories. The reliance on the Poor Law (see Volume 2 Introduction) would

DOI: 10.4324/9780429320323-16

also diminish, they believed, since more people would be put to work and not have to seek relief from the parish.[5] This petition uses rhetoric that was consistent throughout the nineteenth century, connecting factory work with the degradation of the population. Workers, medical practitioners, politicians in favour of factory reform, and others used melodramatic scenes of distress, especially of stunted and weak children, to warn members of Parliament that without controls on factories, the English nation would degenerate. Workers' demands for shorter hours became central to Chartist meetings and then trade union politics later in the century. The 1847 Factory Act was regarded as a victory for the ten-hour movement, restricting the hours of women and young persons (thirteen to eighteen years old) to ten hours a day, which, for practical purposes, limited men's hours as well.[6]

The Petition of The Undersigned Operative Spinners

To the honourable the Commons of the United Kingdom of Great Britain and Ireland, in Parliament assembled.

The petition of the undersigned operative Spinners, and others employed in the Spinning of Cotton Wool into Yarn, in Ashton-under-Lyne and its neighbourhood.

HUMBLY SHEWETH,

That your petitioners have seen with regret, the very injurious effects of protracted labour in Cotton Factories, in a heated and contaminated atmosphere, where the pure air can seldom be permitted to enter. But pernicious to health as is confinement in Cotton Factories, even in the day time, and under the most favourable circumstances, employment in such places in the night, is infinitely more injurious to both the health and morals of the persons so employed.

That your honourable house have already interfered by legislative enactments, to protect persons of tender years from being worked more than twelve hours in such Cotton Mills *in the day;* but there is no law to prohibit the destructive pactice [sic] of working in the night.

That your petitioners are of opinion that the use of Machinery, if rightly directed, is calculated to increase the comforts and conveniences of mankind; but its unrestricted employment, instead of being a benefit, has hitherto tended to the injury of thousands, yea, tens of thousands of the productive classes.

That your petitioners are aware, that to restrict the employment of Machinery without due caution, would interfere with the trade and prosperity of this Kingdom; yet, they humbly submit to your honourable house, that no such injury would accrue from a law prohibiting the working of steam engines and water-wheels more than ten hours and a half on any one day; and eight hours and a half on Saturdays.

That in the present depressed state of the Iron and other branches of trade, greatly dependent upon the Cotton, Woollen, Silk and Linen trades, such a measure would be highly beneficial from the increased stimulas it would give to the erection of new manufactories, and the employment of additional machinery.

That your petitioners know and are competent to prove to your honourable house, that while they are compelled to work in the respective Mills, in which they are employed twelve, thirteen, fourteen, and some even fifteen hours per day, there are thousands of persons out of employ, whose subsistence, if not derived from the Mills, must be derived from the respective parishes to which they belong; thus adding to the burthens of those who cultivate the soil in those parishes. That by shortening the hours of labour in Mills, your petitioners are of opinion that this evil, if not entirely put an end to, would be much lessened by calling into employment a many hands to make up the deficiency occasioned by restricting the hours of labour, ten hours and a half per day.

That the feelings and sympathies of your petitioners are daily outraged on witnessing their emaciated offspring, whose lengthened sallow faces, weak and distorted limbs, clearly indicate that ere long, unless your honourable house interferes, our manufacturing population will become as degraded a race of human beings as ever crawled upon the earth's surface, having no resemblance to our robust and hardy forefathers, to whose industry, valour, and intrepidity, England owes her present high rank and consequence amongst nations.

That the existing laws are totally inefficient in protecting the persons for whose benefit they were passed, as various devices and contrivances are had recourse to, for the purpose of evading their enactments.

That the difficulty of obtaining evidence under the existing laws is another material obstacle in the way of enforcing their enactments.

Your petitioners therefore humbly pray your honourable house to pass a law entirely prohibiting the working of any steam engines and waterwheels, more than ten hours and a half on any one day; and eight hours and a half on Saturdays.

And your petitioners will ever pray.

Notes

1 'Public Petitions, 1833–1918', *ProQuest U.K. Parliamentary Papers,* at https://parlipapers-proquest-com.du.idm.oclc.org/parlipapers/result/pqpresultpage?accountid=14608&groupid=95822&pgId=ab4b8d28-1af3-4f21-a146-1b60f75a33d8&rsId=17DAAD92B29 [accessed 10 January 2022].

2 Anon., *The Petition of the Undersigned Operative Spinners and Others Employed in the Spinning of Cotton Wool into Yarn, in Ashton-under-Lyne and Its Neighbourhood* (Ashton-under-Lyne: T. Cunningham, 1832). The petition was read before the House of Commons on 22 February 1832. U.K. Parliament, House of Commons, *Hansard*, at https://hansard.parliament.uk/commons/1832-02-22/debates/c44d7d39-aa7d-4697-8e7a-43514b8cda98/HouseOfCommons [accessed 10 January 2022].

3 'The Cotton Industry in Ashton', *Ashton-under-Lyne History*, at www.ashton-under-lyne.com/history/cotton.htm [accessed 23 May 2021].

4 D. Fraser, *The Evolution of the British Welfare State: A History of Social Policy since the Industrial Revolution* (London: Macmillan, 1973), pp. 15–23.

5 For an introduction to the Poor Law, see A. Brundage, *The English Poor Laws, 1700–1930* (New York: Palgrave Macmillan, 2001) and L. H. Lees, *The Solidarities of Strangers: The English Poor Laws and the People, 1700–1948* (New York: Cambridge University Press, 1998).

6 On the short-time movement, see R. Gray, *The Factory Question and Industrial England, 1830–1860* (Cambridge: Cambridge University Press, 2002).

13

G. C. BURROWS, 'INTRODUCTION', 'LETTER I', 'LETTER VI', AND 'APPENDIX' IN *A WORD TO ELECTORS. LETTERS TO THE PRESENT GENERATION ON THE UNRESTRAINED USE OF MODERN MACHINERY, PARTICULARLY ADDRESSED TO MY COUNTRYMEN AND FELLOW CITIZENS*

(Norwich: Wilkin and Fletcher, 1832), pp. 3, 4–5, 23–26, and 28–30

G. C. (George Crisp) Burrows (1796–1868) was a general agent (selling insurance) from Norwich who was involved in radical politics.[1] He was deeply concerned about the negative impact of machinery on the working classes. Structured as a series of letters, this second edition of his pamphlet was to correct the 'inaccuracies' of the first edition. Burrows's goal in the pamphlet seems to have been to counter the position of the Society for the Diffusion of Useful Knowledge on machinery, which asked workers to regard mechanization positively. The letters selected here illustrate Burrows's position that machinery was detrimental to the progress of the nation and the well-being of the working class. Burrows argues in Letter I that the destitution his readers saw around them was man-made; nature provided plenty, but the ambition of men created machinery, which had led to 'unnatural starvation'.[2] While the Society for the Diffusion of Useful Knowledge (see Volume 1, Part 2, Chapter 11) asked working men to be rational about machines, Burrows mocks the 'march of reason' that supposedly led to the path of machinery.[3] Machinery, he asserts, answered the call of cheapness, but at the expense of workers, who were left unemployed or employed at a 'pittance'.[4] Countering Say's law that supply creates its own demand,[5] Burrows contends that the endless supply of goods produced from machines would not create demand, because machines made workers destitute, so no one would be left to purchase

DOI: 10.4324/9780429320323-17

new products, the market would become glutted, and workers would starve. Letter VI points to the dangers of thinking only in terms of what is 'cheap',[6] for doing so privileged machinery over humanity. Machinery created a surplus population reduced to eating potatoes and turnips and relying on the Poor Law (see Volume 2 Introduction). If England would limit machinery, labour and capital could come together to produce not only value in land and goods, but happiness. Machinery, according to Burrows, was emasculating, barely covering men in 'effeminating rags',[7] stripping them of their strength, making them idle, and depriving them of their independence, which went against central Victorian values.[8] Between the first printing of this pamphlet and the second, the Society for the Useful Diffusion of Knowledge had published *The Results of Machinery* in the *Working Man's Companion* series, and Burrows added an appendix, included here, directly attacking that publication. Burrows seeks, point by point, to challenge the society's argument that '*cheap production, increased employment, increased consumption*, and *increased enjoyment* go hand in hand with *unrestrained machinery*'.[9] He accuses the society of putting machinery before human beings and demonstrates that his pamphlet was in complete opposition to the society's claims.

'Introduction'

In the following Letters I feel it unnecessary to enter upon a lengthy disquisition, or to search, had I the inclination, into deeply concealed mysteries. Suffice it therefore that mankind inhabit a globe whose surface is fertile, whose inhabitants are numerous, whose wants the spontaneous fruits of the earth will not support; that we live on islands situated in a happy climate, unannoyed by excessive heat, excessive cold, pestilential vapours, noxious insects, or hideous reptiles, whose shores are fertile and of extent sufficient to maintain their population for many generations; that we are associated into a community capable of enjoying the greatest blessings allotted to human nature, but that we are victims of false philosophy, ignorant of, or unable to enjoy these transcendent blessings, of intense intellect, the phantasies of which are in direct opposition to common sense and the wise dispensations of Providence.

It may be said these letters are a mass of plagiarism – assertion without proof; if so, let it pass, good may arise from evil; – whole volumes have been written and may be again to prove 't is taxation, rent, tithes, currency, over production of the fruits of the earth, over population, competition, free trade, high and low prices, the national debt, and national corruption; each writer advocating that as the cause which most affects his own particular interest; but these are effects whose pressure is but relative and subject to local remedies, the effect of machinery is *universal*. To those who espouse the opposite side of the question, I say, let them prove 't is not the earth on which we exist – that the earth is not fruitful, that its fruits are not for the enjoyment of mankind, or that it does not yield to the industry of man a bountiful return. Let them prove the belly has no craving and that food is unnecessary, let them prove raiment is more than food, that the cultivation of the earth is useless, let them prove that one nation cannot rival another, let them prove that the burden of this rivalry is not thrown on the labouring population, let them prove that starvation is the effect of plenty, and I have done. To those who say the mind must progress, I ask, where is Babylon and where the cities of the East? – Were they built without heads and hands? To those who urge that machinery will find its level, I answer, so does every mountain torrent. To those who heap abuse on our country, our soil, our climate, let them leave it – 't is too good for them. To those who love it, I say, let them petition against machinery; for while the creation exists in its present form, while day and night, summer and winter, seed time and harvest remain, so long will the unrestrained use of machinery produce

STARVATION.

'Letter I'

That the want of food creates more of the difficulties and dangers that surround us than aught else, is not disputed; and a little consideration convinces, that of the many conflicting opinions as to the cause, none can be right in the extreme, if any in a degree; and as there is no famine, the natural enquiry is, how is it? – That 't is the earth on which we tread no one denies, nor yet its fruitfulness, nor that its fruits are for the use and benefit of mankind, nor that enough for all his wants it can and does produce by man's industry; this granted, why or how is it, that starvation stalks among us while plenty stares us in the face? How can it be or what is it that so perverts dame nature's laws that so it is? Is it taxation, rent or tithe, competition or free trade, high or low prices, or the currency, or the national debt, or national corruption? If 'tis all these, 't is not dame nature's fault, these are the works of man. Dame nature says the earth is good, increase and multiply is her first law; the Deity made man the Lord of the creation, gave him plain sense and reason, and to his use ordained the earth and its productions. Nature has no hand in this starvation – 'tis man; his intellect has wrought this strange fatality, excessively civilized men, whose exalted minds have marched clean over common minds, all common sense, and left the vile crowd to wonder and admire, not that they are immortal, but that they can't reach the moon. 'T is that queer thing the belly keeps common minds to common sense, 'tis that convinces us men are but mortals. Yes! – the back may be clothed, the head may be sheltered, but unless this belly be fed, pestilence, or famine, or sword will devastate the face of this fair land. In the sweat of his face shall man eat bread, without the sweat of his brow he cannot exist, such is the lot of the human race, but the earth does yield abundantly to his industry, and shall not the labourer be worthy of his hire, when it is said muzzle not the ox that treadeth out the corn? It is not rent, nor tithe, nor taxes, nor the national debt, nor national corruption, nor the currency, nor over population, nor free trade, nor high nor low prices, nor competition, nor fire, nor sword, nor pestilence, nor famine; 'tis not all these combined, nor any one, though of sufficient import to plunge a state in difficulty, has caused this unnatural starvation. 'Tis the march of mind pursuing folly's phantom – universal peace and brotherhood; it is this forgets that nations are but men, each obstinately bent on its own real or fancied prosperity, – that its votaries are men whose schemes and principles war with the philanthropy they teach, – that their own dogmas must let loose a torrent to which they can oppose no barrier, and to which they themselves must fall a sacrifice; is not this march of mind Ambition? – one of nature's ills, – the stumbling block of kings, – the rock on which men, princes, priests, rulers, kings, kingdoms, all have split, – which caused the fall of angels? But is not reason also a gift of Providence, raising man lord of the creation? Does reason guide this march of mind? Does reason teach that all the nations of the earth are one community of universal brotherhood, that Britain shall be the head to whom all the earth must bow? Is it not Ambition, whose mighty engine is in war the sword, in peace machinery? And is machinery her darling offspring? 'England's machinery in the competition shall put down all other;' 'cheap, cheap' is the cry; 'buy where you can buy cheapest,' the order of the day; to attain which end, one portion of the human race must be reduced to the lowest pittance on which it can exist, the other unemployed, beings quite useless in this new creation, are thrown a burden on the vitals of the country, on which they will prey till human nature driven past endurance, breaking through all bonds, sweeps the monster from the earth, its progeny and projectors, and gives good sense her sway. Is this philanthropy, – is this the march of reason, – is this that march of mind and common sense, – or has the march so many routes so near alike? Have reason and folly such close resemblance, that the goal must be possessed ere wrong or right is known? It is not so with common minds; 'tis exquisite refinement, 'tis the march of intellect past common sense, disdaining to look down on common things, on human nature, on human frailty, to consider man as man.

Machinery is the hydra of the present day, starvation is her offspring, and as long as the land is cursed with unrestrained machinery, machinery vying with itself, the inhabitants of the whole earth cannot consume the produce. Every market must be glutted, the industry of the human race be of no avail; and let tithes, taxation, rent, national debt, and extra population be all swept off; free trade and competition have full sway; let there be but currency, let the produce of the earth be reduced to the lowest particle of price, let just one farthing support a family one whole day, let there be but coin, and labour paid in that coin, let that coin be essential to procure the necessaries of life, so long will labour, the means of getting that coin, be warred against by unrestrained machinery, so long must the human race be sacrificed; and the projectors themselves, however they may have grown rich for a time, must be involved in the general ruin, most certainly awaiting the unnatural yet universal competition that must emanate from the unrestrained production and unending power of machinery.

Machinery is a many headed reptile, the hydra of the present day, born of ambition, her foster child is

STARVATION

Monstrum horrendum, informe ingens cui lumen ademptum. [. . .]

'Letter VI'

In conclusion, I beg most forcibly to impress that CHEAP is but a relative term, a term leading to the total destruction of every human enjoyment, and of mankind. Where is the limit to man's invention, – where the limit to the power of machinery? By every new invention, by every improvement, by every increase of its power, it cheapens production, compared to manual labour; fresh bands of population are rendered surplus; fresh tracts of land appear to be required. Hence the schemes of emigration and location! Where can this end? End there can be none; for could another world approach this earth and touch, and then conjoined, could they perform their revolutions, – then could not this new world, if ready peopled, and wanting clothes and every thing but food, – then could not this "new field," opened to the power of machinery, consume its produce. For who will say, the power of machinery could not *instantly be increased*, and increased its produce far beyond the need of such new population, were they bound down by some overruling power eternally to spend their time in agriculture?

Unrestrained machinery must create surplus population. Human competition with machinery is unavailing, and humanity must sink in the unequal contest; the power of machinery must render population surplus; *and while coin is necessary to procure sustenance, and labour the means of procuring coin, so long must the surplus sink also, and cheap to them be mere mockery and delusion.*

The man who drinks *beer*, saves the expense, and can *work cheaper* than he who drinks *wine*, – the man who drinks *water* can *work cheaper* than he who drinks *beer*, – the man who lives on *vegetables, lives cheaper* than the one *indulged with animal food;* and *cheaper he* who denies himself half the plainest necessary sustenance. John Fransham (whose life is in our public library) a character well known here a few years since, by use of potatoes and salt (turnips and spring water he maintained were quite sufficient to support existence) reduced his daily meal in value to just one farthing. To this extremity must unrestrained machinery and *the cry of cheap* reduce mankind (if they can bear it); and even then their competition with machinery must be unavailing, – the poor's rate their only refuge.

Where the earth produces not spontaneously, but yields to the industry of man a fair return, that return is the *intrinsic value* of the labour; yet from the combination of circumstances labour cannot be so paid, for land wants *specie capital* as well as labour. The *intrinsic value* of the produce is equal to the value of the *capital and the labour*. If in such a country climate offers no inconveniences, and labour gets its due proportion, *there* life may be enjoyed to the full measure of happiness allotted to mankind; – that country must command the highest purchase; – THAT COUNTRY IS ENGLAND; and were machinery restrained such must be the lot of her inhabitants.

There are countries yielding *more* abundantly; – there the toil of labour is *less* and *less* the intrinsic value of the produce, although the intrinsic value of that country must be greater, yet a *worse climate* more than counterbalances these advantages. – There are countries yielding almost spontaneously sufficient food for their inhabitants. – There must land be of greatest intrinsic value: but the climate is inimical to human life, rendering its durance scarcely supportable. What can the intrinsic value of produce be in such a country? It is almost nothing, although purchased by the *sacrifice of every comfort known in temperate climes.* And shall the produce of this country be weighed in such a balance? – Shall this fine country, these fair fields, be pitted in such competition? – Is this climate no boon to us? – And are the people to be driven from their native land by this machinery, wandering emigrants in some foreign land, that they may consume the produce of this machinery, or sacrificed at home (their value measured by machinery) to the cry of cheap, the very cheapness purchased at their expence and unavailing to them?

But while unrestrained machinery exists in any country, individual self-defence opposes machinery to machinery, when the baneful effects appear as clear as "sun at noon." On that account alone can the project be countenanced of introducing to this city spinning machinery for wool. Look forward, a little, see the probable result! In Scotland, cabbages and barley form a principal article of diet: in the

North of England, rye, oats, and vegetables: in Ireland, potatoes: to the same fare the people here are fast approaching. Scotch goods are cheap, Yorkshire goods are cheap, the secret is, the *cheapness is purchased at the expence of the inhabitants*. But to compete with Scotland and the North of England, the people here must make a greater sacrifice than just their mode of living The North possesses *natural advantages* not to be purchased here. Machinery, competition, and the cry of cheap, *must render unavailing* every attempt successfully to meet their goods at market in price or quality, unless some greater sacrifice be made. *The attempt must prove abortive, or the rate of wages must be reduced* to pay the difference. No preference will be given to native workmen, *those who will work the cheapest will be the men employed;* Rye, Oat, Barley, Cabbage, and Potatoe diet, will be substituted; these will be found too dear, and Turnip diet, without salt, the less than farthing daily diet, will then be tried. But is this the end of our existence? – For this end were these beauteous isles covered with plenty? God forbid! – But compared to the power of machinery, *may this farthing diet, these turnips be too dear, and "to the cry of cheap," too dear the very oil which keeps the monster moving.*

And now, my countrymen and fellow-citizens, I have endeavoured to discharge, what from the bottom of my heart, I conceived to be a paramount duty, in pointing out the *severest, pressing, all-pervading, never-ending cause*, of your calamities. – I have endeavoured to combat the prevailing cant of the day, *falsely called the* MARCH OF INTELLECT. – I have given you in the meteorological table, a correct and comparative view of your *libelled climate*. – I have shown you the *intrinsic value* of your land. – I have shown you the relative proportion of your country to the inhabitants. – I have shown that for many generations it can supply your wants. – I have shown sufficient of the evil working of machinery, to prove it to be the HYDRA OF THE PRESENT DAY; *and that its pernicious effects far exceed all other grievances.*

Having done this, can I point out a remedy? Most certainly I can. "*Man wants but little here below, nor wants that little long.*" Better had man MARCH LORD OF THE CREATION, in his pristine nudity, or clothed in skins, contented with the *dispensations* of ALLWISE PROVIDENCE, than be cursed with machinery, deprived thereby of the blessings every where by Providence spread around; clothed in machinery's effeminating rags, scarcely sufficient to cover his emaciated form.

MACHINERY MUST BE RESTRAINED.

Unrestrained machinery demoralises society – substitutes idleness for industry – want for competence – immorality for virtue. It has pauperised the peasant, – pauperised the citizen. It has abstracted capital from agriculture; capital from manufactures. – It has abstracted money from circulation, and drawn it into heaps. – *It has created taxes*. – It has destroyed domestic trade, – domestic consumption, – domestic industry. It has concentrated the population, and collected the people into dense masses. Wherever it does give a scanty sustenance, it is in *crowded factories*, prejudicial to health; the nurseries of every evil; setting at defiance every endeavour to work moral improvement; where the very means used to that end, are marshalled in formidable array, dangerous to social happiness. Where *children* are employed in the room of *men;* and the heads of families, instead of leading in the paths of virtue, are starving, turned adrift, to sigh for departed happiness; and to meditate on desperate plans to restore their *cherished, but long-lost independence*.

Such is machinery; and unless restrained, will, ere long, involve this country in every horror and calamity attending the bursting of all the bonds that hold society together.

Fellow citizens! a minister of the crown represents you in parliament; as your representative, HE has pledged himself to listen to your complaints. *Address yourselves to him*, and he will support the prayer of your petition. Fellow citizens and countrymen! should opportunity offer, (and it may be soon,) as you value your existence, return not one man to parliament who will not pledge himself to the restriction or abolition of modern machinery, in all that in him lays. And should such occasion not offer, FORM ANTI-MACHINERY SOCIETIES *to petition, nor let your petitions cease till you get them granted.*

Fellow-citizens! Fellow-countrymen! Fellow-sufferers! Thus have I thrown down the gauntlet in defiance of the *liberal opinions* of the day; and in the hope that men of leisure and acquirements will pursue this subject in all its bearings, I beg to subscribe myself,

Your devoted servant,
THE AUTHOR.

"LET THE POOR PETITION AGAINST MACHINERY, DEPRIVED THEREBY OF DAILY BREAD. LET THE MIDDLE CLASS, FOR BY IT THEY ARE DAILY SINKING INTO POVERTY. – LET THE PHILANTHROPIST, THAT HE MAY RENDER THE HUMAN RACE MORE SERVICE. – LET THE RELIGIONIST, THAT HE MAY ASSIST IN PURGING THE COMMUNITY OF THE PROLIFIC CAUSE OF IMMORALITY; AND LET THE RICH THAT THEY MAY RETAIN THEIR POSSESSIONS."

'Appendix'

A work has just been published "*under the superintendence of a society for the diffusion of useful knowledge*," called the "WORKING MAN'S COMPANION;" or, "Results of Machinery," addressed particularly to the working men of the United Kingdom.

Curiosity has led me to enquire of various booksellers "*if working men had been the purchasers*?" The reply has uniformly been "it is a book in great request, *but working men are not the purchasers*." This one fact is additional evidence against "*cheap production*." This is a proof that machinery giving so much increased employment has not in this part of the country diffused sufficient of its benefits, to enable the *working people* here to give *one shilling* for this very cheap work, this very great bargain, although it contains 216 pages, and about 50,000 words. I almost question if the *working people* would read it if given to them, unless loaves of bread were also distributed gratis, to feed on while wading through such an assemblage of words.

What a mistake does this society labour under! They seem to think people like work for work's sake! They think people dislike machinery, from ignorance of its effects. Let the people be well fed at the expence of machinery! Make that trial! and then hear their opinions about machinery!

On reading over the names of the central and local committees of this society, I felt some misgiving (the foregoing letters were prepared for the printer, they had also been advertised) in publishing my individual opinion in point blank opposition to the doctrines of this society as set forth in this work. I have read their publication attentively, and my firm conviction is, that there are the names of many persons attached to it, who will renounce any connection with a society advocating principles to which are ascribed nearly all the evils which at present afflict society.

With a society who have taken great pains to prove the vast power of machinery! – denied by no one.

With a society who have endeavoured to prove, *cheap production, increased employment, increased consumption*, and *increased enjoyment*, go hand in hand with *unrestrained machinery*, and this in the face of increased crime and increased pauperism! See page 189.

With a society who rather than put the least restraint upon machinery encourage emigration, in other words transportation, when *they* shew the United Kingdom contains 66 acres of land to every agricultural family! See pages 167, 182, 207, 208.

With a society whose doctrine is *buy, buy – sell, sell*, without in any way shewing how sales are to be made or whence is to come the money with which to buy! See pages 74, 77, 79, 117, 186, 187, 184.

With a society whose doctrine is also *change, change, change employment*, as if people could change employments between breakfast and dinner – as if a man could lay down at night a carpenter and as a book-binder earn his next day's bread! See pages 162, 196, 197, 176.

With a society having proved that the composition between manual labour and machinery must be supported by the poor rate, immediately advocate the *propriety* of burdening the community with *eight millions poor rate*, to enable the proprietors of machinery *to make cheap goods!* See page 181.

With a society who prove machinery has it so much in its power to reward the smallest improvement, that it is of importance in making needles to save even the wages of a child! See pages 132, 165.

(Messrs. Taylors, St. George's-fields, London, have invented machines to complete pins without manual labour; these when brought into full operation will displace ten thousand hands, these 10,000 persons will be thrown upon the poor rate, until they can find a change of employment! – to what can they change?)

With a society who set ditchers to work with a mattock! who tell farmers *as they are men of capital* to combine to advance the price of corn, and when they hire land cheap, they are of *necessity to farm carelessly!* See pages 28, 46, 170, 197.

With a society who have discovered England's unhappy climate! See pages 48, 152.

With a society who encourage idleness! See page 197.

With a society who deride old age! See page 134.

With a society who endeavour to prove *strength of body* has been given man *for no purpose!* See pages 157, 158, 193.

With a society who would make mankind mere intellectual beings! See pages 147, 149, 202.

With a society who insinuate that as our forefathers had little or no machinery, they enjoyed neither health, long life, nor the blessings of Providence! See pages 141, 148, 149.

With a society comparing man, made in the image of his creator, to inanimate machinery! See pages 29, 61, 135.

With a society endeavouring to persuade the Lords of the creation that they must submit to be starved by the work of their own hands! See pages 5, 6, 180.

With a society holding up one Joseph Foster as a paragon of excellence, (surely this Foster is pensioned), because he confessed to the committee that as HE could not "*saw with his teeth, nor dig with his nails*," HE could devise no antidote for the starvation of himself, family, and fellow-workmen, by machinery, against which competition is useless! See pages 5, 6, 7, 45, 179, 180, 182.

With a society advocating cheap finery! the certain ruin of the wearers. See page 101, 104.

With a society advocating factories as conducing to health and long life! when it need not be asserted that they are the certain high road to the destruction of all health, morality, virtue, and domestic industry. See page 149.

With a society speaking of men as mere animals, of rearing them and sending them to market! See pages 23, 61.

With a society placing men in unnatural competition with animals, and, with that which is even worse, with machinery! See pages 20, 28, 61.

With a society after having proved beyond doubt that man must be reduced to the extremest misery by unavailing competition with machinery, (see pages 5, 61, 180, 181,) propose that the very men so beggared and very properly relieved as paupers, should become fundholders! should save money to invest in saving banks! to enable them, *not to combine for the advance of wages*, but to enable them to keep out of the *labour market*, "a march of intellect term," *that wages may rise!!!* See pages 197, 198.

With a society crying up the right of capital to exclusive protection!

And, finally, with a society whose watchword is "Knowledge is power!" (as if knowledge was wisdom, as if all men could be learned,) whose doctrines war with the very existence of mankind unless they can live upon iron, cotton, books, or air. God save us from such power of knowledge, and if this be the happiness of knowledge,

"IGNORANCE MUST BE BLISS."

Notes

1 'Died', *Norfolk Chronicle*, 22 February 1868, p. 5; 'Miscellaneous', *Norfolk News*, 8 March 1856, p. 1.
2 G. C. Burrows, *A Word to Electors. Letters to the Present Generation on the Unrestrained Use of Modern Machinery Particularly Addressed to my Countrymen and Fellow Citizens* (Norwich: Wilkin and Fletcher, 1832), Gale, *Making of the Modern World*: GALE|U0104831809, p. 4.
3 Burrows, *A Word to Electors*, p. 5.
4 Burrows, *A Word to Electors*, p. 5.
5 J. B. Say, *A Treatise on Political Economy: Or the Production, Distribution, and Consumption of Wealth*, 6th American ed. (Philadelphia: Grigg & Elliott, 1834, orig. 1803), p. 138.
6 Burrows, *A Word to Electors*, p. 23.
7 Burrows, *A Word to Electors*, p. 25.
8 For Victorian models of masculinity, see J. Tosh, *Manliness and Masculinities in Nineteenth-Century Britain: Essays on Gender, Family, and Empire* (New York: Pearson Longman, 2005).
9 Burrows, *A Word to Electors*, p. 28.

14

DEBATING POLITICAL ECONOMY AND THE CONDITION OF THE HANDLOOM WEAVERS

George Poulett Scrope (1797–1876) was a geologist who also had a career as a member of Parliament (1833–1867) and magistrate for Stroud in Gloucestershire. While he was a proponent of free trade, his familiarity with the struggles of agricultural labourers led him to condemn the Poor Law (see Volume 2 Introduction) and to maintain fairly open views about social welfare. He believed that the fundamental purpose of sound economic measures was to help the poor.[1] This source, which was published by the Hand-loom Worsted Weavers of Bradford, contains Scrope's response to a petition by the weavers and the weavers' reply to Scrope.[2] From Scrope's letter (14.1), we understand that his sympathies towards workers did not stretch so far as to regulate machinery and wages, for that would be a clear violation of classical economics. Scrope tells the handloom weavers that they were 'delusive' to ask for restraints on machinery,[3] since machinery made labour more perfect and thus improved the condition of workers. Specifically, machinery was the product of labour, and the wealth it created went back to the workers. The thing holding labourers back was not machinery, but rather restrictions on free exchange and the overproduction of non-essential goods. Scrope recommends that the handloom weavers and others whose industries could not contribute to the needs of the nation – the production of food – should emigrate to the colonies and become agriculturalists (see Volume 4, Part 1 on emigration). Scrope was known and criticized for seeing emigration as the answer to poverty and social problems more generally.[4] It is worth noting that at the very beginning of the letter, Scrope condemns 'Mr. Maxwell' (the author of Volume 1, Part 2, Chapter 15) among 'men of station' for supporting the handloom weavers' cause.[5]

The Hand-Loom Weavers' Central Committee wrote a biting response to Scrope in the *Poor Man's Guardian* (14.2),[6] telling Scrope that his reply suggested that the weavers either return to a state of barbarism by scrounging a living from the land or blindly follow Scrope's ideas of political economy. They point to Scrope's hypocrisy in claiming that workers would see the rewards of the wealth produced by machine labour, calling the idea 'not apparently honest'.[7] Workers, rather than receiving rewards, were either unemployed or suffering

 DOI: 10.4324/9780429320323-18

from low wages. Free trade and the increase in machinery led to weavers being overworked and experiencing a poorer standard of living. The letter accuses Scrope's economic ideas of destroying English agriculture and his support for unrestrained machinery and emigration of giving preference to foreign goods. Mocking his thinking on emigration, the letter proposes that Scrope should go first to clear the land and make it habitable, rather than leave that work to the 'burdensome' of society.[8] The weavers declare that they would not be leaving England, even if the screws of the Poor Law were tightened. They make their economic position political, demanding the householder vote directly in terms of their relationship to machinery.[9] The weavers ask to limit the hours machines can be worked by law to those 'assigned by the law to the liberated West Indian slaves',[10] in order to have time with their families, presenting themselves as good Christians and men. This source is important in showing the handloom weavers as agents in their own struggle, as opposed to passive victims ruined by the force of circumstances.

14.1 The Letter of George Poulett Scrope, Esq., M.P. to the Chairman of the Central Committee of the Hand Loom Worsted Weavers, of the West-Riding of York: With Their Answer to the Same.

Advertisement

The Hand-Loom Worsted Weavers, having the full permission of Mr. Scrope to publish his Letter, have now to present the same to the Public, with their Answer, which has been discussed and approved by a Special Meeting.

They consider, that both the Letter and the Reply are entitled to the serious consideration of all Working Men, of all Statesmen, of all who value their Liberties as Britons, or their Privileges as Christians.

They will be glad to receive any communications likely to be of any service to them, addressed to Jeremiah Dewhirst, 6, Chapel-Lane, Bradford, Yorkshire.

Bradford, Yorkshire, May 15*th*, 1835.

TO MR. JEREMIAH DEWHIRST, CHAIRMAN OF THE CENTRAL COMMITTEE OF THE WORSTED WEAVERS, OF THE WEST-RIDING OF YORK.

Castle-Combe, Chippenham, Wiltshire,
April 25*th*, 1835.

SIR,

I HAVE lately received, and beg to acknowledge, the Copy of a Petition of the Hand Loom Weavers of Bradford, for a *Legislative Restraint* on *Machinery*, and *Regulation of Wages*.

I am very sorry to find large bodies of the respectable Operatives of the North, entertaining such delusive notions as to the *causes* of their distress, and the remedies to be applied to it. I still more regret to find men of station, like MR. MAXWELL and some others giving encouragement, (though no doubt from the best of motives, and under the influence of similar delusions, to the propagation of such *exploded fallacies*.

If Machinery is to be restrained by law, where will you stop? At the Power Loom? Why there? Was not the spinning Jenny as destructive of the employment of children and women, who used to turn a spinning wheel at their cottage door? MAY THEY NOT WITH AS MUCH RIGHT CALL FOR A RESTRICTION OF *ALL* MACHINERY? And why not put down *all wheels*, and spin with the fingers only? Why not ploughs and spades, and DIG WITH THE NAILS?

Machinery of every kind, is only the instrument more or less perfect, with which man produces what he wants. The more they enable men to produce by the least expenditure of labour, the more perfect the instrument. Are we then to restrain the most perfect instrument in order to keep up the use of the less perfect? Then let us at once prohibit knives, hatchets, and spades, and let us TEAR FROM THE

WOODS AND THE SOIL WHAT WE REQUIRE WITH OUR BARE NAILS AND FINGERS.

All Machinery is itself the produce OF LABOUR, and THE MONEY PAID TO THE PRODUCER OF GOODS WROUGHT BY THE POWER LOOM, GOES JUST AS MUCH TO REWARD LABOUR, AS IF IT WERE PAID TO HAND-LOOM WEAVERS. It goes certainly to one set of labourers instead of another. But these changes and shiftings are necessarily incident to all *improvements*.

EVERY IMPROVEMENT IN THE ARTS OUGHT TO IMPROVE (NOT LOWER) THE CONDITION OF THE WORKING CLASSES OF THE COUNTRY IN WHICH IT OCCURS, and this would be the result, were it not for two classes of obstructions, and these are the real causes of the *distress* your friends complain of. They are,

1. Financial Restrictions on the *free exchange* of the produce of British skill, labour, and ingenuity (in which Britons so far excel all the people of the earth) with the produce of other countries, more fitted by nature than Britain, (through climate, soil, &c.) for their production.

If the manufacturers of Britain could *import, duty free*, or at *low duties*, the corn, cheese, tea, coffee, sugar, timber, tallow, &c. they consume, there would be probably little complaint heard of a want of due remuneration for their industry. THE HAND-LOOM WEAVERS WOULD SET TO WORK AT POWER-LOOMS, to work for the Americans, Chinese, &c. who would pay them well in *their* produce for their labour – and the more goods they were able to produce, by help of the *power-looms*, (or any further invention if such should *happily* be discovered) the more would they receive of good things in return from their foreign customers.

2. But if the *demand* of foreigners be not sufficient (together with the home demand) to take off the goods so made, as fast as British ingenuity and invention allows of their being produced – if the Americans or Chinese cannot produce corn, and tea, and sugar, as fast as we produce cloths, and cottons, and cutlery, for their markets, and our exchange with them is *not* therefore *remunerating* to us, this only proves that we are OVERDOING our peculiar branch of industry – the *manufacturing* as it is called (though every thing is manufactured more or less, corn as well as cotton) and that a part of our productive powers *ought to be diverted* to the production of those articles which are deficient, instead of continuing to add to the glut by producing more and more of those that are in excess. Our industry should be diverted in part to procure those supplies of primary articles of consumption (food especially) of which there is an evident deficiency, since our operatives are unable to get enough for their wants, in return for a continually increasing supply of the actual produce of their industry.

Now the quantity of food produceable *from this island* it is not easy to increase, owing to its limited extent, and that its good soils are all fully cultivated (those yet untilled being too poor to return the costs of cultivation.) But *in our Colonies* – (which ought to be looked upon as *outlying Counties of Britain* – integral portions of our Empire as much as the Isles of Wight or Man,) in our Colonies (especially Canada, which is at no great distance) we have endless tracts of the most fertile soil, capable of returning tenfold the costs of its cultivation. If then the returns of *manufacturing* industry are not profitable to the operatives engaged in it, at any time, if their wages, in other words, are too low, a portion of them ought to betake themselves to AGRICULTURE – to the production of food, for themselves and their brother manufacturers here, *not in this country*, (where the agricultural labour-market is equally glutted with its manufacturing) *but in the Colonies*, where agricultural labour is so valuable from the largeness of its produce. In one word, if your HAND-LOOM WEAVERS cannot earn (as you say) more than five or six shillings a week, clear of charges, in this country, let them EMIGRATE to the Colonies, where their labour in agriculture will bring them in *five* times that sum. This enormous relative difference between the returns of labour on this side and the other side of the Atlantic, is *in itself and alone a proof* of the cause of the evil, (viz. the redundancy of labour here, and its deficiency there,) and an index to the natural remedy, viz. the transference of the excess of the one part of the British empire to supply the deficiency of the other. By this the whole evil would be cured on both sides. The increased production of corn, &c. in the Colonies, will give fresh employment (by exchange) to the producers of manufactures here – the balance will be redressed, and the remuneration of industry of both kinds rendered secure and ample.

Without going further into this question, what I have said will shew you that I agree entirely with the Committee of the House of Commons, who in 1818, I think, declared *Emigration* to be the only true remedy for the distress of the Hand-Loom Weavers.

My recommendation to that class is, that they should petition Government and the Legislature TO AFFORD THEM FACILITIES TO EMIGRATE, I think *every distressed labourer* of this country, who is unable to live and maintain his family by his industry *has a claim on the institutions of his country* FOR A FREE PASSAGE *to such of its colonies*, as offer the certain means of maintenance for them, and where he and they can become useful members of society instead of *a burthen* and a *discredit* to it.

14.2 To George Poulett Scrope, Esq., M.P.

6, Chapel-lane, Bradford, Yorkshire,

May 11th, 1835.

SIR, – The hand-loom worsted weavers are greatly obliged by the reply you have given to their request that you would support their petition; for although you refuse to do so, you have candidly explained the reasons of your conduct. Your letter, in this point of view, has given us all great satisfaction, because, though we cannot subscribe to your doctrines, it is honest and candid, and fairly lets us know what we have to expect, if "the soundest principles of political economy" prevail.

Many public men are not half so honest; and we venture to guess, that several who have fallen in our way would say "Amen" to every part of your doctrine, but for the base fear of being unpopular. You have not recommended us, as a certain M.P. did the Glasgow weavers, "to find other trades;" but you tell us at once that we must clear off, to make way for the machinery of the capitalist. You, Sir, deserve better at our hands than these, for you speak right out. We shall venture, without any intention to be disrespectful, to do the same.

You are opposed to all restraint of any kind of machinery, and that because, in your opinion, its freest and most extensive use is certain to be most beneficial to all mankind.

But, Sir, it was not necessary, in arguing this principle, to [Illegible Text] as you do, into absurdities and extremes, and to set a trap in the way of the unwary labourer, who is not up to the quirks and shifts of logicians and casuists like yourself – who has no time to study those subtleties which are used by you to support and elucidate "the soundest principles of political economy." Is it not a bare imposition to tell us we had as good tear what we want from the woods, and the soil with our nails, thus assuming that a man must be an out-and-out disciple of yours, or else turn barbarian? We could not, if we would, adopt your recommendation. Our barbarous forefathers might and could have done it, for they were Nature's own children, hardy and strong; but we, the children, or we had rather said, the slaves, of so much mis-directed "science," are no longer an athletic race. Our best blood is drained away by scientific avarice, whose prescription of long hours and short wages upon "the soundest principles of political economy," we have been forced to take, till we have degenerated into women in physical strength, and into children in understanding. But, Sir, barbarism, in our estimation, would be preferable to that sort of civilization which you prescribe; and therefore, if yourself and other honest and well-instructed members of Parliament and political economists, whose cupboards and cellars are always well stored, who live well and lie warm, and whose tables are never tainted with "our coarser food," will come and show us how it is done, we are willing to return to a state of nature again; and when you have taught us to "dig with our nails," and other barbarous usages, we will freely consent that you should take all this system of unrestrained machinery and capital to the "outlying counties," and the fairer plains of Canada and Australia. This, we hope, is a modest request; we resign the best part of the empire to such scientific gentlemen as yourself; leave us the secondary and less happy soils of the British islands, and we have no doubt that in a few generations, when our children have ceased to be torn from their beds at five o'clock every morning, and to be confined in the unwholesome atmosphere of these modern bastiles for thirteen or fifteen hours a day, we shall recover our strength both of body and mind, and be able once more to gain the honest point of our ambition – a fair reward for a fair day's work, and reasonable time for the enjoyment of religious, literary, and social blessings.

To one of your principles we fully assent. You say, "Every improvement in the arts ought to improve (not lower) the condition of the working classes of the country in which it occurs." But, of this "improvement," we may say as Pope did – "Alas! my dear Sir, I am dying every day of the most *favourable* symptoms."

The reason you assign for our not experiencing this benefit is, that we have not as yet taken freely enough of free trade and emigration.

Now, Sir, allow us to state our general views of the right use of machinery, and our sentiments upon free trade, and upon emigration.

1. There is a marked distinction between implements used by man, and whose motion is derived from human or animal power, and those machines which are moved by inanimate power.

The human or animal agent, or moving power, consumes in a large degree; the mechanical or inanimate power occasions consumption in a very small degree.

Allow for the consumption of those men or animals who originally contributed their labour or skill to make the machine, and then calculate its production as compared with the consumption resulting from it; and compare that consumption again with what would have been consumed, if the same production had been effected by animate or human power. This comparative view will soon establish a manifest distinction between what is called machinery and such implements as the "spade" and the "plough," the "hatchet" and the "knife," which in your letter are all (excuse us if we say) absurdity confounded together.

"Machinery (to use the words of an eloquent witness before the Committee of last Session) ought to be the slave of man." To this we agree. And if there was a deficiency of population to produce what could be consumed at home, or exported abroad, so as to give a good and sufficient maintenance to the producers, we would consent freely to that portion of work being done by inanimate power, without restraint as to time, or the imposition of taxation, which there were not men in existence to perform. Then machinery would be the slave and the benefactor of man. But your principle, if fairly followed out, is to give machinery its full fling in the midst of, what is called by political economists, "a superabundant population." It is to be allowed to plant its gigantic foot, and to swing its colossal arms where and as it listeth, and to throw out of employ as many human beings as may serve the temporary interests of its proprietors to cast aside. If 800,000 hand-loom weavers obstruct its path, your remedy is to move them off to Canada or Australia, and you tell us a "bridge" of "frigates" is ready. But, Sir, if we do go, will not the monster soon follow us, and chase us nearer still to creation's verge? Did it ever occur to you, Sir, that the world itself has bounds, and that, following up this principle, your steam Leviathan, like a second Alexander, will soon cry out for another world to desolate and to conquer?

But you say – "All machinery is the produce of labour, and the money paid to the producers of goods wrought by the power-loom, goes just as much to reward labour as if it were paid to the hand-loom weavers."

Now, Sir, this is really not apparently honest. You dare not say that "just as much money goes to reward labour" – this, you well know, is not the case. You dare not say – "human labour is supplanted by machinery." You do say, indeed, that we are overdoing our peculiar branch of industry; but you attribute the inconvenience to the scarcity of agricultural produce! And yet our barns, and stack-yards, and granaries, and warehouses are full to overflowing! How is this?

The fact is, Sir, as far as the dense population of manufacturing districts is concerned, there is no lack of room in our stomachs for the farmer's corn, meat, cheese, &c.; but there is lack of money in our pockets to buy them: one cause of which is, that machinery, unrestrained in the time of its working, and untaxed in its productions, has either thrown us out of the market of employment, or else, has reduced us to that condition, that we cannot afford to consume the produce of our agricultural countrymen.

This being the case, the farmer having no demand for his corn, &c., at a remunerating price, he has, in many cases, given up growing it. If we had money to buy it, he would soon grow it again, and we should find him the best customer for our cloths, cottons, and woollens.

You would have us to believe, that our low wages are a proof of the scarcity of food!!!

You, Sir, live in an agricultural district, and we dare say you have seen a vast number of ragged, or half-clad agricultural labourers and families. What is the cause of that? Is it scarcity of cloth, cotton, and worsted pieces? No! It is their poverty – want of money to go to market with. The whole cause of their misery and ours too, is, that the laws of this country have ceased to protect industry; *they tax it, but do not protect it; they protect capital, but will not tax it*. Now, Sir you may be much wiser than we are, but we fancy if corn goes on at five shillings or four shillings a bushel, a little longer, such estates-men as yourself will have to go to the "pop-shops" of the great money-mongers (as we have often had to go to the little ones before you), and you will learn in the dear school of experience, that the way to uphold the pinnacles and ornamental spires of the social building, is not to put the maul into the hands of the great steam-giant, and then to set him, or the capitalist, to bruise and batter the broad stones (the industrious people) which form the firm basis of the edifice. When the rough foundations are destroyed, the polished and gilded superstructure cannot stand, and the capitalist, though perched upon the pinnacles, will fall.

2. But now for our views of the free trade system.

Really, Sir, we are puzzled with your principles. We cannot see of what use it is to go to foreign countries for any thing which we can produce in our own; nor can we see what good it would do, to pull down agriculture in England that we may build it up in Canada. Your project is directly calculated to diminish agriculture here, to increase machinery, to transport the best consumers, depending chiefly upon foreign markets both for corn and for customers. Is, then, England to become the workshop and manufactory of the world? Have the European nations, have the American nations, have the Asiatic nations, agreed to allow us this monopoly, or this precedency? Or do we exclusively possess the means of attaining or maintaining such a position? What, if other nations choose to manufacture for themselves? They have the power to do it to a very great extent; they love and value their independence of us, if we do not appreciate the advantage of being independent of them. Your's, Sir, is a very grand plot – a famous theory – but how will you get at it? The continental manufactures are increasing, the continental competition waxes warmer and warmer. Our machinery is allowed to go abroad by wholesale, our wool is gone, our breed of cattle is gone, our yarns and unfinished manufactures go abroad daily in large quantities; and thus, whilst we are sending work to employ the French, the Swiss, and others, thousands of our own people are wanting employment at home; and you, Sir, bid the British depart to the Canadas! Ship after ship, full of emigrants, sails out, whilst the returning tide brings, either an equal number of Irish labourers in their places, or else, cargoes of continental goods, in weaving which, the continental labourers have been preferred to our own! Truly, Sir, we are puzzled. It seems to us equally foolish, as if the head of a family should send his up-grown sons off, to seek employment and bread, and then set to work those of a stranger in their places.

And pray, Sir, how are we to come on, if we should chance to fall out, and get involved in a war with our continental neighbours! How should we fare if we had no foreign customers for the produce of our machinery, and not sufficient corn on our islands, when hostile fleets were intercepting our exports and imports? Pray, Sir, how do "the soundest principles of political economy" secure us against these very probable consequences? We say, "secure us," for we have heard, or read, of the good luck they promise us in such straits; but we want security, not chance. We have a saying, that "chance provides a poor meal." We ought to trust firmly in Divine Providence; but this we have no right to do, if we neglect to exercise common prudence.

You, perhaps, will reply to this, "If you fetter competition (the living principle of all improvement), you destroy all industry at a blow." (Page 6.) But, Sir, "competition," foreign and domestic, has already nearly "destroyed industry," not "at a blow," but by incessant blows. How will you account for the facts that appear in the return made to Parliament, in the session 1830 (No. 243), and which Professor M'Cullock has inserted in his Commercial Dictionary. We give an extract from it: –

EXPORTS.

British and Irish Produce and Manufactures from Great Britain.

Years ending January 5th.	*Official Value, which is fixed, and refers to the Quantity.*	*Declared Value, which varies, and refers to the Prices.*
	£	£
1799	18,556,891	31,252,836
1809	24,179,854	36,306,385
1815	32,200,580	43,447,373
1825	48,024,952	37,600,021
1830	55,465,723	35,212,873

A weaver will understand this, by supposing that the millions represent so many score hanks in the second column, and so many shillings in the third.

Behold here, how competition has "fettered" industry or else how should a weaver in 1830, have to put in 55 score hanks for 35s., when, in 1815, he had 43s. for putting in 32 score? And yet since then his work has increased, and his wages decreased at least 20 per cent! This general view of our unprofitable foreign trade, on average, is confirmed by the facts, derived from a source equally authentic, referring to the cotton trade.

In the Year.	*The Manufactures had for Wages, Expenses, and Profits*	*For working up every week.*	*According to the Rate of 1815, they ought to have had*
	£	Bags	£
1815	13,007,778	6,500	
1824	12,683,829	11,500	23,013,761
1831	10,925,210	16,300	32,311,812
1832	10,251,926	17,300	34,620,701

Thus is it proved, that the rewards of industry have diminished as its exertions have increased. Nearly three times as much work is done in 1832 as was done in 1815, for considerably less wages than was given for one-third of that quantity in 1815.

Is not this a grand picture of "improvement?" Such are the glorious fruits of the "free-exchange" system, as far as it has gone.

You tell us, that if this system was extended to the utmost, "the more goods we were able to produce by the power looms for any further invention, if such should happily be discovered, the more we should receive of good things in return, from our foreign customer." (Page 4.) If there be any truth in this theory, why have the rewards and profits of industry decreased as production has increased?

You say (Page 6), "the working classes must be the first to profit by any thing which enables them to command more of the good things of life, for a less amount of toil;" and you state that this should be the effect of "every improvement of machinery on the arts." But, Sir, our experience tells quite another tale. This "promise has long been made to the ear, but broken to the hope." Our toil has augmented with the multiplication of machinery. You may tell us that, notwithstanding, great fortunes have been made by manufacturers. True; but how made? By honest means – by giving the labourer his rightful reward? By a humane and Christian use of his services? No, Sir; fortunes, great fortunes have been made, great piles of gold have been raised, but have left a wide waste of poverty and wretchedness all around them.

And does this prove that capital, instead of feeding industry when left unrestrained, feeds like a vampire upon industry.

Again, you say (Page 6) "Depend upon it, the more easily we can produce, the more we shall have among us to consume;" and yet, in another breath, you recommend a million of "consumers" to transport themselves on your "Atlantic bridge" to a distant land! There, they who clear away, will seldom live to sow, they may sow, but not reap; plant, but not gather; build, but not inhabit! And for what? That a few capitalists at home may monopolise the glorious advantage of a "free-exchange" system. [. . .]

3. And now, Sir, we come to your magnificent "cure-all" for all our many woes – Emigration. [. . .]

Really, sir, you do write with marvellous coolness of transporting "every distressed labourer," now "a burden and discredit" to society; and about "the transfer of indigent labourers from the British islands to the British colonies;" and yet labour without capital is declared to be worth nothing! *We* are to sail – we, the "indigent" "distressed" – we that are the "burden and discredit" of our country (and pray who made us so?) and when we get over the great Salt Pond, what are we to have? "Abundance of rich land to be had for asking there!!" In other words, "Live horse and thou shalt eat grass." We are to sit down beside an impenetrable forest – to teach the art of emigration to its present four-footed possessors – to fell its firs and pines – and to "tear from the soil" those magnificent stumps which now encumber it; and when all this is done (ah! "*when*" indeed) we are to have 4s. a day – if – if wages do not drop 15 per cent. several times over before then, by reason of competition and increased "Immigration?" as they recently did in Van Diemen's Land! See *Governor Arthur's Dispatch*, dated January, 1834.

And for a share in this lottery, we are to go down upon our knees to Parliament, and most humbly crave their clemency and charity, to grant to us, out of those taxes which have been wrung from our very sinews and bones, and which have been paid from an "Excise" of almost every morsel we have eaten – we are to implore that the "Atlantic may be bridged over," with the extorted fruits of our own toil, and that we may enjoy "a free passage" in some of his Majesty's "rotting" "frigates" to the delightful regions of the "outlying counties!?" Dear sir! – do set us the example first, and go yourself. It seems to us that the great capitalists want the poor – the "burdensome" and the "discreditable," to go to these wilds, and want to drive out also the little capitalist, to clear the woods, and gather out the stones and stumps "with their nails and fingers; and then they, "the Gods," – will come afterwards, with their long purses and golden sceptres, and say to them, "These lands are ours – we will buy them – without our capital ye can do no good!"

But, sir, we have done for the present: we thank you for your right honest letter; we believe it will do more to open the eyes of the working classes than any thing that has appeared for many years.

We beg you to oppose our petition, since you cannot support it; you are a more honest opponent than we have yet found; as such we respect you. But, sir, do not mistake us – build the "bridge" if you like – we will not go – we'll die here, where we were born. You may twitch the amended Poor Laws tighter, if you can, round the throats and bellies of the poor; and you may send your grenadiers to "dragoon" the conscripts for emigration, but our native shores we leave not, though bullets fly, and bayonets bristle all around us. Here we will die, here we will live. So find another scheme. We have found one already. Our request is reasonable. If you will tax labour, then give direct representation to labour, and let each householder have a vote, and the Ballot to protect it. And if you will not tax machinery, either by limiting its time, or otherwise, then let every holder of it be disfranchised. If you will not tax property, then let industry have the power of taxing itself. We ask but for fair play – we are willing to work, to live in peace, and obey the laws – but not to starve, and not to "shove off."

Let there be a "bridge" of "free conveyance for those who *choose* to go," as you say, but let there be also a good day's wages for a fair day's work for those who "*choose*" to stay.

Restore the constitutional principle of the Poor Laws.

Restrain the working of machinery to reasonable hours – not exceeding those assigned by the law to the liberated West Indian slaves. Give us time to worship God, to instruct our families, and to learn our duties, as Christians and as citizens.

Ye legislators! "Cease to do evil, learn to do well, seek judgment, relieve the oppressed;" practice Christianity, that it may be respected and honoured, and that this nation may enjoy the smile of that God, who is the patron of the poor and the avenger of the oppressed.

Signed for the Hand-Loom Weavers' Central Committee,
Jeremiah Dewhirst, Chairman.

P.S. We understand you are a great advocate for Irish poor laws. We wish for them too. But would it not be much more consistent with "the soundest principles of political economy," to send the "burthensome" and "discreditable" Irish over your "bridge" to Canada at once?

Notes

1 M. Rudwick, 'Scrope, George Julius Poulett [*formerly* George Julius Thompson]', *Oxford Dictionary of National Biography*, 4 October 2007, at https://doi-org.du.idm.oclc.org/10.1093/ref:odnb/24956 [accessed 13 June 2021].

2 On the condition of the handloom weavers, see Volume 1 Introduction.

3 G. P. Scrope, *Political Economy versus the Hand Loom Weavers, the Letter of George Poulett Scrope, Esq., M.P., to the Chairman of the Central Committee of the Hand Loom Worsted Weavers* (Bradford, UK: H. Wardman, 1835), Senate House Library: [G.L] B.835.

4 Rudwick, 'Scrope'.

5 Rudwick, 'Scrope'.

6 The *Poor Man's Guardian* was 'Published in protest of the stamp tax and vendors were often imprisoned' (quoted in '*Poor Man's Guardian*', British Newspaper Archive, at www.britishnewspaperarchive.co.uk/titles?title_search=poor+man [accessed 5 June 2021]).

7 J. Dewhirst, 'To George Poulett Scrope, Esq., M.P.', *Poor Man's Guardian*, 1 August 1835, British Library, p. 619.

8 Dewhirst, 'To George Poulett Scrope', p. 621.

9 Chartists would soon be tying the economic condition of the working class to their disenfranchisement. See Volume 1 Introduction.

10 Dewhirst, 'To George Poulett Scrope', p. 621. On the rhetoric of slavery in relation to factory work, see M. Cunliffe, *Chattel Slavery and Wage Slavery: The Anglo-American Context, 1830–1860* (Athens: University of Georgia Press, 1979).

15

J. MAXWELL, *MANUAL LABOUR VERSUS MACHINERY*

(London: Cochrane and M'Crone, 1834), pp. 6–9, 12–15, 17–29, 31

Sir John Maxwell (1791–1865) was a great advocate both in and out of Parliament for protecting the unemployed handloom weavers.[1] He served as the Whig member for Renfrewshire from 1818 to 1830 and then represented Paisley from 1832 to 1837 in the first reformed Parliament (see General Introduction), for which he was an active campaigner. The committee he called for in the document included here was indeed seated as the Select Committee on Hand-Loom Weavers (1834–1835), and Maxwell served as chairman. Government opposition to state intervention and wage controls was strong, however, so the bill Maxwell introduced for protection went nowhere. He led a second committee and introduced a second bill, with the same result.[2] Maxwell believed in the protectionist power of government to regulate wages, going against free-market, liberal currents. He mentions in his preface that the weavers were requesting some kind of legislative interference to help them, rather than resorting to 'factious and intimidating associations',[3] which Maxwell most likely broadcasted to promote their respectability.[4] He was taking his case to the public, since he initially received little attention in Parliament or the press. He believed that the fact that weavers were suffering while manufacturers prospered was an 'imperfect prosperity',[5] a potential danger to the nation and empire, as workers left England to find better jobs abroad or starved at home. Maxwell declares that strict economist positions went against utilitarian theory that promised 'the greatest possible happiness to the greatest number', stating that theory should always be subsumed to human needs and not vice versa.[6] He contends that if one manufacturer lowered wages, all others would follow, leading to a constant downward pressure on wages. Arguing that the government had already intervened in the economy by 'increas[ing] the salaries of judges, the pay of troops, and the value of money; fix[ing] a minimum price of corn, and even on the fares of wherries and hackney coaches', Maxwell asks, 'why should man alone be excluded from your system of protection?'[7] In asking this question, he makes John Locke's argument that labour, for a working man, is his property.[8] He then extends this argument to claim that protecting wages was

DOI: 10.4324/9780429320323-19

like protecting property rights. He condemns the idea, which he believes was prevalent in the House of Commons, that increased wages would damage trade. He also uses rhetoric emphasizing the sacrifices the weavers had made by serving the nation in war, appealing emotively to the distress of wives and children and stressing the humiliation of the Poor Law's workhouse (see Volume 2 Introduction). Maxwell appends documents of affidavits to provide 'first-hand' evidence of the suffering of the weavers from their own testimony and the testimony of those, like churchmen, who witnessed their experiences.

Manual Labour Versus Machinery

Preface.

It may be necessary to state *why* this Speech, and the appalling Facts contained in the Appendix, are laid before the Public.

No one who looks to the structure of society will deny, that on the well-being and content of the working classes depend the prosperity and happiness of the nation in the aggregate: the hand-loom weavers form a large and exceedingly valuable portion of the community; their numbers (including families) have been estimated, by competent authorities, at 800,000, but reducing the number so low as 500,000 it may be fairly contended that the condition of half-a-million of our fellow-subjects is deserving of the prompt and assiduous interference of the government and legislature: – not merely in reference to numbers, but because the existence of rapidly progressing misery, in a large section of the people, cannot long remain confined within the originating sphere, like contagious physical miasmata, it is scattered around with fearful velocity, thus extending and implanting the germs of moral disease and disorganization, among the more healthy, or rather less tainted, members of the social fabric.

To obtain a Committee of Inquiry, into the cause of this misery, and into the practicability of the measures proposed for its relief, by the suffering petitioners, was the object of the following Speech, which (together with the facts adduced in support of the motion), was scarcely, if at all, noticed by the "*Press*," from the late hour at which it was unavoidably brought forward. The case of these unfortunate petitioners is now therefore presented to the public, in the hope that the positive existence of a great amount of human misery, will command, not merely sympathy, but an active interference, on behalf of sufferers, who, depending less upon factious and intimidating associations, wisely (it is to be hoped) preferred seeking an alleviation of their distress, from the beneficence and forethought of Parliament.

The facts given in the Appendix speak volumes – they indicate, more strongly than language can express, the imperative necessity of demonstrating to the People, that a British Parliament, is omnipotent to save, as well as to destroy.

SPEECH

ON MOVING FOR A

Committee of Parliamentary Inquiry

INTO THE PETITIONS AND DISTRESS OF

HALF-A-MILLION HAND-LOOM WEAVERS.

Sir,

IN asking for a Committee of Inquiry into the causes of the distress of 500,000 hand-loom weavers,[1] I shall remind the House of the passage in the Speech of our

Gracious Sovereign, wherein His Majesty says, "I shall feel it my duty to co-operate with you in such legislative improvements as may be necessary to remove any grievances under which *any portion* of my subjects may be labouring." I remind the House of this emphatic and encouraging announcement in order that these artisans may not impute any want of sympathy, – any wish to withold them relief where a contrary desire is not only felt but declared at the very commencement of the Session, and in order to let the representatives of these most suffering and meritorious artisans know that every proposition for their benefit would receive a prompt and willing support and sanction from the Crown.

I am aware that there is in this branch of the Legislature a real or an assumed opinion that no aid can be given to these petitioners, and that the mode of relief which the prayer of their petitions point out,[2] would introduce a system of regulation of the prices of their productions and of their labour, which would fetter trade and not secure the object they seek – "the best wages that their employers could afford *without injury to the general interests of manufactures and the welfare of the empire.*"

It is to bring this difference of opinion between the working classes and this House under discussion, that I have felt it my duty to move for a Committee of Inquiry, more particularly because many of these artisans have no direct representation, and therefore have a stronger claim to the attention of every individual in this assembly, who has the maintenance of existing institutions at heart.

That my impression of the justice and the expediency of complying with these petitioners' wish may have some weight, I shall quote the words of Mr. Pitt on the subject of the Arbitration Act: "*The time will come when manufactures will have been so long established, and the Operatives not having any other business to flee to, that it will be in the power of any one man in a town to reduce the wages, and all the other manufacturers must follow. Then, when* YOU ARE GOADED WITH REDUCTIONS AND MADE WILLING TO FLEE YOUR COUNTRY, FRANCE AND AMERICA WILL RECEIVE YOU WITH OPEN ARMS, AND THEN, FAREWELL TO OUR COMMERCIAL SUPERIORITY. IF EVER IT DOES ARRIVE AT THIS PITCH, PARLIAMENT, IF IT BE NOT THEN SITTING, OUGHT TO BE CALLED TOGETHER; AND IF IT CANNOT REDRESS YOUR GRIEVANCES, ITS POWER IS AT AN END. TELL ME NOT THAT PARLIAMENT CANNOT, IT IS OMNIPOTENT TO PROTECT."

The time to try the power of this House is arrived. The petitioners declare that, "it is in the power of any one man to reduce the wages, and all the other manufacturers must follow." No manufacturer will deny this necessity to follow reduction; no theorist can deny it. I will add that the hand-loom weavers are not only goaded by these reductions, but that *many of them have fled to France and America,* that those who have not yet fled, and "have no other trade to flee to," – are too ill clothed in many instances to be able to go to church, to send their children to school, or to enforce those habits of life and principles of morality, without which this empire can neither be happy nor powerful. I will leave to the manufacturers to say, whether we are or are not "bidding farewell to our commercial prosperity." It appears to me that *if there be prosperity to the employer*, there ought *not to be such adversity to the employed:*[3] let us at all events devote our immediate and fullest efforts to ascertain the causes of such imperfect prosperity, to demonstrate the necessity or advantage of its continuance – or endeavour to make the alleged prosperity mutual.

If the nation or the state derive benefit by this paralytic sort of prosperity, let that benefit be made manifest to these petitioners. Let it be proved that their privations contribute "to the safety, honour, and welfare of his Majesty and his dominions." Let them have no doubt that such sacrifices are beneficial to their neighbours, – that the desire of their Sovereign to "*co-operate in removing their grievances*," must neither be gratified, nor awaken corresponding feelings in Members of this House, because the interests of humanity and the dictates of religion impede the march of sound principles and an enlightened policy!

Let us not for some temporary or abstract doctrine of political economy, forget the first and unalterable principles of good government – encouragement to virtue and industry, and the greatest possible happiness to the greatest number. If the Sabbath was made for man, and not man for the Sabbath, how much more should any mere human theory be made subservient to his well being. [. . .]

This lamentable ambition, lauded under the title of *enterprize*, may proceed from no higher source than an overreaching and mercenary spirit. The petitioners tell you that this avaricious spirit exists, and that a destructive practice, emanating from such unworthy feelings, is in extensive operation. They implore you not to leave them a prey to it. They do not ask you to force their employers to give a price for their labour which their employer cannot, with adequate profit afford, or the consumer pay; but they do ask you *to foster their nascent efforts, to secure unto themselves as much remuneration as their labour fairly entitles them to, or as machinery and taxes will permit, and the alledged prosperity of commerce justify*. In this request, let me remind the house, is conveyed a mark of confidence which it should not rashly impair, lest, like Mr. Pitt, these confiding sufferers may exclaim "Our powers are at an end!"

Did they ask to be relieved from all taxes on their industry, the fundholder, the civil and military and naval servants of the state might refuse them enquiry. – Did they ask for free trade in corn, sugar, woollens or banking, the landowners, colonial proprietors, manufacturers, and London bankers, who fill this House, might be opposed to their request. On the contrary they seek to become contributors to the revenue, to invigorate the markets for agricultural, manufacturing, and colonial produce; and let me add, that neither corn laws[4] nor protecting duties will give you remunerating prices while the artizans from Coventry to Perth are restricted to half prices for their labour. They only ask the same protection for their property, *which is labour*, that you give to all other descriptions of property. Have you not increased the salaries of judges, the pay of troops, and the value of money; fixed a minimum price of corn, and even on the fares of wherries and hackney coaches? WHY SHOULD MAN ALONE BE EXCLUDED FROM YOUR SYSTEM OF PROTECTION? Alas! your very scheme of finance is based upon a principle *hostile to his interest* – as remarked by Adam Smith, excessive taxation (like the sterility of the soil, or the inclemency of the heavens) rendering man like the field he tills, less productive to him who cultivates his powers of industry. For instance, let us look at the power loom: this machine, with *one person*, is able to perform the work of *three* hand-loom weavers; but as the cloth made by it ESCAPES TWO-THIRDS OF THE TAXES levied on articles of subsistence, it gains a *premium* to that extent in its favor. This *premium* enables it to work at such terms that the business of hand-loom weaving is overstocked, and inferior artisans, whose coarser fabricks it can produce, constantly seeking to press into the finer branches of the trade, are ever accessible to the artifices of gambling and reckless, speculators. Yet with that moderation, so remarkable in these men, they have not asked you even to tax machines so severely as you do men, though they had an undoubted right to do so! They put it to your sense of justice, whether you should not enable them to enjoy the countenance and sanction of the law, and to *reap the benefit contemplated for them by* A MAJORITY[5] *of the manufacturers*, who have the feeling, wisdom, and sense of honor not to wish their workmen to be depressed and goaded to despair by useless and reckless competition.

Undoubtedly those who live upon the taxes may exclaim, you will raise prices, and our money will not command so much muslin for our families as they now do. I answer that the value of *your money has been nearly doubled*, while the wages of these men have fallen more than one half; and I am certain that none of you have a wife or daughter who would not pay a reasonable price for their dresses, and scorn that it should be moistened by the tears of a mother.[6]

Indeed I am confident that there are few of our political economists who would not support this motion, could I but bring them to view the consequences of their preferring theory to practice and machines to men. They lose the end by mistaking the means of promoting the wealth of the nation. It is not merely vast exports, or unlimited freedom of trade, that give greatness or happiness to empires. It is freedom from degrading poverty, – freedom from its consequences, vice and crime[7] – freedom from that inevitable insecurity of property, disrespect for the law, want of attachment to the government, and mutual distrust between the different orders and grades of society – I say it is freedom from these restrictions on moral and national grandeur, that alone can confer strength abroad and happiness at home.

I shall conclude, Sir, with stating that there are among these petitioners many gallant men who have contributed to raise the glory of the British name – who have planted the standard of their country under Nelson and Wellington wherever honour or liberty required it to wave. They have never hesitated to risk their life for their native land – they would still shed their blood in its defence; but they think it hard to pine in daily suffering – to see their wives and children losing health and virtue, and in vain imploring those decencies of life which even incessant labour cannot procure. They feel wounded by the apparent neglect of the nation; they think that an adventurous life should not terminate with the loss of independence in the gloomy precincts of a workhouse, on the degrading and demoralizing pittance of parochial alms! Let us tell them we will try to find for them here a less gloomy future, or enable them to emigrate[8] to some happier isle in the watery waste – let us, in the words of their own Campbell, assure them,

> "That when the silent years have passed away,
> That when the eye grows dim – the tresses grey –
> These busy hands a lovelier cot shall build,
> And deck with fairer flowers their little field."

APPENDIX OF DOCUMENTS

IN

CONFIRMATION OF THE STATEMENTS MADE IN THE FOREGOING SPEECH, AND ILLUSTRATIVE OF THE CONDITION OF THE HAND-LOOM WEAVERS.

(A.)

AFFIDAVITS OF THE GENERAL AND INDIVIDUAL DISTRESS.

Kilsyth, April 5.

CONDITION OF THE OPERATIVE WEAVERS. – The subject to which the following affidavits have reference, is so extremely imimportant and interesting, that we stretch a point, notwithstanding their length, to give them a place. – In explanation it may be necessary to state, that in consequence of the incongruous information which has been elicited of late in the House of Commons, respecting the real condition of the labouring classes, it was thought proper, at a public meeting, to appoint a Committee to inquire into the state of those in and around this place. As the population, with few exceptions, consist altogether of hand-loom weavers, the committee considered it unnecessary to carry their researches farther than that class; and to arrive with accuracy at their real earnings, a number of weaving agents were desired to examine their books with the greatest care, and find out what was the net money each weaver had got, whom they had employed, during the last three months. The average is seen in their depositions; and, to put it beyond the possibility of a quibble, it was thought proper to take them upon oath. A petition founded on the facts is in course of preparation, praying for inquiry into the cause of distress, and will be despatched to Mr. Gillon immediately. If many such petitions and affidavits were laid before the House, a motion similar to that of Mr. Attwood's would not be rejected a second time. – *Glasgow Free Press, April 6th*, 1834.

Affidavits

Upon this 26th day of March, 1833, appeared before the Bailie and Councillors of the Burgh of Kilsyth, James Morrison, weaving agent, who depones and saith, that he has been employed as a weaving agent in Kilsyth for several years. That it is consistent with his knowledge, that the price paid for hand-loom weaving during said period, has, compared with the former state of trade, house rent, and provisions, been very low. That, from daily intercourse with those employed by him, he is aware that great destitution and poverty prevails among them. And he farther depones and saith, that in order to ascertain the average amount of wages received by said hand-loom weavers, deponent hath examined and collated his books and accounts, and findeth, that, during the last three months, the said average rate of wages paid to, and received by said hand-loom weavers, amount to, and does not exceed the sum of 3s. and 10½d. per week, from which 1s. per week must be deducted for loom-rent and candles, leaving them only 2s. and 10½d. per week, for house rent, food, clothing, children's education, church accommodation, and other numerous incidental charges. And deponent farther saith, that it is consistent with his knowledge and belief, that the said average amount of wages has been lower than just now stated within, and during the last twelvemonths. And this is truth, as deponent shall answer to God.

James Morrison.
James Inglis, Bailie.

Upon the same day and manner compeared Alexander Abercrombie, agent, who, being examined *ut supra*, depones and saith, that he agrees with the preceding witness in all things, with this difference, that the wages paid to the weavers employed by him amounts to, and does not exceed the sum of 2s. 11½d. after deducting the necessary expenses incurred in finishing the work. And this is truth, as deponent shall answer to God.

Alexander Abercrombie.
James Inglis, Bailie.

Upon the same day and manner compeared Robert Anderson, weaving agent, who, being examined *ut supra*, depones and saith, that he agrees with the preceding witnesses in all things, with this difference, that the wages paid to the weavers employed by him, amounts to, and does not exceed the sum of 3s. 4¾d. per week, after deducting, at a very moderate calculation, what is necessary for finishing the work. And this is truth, as deponent shall answer to God.

Robert Anderson.
James Inglis, Bailie.

Upon the same day and manner compeared Henry Rankin weaving agent, who, being examined *ut supra*, depones and saith, that he agrees with the preceding witnesses in all things, with this difference, that the wages paid to the hand-loom weavers employed by him, amounts to, and does not exceed the sum of 3s. 3d. per week, after deducting the necessary expenses incurred in finishing the work. And this is truth, as the deponent shall answer to God.

Henry Rankin.
James Inglis, Bailie.

Council Chambers, Kilsyth, March 26, 1833.

Upon the day compeared William Jack, weaving agent, who, being examined *ut supra*, depones and saith, that he agrees with the preceding witnesses in all things, with this difference, that the wages paid to the weavers employed by him, amounts to, and does not exceed the sum of 2s. 10d. per week, after deducting the necessary expenses incurred in finishing the work. And this is truth, as deponent shall answer to God.

WILLIAM JACK.
JAMES INGLIS, Bailie.

At Kilsyth, this 26th day of March, 1833, appeared before the Bailie and Councillors of the Burgh of Kilsyth, Daniel Taylor, weaver, Kilsyth, aged 49 years, who depones and saith that he has been a weaver for thirty-four years. Recollects that a descriprion [sic] of goods called lappets was introduced at that period; that these goods were at that time paid at the rate of 1s. 6d. per ell: and the deponent is not aware of any goods of precisely the same description now going, but from his knowledge of the rates presently paid for goods of a nearly similar description that were these now in demand, they would not be paid at more than 2½d. per ell, and deponent farther states, that the depreciation has been in the ratio just now stated.

And deponent farther saith, that pullicates, wrought in a 1200 reed, have been a common kind of work wrought in and about Kilsyth for more than thirty years; that within said period he has known 9d. per ell paid for weaving this description of work; that during the last twenty years and more, the prices paid for weaving have been generally on the decline; and that 1¾d. is all that is given for what was formerly paid at 9d. per ell.

And deponent farther states, that all descriptions of goods with which he is acquainted, have fallen in the price paid for weaving in the same proportion. And deponent saith, that certain incicental [sic] charges, such as loom-stead rent and candles, cannot be furnished for less than 1s. per week. And all this is truth, as he shall answer to God.

DANIEL TAYLOR.
JAMES INGLIS, Bailie.

Upon the same day compeared James Bankier, weaver in Kilsyth, aged 48, who, being interrogated, depones and saith, that he agrees with the preceding witness in all things, with this difference, that starching webs, carriage, and twisting, amounting to five per cent. appears not to be included in the statement made by the preceding witness. – And all this is truth, as he shall answer to God.

JAMES BANKIER.
JAMES INGLIS, Bailie.

Upon the same day compeared Andrew Findley, weaver in Kilsyth, aged 42, who depones and saith, that he has been employed as a weaver for thirty years; has been paid for weaving 1200 pullicates ninepence per ell, and has known others paid ninepence-halfpenny for weaving a similar description of goods; and he farther states, that, within these last few years, he has wrought the same description of work as low as one-penny farthing per ell. In all other things he agrees with the last witness. And all this is truth, as he shall answer to God.

A. FINDLEY.
JAMES INGLIS, Bailie.

Upon the same day compeared Daniel M'Farlane, weaver in Kilsyth, aged 54; he has been employed as a weaver about forty-three years, is generally acquainted with the different descriptions of work that have been wrought in and about Kilsyth for more than twenty years; that he had been acquainted with the condition and habits of the working population during the period above stated; and that he observed a great deterioration in the domestic comfort of the people around him, arising in his apprehension from the great reduction in the rate of wages paid to workmen, in all departments that he is acquainted with in the manufacture of cotton goods. That the people generally are poorly fed, and worse clothed; that the people in his situation of life are frequently compelled to neglect the education of their children, partly from poverty, and partly from the pressing demands made upon them, to avail themselves of the earliest possible opportunity of increasing their income, by the labours of their infant children. And deponent further states that he agrees with the preceding witnesses in all other things. And all this is truth, as he shall answer to God.

DANIEL M'FARLANE.
JAMES INGLIS, Bailie.

Council Chambers, Kilsyth, March 26th, 1833.

Kilsyth, 28th March, 1833.

I have long been acquainted with the above deponents, and have no reason to question the truth of what they have said. In course of discharging his duty, the subscriber has been called for more than thirty years, statedly and occasionally, to visit many families in this place and neighbourhood, and is well acquainted with their circumstances. He has of late years observed a progressive deterioration in household furniture, and the dress of parents and children. He knows that in various cases the education of the young has been neglected through poverty, and the attendance of the aged on the public services of religion has been given up through want of proper clothing. That friendly and charitable institutions are allowed to languish, and the necessaries of life in many cases procured with difficulty. Every thing, indeed, bespeaks a state of wretched destitution, and unless some means be devised for alleviating the public distress, the most deplorable consequences may be expected.

JOHN ANDERSON, Minister.

I feel myself called upon to declare that the preceding facts and statements are consistent with the knowledge and experience of seventeen years, which I have had among the class of the community referred to.

JAMES INGLIS, Bailie.

Kilsyth, 1st April, 1833.

Kilsyth, 1st April, 1833.

I have examined the above statements, and am acquainted more or less with the individuals who have made said statements upon oath, and I attach entire credit to the fidelity and accuracy of their report as to the lamentably low state of the weaving department of our trade. I have known this place for nearly twelve years past, during which period the weaving conducted here has been all along in a depressed state, and the effects are but too apparent in the diminution of comfort in domestic life, neglect of education, and attendance on religious ordinances, occasioned in many instances by depressed circumstances.

William Burns,
Minister of the Parish of Kilsyth.

We, subscribing to the above statements as consisting with our knowledge, have, in addition, to state, that the weekly earnings as above, low as they are, go on the supposition that the weavers have constant employment, and labour the usual hours, that is 14 hours a day.

James Lang, Elder.
Alex. Henderson, Elder.

Kirkintilloch, April 18, 1834.

In compliance with a requisition to the Magistrates, a public meeting of the inhabitants of this town and parish was held this day, for the purpose of petitioning the Commons' House of Parliament, to institute a Committee of Inquiry into the distressed state of the nation. Bailie Gemmel was called to the chair, and, to show the existing distress, a number of affidavits by the manufacturers and weavers were then read, after which Mr. George Walker, teacher, moved the resolutions, and enforced them by a most pointed address, and Dr. Wallace, from Kilsyth, supported them in a lengthened and animated speech, which was received by the meeting with great applause, after which a petition, founded on the resolutions, was agreed to, and that it be sent by the chairman to J. C. Colquhoun, Esq., member for the county, for presentation, and that he be requested to support the prayer thereof. – *Glasgow Free Press, April* 24*th*, 1834.

Affidavits.

Upon the 18th April, 1833, appeared before us, David Gemmel and John Dickson, Bailies for the Burgh of Kirkintilloch, within the Court Hall thereof, Robert Muir, manufacturer here, who depones and saith, that, having carefully compared his books, finds that the average rate of wages paid to his weavers for six months prior to 6th inst., amounts to, and does not exceed, the sum of 4s. 10¾d. per week each, from which sum the necessary expenses of loom-rent and candle must be deducted, to show the net weekly wages on which the weaver, and perhaps a numerous family, has to subsist; and all this is truth, as the deponent shall answer to God.

(Signed) Robert Muir.
John Dickson, Bailie.
David Gemmel, Bailie.

Same day and place appeared William Cooper, weaving agent, who depones and saith, that he agrees with the former deponent in all things, with this difference, that the average rate of wages paid by him to his weavers, for six months prior to 1st January last, amounts to, and does not exceed, the sum of 4s. 10½d. per week each; and this is truth, as deponent shall answer to God.

(Signed) WILLIAM COOPER.
JOHN DICKSON, Bailie.
DAVID GEMMEL, Bailie.

Same day and place appeared Hugh Pollock, weaving agent, who depones and saith, that he agrees with the former deponents in all things, with this difference, that the average rate of wages paid by him to his steady weavers, for three months prior to 12th inst., amounts to, and does not exceed, the sum of 4s. 11¾d. weekly each; and this is truth, as the deponent shall answer to God.

(Signed) HUGH POLLOCK.
DAVID GEMMEL, Bailie.
JOHN DICKSON, Bailie.

Same day and place appeared William Gray, manufacturer here, who depones and saith, that he has carefully compared his books for the last twelve months, and that he has examined a considerable number of his most steady workmen, and finds, that the average rate of wages per week for steady workmen, working 12 hours per day, does not exceed 4s. 6d., deduct 1s. for loom-rent and charges, making their net wages 3s. 6d.; and this is truth, as the deponent shall answer to God.

(Signed) WILLIAM GRAY.
DAVID GEMMEL, Bailie.
JOHN DICKSON, Bailie.

At Kirkintilloch, this 18th day of April, 1833, appeared before the Bailies of the Burgh of Kirkintilloch, David Horn, aged forty-one years, who depones and saith, that he has been engaged at the cotton weaving since the 13th day of September, 1803, which is nearly thirty years. Recollects that in 1805 he was working at a 900 lappet, 18 heddles, 10 shots weft, weaving per ell, 8d., and 1½d. on the shilling, which amounted to 9d.; and that in the summer of 1832, he had under his charge a 900 lappet, 38 heddles, 8 shots weft, for which he was paid the *miserable pittance* of ⅞ of a penny per ell weaving; and deponent saith, that in the same shop with him is a 900 lappet, 34 heddles, 11 shots weft, weaving per ell, 1¼d.; and deponent farther saith, that a short time after the memorable battle of Leipsic, (in 1813) he was working at a 1200 twilled and veined stripe, weaving per ell, 1s. 4d., and that the same kind of work is going at the present day at 2½d. per ell weaving, with lappetting additional to the former; and deponent further declareth, that all descriptions of cotton goods with which he is acquainted, have fallen, in the price paid for weaving, in nearly the same proportion; and deponent saith that certain incidental expenses, such as loomstead rent, candles, dressing, carriage, &c. &c., cannot be furnished for less than 1s. 3d. per week; and deponent saith, that it is consistent with his knowledge that many severe and ruinous privations are felt among many employed in the same occupation as himself, particularly those who have a wife and four or five small children to support. They are necessitated to work 14, and in some cases, 15 or 16 hours per day. They are poorly fed, and a replacement of clothing is almost out of the question, and all this ariseth, in his opinion, from a want of a proper remuneration for labour; and deponent farther states, and saith, that he would most willingly have abandoned a profession that has long been unprofitable, and in following which he has suffered many severe privations; but from the channels of industry being full and overflowing, deponent has hitherto been unsuccessful in finding employment in any other trade or profession; and all this is truth, as he shall answer to God.

(Signed) DAVID HORN.
DAVID GEMMEL, Bailie.
JOHN DICKSON, Bailie.

Same day and place, appeared James Cooper, weaver here, who depones and saith, that having been a weaver upwards of 41 years, he in course of that period, has from time to time beheld, amid the various fluctuations of trade, the most overwhelming disparity of prices paid for weaving at different times, which the following will in some measure attest: Recollects in 1792, was weaving a book muslin at 1s. 7d. per ell, at present paid only about 2½d. – in 1803, was weaving a vein lappet, at 1s. 8d. per ell, at present paid about 2¼d. and in 1809, and 1810, was in the habit of giving out webs – recollects 11-8ths lappet shawls paid at 10½d. at present about 2d. – 6-4ths gauzes at 8d. per ell, at present 1¼d per ell – and 6–4ths lappets, at 7½d. per ell, at present 1¼d. per ell – only 10d. per piece of 10 yards weaving, instead of 5s. formerly; however, these statements are only a few specimens amongst the number and variety of fabrics that might be produced, and except amongst those connected with the trade, by the public in general (as we are extremely averse to believe any thing that gives pain) would scarcely be credited; however, the above, to the best of my knowledge, is as near the truth as I can recollect, to which I here depone, and being farther interrogated how workmen continue at that unprofitable employment, answers, because they cannot find a better; and all this is truth, as deponent shall answer to God.

(Signed) JAMES COOPER.
DAVID GEMMEL, Bailie.
JOHN DICKSON, Bailie.

Same day and place, compeared James Hutchison, weaver here, who depones and saith, – that in the following statements, as to particular dates he is not perfectly certain, he only states from memory, but he thinks he comes pretty near the different periods mentioned, with respect to prices referred to. He is perfectly certain, he likewise admits, of some difference, and the time specified respecting the various fabrics of work mentioned; but it goes for almost for nothing to the weaver, it amounts to nearly the same thing as the different fashions of a coat in the 17th and 18th century. He commenced weaving about the year 1797 – shortly after that period, say 1798, the weaving of lappets was introduced to Kirkintilloch; at that time an 1100 plain lappet was paid 1s. 6d. per ell, and 1½d. on the shilling, which made 1s. 8¼d. per ell. In January, 1833, an 1100 plain lappet was wrought in his shop at 1½d. per ell. In 1806, he wrought an 1100 lappet shawl at 1s. ½d.; in 1826, the same kind of work was wrought at 3½d.; and in 1832, under his charge, at 2d. per ell. In 1813, a species of figured gauze, called bird's-eye crape, was wrought in a 700 reed at Kirkintilloch at 1s. 1d. per ell; in 1833 the same kind of work was wrought in a 600 reed at 1⅛d. In 1813, he wrought a 1300 one in the breadth, twilled vein lappet at 1s. 1d. per ell; in January 1833, he wrought work of nearly the same description in a 1400 reed, at two in the breadth, at 5d. per ell; since January, has got an advance of ¼d. per ell. So much for the present advance of wages. He thinks 1s. 3d. per week but barely sufficient for loomstead rent and other incidental expenses, necessary in carrying on his business; and being further interrogated how workmen continue at so unprofitable an employment, answers, because they cannot find better; and this is truth, as deponent shall answer to God.

(Signed) James Hutchison.
John Dickson, Bailie.
David Gemmel, Bailie.

Same time and place, compeared Thomas Cooper, weaver here, who depones that he has been a weaver in Kirkintilloch for thirty years; is aware that a great reduction has taken place in the price of weaving within that time; remembers, when a boy, of working a lappet at 6¾d. per ell, and that in 1832, had one of same kind wrought under his charge, at 7-8ths of a penny. Deponent further saith, that he is fully persuaded that it takes as much, if not more, exertion to work an ell of the latter as of the former; and is persuaded that the prices of weaving lappet of every description are fallen in nearly the same proportion, and in many instances much more. Does not mean to say that prices have been falling gradually these thirty years. Has known prices fall very rapidly. In one instance, viz. in 1818, had a web at 1s. 5½d. per ell; but before six months expired, was offered the same kind at 9d. per ell, and has known work of a similar kind wrought at 4½d. per ell since; and this is truth, as deponent shall answer to God.

(Signed) THOMAS COOPER.
DAVID GEMMEL, Bailie.
JOHN DICKSON, Bailie.

We certify that the individuals who have this day been examined on oath, in the presence of the magistrates, are known to us, all of them to the one or the other of us, and that we regard them as men of strict probity, whose declaration even without an oath, would be entitled to the amplest credit. We can add from our own knowledge, that the class of the population employed in hand-loom weaving, who in this town are the most numerous class, have, owing to the melancholy depression of that branch of trade, been gradually sinking in the scale of comfort, till they are now, generally speaking, reduced to a state which may be termed, with too much truth, a state of privation. Many have disappeared from the public ordinances of religion, who assign as the reason, that they are no longer able to provide themselves and their families with decent apparel, and though this perhaps may in some instances be falsely pleaded as an excuse by the careless, we have not the smallest doubt that, in the great majority of cases, it is pleaded in good faith.

(Signed) ANDREW MARSHALL, Minister.
WILLIAM TURNBULL, Minister.

Letter from the Parish Minister of Balfron to Lord Althorp, in behalf of the Hand-Loom Weavers, and representing their deplorable condition.

My Lord,

I have the honor to forward to your Lordship, with a request that you will have the goodness to present it to the House of Commons, a Petition, agreed to at a public meeting of the inhabitants of this parish, in behalf of the hand-loom weavers. It is signed by above 535 persons, either weavers themselves, or those interested in the welfare of that sorely depressed and industrious part of the community. As chairman of the meeting at which the petition was agreed to, will your Lordship forgive me when I offer my testimony to the industry which is the marked characteristic of the weavers in general in this district of country, and to the patience with which they have borne their protracted sufferings. They in general work very long hours, not unfrequently from five in the morning till eleven at night; and with all their endeavours, their average wages for the week are only 4*s*. 1*d*! But, my lord, not merely as chairman of the late meeting would I take the liberty of presenting the claims of the distressed weavers to your Lordship's favourable consideration, as minister of the parish, and, of course, as such, feeling a deep interest in all that pertains to so large a portion of my parishioners, I entreat your forgiveness whilst I would lay their claims for sympathy before you.

There are in my parish upwards of 2000 souls. Of these, 1800 are in the parish of Balfron, wholly depending, either directly or indirectly, on manufacturing goods. From holding, professionally, perpetual intercourse with my people, no man can know their condition better than I do, and it is from this intimate knowledge of their condition, of their privations and sufferings, and of the patience and resignation with which they have endured these, and being perfectly aware too of their, generally speaking, industrious habits, that I take it upon me to recommend them to your attention, and entreat your Lordship to take up their cause. From the wages that he receives (and I challenge contradiction to the average as stated by me, viz. 4*s.* 1*d.* weekly,) it is quite impossible for the weaver to provide the common comforts of life for himself; much less is it possible for him to bring up his family either comfortably for themselves or usefully for the state. The moment the child of a weaver can be of use to its distressed parent, instead of being at school it is sent to the workshop, to help, by its miserable toil, to eke out the miserable pittance of the family, at the point of starving. The consequence is, the child is brought up in ignorance, destitute wholly of that instruction and moral training so necessary for the comfort of this world, and, ten to one, reckless of the concerns of the world to come. Nor is the parent, in point of privileges, in general very much superior to the child. The Sabbath comes round, but, in as far as respects its external privileges, it brings none of its delights or its comforts to the poor weaver. No! he is excluded from those enjoyments which other Christians have throughout our favoured land. He cannot go to church; and why? Because he has but the same dress in which he has been toiling during the past week. He cannot bear to tell the world that he has but the one self-same dirty and greasy jacket for Sunday as for Saturday. He can bear the pinchings of hunger, but he cannot bear to tell the world that he is poor, or so poor at least as in reality he is. The consequence is, that he either sits a prisoner in his own miserable dwelling, or he is seen sculking about the moors, or roaming on the highways, breathing the fresh air, as he says, and fitting himself for a renewal of another week's labour. Now I most humbly submit that such a state of things ought not to be: it is ruinous to the individuals themselves, and ruinous to society at large. And if there is one object that ought more than another to engage the consideration of a patriot, it is the question how the weaver is to be rescued from his sad condition.

I have the honour to be,
My Lord, &c.

WARWICKSHIRE HAND-LOOM WEAVERS' PETITIONS, IN 1834.

In Nuneaton, Poleshill, Bedworth, Coton, Bulkington, ribbon weavers suffering the greatest privations; 80 out of every 100 Hand-looms unemployed!! earnings per head each day twopence farthing!!

In Nuneaton, containg 8000 inhabitants, 6000 depend on ribbon trade; average earnings, three shillings or three shillings and sixpence per week!

In Bedworth, 300 only of 1500 employed at three shillings per week.

Pray for adequate wages and employment or means to emigrate.

Editorial Endnotes

1 On handloom weavers, see Volume 1 Introduction.
2 I. Maver, 'Maxwell, Sir John, of Pollok, eighth baronet', *Oxford Dictionary of National Biography*, 23 September 2004, at https://doi-org.du.idm.oclc.org/10.1093/ref:odnb/75306 [accessed 13 June 2021]; 'Death of Sir John Maxwell, Bart. Of Polloc.', *Paisley Herald and Renfrewshire Advertiser*, 10 June 1865, p. 1.
3 J. Maxwell, *Manual Labour versus Machinery* (London: Cochrane and M'Crone, 1834), Gale, *Making of the Modern World*: GALE|U0105373820, p. 5.
4 Maxwell was writing in the context of much political unrest surrounding agricultural riots against machines, protests against the passage of the New Poor Law, and the case against the 'Tolpuddle Martyrs' in Dorset, agricultural labourers who refused to work for low wages. See, for example, N. C. Edsall, *The Anti-Poor Law Movement, 1834–44* (Manchester: Manchester University Press, 1971); J. Horn 'Machine Breaking in England and France during the Age of Revolution', *Labour*, 55 (Spring 2005), pp. 143–166; C. Griffiths, 'From "Dorchester Labourers" to "Tolpuddle Martyrs": Celebrating Radicalism in the English Countryside', in Q. Outram and K. Laybourn (eds), *Secular Martyrdom in Britain and Ireland: From Peterloo to the Present* (New York: Palgrave Macmillan, 2018), pp. 59–84.
5 Maxwell, *Manual Labour*, p. 9.
6 Maxwell, *Manual Labour*, p. 9.
7 Maxwell, *Manual Labour*, p. 13.
8 J. Locke, *Two Treatises on Government*, book 2, chap. 5, sec. 27 (Project Gutenberg ebook), at www.gutenberg.org/files/7370/7370-h/7370-h.htm [accessed 20 June 2021].

Source Endnotes

1 Vide Appendix A.
2 Vide Appendix B [not included].
3 Vide Appendix C [not included].
4 Vide Appendix F [not included].
5 Vide Appendix H [not included].
6 Vide Appendix G [not included].
7 Vide Title-page Table [not included].
8 Vide Coventry Weavers' Petition in Appendix A.

16

ANON., 'THE PRESENT CONDITION OF BRITISH WORKMEN'

Broadside, 1834

This broadside ballad (unknown origin) blames machinery for creating a situation in which poor men can find no work. Not only had machines reduced the numbers of labourers required to produce needed goods, but they had also destroyed community relations. Unemployed men and their families were reduced to seeking help from the harsh 1834 New Poor Law (the Union), which separated 'man and wife' in its dreaded workhouse and forced men to break stones for their relief.[1]

DOI: 10.4324/9780429320323-20

'The Present Condition of British Workmen'

Now Poor Laws thus breaks God's commands
For it parts man and wife,
Though at the altar hand in hand
Vowed they ne'er would part in life.
And thus they treat an Englishman,
Where they boast of Christianity,
Where Liberty's flag it is unfurled,
No one knows their destiny.

Now when in work relations will
In numbers visit you,
But if unemployed or taken ill,
Then your company will not do.
Its neglect, or else he is lazy,
Or fresh work he might procure,
The only friend left is your wife,
She stands by you when you are poor.

Trade everywhere is at a stand,
The poor man's hopes destroyed,
Let us hope that they'll find labour soon
To support the unemployed.
Now wives and suffering children dear
Before their Maker kneel,
They ask of God what they're to do,
They must neither beg nor steal.

Now men you'll find in every trade,
In towns both far and near,
Without a place to lay their heads,
And know not where to steer.
The planets we are born under
There's no one can tell true,
We'll put our trust in Providence,
Our friends are but few.

Our master, shopmates, and our friends,
Have changed since we've grown poor,
They have nothing they could give or lend,
With spirits broken left their doors.
Let us hope that trade will flourish soon,
And all bad times away,
Perhaps a cloudy morning may
Bring a sun-shiny day.

Mechanics and poor labourers
Are wandering up and down,
There is nothing now but poverty
In country and in town;
Machinery and steam-power has
The poor man's hopes destroyed,
Then pray behold the numbers of
The suffering unemployed.

The invention of machinery
Has caused many to weep and moan;
It has thrown thousands out of work,
And drove them from their homes.
Where a hundred hands were once employed,
Now there's not more than ten,
And this is through machinery –
God help poor working-men.

There is nothing but starvation now
In all parts of England,
Shopmates cannot assist now,
Though we once went hand in hand.
Our friends then used to treat us kind,
When we could pay our way;
But you know friends change with the times,
Now tell us they poor-rates pay.

Poor people has no comfort now,
There is no bread upon the shelves,
Let us pray to God to help the poor,
For the rich can help themselves.
Now if we to the Union goes,
How they will sweat our bones,
For a night's shelter or a loaf of bread
They will send us breaking stones.

The parish says they wont relieve
Us without we go in,
Which caused our families for to grieve,
But poverty it is no sin.
In the House we are treated worse than slaves,
The truth I will impart,
If we look or speak we're bad behaved,
From our families forced to part.

Note

1 For an introduction to the Poor Law, see A. Brundage, *The English Poor Laws, 1700–1930* (New York: Palgrave Macmillan, 2001) and L. H. Lees, *The Solidarities of Strangers: The English Poor Laws and the People, 1700–1948* (New York: Cambridge University Press, 1998).

17

H. LEGGETH AND S. COWLE, 'THE ADDRESS OF THE FEMALE CHARTISTS OF MANCHESTER TO THEIR SISTERS OF ENGLAND, IRELAND, SCOTLAND, AND WALES'

Northern Star, 24 July 1841, p. 8

The demands of Chartism (see Volume 1 Introduction) focused on political progress for men, especially universal male suffrage. While women did not belong to official Chartist groups, they were powerful allies in their female auxiliary organizations. Historian Anna Clark argues that they developed 'militant domesticity' as a political identity, which extended women's role as mothers to include working and activism to improve their children's lives.[1] Women helped with the domestic tasks of the movement, but they were also engaged at meetings, demonstrations, and marches, and some became important lecturers on the Chartist circuit. Most of the women's groups were formed in order to support the points of the Charter, but some women, and a very few male Chartists, believed that universal suffrage should include women, too.[2] This article, from the Chartist newspaper the *Northern Star*, reproduces the text from a meeting of the Female Chartists of Manchester. The tone is typical of many other female Chartist petitions and meetings. The authors of this appeal present themselves both as independent political actors and as representing their starving children and unemployed husbands. They argue for a 'right to subsistence', in 'circumstances over which [they] have had no control',[3] pointing to the intersection of class and gender in their position as poor women. Even though they saw themselves as somewhat helpless in these circumstances, they believed that it was their right to fight for the good of the country and their families. As was the case with many Chartist meetings, the Manchester women compared the poverty of workers with the cost of maintaining the royals, but they also drew power from the fact that a woman was on the throne. Because many of their husbands were absent due to imprisonment, it was the wives' responsibility to carry on the Chartist cause. The 1839 law referred to in the women's appeal is most likely the County Police Act of 1839, which was the result of a Royal Commission recommendation. The act allowed county justices of the peace to set up

DOI: 10.4324/9780429320323-21

police forces just at the time when Chartist demonstrations were increasing.[4] John Frost, Zephaniah Williams, and William Jones were tried for treason as a result of the mass Newport Rising in Wales. They were found guilty and transported to Australia.[5] While the women's appeal identifies both men and women as unemployed, the authors quickly shift their language to focus on husbands who had lost work because of machinery. Husbands were willing to work, which was a sign of their respectability, but no work existed because of mechanization. Men's lack of work, the women claim, then caused their wives to suffer from the inability to feed starving children. They worried that because of machinery, their life choices would be reduced to emigration or the workhouse.[6] The productive class, those who 'have produced everything valuable in society', were 'willing to work', but instead they were starving when the country had plenty of food.[7] The women argued that the evil system existed because working men were disenfranchised: they had no voice to determine how wealth was distributed. The appeal called on the women of Britain to demand the Charter, 'which will protect labour',[8] linking their political and economic conditions. They asked women to support the Chartist champions who were about to be released from prison.[9]

'The Address of The Female Chartists of Manchester to Their Sisters of England, Ireland, Scotland, and Wales'

***Passed at a Public Meeting of their Sex, holden in the Chartist Room, Tib-street, on Wednesday, July* 21*st,* 1841.**

Sisters in Bondage, – We, the females of Manchester, feel it our duty, at this important crisis, thus to address you, from a conviction that our principles and motives need only to be known to gain your assistance, appreciation, and co-operation, in gaining our object.

Our principles are justice to all, and injustice to none; a right to subsistence in the land of our birth. It may be asked by those who wish for things to remain as they are – by those who are not actuated by a desire to save their country from impending ruin, why we engage in and concern ourselves about politics? In reply to which we say we have an interest in the prosperity of the country. We all spring from one common parent – are the children of one all-wise Creator, who has provided for all; therefore we have the same right to subsistence, though dwelling in a con, cellar, or garret, where forced by circumstances over which we have had no controul, as the lady in the drawing-room, or the ballroom, or the Queen upon the throne.

A love for ourselves, our husbands, our children, our country, and everything valuable in existence, stimulates us to take a part in a struggle which we conceive calculated to end in success, and thus avert the awful calamity that has been for some time, and is now pending over us; and which will certainly overtake us if not thus averted.

We take our stand, also, as a matter of right; as fully and fairly illustrated by circumstances before our eyes. Surely, if by our labour we are compelled to maintain two Queens at the expence of £570,000 a year; and if a female is allowed to take the highest seat in the state, and give directions for the government of the country, we have a right to struggle to gain for ourselves, our husbands, brothers, and children, suitable houses, proper clothing, and good food. Then, Sisters, we call upon you in behalf of upwards of four hundred females, who had their husbands torn from them at the instigation of class-made law in 1839, and placed in dungeons for merely wishing to redress the grievances which press upon both you and us; – left without their guardians and protectors at the mercy of the public, with a forlorn, sorrowful, and agitated mind by day, weeping and mourning and sighing over their husbands' sufferings; and dreary, restless, and sleepless hours by night, their children bereft of kind and affectionate fathers, and the long affection and concord which existed betwixt them cut asunder by the tyrants. We call upon you on behalf of the wives of those unfortunate men, Frost, Williams, and Jones, who are left disconsolate, heart-broken, and in a state of anxiety for their husbands, who are sent across the seas; subject to insult, torture, and slavery; on behalf of the widow, Mrs. Clayton, whose husband died in Northallerton prison; and on behalf of the good, true, and virtuous men who have suffered, and are now suffering imprisonment.

Sisters, if ever there was a time when it was our duty to shake off our lethargy, and engage in a grand struggle for liberty, surely it is now. Does not the sword of persecution draw nearer and nearer every day, tyrannising over us in various ways? Thousands of both males and females are walking the streets for the want of employment, compelled to pledge and sell their clothes and furniture to purchase food to supply their physical wants, until their houses and clothes boxes are nearly empty, while the pawn-brokers and furniture-brokers' shops are wedged and crammed with the furniture and clothes of the industrious poor. Our granaries are full of the food which providence has sent, and the warehouses are full of clothing, while thousands are starving. How grievous must it be to see our husbands wandering the streets, willing to work but unable to procure it, thrown out in consequence of the improvements which have been made in machinery! What can be more piercing and heart-rending to a woman than to hear her offspring crying for food to satisfy the cravings of hunger, and she none to give to them! And after pledging and selling all they have, driven to begging from their neighbours, who are in the same condition as themselves, or nearly so!

What prospect is there for us, when our husbands are supplanted by machinery, except to emigrate to a foreign land, or be inmates of a Poor Law bastile, which will be inevitably the lot of a large number of our fellow creatures without a speedy change?

Sisters, suffering humanity cries for your assistance at this most important crisis, to endeavour to alleviate the miseries which every where abound amongst the industrious, yet starving millions.

We ask for nothing but what is consistent with the laws which God has laid down in the unerring standard of divine truth – the Scriptures, and exemplified in the laws of nature.

The fowls of the air, the fishes of the sea, the beasts of the field, and every other living agent, have enough, without either toiling or spinning, while we can scarcely get sufficient to keep body and soul together, for working twelve or thirteen hours per day. Should such a state of things exist, when there is sufficient for every man, woman, and child in existence? Justice and common sense say no! Then why is it that, in the midst of plenty, we are in such a condition! Why is it that those who are willing to work, that those who have produced everything valuable in society, without whom the factories would not have been built, the machinery made, the railroads constructed, the canals cut, who build and man the ships, who fight the battles, make their hats, shoes, and coats, and till the land – cannot get enough to quell the ravings of hunger? Why, because they have no power to make laws that influence the distribution of such wealth.

It rests with the industrious people whether they will any longer submit to a system so wicked, fraught with injustice and misrule.

Up, then, brave women of England, Ireland, Scotland, and Wales, and join us in the cry for the Charter, which will protect labour, and secure plenty, comfort, and happiness to all! Give us your support in paying due respect to our champions who are about to be released from their dungeons, and lead us on to victory, namely, O'Connor, O'Brien, and Benbow.

Sisters, in the cause of democracy, we remain,
Yours, in the bonds of affection,
THE FEMALE CHARTISTS OF MANCHESTER.
HANNAH LEGGETH, Treasurer. SARAH COWLE, Secretary.

Notes

1 A. Clark, *The Struggle for the Breeches: Gender and the Making of the British Working Class* (Berkeley: University of California Press, 1995), p. 229.
2 Clark, *Struggle for the Breeches*, pp. 220–247. Also see, D. Thompson, *The Chartists: Popular Politics in the Industrial Revolution* (New York: Pantheon Books, 1984) pp. 120–151.
3 H. Leggeth and S. Cowle, 'The Address of the Female Chartists of Manchester to Their Sisters of England, Ireland, Scotland, and Wales', *Northern Star*, 24 July 1841, p. 8.
4 A. Brundage, 'Ministers, Magistrates, and Reformers: The Genesis of the Rural Constabulary Act of 1839', *Parliamentary History* 5 (1986), pp. 55–64.
5 J. A. Cannon, 'Newport Rising', in *Oxford Companion to British History* (Oxford: Oxford University Press, 2015).
6 On emigration, see Volume 4 Introduction, and, for example, G. Howells, 'On Account of Their Disreputable Characters': Parish-Assisted Emigration from Rural England, 1834–1860', *History* 88:4 (2003), pp. 587–605; on the Poor Law's workhouse, see, for example, *The Workhouse System, 1834–1929: The History of an English Social Institution* (London: Batsford, 1981).
7 Leggeth and Cowle, 'The Address of the Female Chartists', p. 8.
8 Leggeth and Cowle, 'The Address of the Female Chartists', p. 8.
9 Feargus O'Connor, the editor of the Chartist *Northern Star*, had been found guilty of seditious libel for publishing subversive speeches in his newspaper and sentenced to eighteen months imprisonment. Bronterre O'Brien had been found guilty of sedition for his part in the Newport Rising, an armed Chartist uprising, and William Benbow was convicted of sedition for anti–Poor Law and Chartist demonstrating. J. Epstein, 'O'Connor, Feargus Edward', *Oxford Dictionary of National Biography* (hereafter ODNB), 8 October 2009, at https://doi-org.du.idm.oclc.org/10.1093/ref:odnb/20515 [accessed 13 June, 2021]; M. Taylor, 'O'Brien, James [*pseud.* Bronterre O'Brien], *ODNB*, 23 September 2004, at https://doi-org.du.idm.oclc.org/10.1093/ref:odnb/20457 [accessed 13 June 2021]; M. Chase, 'Benbow, William', *ODNB*, 17 September 2015, at https://doi-org.du.idm.oclc.org/10.1093/ref:odnb/47096 [accessed 13 June 2021].

18

W. CARPENTER, 'THE QUESTION OF MACHINERY FAIRLY STATED', 'MACHINERY CREATES A DEMAND FOR MANUAL LABOUR', AND 'CONDITION OF THE HAND-LOOM WEAVERS', IN *MACHINERY AS IT AFFECTS THE INDUSTRIAL CLASSES AND THE EMPLOYMENT OF CHILDREN IN FACTORIES*

(London: E. Lloyd, 1844), pp. 10–11, 21–24, and 28–30

William Carpenter (1797–1874) was an author and journalist who became involved in various radical reform causes, including early Chartism (see Volume 1 Introduction). Over the course of his life, he edited seven journals and actively campaigned for freedom of the press, which led to his brief imprisonment.[1] In this selection, in order to convince the labouring classes of his credentials, he prefaces his text by 'appeal[ing] to all his past labours – and they have not been few – in proof of his sympathy with the less favoured classes of society, and of his sincere desire to see their condition improved'.[2] Carpenter was probably referring to his support of the Dorchester Labourers, also called the Tolpuddle Martyrs, a small group of agricultural labourers who formed a trade union and were transported to Australia after their death sentence was commuted, as well as his battle for an unstamped (untaxed) press.[3] He needed to present himself this way, because he would make an unpopular argument: that machinery benefited everyone, including labourers. In Chapter 3 of his text, Carpenter directly attacks Richard Oastler (see Volume 1 Introduction) for blaming machinery for the destitute condition of the labouring classes. He argues that machinery both increased production and cheapened the cost of goods, fuelling jobs and consumption. In Chapter 7, Carpenter counters

DOI: 10.4324/9780429320323-22

the idea that machinery diminished the demand for labour. Machines actually multiplied the types of employments available to workmen and increased jobs. This argument, he insists, was supported by the growth of cities built on manufacturing, such as Manchester. He finds it incredible that anyone could claim that machinery was a danger to the livelihoods of the labouring class, since he had demonstrated that machines make goods cheaper and increase the number of jobs. This argument is in direct contradiction to Burrows (see Volume 1, Part 2, Chapter 13), who claims that even though machinery lowered prices, it also forced down wages and increased poverty so that working-class consumption decreased. Carpenter looks specifically at the case of the handloom weavers (see Volume 1 Introduction) in Chapter 10, since theirs was the case most often seen as proving the evil effects of machinery. He admits that when machinery was initially introduced into a trade, it did have a negative impact on the workers by displacing hand labour by machine labour, but this did not counter the positive effect machinery had on the working class as a whole. He also points out that the handloom weavers had already started their decline before the introduction of the power loom.[4] Additionally, Carpenter attributes the poor condition and low wages of handloom weavers in Manchester to the fact that their industry was dominated by the Irish. He links the 'wretched condition of the labourers in Ireland' with the condition of the work the Irish took on in England.[5] Rather than looking to structural issues, he thus blames the character of the workers themselves. This image of the Irish as the source of destitution was common in Victorian England and was especially prevalent in mid-century as a result of extensive Irish immigration due to the Irish famine.[6]

Machinery as It Affects the Industrial Classes and the Employment of Children in Factories

Chapter III

The question of machinery fairly stated

BLUNDERS MADE AT THE THRESHOLD OF THE INQUIRY. – PROBABLE CONDITION OF THE INDUSTRIAL CLASSES HAD MACHINERY MADE LESSER ADVANCES. – THE STOCKING-FRAME AND THE POWER-LOOM.

To determine in how far machinery affects the condition of the working classes, one way or the other, it is not enough to compare the condition of those classes now, and their condition at some antecedent period, when they were placed, by other causes than machinery, under different circumstances; as previously to the continental war, when their numbers were much fewer, or during the war, when the demand for their services was much greater. And yet, this is the course usually taken by the opponents of machinery. It is thus that Mr. Oastler – the ardour of whose benevolence frequently runs away with his judgment – expatiates upon the deteriorated condition of the labouring classes, attributing the change to what he calls the "unlimited use" of machinery – a phrase, by the way, not very intelligible. But let that pass. Here is his plaint: –

"It has produced havoc in the districts where it abounds; and, like the fiend, whom Shakspere represents as 'coming hot from hell,' it has let slip the dogs of war. It has driven the aristocracy from their estates, and now keeps them away, under the hint that residence is dangerous; and has thus left the people in the hands of mercenary tyrants, who, like the middle men of Ireland, fatten on the wasting property of the absentee lords of the soil. It has unsettled all the old foundations of justice and humanity, united and raised up a power that tramples upon law, and sneers at the simpleton who pleads for the poor. It has razed to the ground the former refuge for the weary and heart-broken traveller through life's thorny road, and built for them a bastile, which, frightful as is appeared at first, has become at last so familiar, that the poor will walk into the den rather than die in a ditch. It has converted the once happy hives of busy bees into a nest of hornets; and the land which was formerly the cradle and the castle of freemen, has become the grave and the dungeon of slaves."

That is a specimen of the way in which the use of machinery is assailed, and of the kind of reasoning by which it is made responsible for nearly all "the ills that flesh is heir to." That it is utterly fallacious, as proceeding upon narrow and inadequate grounds, it will be easy to show.

In order to form a just estimate of the benefits which machinery has conferred upon that class of persons who are dependent upon their industry for the means of subsistence, we must endeavour to ascertain what they would have been, and what their condition, had no such means of production enlarged the sphere of manufacturing industry. Let us, with an eye to this, divide the working population into the two great branches of industry – manufactures and agriculture; and see what our daily growing population would have been, had it not been provided for by manufacturing processes. And let it be remembered, as we have already shown, that these processes would have been utterly insignificant, compared with their present magnitude, had it not been for increased consumption, promoted by the cheapness occasioned by the employment of machinery, in conjunction with manual labour.

It is scarcely necessary to accumulate facts to show, that, as prices have been reduced by cheapening and enlarging the power of production, the consumption of the articles thus more cheaply and plentifully produced, has been proportionately increased. At the time when a pair of silk stockings were presented to Queen Elizabeth, they are said to have been worth their weight in gold; and not another person in the kingdom, probably, wore so costly an article. By the improvements subsequently introduced into the process of manufacturing silk stockings, – first, by Sir Thomas Lombe's mode of "organising" (or preparing for the weaver) raw silk by machinery, and next, by the invention of the machine known as the "stocking-frame," which largely superseded manual labour in knitting, the article has long been produced at so low a price, that it has become one of ordinary use, and many thousands of hands have been constantly employed in its fabrication. (Mr. M'Culloch estimates the consumption of silk stockings and gloves in England to amount, annually, to 2,500,000*l.*)

It is the same in other branches of production. Before Richard Arkwright invented his machinery for spinning cotton, and Dr. Cartwright his powerloom for weaving it, the prices of cotton fabrics were so high that the demand for them gave employment to comparatively few hands. I have already stated the number at forty thousand. The number now employed is estimated at more than half a million, independent of those employed in making and repairing the machinery used, in carrying away and disposing of the raw and manufactured material, &c.

Now, without at all adverting to the benefits conferred upon the consumers of these and other commodities – these consumers being *the whole* population, working classes included – let us try if we can form an idea of the possibility there would have been of disposing of our increased and increasing population, had no new channels of employment been created by that extension of manufacturing industry which has been consequent upon the employment of machinery. [. . .]

Chapter VII

Machinery creates a demand for manual labour

ABSURD NOTIONS ENTERTAINED AS TO THE CAPABILITIES OF MECHANICAL POWER. – INCREASE OF THE MANUFACTURING POPULATION. – EMPLOYMENT FURNISHED BY THE ERECTION OF COTTON MILLS. – INCREASE OF THE COTTON MANUFACTURE. – DEMAND FOR HUMAN LABOUR KEEPS PACE WITH THE EXTENSION OF MECHANICAL POWER TO THE PURPOSES OF PRODUCTION. – WAGES CANNOT BE REDUCED BY ANY AUGMENTATION OF THE PRODUCTIVE POWER.

To hear some persons talk of the effects of machinery upon the condition of the labouring classes, it might reasonably be inferred that some power had been discovered by capitalists, by which they would create and work the machinery they employ for productive purposes, without the aid of human labour.

At an agricultural dinner some time since held in Berkshire, to entertain the kind-hearted but short-sighted Earl of Stanhope, the chairman assigned the employment of machinery as the cause of manufacturing distress, and spoke of that power in terms which might fairly warrant a belief in those who confided in his representations, that nothing is required in the present state of machinery but to put a fleece of wool or a bundle of cotton into a machine, and receive it back a well-manufactured coat or a fashionable gown. Such a belief may be too absurd for general reception, but not a few are infected with a belief, almost as absurd, namely, that the employment of machinery in manufacturing business, tends to diminish the demand for human labour.

All the facts that have been stated relative to the increase that has taken place in the population of manufacturing towns and districts, show that such cannot have been the case. The manufacturing population has increased much more rapidly than the agricultural, and even than the general population of the country; which shows clearly enough that the application of machinery to manufactures has not had the effect of lessening the aggregate amount of employment of the working classes. In point of fact, almost everybody knows, although many strangely overlook the fact, that the machine, while it performs an herculean task, creates an infinite variety of employments, whose combined power nearly equals its own operative production, and which cannot be performed and sustained without the attendance, preparation, and assistance of innumerable attendants.

It seems almost superfluous to add anything further upon this point; but we will mention one very striking fact, out of a large number that might be adduced. In the first report of the Poor-law Commissioners is one from Dr. Kay, dated June 22, 1835, in which he enumerates the steam-power which had either recently been erected, but was not then supplied with hands, or which was to be erected within the following year and a half, or two years, in the cotton districts of Lancashire and its immediate vicinity. It appears, from the facts stated in this report, that 7,507 horse power was about to be erected, and brought into operation in this district alone, in the course of two years from June, 1835. "Ah," say some of the antagonists of machinery, "thus it is that the labour of those whose subsistence depends upon their employment is superseded, and iron and steam are made to do the work of human beings." But how stands the fact? "Within whatever period this power is brought into complete activity," says Dr. Kay, "six mill hands, at least, will be required for every horse power." On the introduction of this power depended the employment of 45,042 mill hands; and if we take into account the unemployed members of the families of mill hands, as well as mechanics, labourers, handicraftsmen, warehousemen, dyers, calenderers, finishers, shopkeepers, &c.; in fact, the whole population necessary to complete the said fabric, of which these 45,042 mill hands would form a part, we must add an equal number. The erection of this steam-power, or machinery, therefore, so far from displacing human labour, or throwing persons out of employment, would place in immediate relation with itself a population of 90,084 persons!

But, in addition to the demand for operatives, which this new machinery would thus create, look at the employment it would furnish in its erection. The outlay in buildings and machinery necessary to bring this power into operation, is estimated at 500*l*. per ten-horse power, without taking into account the capital necessarily employed in trading transactions in connection with the power; or, in other words, the erection of this power presupposes an outlay of 3,753,500*l*. in buildings and machinery; which outlay is made upon the working classes, by whose hands the buildings are raised, and the machinery made. Let me, to strengthen this position, refer to an admirable little work, translated from the French of Leon Faucher, with notes, by a member of the Manchester Athenæum. It is to the notes that I would refer for some clear and unanswerable reasonings touching the economies of machinery, as applied to the purposes of manufacture; but the text of M. Faucher supplies some facts which illustrate, in a very striking manner, the great extent to which the field of industry has been enlarged, and, therefore, employment created for the industrial classes, by the extension and improvement of mechanical power. Thus, whilst the number of inhabitants of the county of Lancashire increased from 300,000 to 1,667,000 – drawn thither by the sources of employment which the improvements in machinery opened up – the inhabitants of Manchester increased from 40,000 to 306,000! In 1792, when Arkwright formed those projects which seemed to authorise the greatness and rapidity of his fortune, England did not import, annually 30,000,000lbs. of cotton wool; the products of the manufacture were estimated at from 3,200,000*l*. to 4,000,000*l*., and employed fewer than 100,000 hands. What is the state of the manufacture now, notwithstanding its restrictions and depression, through the operation of absurd and unjust commercial laws? The importation of cotton wool has increased from 30,000,000lbs. to more than 600,000,000lbs; the value of the products have increased, notwithstanding the continual reduction of price, from 3,200,000*l*. to 36,000,000*l*., while the various classes of the operatives constitute 75 per cent. of the whole population of the borough. And so of the other great seats of the cotton manufacture, where the population has enormously increased within the last quarter of a century. In Salford, the operatives constitute 74 per cent. of the population; in Ashton, 81 per cent.; in Staleybridge, 90 per cent.; and in Dunkenfield, nearly 95 per cent. Thus has the population of the agricultural districts, unable to find employment in the places of their birth, and in the pursuits to which they were born, migrated to those parts of the country where the processes of manufacture, aided and augmented by mechanical power, have opened a wide field for the exercise of their industry, and supplied them with the means of living.

It was stated in the *Manchester Guardian*, the other day, that the Mersey cotton-mill, in Heaton-lane, Stockport, had recommenced work, after a stoppage of eighteen months. Surely the bringing into operation of so much additional machinery as these mills contain, must greatly injure the labourers in the district and trade to which they belong? No. The re-employment of this machinery, which had been lying idle for eighteen months – which had for that space of time produced nothing which the skill and hand labour of man might have produced – gives occupation to upwards of *one thousand* hands! The same journal also stated, that the large establishment in Chestergate, last worked by Mr. T. S. Knowles, which had been standing idle since 1842, was likely to be again brought into work, which, instead of throwing labourers out of employment, would afford occupation and wages to upwards of *seven hundred* hands.

I have already stated that inanimate agencies, such as steam, air, and water, joined to machinery, do the work of some 600,000,000 of labourers in Great Britain alone. Are there, then, fewer labourers in the kingdom now than before machinery was so largely employed? On the contrary, who does not know that the population has more than doubled itself. Monsieur Say calculates that, by the invention of printing, a *thousand* copiers of MSS. were thrown out of employment. But, then, look at the compensatory power of the machinery which has been introduced for printing, by which these copiers were displaced. More than a *million of persons* are now employed in the various processes connected with printing; and their numbers are every year augmenting. Lord Monboddo contended that the plough, by superseding spade cultivation, was the most pernicious invention ever made. This world would be a rare place, if such people had the management of it! They are confident enough in themselves, and, with Sir Godfrey Kneller, think that things would have been better ordered had they been consulted at the creation; but for all real emergencies, or even for ordinary practical measures, they are, of all persons, the most inefficient.

Look, say some such acute reasoners, look at what an immense number of persons the cotton trade, for example, would employ, were machinery dispensed with, and manual labour only employed. This has been answered in part already. Let us just add, that the reasoning is based upon the merest fallacy. Had it not been for the machinery, we should have had *no* cotton trade. Even *with* the aid of machinery in an imperfect state, the trade could afford employment to but about 50,000 in the United Kingdom. As the machinery has been improved and extended, these numbers have increased to 500,000! "Experience has proved," says Colonel Thompson, "that when the production of any commodity is facilitated by machinery, the increase of consumption consequent on the reduction of price, in a state of freedom, and under the existing circumstances of the world, in respect of the desire to consume, is such as in the end to increase the demand for labour in the production of that particular commodity. If power-looms could bring down the price of broadcloth to a shilling a yard, and the corn of foreigners might be taken from them in return, so many people in different parts of the world would wear broadcloth who now do not, that there would be more employment for makers of broadcloth in the end than ever. If men cannot exchange the cloth because the agriculturists will not let them, the case is certainly altered. But then the fault is not in the machinery."

Is it not astonishing to find men, with these and numberless similar facts staring them in the face, gravely contending that machinery *displaces* human labour, and militates against the interests of the poorer classes! [. . .]

Look at the question in what light soever we may, the contrary is seen to be the case. The faculty of invention, in which it takes its source, is one of Heaven's best gifts to man. Like all other boons, it is capable of being misused; but they who would deny its exceeding value, give but poor evidence of their rationality. [. . .]

Chapter X

Condition of the hand-loom weavers.

NUMBER OF ADULT HAND-LOOM WEAVERS. – INVENTION MAY BE INJURIOUS TO PARTICULAR CLASSES, BUT IS BENEFICIAL TO THE WHOLE. – PECULIARITY IN THE CONDITION OF THE HAND-LOOM WEAVERS. – HAVE ALWAYS BEEN IN A LOW AND SUFFERING CONDITION. – VARIATIONS IN WAGES FOR HAND-LOOM WEAVING. – THE POWER-LOOM DOES NOT COMPETE WITH THE HAND LOOM. – CAUSE OF THE MISERABLE CONDITION OF THE HAND-LOOM WEAVER.

THE case most commonly referred to, as furnishing proof of the injurious effects of improved machinery on the condition of the working classes, is that of the hand-loom weavers, whose reduced and truly pitiable condition has been fully shown in a variety of ways. The number of adult hand-loom weavers in the United Kingdom, is, probably, somewhere about 250,000, and their earnings have been reduced from what was at one time a competency, down to a sum, which, if not increased by the labour of their wives and children, would be wholly inadequate to supply a family with even the smallest amount of the bare means of existence. This deplorable fact is admitted; the question is, whether improved machinery is to bear the blame of it.

It may be deemed unnecessary to discuss this question, after what has been said upon the general subject of the compensatory power of machinery, inasmuch as the displacing of the labour of the hand-loom weaver, by the application of an improved mechanical weaving apparatus, however deplorable in its immediate, or even in its permanent, consequences to the displaced individuals themselves, might be quite compatible with the improved condition of the working classes, as a whole. The invention of printing was, no doubt, injurious to the copyists, who, as exercising a lucrative profession, were exterminated by the introduction of the new mechanical art. The invention of the threshing-machine was equally injurious to those who made flail-threshing one source of their subsistence. And the same thing may be said of the effects of the new processes of manufacture, which have displaced "shearmen" in the woollen trade, and "flax-dressers" in the linen trade; with numerous other occupations or professions.[1] But to admit this, is not to admit that these new inventions, by which the classes, *as classes*, have been injured, have been injurious to the working population at large; nor even ultimately injurious to those who have at first suffered from them.

But, not to insist upon this view of the question, it is by no means so clear as is generally thought, that the deplorable condition of the hand-loom weavers has been brought about through the introduction of the power-loom.

There is something very peculiar in the case of the hand-loom weavers, which induces strong difficulties in the way of deciding on the precise cause of their distress. The hand-loom weavers were in a very wretched condition long before the use of the power-loom.

In 1799, no fewer than 500,000 persons connected with this occupation were represented in a petition to Parliament, setting forth the miserably low rate of their wages, and praying for the protection of Parliament, in their state of "distress." In 1808, Mr. William Ratcliffe, one of the inventors of the dressing-machine, and intimately acquainted with the manufacture, was examined by the Committee of the House of Commons, appointed to inquire into the claims of the Rev. Dr. Cartwright, the inventor of the power-loom, to a public reward, when he made the following statement: – "To that part of your question, whether I think the general adoption of the loom by power will operate to the prejudice of the weavers in the old way, I answer, no. In the first place, their situation has been such, for the last 12 or 18 months, that it cannot be made worse; as, during that time, generally speaking, they have neither been able to pay rents, nor to buy themselves clothes; all their earnings have barely been sufficient to keep them alive; and men, who have families to support, are obliged to work from 16 to 18 hours in the day to do this."

This distress was not temporary, merely. From 1808, when this evidence was given, down to 1818, when there were not more than 2,000 power-looms in Lancashire, the hand-loom weavers were exposed to similar privations. The use of the power-loom down to this period was too limited to make any material impression on the market price of cloth; nevertheless, the price paid for weaving a particular fabric, in the woollen trade, varied in the following proportions, according to the Lords' Report, of 1814: –

1792	8s.0d.
1802	10s.0d.
1808	5s.6d.
1809	9s.0d.
1811	5s.6d.
1812	6s.6d.
1813	8s.0d.
1814	10s.0d.

Now, as but few power-looms existed in 1808, and not many, compared with the number of hand-looms, in 1811, the fall of wages, at these periods, respectively, cannot be attributed to the use of the power-loom. But, besides this, it is observable, that notwithstanding the gradual introduction of the power-loom, up to 1814, the wages for weaving the particular article referred to, had risen, at that time, to 10s.

All these facts are irreconcileable with the notion, that the wages of the hand-loom weaver were depressed, and finally reduced to their present deplorably low rate, by the employment of the power-loom.

Another fact to be noticed here, is this, that the power-loom is improperly represented to "come into competition with the hand-loom," inasmuch as it cannot be profitably applied, and is not applied, therefore, to the production of the particular descriptions of articles upon which hand-loom weavers are employed. The power-loom is not applicable to figured nor to fine articles – "fancy goods," as they are termed. The necessity there is for constantly changing the shuttles, for the production of any figured or cross pattern in silks, and the increased breaking of the fine yarns, in cotton and worsted, render the use of the power-loom unprofitable in the production of any but the commoner and stronger tissues, whether of cotton, linen, woollen, or silk.

After the statement of these facts, it will not appear strange that there has been no reduction in the number of hand-loom weavers, in consequence of the increase that has taken place in the number of power-looms. Mr. Babbage states, from information gathered to be laid before Parliament, that, in 1830, the number of hand-looms in use, in Great Britain, was 240,000, and that nearly the same number existed in 1820; whereas the number of power-looms, which was only 14,000 in 1820, was increased to 55,000 in 1830. The number is now much larger.

But this fact, though quite consistent with what has been said here, is wholly inconsistent with the assumption, that the hand-loom weaver has been brought down to his present position by the operation of the power-loom.

Another striking fact was stated to the committee of 1834, by Mr. Makin, a manufacturer of Bolton. It was this, that there is often a demand for thousands of hand-loom weavers, beyond the number that can be obtained; but that, notwithstanding this, their wages never rise. This fact, which is seemingly at variance with the ordinary law of supply and demand, is supposed by Mr. Porter (Progress of the Nation) to be accounted for on the assumption, that when hand-loom woven goods can be furnished within a certain price, they admit of an extensive sale; but that when that limit is passed, other goods, of home production, or foreign goods of similar make, come into successful competition with them. If this supposition be well founded, then, and to that extent, the hand-loom weavers are certainly affected by the use of the power-loom, since, but for this, no such limit would exist as to the price obtainable for their productions. I do not think, however, that Mr. Porter's mode of accounting for the phenomenon is of any value. If it were, it would hold good in other branches of industry, which is not alleged.

Looking carefully at all the circumstances of the case of the hand-loom weavers, I am strongly disposed to think that the deterioration that has taken place in their condition, as compared with what has taken place in the condition of other classes of operatives employed in the staple trades of the country, is attributable, almost exclusively, to the nature of their employment, and the comparative facility with which the lowest class of labourers may transfer their labour to it. Common weaving is an employment to which unskilled persons, and even young children, may readily adapt themselves. If the power-loom had never been invented, there would, no doubt, have been a demand for a greater number of hands for the hand-loom; but what reason is there to believe that the greater number would not have been forced to work at wages equally low as those now paid?

From an analysis of an inquiry into the condition of 10,000 families of the working classes in Manchester, made in the spring of 1840, and published by Mr. Ordshead, it appears that of 6,978 hand-loom weavers, no fewer than 4,157 were Irish, or their immediate progeny; while of 38,613 persons, employed in other and more skilled branches of industry, only 15,642 were Irish, or their immediate progeny. It is computed that there are, in Manchester and its immediate neighbourhood, 60,000 Irish,[2] or their immediate descendants, a large proportion of whom depend upon weaving for a living; and if any additional number had been wanted, they would doubtless have been there. The wretched condition of the labourers in Ireland has not a little to do with the condition of the hand-loom weavers here.

Editorial Endnotes

1 J. H. Wiener, 'Carpenter, William', *Oxford Dictionary of National Biography*, 23 September 2004, at https://doi-org.du.idm.oclc.org/10.1093/ref:odnb/4741 [accessed 13 June 2021].

2 W. Carpenter, *Machinery as it Affects the Industrial Classes and the Employment of Children in Factories* (London: E. Lloyd, 1844), London School of Economics Library: OU1844/4F, p. 4.

3 Wiener, 'Carpenter, William'. On the Tolpuddle Martyrs, see C. Griffiths, 'From "Dorchester Labourers" to "Tolpuddle Martyrs": Celebrating Radicalism in the English Countryside', in Q. Outram and K. Laybourn (eds), *Secular Martyrdom in Britain and Ireland: From Peterloo to the Present* (New York: Palgrave Macmillan, 2018), pp. 59–84.

4 E. P. Thompson demonstrates this as well in *The Making of the English Working Class* (New York: Vintage Books, 1966), p. 286.

5 Carpenter, *Machinery*, p. 30.

6 See, for example, D. M. MacRaild, 'Irish Immigration and the "Condition of England" Question: The Roots of an Historiographical Tradition', *Immigrants and Minorities* 14:1 (1995), pp. 67–85.

Source Endnotes

1 There is great inconsistency in all the reasoning advanced against improvements in machinery, as being injurious to the labour classes. The power-loom in weaving, and the mule in spinning, are said to have displaced manual labour, to the prejudice of the operatives. But has not every machine, however simple, done the same thing? If the only

object be to give *employment* to the people, let us break up all our machines, from the spade to the steam-engine, and dig, as well as spin and weave, after the primitive fashion, before machines of any kind were thought of. But no; the opponents of machinery would not go that length, although they do not exactly know where they would stop short of it. They object to the "mule," because "it supercedes human labour;" but so also did the "jenny;" yet they do not propose to go back to the use of the distaff and one-handed spinning wheel. They assail the "power-loom," because it has reduced the value of the "hand-loom;" the hand-loom, however, was as great an improvement upon the old and rudely-constructed weaving apparatus, which may still be seen in India, and by the use of which a weaver might, perhaps, earn 1s. per week, as the power-loom is upon the hand-loom. All the arguments against improved machinery rest upon mistaken or limited views of the facts involved in the question.

2 Dr. Kay estimates the number of Irish employed in the cotton trade, in Lancashire, at 150,000, or 160,000. – Poor-law Report, I, 305.

19

LITERARY DEPICTIONS OF MECHANIZATION

The two sources here are literary depictions of the effect of industrial society on workers and their environments. Charles Dickens's *Hard Times* (19.1) is a quintessential 'condition of England' novel of the mid-nineteenth century, querying class relations and the social impact of industrialization. Charles Dickens (1812–1870) grew up in a family of eight children, with a father who often faced debt. When Dickens was twelve, his father was sent to debtor's prison, which meant that Dickens had to leave school. He went to work in a blacking factory (shoe polishing) for several months, until his father was released from prison. This experience of poverty shaped his literary career and made him a sensitive and important voice for the working class. *Hard Times* (1854) was first serialized in Dickens's weekly periodical *Household Words*.[1] It was aggressively topical, aiming to 'shake' people into awareness of the 'mistake of these days'.[2] The novel is a critique of industrial degradation, political economy, and Jeremy Bentham's utilitarian theory, all of which Dickens saw as destroying the capacity for human feeling and imagination.[3] In this brief selection, Dickens paints a picture of Coketown, his fictitious northern industrial town, where the action of *Hard Times* takes place. The chapter is titled 'The Key-Note', for it demonstrates the centrality of Fact, conformity, and industry to the rest of the story. Dickens connects machinery to environmental destruction, with blackened water and unending smoke produced from factory work. Workers are like cogs in the machine, who all look exactly alike and do exactly the same thing. The entire town of Coketown is devoted to work and fact, and everything in it appeared 'workful', with no embellishment.[4] While Coketown was supposed to be supremely orderly, Dickens notes that there were cracks in the construction: the working class did not attend church or chapel, they drank and took drugs, and they resorted to 'low' entertainments.[5] All of this was, of course, tabulated carefully to create facts. Dickens introduces Gradgrind, who represents hard facts and utilitarian philosophy, and Bounderby, a factory owner, who falsely claims to be a self-made man. Here they are suspicious of the working class and poor, who seem to always want more than they are due and were never satisfied. Dickens then compares this picture of the working class to Gradgrind's children, who their father was raising solely on Fact with no Fancy. Just as workers were mechanized through factory labour, the little Gradgrinds had

DOI: 10.4324/9780429320323-23

become mechanical through their education. Both, Dickens argues, needed some kind of 'holiday' to find their humanity.[6]

The next source is a selection from Benjamin Brierley's 1885 *Tales and Sketches of Lancashire Life* (19.2). Brierley (1825–1896) was born to a very poor family in Failsworth, near Manchester. His father was a handloom weaver, and Brierley went to work very young as a bobbin winder, at one point becoming a handloom weaver himself and finally a silk-warper. He was self-taught, having left school before the age of six, and helped found the Manchester Mechanics Institute, a self-help society. He was known as a Lancashire poet and author, writing in the dialect from where he came.[7] The selection here comes from 'Out of Work', in *Tales and Sketches of Lancashire Life* (1885). In the tale included here, Jenny, a Lancashire factory worker, receives a letter from Agnes, who has recently rejected her job as a servant in Lancashire and moved to London to take up dressmaking.[8] Agnes chides Jenny for staying in Lancashire doing factory work, where the operatives' hours had been reduced, when she could be using her 'good fingers' at needle-work.[9] Agnes invites Jenny to come to London to visit and see how well set up she is, with her 'young man' and her own house.[10] Brierley uses the delivery of this letter to describe the setting in which Jenny finds herself: an area filled with the lovely cottages of the once well-to-do handloom weavers of 'forty years ago'.[11] The picture Brierley paints is a sharp contrast with that of Coketown. Here was an idyll, with gardens and flowers, where wives used to spin and husbands wove. The narrator comments that he understands why 'old people' think of these times nostalgically and lament 'the passing away of "old times"'.[12] Jenny has been raised in the 'old-fashioned ways' of her parents, in this neighbourhood, 'where the rattle of the looms is heard no more'.[13] Jenny's father, Walter Fairclough, was one of the weavers put out of work. While so much has changed around him, including 'foreign competition', the rule of 'unfeeling' economics, and the development of the music hall, Fairclough's garden and demeanour remained the same.[14] He 'never loved the sight or sound of a factory', but he recognized that handloom weaving was 'dead' and his children had to make a living.[15] Even though Jenny worked at a factory, the narrator tells the reader, she was not corrupted by factory culture, paying no attention to trivialities like fashion. Yet a trade depression in the region began to pull Jenny toward the city, where she heard she could earn higher wages and better support her family. In these few pages, Brierley offers a critique of mechanization, not only in terms of the destruction of handloom weaving as a trade but of the culture of the region. His is a backward-looking vision that idealizes a lost preindustrial past.

19.1 Charles Dickens, *Hard Times*, chapter 5, 'The Key-Note'

[. . .] Let us strike the key-note, Coketown, before pursuing our tune.

It was a town of red brick, or of brick that would have been red if the smoke and ashes had allowed it; but as matters stood, it was a town of unnatural red and black like the painted face of a savage. It was a town of machinery and tall chimneys, out of which interminable serpents of smoke trailed themselves for ever and ever, and never got uncoiled. It had a black canal in it, and a river that ran purple with ill-smelling dye, and vast piles of building full of windows where there was a rattling and a trembling all day long, and where the piston of the steam-engine worked monotonously up and down, like the head of an elephant in a state of melancholy madness. It contained several large streets all very like one another, and many small streets still more like one another, inhabited by people equally like one another, who all went in and out at the same hours, with the same sound upon the same pavements, to do the same work, and to whom every day was the same as yesterday and to-morrow, and every year the counterpart of the last and the next.

These attributes of Coketown were in the main inseparable from the work by which it was sustained; against them were to be set off, comforts of life which found their way all over the world, and elegancies of life which made, we will not ask how much of the fine lady, who could scarcely bear to hear the place mentioned. The rest of its features were voluntary, and they were these.

You saw nothing in Coketown but what was severely workful. If the members of a religious persuasion built a chapel there – as the members of eighteen religious persuasions had done – they made it a pious warehouse of red brick, with sometimes (but this is only in highly ornamental examples) a bell in a birdcage on the top of it. The solitary exception was the New Church; a stuccoed edifice with a square steeple over the door, terminating in four short pinnacles like florid wooden legs. All the public inscriptions in the town were painted alike, in severe characters of black and white. The jail might have been the infirmary, the infirmary might have been the jail, the town-hall might have been either, or both, or anything else, for anything that appeared to the contrary in the graces of their construction. Fact, fact, fact, everywhere in the material aspect of the town; fact, fact, fact, everywhere in the immaterial. The M'Choakumchild school was all fact, and the school of design was all fact, and the relations between master and man were all fact, and everything was fact between the lying-in hospital and the cemetery, and what you couldn't state in figures, or show to be purchaseable in the cheapest market and saleable in the dearest, was not, and never should be, world without end, Amen.

A town so sacred to fact, and so triumphant in its assertion, of course got on well? Why no, not quite well. No? Dear me!

No. Coketown did not come out of its own furnaces, in all respects like gold that had stood the fire. First, the perplexing mystery of the place was, Who belonged to the eighteen denominations? Because, whoever did, the labouring people did not. It was very strange to walk through the streets on a Sunday morning, and note how few of them the barbarous jangling of bells that was driving the sick and nervous mad, called away from their own quarter, from their own close rooms, from the corners of their own streets, where they lounged listlessly, gazing at all the church and chapel going, as at a thing with which they had no manner of concern. Nor was it merely the stranger who noticed this, because there was a native organization in Coketown itself, whose members were to be heard of in the House of Commons every session, indignantly petitioning for acts of parliament that should make these people religious by main force. Then came the Teetotal Society, who complained that these same people would get drunk, and showed in tabular statements that they did get drunk, and proved at tea parties that no inducement, human or Divine (except a medal), would induce them to forego their custom of getting drunk. Then came the chemist and druggist, with other tabular statements, showing that when they didn't get drunk, they took opium. Then came the experienced chaplain of the jail, with more tabular statements, outdoing all the previous tabular statements, and showing that the same people would resort to low haunts, hidden from the public eye, where they heard low singing and saw low dancing, and mayhap joined in it; and where A. B., aged twenty-four next birthday, and committed for eighteen months' solitary, had himself said (not that he had ever shown himself particularly worthy of belief) his ruin began, as he was perfectly sure and confident that otherwise he would have been a tip-top moral specimen. Then came Mr. Gradgrind and Mr. Bounderby, the two gentlemen at this present moment walking through Coketown, and both eminently practical, who could, on occasion, furnish more tabular statements derived from their own personal experience, and illustrated by cases they had known and seen, from which it clearly appeared – in short, it was the only clear thing in the case – that these same people were a bad lot altogether, gentlemen; that do what you would for them they were never thankful for it, gentlemen; that they were restless, gentlemen; that they never knew what they wanted; that they lived upon the best, and bought fresh butter; and insisted on Mocha coffee, and rejected all but prime parts of meat, and yet were eternally dissatisfied and unmanageable. In short, it was the moral of the old nursery fable:

> There was an old woman, and what do you think?
> She lives upon nothing but victuals and drink;
> Victuals and drink were the whole of her diet,
> And yet this old woman would NEVER be quiet.

Is it possible, I wonder, that there was any analogy between the case of the Coketown population and the case of the little Gradgrinds? Surely, none of us in our sober senses and acquainted with figures, are to be told at this time of day, that one of the foremost elements in the existence of the Coketown working-people had been for scores of years, deliberately set at nought? That there was any Fancy in them demanding to be brought into healthy existence instead of struggling on in convulsions? That exactly in the ratio as they worked long and monotonously, the craving grew within them for some physical relief – some relaxation, encouraging good humour and good spirits, and giving them a vent – some recognized holiday, though it were but for an honest dance to a stirring band of music – some occasional light pie in which even M'Choakumchild had no finger – which craving must and would be satisfied aright, or must and would inevitably go wrong, until the laws of the Creation were repealed?

19.2 Benjamin Brierley, 'Out of Work'

DEAR JENNY, – i rite these few lines hopeing To find you in hood Helth as it leeves me at Present thank god for it i hear as how you isnt doing So well as you was through Short time at the factry. i wonder how you have paichance to go to the dirty Mill when you have Such good fingers beside if i Had as good figgur as you wich i dont think as im a frite i woud never stop To hide myself in the countery as you is Hiden come and Spend a day or tow with me i Have got an House to myself wich i pays tree and Six for and i am so comfutable if you will come by the Buss which comes by the Park Wall and get out at lord street cheetham hill roade and ask for Miss St. Clair i dont go in My own name as works the sewing mechine land of juda you will find me come Tomorrow if you can fred that is my yong Man is coming you Will be So Pleosed with him hes quite a gentleman a byer at a warhouse wich is a good sittuation hel take us To the music hall wich is a grand place and he never thinks hes done enogh for me do come So no more at Present from your old companyon Agnes Meadowcroft.

land of juda red bank.

Manchester october – 1867.

Such were the contents of a letter delivered over the gate leading to one of those substantial-looking cottages that, forty years ago, were the homesteads of the better-to-do class of Lancashire weavers. There was nothing on earth that had the neatness and comfort of the dwellings at that period. They were mostly built in a detached form, completely surrounded by garden plot – the indispensable pear-tree nailed against the sunniest gable, and the honeysuckle trailing in wanton luxuriance about the door and windows. The front garden was usually devoted to the growth of gooseberries, currants, and that emblem of the purity of such homes, the white rose. The gates and hedges were all of one pattern, the latter of mixed thorn, box, and privet, with here and there a limb of wild-briar, creeping round, and lacing the bushes together, as if wishful to form a sylvan brotherhood. Strips of flowered border invariably hemmed each side of the path leading from the gate to the door; and occasionally a straw-plaited cone, resting on a rude wooden structure, sheltered its humming colony under the house window. On fine summer mornings cages would be hung about the walls, or stuck in the hedges, that their feathered tenants might feel the sunshine, and breathe the air their wings ought to have been cleaving; and the song would be poured forth in full-throated thankfulness for such a boon. Behind the house, on lines reaching from tree to tree in a small clump of orchard, the family linen would be flapping – the winter's snow woven into fluffy garments that, when "taken in," would smell of the blossoms they had hung amongst. And the well-ordered household, the busy whirl of the old dame's wheel, the cheerful rattle of the looms, and the song that would now and then break forth from the weavers, made these little colonies such charming bits of earth-embroidery, that I do not wonder at old people sighing over the remembrance of them, and placing them foremost among their regrets for the passing away of "old times."

In one of these cottages, that still preserve a little of the olden flavour, lives "Walker Fairclough," a man, of whom it may be said, as was sung of "Old Ralph" – "He had walked with his God from the morning of youth," and still held on in the path that leads up to heaven's gates. Walker's wife is to him as Eve was to Adam – truly a "rib" from his very soul, if we may give that subtle element a substantial character. And both have been as true to their own hearth; as true to their old-fashioned friendships, and as true to the even line of pure purpose, as the unerring law that awards happiness only to the good. A son and a daughter, "Squire" and "Jenny," their only offspring, have been brought up in the old-fashioned ways of their parents, and the new world, with its shifting modes, its flimsy toyishness, its ephemeral attachments, and the dissimulation that is making a liar of almost every face, has been until now a sealed book to them. Coyly have they approached the fashions as they have changed – in dress, in manner, in speech – and the hat, the coat, the bonnet, the frock, have always been the relics of long-departed tastes, so that each was a sort of museum, or repository, of dead fashions. Their inner furnishing kept pace only with their outer garb. Their loves were not of the early spring. They came when the snowdrop and primrose had buried their first passions, and subsided into the sere of a forward autumn. With Jenny it came not until it was wooed; and with Squire it was a plant of such slow growth, that even when matured he scarcely knew of its presence. There was a youth, however, who years ago saw in Jenny a wife, a mother, and a companion that would have been to a poor man's heart and hearth a treasure of priceless worth. But the girl's eye replied not to his, and his tongue could not fashion the word that was to win her affections; so he was content to regard her as a saint, that to defile with human breath would be to call down the anger of Heaven, and the tears of such angelic natures as dwelt therein. He placed her image in a higher receptacle than his breast, and with it enshrined there, among bright hopes and holy aspirations, left the village, and sought the less genial atmosphere of town life, where we will leave him for the present.

Old Fairclough's cottage is one of a cluster of such dwellings as I have attempted to describe, and stands in a lane that seems to have been shaped and stocked out of old memories. The garden is as sweet and as prettily kept as when its owner trimmed it with a youthful hand. The colony of honey storers flourishes, even with foreign competition in the market; and the several families of feathered bachelors pipe their melodies as sweetly and as merrily as they did before "Vance" and "Claribel" gave a tone to our national minstrelsy. But the rattle of the looms is heard no more, and the bobbinwheel is laid by. What boots it, however, to Walker Fairclough if "trade's unfeeling train" hath swept his little workshop of the busy life that it was once a joy to dwell among? He has just enough for himself and old dame wherewith to refresh at every resting-place on their shortening journey to the churchyard. The old man has more time now to think of God, his neighbours, and his duties to both; but he cannot help sighing over the remembrance of a time when Squire and Jenny grew up under his watchful eye, and their constant presence and daily fulfilment of the better purposes of life was a comfort and an assurance to him that few parents can now enjoy. He never loved the sight or sound of a factory; and it was with the greatest reluctance that he permitted his children to go to work at one; but hand-weaving appeared to be dead, and its resuscitation very doubtful; so there was no other course open but to attend the summons of the bell, and to submit to the encroachments of all-pervading steam.

For years had Jenny Fairclough worked at ——— Mill, Radcliffe, and yet her outward manner had never lost one line of its grace and modesty. Still no prettier girl walked the lanes of "Besses," nor one who appeared to be less conscious of her beauty. Her hair done up in the simplest style; her bonnet a compromise between the one worn by our foremothers and the bit of straw and ribbon of the present day; her dress without a single gew-gaw, save an unobtrusive gold pin that had been her grandmother's, and worn on that account; the shawl that she drew round her with so much unaffected art; her quiet, yet gracefully agile gait, and the eye that never watched herself or others, but found more things between heaven and earth than Fashion's votaries to look upon and admire, stamped her as a woman who deemed her sex had a higher mission in this world than merely flaunting through it, with no worthier ambition than to become the packhorse of the jeweller and the artificer in silks and sables, and with the inevitable certainty of becoming a victim to the thousand and one jealousies that follow in the train. If she had admirers, she knew it not, as she courted no eye, nor allowed her own to wander the least in search of the blush and confused manner that betrayed the presence of love's emotions. She read no books that fostered the tender passion. Her library-companions "breathed not the words that burn" – awoke not the flame that consumes the heart. If her breast throbbed, it was in sympathy with misfortune; if the tear fell, it was in pity for some wounded dove that the sport of the world had made its quarry and robbed of the innocence it pretends to prize.

And such might Jenny have continued to be had not the tempter crossed her path. But the turn came for steam to have its holiday. Trade went bad; "short-time" set in, and the fortnightly wage list had an impoverished look. Old Fairclough grunted over the diminished receipts, and the daughter began to feel as though she was a burden where she ought to have been a support. She had heard "great sayings" of what young women could earn in Manchester, and her ear inclined more and more to listen to these tales.

Notes

1 'The Late Charles Dickens', *Illustrated (London) News*, 18 June 1870, p. 2; M. Slater, 'Dickens, Charles John Huffam', *Oxford Dictionary of National Biography* (hereafter

ODNB), 12 November 2020, at https://doi-org.du.idm.oclc.org/10.1093/ref:odnb/7599 [accessed 13 June 2021].

2 C. Dickens, quoted in Slater, 'Dickens'.

3 For a nuanced reading of Dickens on political economy, see C. Gallagher, '*Hard Times* and the Somaeconomics of the Early Victorians', in *The Body Economic: Life, Death, and Sensation in Political Economy and the Victorian Novel* (Princeton, NJ: Princeton University Press, 2009), pp. 62–85; on Dickens and utilitarianism, see, for example, R. J. Arneson, 'Benthamite Utilitarianism and *Hard Times*', *Philosophy and Literature* 2:1 (1978), pp. 60–75.

4 C. Dickens, *Hard Times* (London: Bradbury & Evans, 1854), Google Books, p. 29.

5 Dickens, *Hard Times*, pp. 30–31.

6 Dickens, *Hard Times*, p. 32.

7 'Death of Ben Brierley', *Manchester Courier and Lancashire General Advertiser*, 25 January 1896, p. 15; C. W. Sutton, 'Brierley, Benjamin [Ben]', *ODNB*, 4 October 2008, at https://doi-org.du.idm.oclc.org/10.1093/ref:odnb/3405 [accessed 13 June 2021].

8 On women's work in factories and needlework, see Volume 1, Part 3.

9 B. Brierley, 'Out of Work' in *Tales and Sketches of Lancashire Life* (Manchester: Abel Haywood & Son; London: Simpkin, Marshall, & Co., 1885), Google Books, p. 27.

10 Brierley, *Tales and Sketches*, p. 27.

11 Brierley, *Tales and Sketches*, p. 27. On handloom weavers, see Volume 1 Introduction.

12 Brierley, *Tales and Sketches*, p. 28.

13 Brierley, *Tales and Sketches*, pp. 29, 30.

14 Brierley, *Tales and Sketches*, p. 30.

15 Brierley, *Tales and Sketches*, p. 31.

20

J. SAMUELSON, 'INTRODUCTORY', 'THE DISPLACEMENT OF HAND-LABOUR IN AGRICULTURE', 'DISPLACEMENT OF GENERAL LABOURERS BY MACHINERY', AND 'INFERENCES – THE GENERAL QUESTION OF LABOUR – CONCLUSION', IN *LABOUR-SAVING MACHINERY*

(London: Kegan, Paul, Trench, Trübner, & Co., 1893), pp. 1–13, 66–80, and 91–94

James Samuelson (1829–1918) had a seed-crushing firm, James Samuelson and Son, which gave him the opportunity to interact with working people, and he became a close ally of trade unionists. He studied law in order to have the legal knowledge to support legislation to improve conditions for labourers and mediate trade disputes. Having a strong interest in technical education, he founded courses at the Liverpool School of Science. He stood unsuccessfully for Parliament twice as a Liberal. His obituaries refer to him as a 'well-known local leader' and 'a noted social reformer'.[1] In these selections, Samuelson provides a sober study of labour-saving machinery. In chapter 2, Samuelson argues that no industry had been so affected by mechanization as much as agricultural labour. Machines had almost entirely displaced manual labour, which had caused agricultural workers to emigrate to towns, creating problems of un- and underemployment in urban areas.[2] From the 'economic view', Samuelson argues, machines had improved agriculture, with far less time required in almost all agricultural processes and less dependence on the weather in order to work.[3] While the new industry of machine making had evolved and required skilled workers to build the machines and semi-skilled workers to operate them, the whole enterprise needed far fewer workers than the over 100,000 displaced agricultural labourers. Interestingly, Samuelson

DOI: 10.4324/9780429320323-24

also points out that the boredom arising from village life without work had led rural men to desire more education and a 'more rational existence', which he sees as a positive step forward, improving on a life that 'begins with the taproom and ends in the workhouse'.[4] He also notes that women felt less comfortable in the new model of working in the fields. In Chapter 6, Samuelson turns to the question of unskilled labour and warns that employers were using strikes as an excuse to permanently displace workers by machinery.[5] He indicates, however, that the extent of savings in the cost of production would have led to mechanization in any event. Indeed, he seems to regard the displacement of manual labour as inevitable, providing examples from a variety of different industries across England and even mentioning the U.S. While warning that the census had difficulties measuring unskilled labour, Samuelson uses census numbers to show the growth of casual positions between 1861 and 1881, attributing this growth to mechanization. In the conclusion, Samuelson argues that the two biggest forces driving employers to embrace machinery were competition and consumption. He states that mechanization was not just about manufacturers trying to supplant men with machines: 'the masses' demanded cheaper goods,[6] and the only way to produce these was through mechanization. Samuelson makes a point of warning labour leaders that strikes gave employers an incentive to develop machinery to replace men and warning employers not to use machinery as a weapon against their employees. He urges technical education 'to elevate the masses' and desires a future with a more equitable distribution of wealth.[7] His overall picture is utilitarian, urging the state to play a role to relieve unemployment, such as the public works circular of 1892 (see Volume 2, Part 3, Chapter 37), to bring the greatest happiness to the greatest number. He favours a measured adoption of machinery and the public recognition of the disruption the process of mechanization caused to manual workers.

Labour-Saving Machinery.

Chapter I.

Introductory.

THERE has been no period in English history when the labour question has attracted such widespread attention as at the present time. There have been agrarian and servile revolts against the tyranny and exactions of feudal lords and landowners; scarcity and high prices of the necessaries of life have driven the poor to desperation, and have caused riot and outrage; the adoption of machinery to meet the advancing needs of civilisation has led to futile attempts to suppress its use; prosperity in trade has caused strikes for higher wages, and its depression has been the means of creating lock-outs to enforce a reduction. But all these uprisings of labour have been either partial in time or space, and it may have been that disturbances existed in one county which were hardly heard of in a neighbouring one. Now, however, all that is changed. The unequal distribution of property continues, and the extremes of wealth and poverty are held up to view, not alone by those who suffer, but by the Press, by philanthropic and political organisations, by preachers, and by writers on political economy in books and in magazines. The proverbial one-half of society is beginning to learn, not how the other half lives, but how it starves; and nostrums of every kind are being advertised, gratuitously or otherwise, for the amelioration or reconstruction of society. In our villages, life is so dull and monotonous that people are migrating into large cities, tempted by nominally higher wages, to find only partial employment. There, in the large towns, the most glaring inconsistencies are to be witnessed. In London, one-third of the labouring men earn less than 1*l*. per week (to say nothing of those who starve); in Liverpool, the proportion is two-fifths, whilst within a mile or two there are to be found persons with thousands a year who never did a handstroke in their lives. In some of our large towns there is a demand for improved dwellings to be erected by the local authorities for the benefit of the unemployed; but whilst there are hundreds upon hundreds of houses in which five or six families herd together, there are thousands completely untenanted.

On the one hand we find large employers of labour complaining of the dulness of trade, arising from prohibitory tariffs abroad or reckless speculation at home, and seeking to enforce reduced wages; on the other hand, the labouring classes are banding more closely to resist a reduction, and complaining of competition in *their* class through surplus labour, skilled and unskilled. Whilst the labouring classes are seeking by every possible means to strengthen their position, the employing class is doing the same, not only by federation, but by an effort, as far as possible, to dispense with hand-labour altogether, through the adoption of mechanical appliances.

Enough, and to spare has been said and written about trades unions of employer and employed, and it seems to me that a word in season with regard to the adoption of labour-saving machinery may now be added, with advantage to all classes who are interested. The following pages are, however, intended simply to draw attention to the subject, and not by any means to treat it exhaustively. Its complete treatment is surrounded with many difficulties. Makers of machinery are ready enough to give every information that is desired, and I am bound to say that, with one or two exceptions, I have found on inquiry from users of the machinery that there is little trade exaggeration in what has been told me. On the other hand, some of the users were unwilling to give me the results of the employment of mechanical appliances for the displacement of hand-labour, either because they wish to retain an advantage over their neighbours, or from fear of the unions. On the whole, however, I think the high position of the firms from whom I have received the data which will be found in the following chapters is a sufficient guarantee for their accuracy.

Another difficulty that is encountered is the unmethodical system of compiling the census returns, and it may be added, the delay in their publication. The volume containing the 'Occupations of the People,' in 1891, is not yet issued, and although it may be difficult to bring it out in its completed form without considerable preparation, the information published two or three years after date can hardly be used with safety. But although some of the figures given in reference to the various industries indicate their condition in 1881, that is to say, such figures as have been extracted from the census tables, the reader will find that where those figures deal with important changes now proceeding, as for example the introduction of machinery into mines, or the substitution of mechanical appliances for hand-labour in navvy or general labourers' work, I have been enabled, from private sources, to give a faithful statement of the facts bearing upon the inquiry.

Two or three references to my own experience and observation (extending over about thirty-five years) may be considered egotistical, but I have made them to show the reader that my knowledge of the subject is more than theoretical; and it may here be added, that in the majority of examples cited I have not been satisfied with hearsay evidence, but have seen the appliances in use; and I should like to thank those firms and friends in various parts of the country who have helped me in my work, and without whose aid it could hardly have been accomplished.

As already stated, the following chapters are merely suggestive, and are intended to indicate the direction which the inquiry should take. Most of the appliances referred to serve a double purpose; to do the work more speedily and efficiently, and to save hand-labour; and typical examples of these appliances in several prominent industries are described in all but the last chapter. In the last chapter but one, I have briefly summarised the information contained in the United States Labour Report, compiled by Colonel Carroll Wright, and any one who wishes to enter more fully into the subject should procure and carefully study that report, where a number of industries are dealt with which are here merely mentioned.

In the last chapter I have sought to bring before the reader such inferences and conclusions, in regard to the effects of labour-saving machinery upon the future of our working classes, as have been suggested by the consideration of the whole subject. No attempt has been made to propose new remedies for existing evils, but I have endeavoured, by accentuating movements already in progress, to point out to well-meaning philanthropists and employers how they can best contribute to the solution of one of the most difficult problems of our age. At present the labour question is in a chaotic condition, but a settlement will not be helped forward by abuse of the working classes on the one hand, or of "Capital" on the other. It has to be faced – by employers, by local authorities, by the legislature, by all who are interested in the welfare of the community – and inasmuch as we have in this country no "paternal government" to take charge of the interests of the masses, it behoves all who by word or act can exercise any influence, to do so unselfishly, and with a view to the national advancement.

Chapter II.

The displacement of hand-labour in agriculture.

It is difficult to point to any one of our industries, and to say, that particular branch has been the most largely affected by the introduction of machinery as a substitute for hand-labour; but for various reasons the one which appears to be the most striking and important is agriculture. Of the vast number of men who have been displaced by machinery, a certain proportion figure in the emigration records, but the change has made itself more sensibly felt in the immigration of farm labourers into our large towns, where they overcrowd the labour market, and add largely to the tale of the semi-employed or the entirely unemployed. Every branch of agriculture has been revolutionised by the introduction of machinery, which has largely displaced hand-labour, and the very manufacture of the machinery itself has undergone great changes from the same cause. For this reason alone, it is necessary to limit our inquiry as much as possible, and to select one or two striking illustrations of the changes that have affected our labouring community.

Thrashing machines probably first superseded the flail in Scotland about the end of the last century; improved ploughs were first introduced by the Ransomes at the beginning of the present one; reaping and mowing machines came largely into use between 1860 and 1874 (their introduction being stimulated by the prosperity of farmers, and the universal demand for labour about that period) with what effect on hand-labour we shall see presently. Added to the mere reaping operations, we have now the so-called "binders," which reap, collect and bind the grain; we have the steam plough, the mechanical drill, the horse-rake, a substitute for the hand-rake, winnowing machines worked by steam, chaff-cutters, turnip-cutters, cake-breakers, and a variety of other appliances in the field, the dairy, and the farmyard.

Let us take, first, as an illustration of the displacement of hand-labour, the effect of the introduction of machinery in the cultivation of grass and cereals.[1]

Comparison between the labour employed in Agriculture, when work is done by machinery and by hand-power only.

A full day's work.	*In acres.*	*Men employed.*	*Same work done by manual labour.*	*Number of men displaced by machinery.*
2 H.P. grass-mower	12 acres	2 men	9 men	7 men gained
2 H.P. reaper	16 "	3 "	12 "	9 " "
Binder	12 "	2½ "	12 "	9½ " "
Hay-rake or corn-rake	16 "	1 man	2 "	1 man "
Seed-drill (small seeds)	20 "	2 men	1 man	1 " lost

In this estimate, all preliminary and subsequent work is considered, and it must be mentioned that the work done by mechanical drill is superior to that by hand-labour. An immense gain to the agriculturist is the speed with which farming operations can be carried on by machinery, rendering him less dependent upon the weather, and, to some extent, more independent of trades unions. This is, of course, looking at the question from what is called the "economic" point of view alone.[2]

Let us now turn from this limited aspect of the question to the wider one of the general divorcement of a great mass of labourers from the soil; bearing in mind that the years when reaping and mowing machinery most largely superseded hand-labour were from 1860 to 1874.

Agricultural labourers reported as employed, in the Census Tables.[3]

	Men.	*Women.*	*Total.*
In 1861	914,301	43,964	958,265
In 1871	764,574	33,513	798,087
In 1881	807,608	40,340	847,948
	Decrease, 1861 to 1881, 110,317		

More than 110,000 persons, therefore, have been displaced, largely by the introduction of machinery. It is necessary to qualify this statement, because during some of those years considerable changes were made in the nature of the crops cultivated. The agricultural returns are imperfect in this respect until the year 1871, but it will be found that out of every 1000 acres of arable and pasture land in Great Britain –

	In 1871.	*In 1881.*	*In 1891.*	*1871 to 1891.*
The total permanent pasture was	403	455	499	+ nearly 10 p. c.
" of arable was	597	545	501	– nearly 16 p. c.

involving a considerable diminution of field labour.

But we are also enabled to judge of the increase in the use of machinery as a substitute for manual labour by the growth of the implement manufacture. According to the census returns there were employed in this industry: –

	In 1861.	*In 1871.*	*In 1881.*	*Increase between 1861 & 1881.*
Artisans and dealers in implements	1034	3617	4119	2583
Labourers *with* implements	1205	2152	4260	3055

Thus we find that between 1861 and 1881 more than 110,000 comparatively skilled and unskilled farm labourers have given place to about 4000 skilled artisans making machines, which were worked by 4260 semi-skilled labourers. And it must not be forgotten that a very large number of additional machines of various kinds have been annually imported from the United States, a fact which probably accounts for the comparatively greater increase of labourers using implements over that of the artisans making them.

It may be of interest also to inquire whether hand-labour has not been superseded by machine labour even in the fabrication of the improved labour-saving implements themselves. In this connection I have received information from several eminent firms of agricultural implement makers.

Messrs. Ruston, Proctor & Co., Limited, of Lincoln, say: –

> "All the machinery we make saves labour immensely on old methods, and all we use in our factory is of the most advanced description. We employ 2000 hands and are extremely busy . . . . Our works and output have increased so steadily in size and quantity that it is quite impossible for us to distinguish on the output what is due to an enlarged staff and additional tools, and what is due to labour-saving machinery; the process has been one of such steady development. We can only say we are employing more men than ever we did, and their wages are higher than they ever have been."[4]

More aggregate labour employed, therefore, at higher wages.

Messrs. James and Francis Howard, of Bedford, say: –

> "We are constantly adopting new appliances for reducing hand-labour, with a view to economy, accuracy of fit, and quickness of execution. This machinery is used for the purposes of pressing and shaping metal plates, bars, and other forms of material. The tendency is toward an advance of wages for individual workmen, especially unskilled workers . . . . The number of men

> and boys employed here has been reduced by the adoption of labour-saving appliances. No opposition has been met with from the unions."

Here we have a reduction of labour therefore, along with an increase of wages of unskilled labour.

Messrs. Robey & Co., of Lincoln, write: –

> "Generally we may say, we have never ceased since these works were first established, and particularly so during the last 28 years, to continually add labour-saving plant in every department of our works. The mechanical results of such are that the machinery we turn out has continually improved, both in design and finish. The financial results of this large additional expenditure of capital have been that the benefits therefrom have gone partly to increased wages to labour and partly to the public, who are now purchasing better machinery at a much lower price than in former years. Capital itself has derived no reproductive benefit from this large additional outlay."

With regard to these last sentences, which may perhaps appear to some persons to be rather diplomatic, I would say that they are entitled to complete credence. Whoever has followed the course of our manufacturing industries, knows that in many of them, respectable firms who have improved their products, enlarged their premises, and employed more perfect plant, are now earning considerably less than with a smaller capital and less perfect appliances. Competition has reduced the margin of profit, and large additional sums have been expended in wages, coal, and other indispensable elements of manufacture.

From another large firm of agricultural implement makers I have received confirmation of the preceding statement. They say that looking back over the last ten years they have employed labour-saving machinery in the foundry, such as moulding machines, in the carpenter's shop for mortising, tenoning and shaping; and in the fitting shop various machines for simplifying and economising labour. After taking all items of expenditure into consideration, such as interest and wear and tear of machinery, driving power, &c., they estimate an average gain of 33 per cent. on working expenses. Trade, they say, has not been good of late, but their improved machinery has enabled them to maintain their output without reduction of wages or diminution of the number of men employed.

The general effects of the introduction of machinery into agriculture in this country have been, as already stated, to shorten the time for farming operations; to enable the British agriculturist to meet to some extent the grave competition of distant lands which send their products into our markets; to displace vast numbers of hand-labourers in the fields, thereby diminishing the periodical immigration of Irish immigrants during harvest; of driving English labourers into our large towns or compelling them to emigrate. On the other hand, it has created a new and rapidly increasing industry, that of agricultural implement making, which is calling into existence a new class of skilled artisans, and perhaps a higher class of labourers in field and farm. I hear also that it is causing a growing disinclination in women to take part in field-labour; is making the male agricultural population dissatisfied with the prevalent dulness of village life and their surrounding ignorance, and thus calling for higher education and a more rational existence than that which begins with the taproom and ends in the workhouse; and generally that it is raising the whole class. To put it tersely, as my friend Joseph Arch has done on the back of a post-card which I have received from him: –

> "No doubt but the introduction of machinery woke the rural labourers and set them thinking, and did, I believe, a great deal towards their combination." [. . .]

Chapter IV.

Displacement of general labourers by machinery.

THERE is one important phase of this question to which we have not yet directed our attention. In most of the cases hitherto considered, machinery and improved processes have been necessitated by increased demand, or by keen competition, or by both; but as having a more direct bearing on our inquiry, we must now look at those examples where the action of the labourers themselves has caused employers, in the first instance at least, to resort to the use of mechanical contrivances, in order to render themselves as independent as possible of hand-labour. This has been chiefly the case in unskilled trades, and although I have naturally enough found less readiness on the part of employers to supply me with data for comparison, quite sufficient have been given to me, coupled with the results of my own experience and observation, extending over more than a quarter of a century, to enable me to show conclusively, that the opposition of employers to strikes is by no means confined to the displacement of unionists by non-unionists. The secretary of an extensive federation of employers naïvely tells me that machinery is the answer of the employers to the workmen's demands for shorter hours and higher wages. To what extent this is so, my readers will be able to judge for themselves, but it may be at once admitted, that the facts, as they stand, make it advisable that the leaders of labour should consider well whether, and to what extent, those who look up to them for counsel are likely, in case of a strike, to be *permanently* displaced by mechanical appliances. For in the interest of the men themselves, I would add that there may be cases, when even from their point of view it would be better for unionists to work with non-society men, than to be permanently deprived of the means of earning their livelihood by the introduction of machinery into their particular industry. And now to give a few examples in support of this view.

It was last year, I think, that the Directors of the Western Counties Agricultural Co-operative Association informed their shareholders in their annual report that much labour-saving apparatus had been erected, and in reply to inquiries I was told that this had been necessitated by a strike of piece-work labourers under the direction of what were called "Union Agitators," and the following details of the changes in working were furnished to me: –

> "Elevating and distributing machinery, by which grain delivered in bulk into hopper at the quay side is carried to the top of the building and distributed on an endless band into bins in the top loft, and gravitates into bins on the lower floors as may be required for feeding, direct into grinding mills or re-delivering into sacks through shoots. Said grain can be re-delivered into the elevator by means of the conveyor-worm, so as to remove the contents of one part of the warehouse to another without hand-labour, or for cooling grain instead of turning by hand."

In this case, the estimate of labour-saving is as follows: –

> "This entirely displaces four men, saving in labour 10*s*. per 100 quarters of grain delivered into warehouse, and 12*s*. 6*d*. per 100 quarters on all grain which may be required to be shifted from one part of the warehouse to another, or into the grinding bins. In addition to this there is considerable saving in respect to day-labour when the grain requires to be turned or shifted to keep it cool, for by means of the machinery it is allowed to run from the bins by gravitation into the conveyor-worm which re-delivers it into the elevator, and it is again carried to the top of the building and redistributed into any part of the warehouse required. This process cools the grain far more effectually than is at all possible by hand-power. The contract for fixing our grain elevating and distributing machinery is 670*l*."

There is a little repetition here, which I have intentionally given, in order to show the reader how completely a substance like grain, which is liable to heating, can be handled by automatic machinery; but now I propose to show in detail, on what an enormous scale such machinery is being employed elsewhere, to the disadvantage of the hand-labourer, and the gain of the employer.

Until the year 1880, the Mersey Docks and Harbour Board did not use any of the new elevating machinery at their grain warehouses, but during the great strike in 1879, their regularly employed "bushellers" ceased work in sympathy with other labourers on strike, and were guilty of violence towards imported labourers (probably paupers, &c.) who were set to work to discharge the grain vessels.[5] As a consequence, the Board fitted up its grain warehouses with grain elevators, patented by Mr. Brice, the superintendent, at the suggestion of Mr. James Spence, a member of the Board, and manufactured by Messrs. S. Stott & Co., Haslingden (of whose labour-saving machinery more will be said hereafter) (Fig. 15). The elevators are of two kinds, fixed and floating, and the latter are also largely employed by some of the leading Liverpool steamship-owners. In addition to the

FIG. 15.—BRICE'S ELEVATOR FOR DISCHARGING GRAIN FROM SHIPS AND BARGES. BIRKENHEAD GRAIN WAREHOUSES.

Figure 20.1 Brice's Elevator for Discharging Grain from Ships and Barges. Birkenhead Grain Warehouses.

elevator, the grain is shifted by a "trimmer," also Brice's patent, and a galvanised iron hopper for weighing the grain.[6]

The following data will give an idea of the displacement of labour, and the saving of expense by the use of these three contrivances as compared with the old system of hand-labour.

1. The use of an "Elevator" means an average discharge of 400 tons per day, and calls for the employment of 5 men, together with the use of steam or hydraulic power for the working of the "Trimmers." For this work, a tonnage rate of 1¼*d.* is paid to the men, or say 8*s.* 4*d.* per day on the basis of 400 tons per day. The *average* work discharging by hand-labour and the *bushel* would be 200 tons per day, and the gang would consist of 16 to 18 men, 8 of whom would receive 6*s.* 8*d.* per day (being piece-work), and the 10 men each 4*s.* 6*d.* per day.

2. The "Trimmer" is used for moving the grain in the hold of a vessel to the foot of the "Elevator," and needs, as before stated, 5 men. Should it be attempted to do the same work without the aid of the "Trimmer," i.e. by the use of corn-shovels, the employment of 12 to 20 men would be necessary at 4*s.* 6*d.* per day each.

For the storing of grain in the warehouse rooms, turning by machinery, weighing over, and delivery to craft, 3 men and a "Trimmer" do the work which otherwise would call for the services of at least 8 men (3 men at 4*s.* 11*d.* each, instead of 8 men at 4*s.* 3*d.*).

3. The "Hopper" for weighing grain in bulk is used for effecting deliveries to carts and to craft, in the former instance by means of a platform which is made on the quay and stands to the height of the cart. The "Trimmer" and "Hopper" combined require a gang of 6 men (at 4*s.* 3*d.* each), and deliver to carts, say 1000 sacks, and to craft 1200 sacks per day. Similar work performed without these two inventions would require 12 men at least: i.e. 10 men at 4*s.* 3*d.*, and 2 men at 8*s.* 8*d.* per day.

To put this calculation before the reader in a more concrete form, we will suppose a vessel to have entered the dock with 400 tons of grain, which had to be discharged, trucked to the nearest warehouse, handled in warehouse, weighed and delivered, all by hand-labour; and the same operations to be performed with the aid of machinery. And inasmuch as the work is done under the new system in one day whilst it formerly occupied two, the number of men and the wages under the old system must be doubled.

Under the old system there were employed: –

On Ship.	*Wages.*	*Truckers.*	*Wages.*
36 men	£9 14 8	24 men	£5 2 0
Handling in Warehouse.	*Wages.*	*Weighing and Delivering.*	*Wages.*
16 men	£3 8 0	32 men	£6 8 8

With modern machinery: –

Trimming Machine in Hold.	*Wages.*	*Working Elevator.*	*Wages.*
5 men	£2 18 0	4 men	£0 18 4
Handling in Warehouse.	*Wages.*	*Weighing and Delivering.*	*Wages.*
3 men	£0 13 9	24 men	£6 2 0

Or, all operations: –

Under the old system 108 men	£24	13	4
" new " 36 "	10	12	1
Equal to men saved 72.[7] Wages saved	14	1	3

Although it is of no advantage to the men displaced, there must be put against this gain to the Board, the cost of hydraulic power, and the interest, and wear and tear of the machinery. It will be remembered that the cost of the machinery in the case first cited was 670*l*. From other data which I have received, I estimate that the proportion of first cost of machinery doing 400 tons per day would be about 1280*l*.

The following are particulars of the number of elevators in use on the Mersey, which have enabled the Board to reduce the charge for handling grain 20 per cent.: –

Stationary	belonging to the M. D. and H. Board	3
"	" " Grain Storage Company	4
Portable	" " Liverpool Grain Elevator Company	15
Floating	" " Liverpool Grain Elevator Company	3
"	" to Mr. McCabe	1
New Portable	" " S. S. Stott & Co., Haslingden	1
		27

But whilst it is an undeniable fact that the men themselves were the cause of the introduction of this labour-saving machinery, it would not be fair to them to omit saying that sooner or later something of the kind would have happened. This will be best understood from the remarks of the engineer of the Mersey Docks and Harbour Board, Mr. G. F. Lyster, in a letter which I have received from him in answer to inquiries: –

> "For the last 32 years, in my capacity of engineer-in-chief to the Mersey Dock Estate," he says, "I have largely constructed, purchased, and applied mechanical contrivances of various kinds for the purpose of facilitating the working of the Dock Estate, primarily with the object of expediting the work to be done, and as a consequence the diminishing or dispensing with hand-labour. The *necessity* for such contrivances will readily present themselves to your mind when you consider the class of work to be performed on such an estate as ours, and the impossibility of adhering to the old-fashioned man-power which prevailed in the early stages of the docks, when the exigencies of the public were not so pressing as they are now. For instance, the conditions of trade now demand that the greatest possible expedition should be used in passing shipping in and out of dock. This involves a special class of machinery for actuating dock-gates, capstans, &c.; a like necessity arises for moving (opening and closing) the bridges which cross the passages into the docks, and by which the thoroughfares about the quays are intersected. If undue delay were permitted in these operations the shipping interest and the public convenience would naturally suffer, and a public outcry would be the result. Let me give you two instances of these new methods of working. When the 100 ft. bridge was placed across Duke Street passage, between the East and West Floats, Birkenhead, it was worked by hand, and I recollect that it took 12 men 15 minutes to open against a moderate breeze. I, however, applied hydraulic machinery to effect the object, thereby reducing the time under similar conditions of wind to about 3 minutes.[8] Somewhat the same effect was experienced at the gates across the 100 ft. entrances. For reasons such as are illustrated by these examples I have largely adopted hydraulic machinery actuated by steam-power as the simplest and most efficacious method of dealing with such matters on those parts of the Dock Estate where imperatively needed; in fact, I have no hesitation in saying that the business of the port of Liverpool could not be carried on without such appliances. Innumerable other matters inseparable from the working of such an estate also demand mechanical contrivances in lieu of the old-fashioned methods of manual labour. I allude to pumping machinery necessary for the drying of the graving docks (of which I have introduced a great variety), of machines for raising cloughs and paddles,[9] for working cranes and grain machinery, hoists for lifting buckets and barrels, machinery for dredging and removing sand; in fact, I feel safe in asserting that there is more machinery, and of a greater variety for expediting work and economising labour, on the Liverpool Dock Estate than in any other similar area in the world."

And what exists on a large scale in the Mersey Dock Estate is to be found equally in almost every modern factory and workshop. I have already referred to the labour-saving apparatus in a great west of England store, and similar appliances are to be found in oil-mills, sugar-refineries, flour-mills, &c. One large seed-crushing firm writes me that their machinery is for "saving of labour generally, and making our manufacture as much automatic as possible" to reduce working expenses. In that mill the seed is largely handled by machinery in all but the hydraulic pressing. Another seed-crusher gives an estimate of labour saved by recent improvements in machinery whereby the work of 19 men is now performed by 10, a little over 50 per cent., and this was mainly caused by the necessity for expediting work and economising labour in competition with foreign seed-crushers.

The well-known firm of Aveling & Porter makes road and street rollers, and supplants thereby another form of pauper labour. The necessity for this labour-saving appliance no one will deny, both to prevent the cruelty of compelling horses to trample down the sharpened stones in what is mis-named macadamising, and to save wear and tear of the wheels of every kind of conveyance. These steam-rollers are in use over the whole civilised world and the testimony to their efficiency is universal. The users all speak of their economical working, the surveyor of the Stirlingshire roads saying, "The saving of material in a rolled road is at least 30 per cent. and that in surface-labour still more;" whilst the street superintendent of an important town in Massachusetts says,

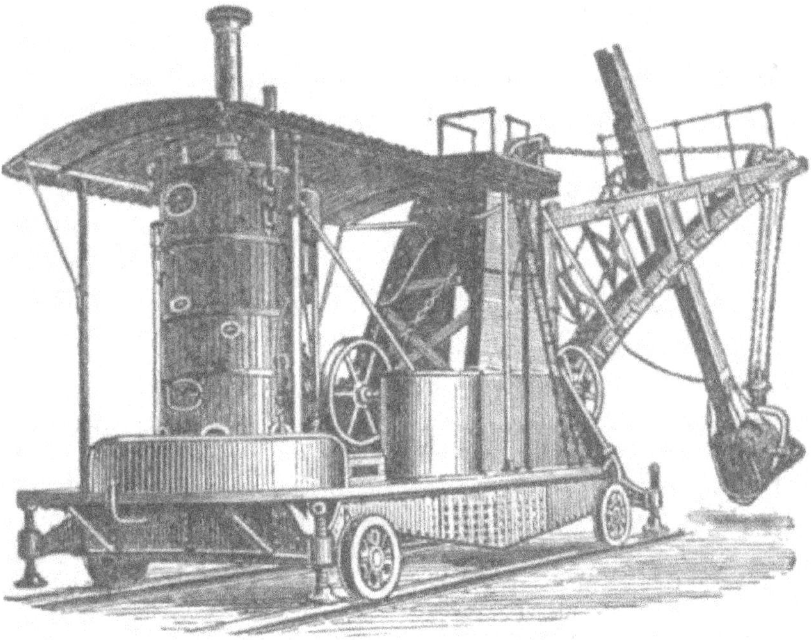

Figure 20.2 – Ruston, Proctor & Co.'s "Steam Navvy."

"I estimate that the steam-roller, with the pick attachment, and two men with hand-picks, will do the work of from 20 to 40 men with hand-picks alone, according to the hardness of the road-bed." As to their own work Messrs. Aveling & Porter tell me, "Our plant, i. e. the tools and machines we have from time to time bought, have been of a general character. The wages of our men have not decreased. The number of men has gradually increased, but there has been no decrease of hours."

Again, one of the most important branches of civil engineering in which powerful machinery has largely supplanted manual labour is the excavation of docks, canals, &c. This has been accomplished chiefly by the "steam navvy," the operation of which I have had frequent opportunities to observe, notably in the works of the Manchester ship-canal, and the new works at the Canada Docks, Liverpool. In both these great works the "Steam Navvy" of Messrs. Ruston, Proctor & Co. has been found the most efficient, and the following is an estimate of the difference between its working and hand-labour. The weight of the machine is 34 tons, and the bucket for excavating and lifting holds 1½ cubic yards. At the Canada Dock works I was told that the average quantity of "soft muck" excavated in a day of ten hours is 1000 cubic yards; but the engineer of the Manchester Ship Canal (Mr. Leader Williams), in a testimonial which he has given to Messrs. Ruston, Proctor & Co., says that about 2000 yards of good material has been excavated in 10 hours.[10]

To be quite within the mark, however, it will be as well to estimate the quantity worked at 1000 cubic yards, which gives the following results: –

Men Employed and Wages per Diem with Steam Navvy.

Engine driver, 7s. 6d.; 3 labourers, 4s. 3d. each, together	£1	0	3
Men laying rails and working about the machine, 12 at 4*s.* 3*d.*	2	11	0
	£3	11	3
The same work done by hand-labour would require 50 men at 3*s.* 10*d.*	9	11	8
Men displaced, 34. Wages saved	£6	0	5

Against this must be placed cost of coal, interest, and wear and tear of machinery, as the hand-labourers find their own tools.

I have already spoken of the labour-saving machinery in the works of Messrs. Tangye Brothers, Birmingham, and amongst the appliances made by that firm are hydraulic jacks for moving large objects. This is the quaint advertisement which they have forwarded to me, and, whilst they are responsible for its absolute historical accuracy it exhibits in a striking manner what changes have taken place through the introduction of labour-saving appliances.

How Obelisks have been Raised.

A.D. 1586. Fontana raised an obelisk at Rome with 40 capstans worked by 960 men and 75 horses.

A.D. 1836. Le Bas raised the Luxor obelisk at Paris with ten capstans worked by 480 men.

A.D. 1878. John Dixon raised Cleopatra's Needle in London with 4 of Tangye's patent hydraulic jacks worked by 4 men.

All kinds of unskilled labour have been superseded in a greater or lesser degree by machinery. Messrs. S. Stott & Co., of Haslingden, the manufacturers of the grain elevators, also make elevators and conveyors for supplying coal to stoked boilers, for transferring bundles of cloth from one part of a manufactory to another, for removing barrels and boxes either from warehouse to warehouse, from warehouse to trucks, or even from the ground over a line of railway with its waggons into the upper stories of a warehouse . . . It would be possible to mention a variety of other labour-saving contrivances made by that and other firms, but enough has been said to show how such appliances, actuated by steam or hydraulic power, are gradually superseding hand-labour.

As regards the statistics of unskilled labour, it must be mentioned that the Census tables are an unsafe guide, first, on account of the uncertain and changing methods adopted in successive enumerations, and secondly on account of the much larger and indefinite number of unemployed. With these reservations the following may be taken as the statistics of England and Wales: –

	1861.	1871.	1881.
Labourers: Dock, Dock-yard, Road, Cotton-porter, Coal-heaver, and "General." }	375,783	565,234	685,077

In each of these three enumerations the labourers are differently classified in the Census tables, but I have endeavoured to reduce them, as far as possible, to uniformity, and before passing on to the conclusions to be drawn from this and the preceding chapters, and discussing the general situation, it is right once more to mention the fact that in the numbers of labourers given above there must be included a large percentage of those who were divorced from the soil, and who migrated into our large cities and seaports. [. . .]

Chapter VIII.

Inferences – the general question of labour – conclusion.

[. . .] The hand of man has been unable to supply the wants of man, and he has been compelled to call in the forces of nature to his assistance. It is a mistake to suppose that manufacturers are always on the look-out to save labour through the application of machinery. They are in this respect conservative; many are lazy laggards, and it is not an infrequent occurrence that a whole industry finds itself extinguished by the enterprise of one clever and enterprising inventor. It is a truism to say that what drives manufacturers, shipowners, and others to employ improved machinery is competition, or more frequently the clamorous demand for cheaper articles of consumption. The requirements of the masses themselves necessitate the machinery which they frequently denounce. As I have sought to show, however, one phase of this revolution in our industrial life is the employment of mechanical contrivances to cope with the demands of labour, and the men are then fighting, not the employer but the forces of nature which are at his disposal. The lower and less skilled the description of labour the more readily do those forces lend themselves to his service, and, as I have already said, this is a factor in the labour question which should not be lost sight of by those to whom the great mass of working men look for guidance and support. There is perhaps no need to convey any hint of the kind to many of the enlightened and intelligent leaders, as Burt, Henry Broadhurst, and others who might be named, inside and outside the walls of Parliament, whose long experience and knowledge of machinery must be a serious consideration with them when they have to advise their followers and clients in matters appertaining to labour and wages. But there are other prominent men coming to the front who are too ready to promote strikes as a cure for the grievances of the working classes, and this policy it is that gives the greatest stimulus to the invention and application of certain kinds of labour-saving machinery, and the consequent displacement of hand-labour *in perpetuity*.

On the other hand, whilst the working classes should be careful not to dishearten employers, employers should not forget that there are forces at work which make it undesirable that they should hastily use machinery as a weapon to fight the men. It may not be correct to say that "the introduction of machinery is of course the natural answer of all employers to attempts of men to shorten the hours of work," as the secretary of the employers' organisation already referred to writes to me, but if such sentiments as these are known to exist, they embitter the relations between the employer and his workmen, and cause the latter to fall back upon the combative leaders for help.[11] Whilst on the one hand we have combination (Employers' Federations), wealth, and all that wealth can purchase, we have on the other side Trades Unions, Co-operative, Land-nationalisation, Labour-nationalisation, Independent Labour, Fabian, Socialist, and many other societies; we have labour representatives in increasing numbers in Parliament, amongst local authorities, on the Bench, and wherever political influence can place them, and the Legislature is compelled, as a matter of self-preservation, to further the interests of the labouring classes in various ways, without reference to their bearing upon those of the employers. A writer on political economy has said that "Capital has taken full advantage of its increased means of obtaining knowledge, Labour scarcely at all."[12] To remedy this state of things the President of the Board of Trade, following the example of the United States Government, has established a Labour Department, which has issued a special Gazette,[13] and it will be the fault of the labouring classes themselves if, during the next few years, every great industrial centre is not furnished with an Intelligence Office for their benefit.

Again, what is the significance of the increasing facilities for giving "technical" instruction to the labouring classes? The State has taken this duty upon itself, to enable this country to compete with its neighbours; but technical training means the training of vast numbers of artisans to become (either themselves or their children) masters in the industrial world, masters as individuals or as co-operators; and although at the present moment the outlook for productive co-operation may not be promising, there can be no doubt this will be one of the most important agencies for the better distribution and greater equalisation of property. Without reference, therefore, to the schemes of those socialists who would seek, by violence or by revolutionary measures, to partition the wealth of the few amongst the many, it must be clear to all thinking men that a more equal and equitable distribution must result from the elevation of the masses, and every means should be employed to bring about this change peaceably. The establishment of Boards of Conciliation and Arbitration; Joint Committees for Regulating Wages, &c.; Bureaux for the Unemployed, all are admirable palliatives. The introduction of new machinery, as we have seen, and as the men themselves admit, usually causes temporary displacement of hand-labour and consequently temporary distress, and to meet this, temporary relief alone is requisite. Here, too, the State has beneficently stepped in, and if the recommendation of the Local Government Board which was issued in November 1892 to Local Authorities throughout the country, meets with the response which it deserves, much will have been done to conciliate the suffering poor, and to provide employment for those who, through no fault of their own, have been temporarily deprived of the means of subsistence.[14] Expediency then, philanthropy, and bare justice require that every means should be taken to secure "the greatest happiness to the greatest number."

Editorial Endnotes

1 'Mr. Samuelson: Death of Former Well-Known Local Leader', *Liverpool Echo*, 15 April 1918, p. 3; 'Death of Mr. James Samuelson: A Noted Social Reformer', *Liverpool Daily Post*, 16 April 1918, p. 3.

2 For more on this issue, see G. Stedman Jones, *Outcast London: A Study of the Relationship between Classes in Victorian Society* (Oxford: Clarendon Press, 1971), pp. 127–151.

3 J. Samuelson, *Labour Saving Machinery* (London: Kegan, Paul, Trench, Trübner, & Co., 1893), Google Books, p. 8.

4 Samuelson, *Labour Saving Machinery*, p. 13. For this image of rural workers, see M. Freeman, 'The Agricultural Labourer and the "Hodge" Stereotype, c. 1850–1914', *Agricultural History Review* 49:2 (2001), pp. 172–186.

5 Samuelson was writing during a time of trade depression when employers were pushing back against the growth of unions and strikes from 1889 to 1900. See, for example, J. E. Cronin, 'Strikes and Power in Britain', *International Review of Social History* 32:2 (1987), pp. 144–167.

6 Samuelson, *Labour Saving Machinery*, p. 91.
7 Samuelson, *Labour Saving Machinery*, p. 94.

Source Endnotes

1 The estimate which follows, and other valuable information, has been given me by F. C. Marshall, Esq., of Riseholme Grange, Lincoln.
2 It will be found from the sequel that this "expedition" is a necessity which, in one way or another, affects every department of industry.
3 Vol. III. 'Occupations of the People.' The volume for 1891 is not yet completed.
4 In a subsequent chapter will be found an account of labour-saving by steam navvies, made by this firm.
5 On this occasion the dock labourers were beaten after a three weeks' strike (or rather lock-out) against reduced wages, and about a year afterwards they would have struck again, but I induced them to resort to arbitration, and acted as their arbitrator along with the late Mr. R. Lowndes, nominated by the ship-owners, and Lord Derby as umpire. Their wages were restored to them and they have since been further raised.
6 For the information of readers who are unacquainted with these appliances, I may mention that grain is lifted *perpendicularly* by "buckets" running upon an endless strap or chain; that it is conveyed *horizontally* by broad endless belts on which it settles; and is *trimmed* by a large scoop which is hauled along by machinery, when full, and guided by a man who drags it back empty for refilling.
7 Perhaps it would be more correct to say that 36 men are displaced for 2 days.
8 Mr. Lyster omits to say with the aid of three men, one to work the hydraulic machinery, and two to adjust the chains to prevent carts, &c., from attempting to cross.
9 Two kinds of sluice-gates.
10 In 1891, there were 58 of these machines in use on the works of the ship canal, and I believe more were added at a later period, and the engineer speaks of Messrs. Ruston & Proctor's machine as being the best for removing hard materials.
11 The reader will have noticed that I never use the expression "capital and labour." Capital is nothing without brains, and the relations between the two classes should always be regarded as between intelligent active members of society.
12 'The Effects of Machinery on Wages,' Professor Nicholson, D.Sc., p. 111. London: Swan Sonnenschein & Co.
13 The best labour journal that has ever come under my notice.
14 "Pauperism and Distress," Circular of the Local Government Board.

Part 3

WOMEN'S WORK

Productive and reproductive

21

J. LIVESEY, 'TO THE FEMALES EMPLOYED IN FACTORIES AND ALL OUR LARGE MANUFACTURING ESTABLISHMENTS'

Moral Reformer 2 (1 February 1832), pp. 37–46

In this selection, typical of the advice literature of the time, the temperance reformer Joseph Livesey (1794–1884) (see Volume 1, Part 1, Chapter 2) writes to young women working in factories to try to convince them to reform their behaviour. Factory women became central to ideas about the improvement of the working classes in the early nineteenth century because, as Livesey and others believed, women were the moral centre of the home. Sarah Stickney Ellis, a Victorian author on conduct books for middle-class women, wrote that 'the customs of English society have so constituted women the guardians of the comforts of their homes, that, like the Vestals of old, they cannot allow the lamp they cherish to be extinguished, or to fail for want of oil, without an equal share of degradation attaching to their names'.[1] Factory women became equated in many ways with the ills of industrial society and, in particular, the destruction of a nostalgic vision of the family, where men and women worked together in cottage industries and agricultural pursuits.[2] In this source, Livesey reads the factory woman's experience through the lens of middle-class morality. He sees these young women as 'objects of pity rather than censure' because they had grown up in 'poverty, misery, and crime', which had subjected them to various temptations they were never instructed to avoid.[3] Even though these pitiable women worked in factories, Livesey writes, they were still women and therefore deserved respect. He regards his message to female factory workers as essential because of his assumptions about the influence women had on society through their higher morality.[4] In doing so, he does not condemn factory work altogether, but tries to teach young women workers how to improve their conduct in the context in which they exist. Livesey commends the industriousness of women's work in factories and understands that circumstances necessitated that they must do industrial labour. In this way, Livesey normalizes women's need to work and recognizes that industrial society

DOI: 10.4324/9780429320323-26

has produced a particular labour market for women. Yet he still abhors women's factory work and believes it kept women from learning proper domestic skills and corrupted their feminine conduct.[5] According to Livesey, working in factories threw men and women together, taught women immodest behaviour and the use of bad language, and put women on the edge of prostitution. Factory women treated their parents badly and had no sense how to choose a husband. He has a nostalgic vision of rural families and labour that was destroyed with emigration to the towns. Livesey urges women to choose domestic service over factory work to prepare them for their futures as mothers and housekeepers for husbands, the roles they were meant to play. However, because his audience was young, Livesey sees the hope of transformation. When these women changed their behaviour, they would be at the frontlines of reform of the whole working class. This suggests that immoral conduct would not taint a woman forever; rather, her recovered morality would have the power to influence those around her.

'To the Females Employed in Factories and All Our Large Manufacturing Establishments.'[1]

When you hear that I have printed an Address especially intended for you, do not consider that I am actuated either by a meddlesome or an unfeeling disposition. Conscious of the purity of my intentions, I make no apology for commencing a communication, which an excess of delicacy might deter some persons from attempting. I know the temptations of youth, and though I have been spared to see my children approaching the age of some of those included in the objects of this address, I cannot forget how immensely valuable were those admonitions which I received from experienced friends, at your time of life. Give me, then, your candid attention, while I advise you in reference to your best interests. I address you as a sincere friend, – as one who has marked your conduct, who laments your vices, and who can never recount the miseries of society to which your example has contributed, without an anxious solicitude to assist in effecting your moral improvement. If I praise you, it is not in the spirit of flattery; if I censure you severely, it is that you may see your errors and be persuaded to amend. Considering your numbers, your circumstances, and your age, you claim the special attention of every one who wishes to trace the maladies of our moral constitution, or to discover the true cause of much of the physical evil which prevails in society. In Lancashire, you constitute, as it were, a distinct class; and a stranger would be surprised to notice the vast number of girls, from fourteen to twenty and upwards, who throng the streets at the dinner hour in such towns as Preston, Bolton, and Manchester. In reference to the formation of character, this is the most critical period of your life; and from this age may be dated the commencement of those habits which, in many instances within your own knowledge, are now producing, poverty, misery, and crime. Nursed and brought up, generally, beneath the chilling influence of poverty, and without the inculcation of Christian principles, you become an easy prey to the influence of bad example. The daughters of the rich have many motives for watchfulness which have little weight with persons in your circumstances, and many opportunities of improvement with which the children of the poor are not favoured. Indeed, whilst I have often joined others in passing censure upon your conduct, I am afraid we have not made sufficient allowance for the unfavourable circumstances with which you have been constantly surrounded. Corn will not grow upon sand, nor potatoes upon pavement: and where you have never been favoured with the teaching and fostering care of pious parents; when labour and toil have been your lot from childhood; and when all that is calculated to influence character has been on the wrong side, – I am disposed to make great allowances, and to regard you as objects of pity rather than censure. The melioration of the condition of the inmates of factories has attracted the attention of the legislature, and will continue, I trust, a subject of agitation till both male and female regain that dignity and moral character, which, as rational beings, they ought to enjoy.

Your sex is called the *weaker* sex, and in all polished society claims the polite attention and special regards of the *men*. In the intercourse of life, he who slights a female, or omits any necessary service, is considered a man of no breeding, and unfitted for the connubial enjoyments of life. Though confined within the walls of a factory, and though deficient in the polished manners of the age, you are still entitled to our respect, and to that civility of treatment which gives point to admonition. Though in many instances sadly depraved, you are endowed with all the excellences of nature, and are not less the splendid workmanship of your Creator than the young ladies whose education and connections have raised them so much above you in the scale of society. Your lot has been cast for labour; and resigned to your condition, and contributing daily to the supply of our comforts, it were inhuman to cultivate towards you any feeling but that of friendship and respect.

But why do I address *you* especially? Because, in the various circles of the labouring part of the people, you are capable, every step that you take in life, of exercising an extensive influence upon the well being of mankind. To whom do we look for the happiness of the poor man's house, but to his *wife?* On whom are children to depend for the best instruction and care but the *mother?* On whom, principally, do aged parents rely for comfort and support in old age, but on their *daughters*? Who are most capable of diffusing a sweet influence over the manners, morals, and general demeanour of mankind? Our *females*. Who can, by the potent spell of a look, a word, or a smile, soften the heart, and make obedience a pleasure? *Woman*. By whom is the world of fashion governed, and who are the conservators of the laws of etiquette? The *ladies*. And in accordance with all this, I venture to say, that in attempting to reform the character of our factory population, we shall utterly fail, unless sanctioned by the powerful influence of *your* example. It were easy to shew, in analyzing the causes of the present immorality, the influence *you* have had, directly and indirectly, in producing this result; and, controled by different principles, it is perfectly plain that your efforts will be a valuable auxiliary in all our attempts at reform. If, through the blessing of heaven, this address should be the means of changing the conduct of a few of your class, the effects will probably be reflected where the labour of others could never reach. Through *you* I seek the reformation of fathers and mothers, sisters and brothers, and, prospectively, husbands and children, and generations yet unborn!

I proceed to remark on the nature of your *employment*, and to commend your *industrious* habits. Though I have strong objections to the kind of labour in which you are engaged, as being injurious to health, destructive to good morals, and productive of the subversion of the order of nature as it regards the influence of family ties, yet seeing no chance of any material change, you must reconcile yourselves to your lot. This, and every other manufacturing town, swarms with families who have migrated from the country, where at one time they enjoyed their seclusive homes, and pursued their rural occupations, without so much as a knowledge of many of the vices which, in their present situations, stare them in the face every day. However, in the present changed circumstances of the country, it would seem difficult for many of you to earn a livelihood in any other way. Placed at the factory at the age of nine by your parents, your habits have been formed for nothing else; and though liable to great objections, it is, after all, much better than to be brought up, like thousands of young girls in the sister country, amid sloth and idleness. In Ireland the young women suffer for want of employment, and you from its excess. Barefoot, ragged, and dirty, you may see hundreds, who have no employment, and who seem never to have felt the necessity or the honour of obtaining a livelihood by labour. Compared to you, they are the most miserable of beings. Labour at the spinning factories, power looms, winding frames, and especially at the *dandy* looms, is, in many cases, excessive, yet it is evident that it agrees better with your constitutions than it does with boys. While many of you are full grown, exhibit comparatively healthy countenances, and generally seem cheerful and content, the boys are often diminutive in size, are pale and wan, and appear much more dejected. It is also evident to every observer, that you are much better *clothed* than formerly. Whatever blame I may attach to some parts of your conduct, I will award to you what I am sure you deserve, unmeasured praise for your *industry*. When I see the factories in full operation at six o'clock these cold winter's mornings, and continuing till half after seven in the evening, I cannot overlook the extent of your labour, or avoid lamenting that fortune has not favoured you with a sphere of operation both more easy and more favourable to the growth of good morals. Both your domestic interests and those of the upper classes, it is well known, are much abridged through your partiality for this sort of employment. Good household servants have long been scarce, and are every year getting more so, entirely owing to the disposition of young women preferring factory work to household labour. But though the families of the rich experience much inconvenience from this circumstance, it is upon yourselves that the greatest weight of the evil will fall. While young and giddy, you may be pleased with the excitement of tumultuous association, you may think it a great privilege to have your evenings and your Sundays at your own command; but when you come to think soberly, and live to see the consequences of your choice, you will deeply regret having lost the only opportunity of learning the essentials of domestic management. While you have experienced mothers to wash, clean, and cook, you seem unconcerned; but if you should become mothers yourselves, where are your abilities to manage as you ought to manage? You were created as "help mates" to man; and the task allotted to you is "to keep the house;" but if we must judge from the specimens which daily appear, we come inevitably to this conclusion, that you are at a wrong school for this kind of learning. Your natures and faculties adapt themselves to the work of the cottage, and no cottage is complete or comfortable without the superintendence of a female mind. In my estimation, neither rank, nor beauty, nor money, in the qualifications of a wife, is fit to be put in comparison with a full acquaintance with domestic economy. Give me the wife who can wash, and clean, and mend, who keeps her own house, who knows the wants of a family, the quality and value of every article of consumption, who can lay out the husband's earnings with discretion, and who will always take care that the expenditure never exceeds the income. Such qualifications you ought to aspire after, and as few of you miss becoming wives (in many instances sadly too soon) never consider yourselves deserving this honour till you are qualified to perform the duties required. And if young men were more careful in making their selections, those who found themselves rejected through a lack of household talents would feel a necessity for improvement; and I think I may venture to surmise, that if this stimulus should fail, it would be in vain to try any other! As many girls as possibly can, I advise to become servants in respectable houses, and those who may not change their employment should embrace every opportunity of learning and practising the proper duties of their station. I have seen so much wretchedness, so many poor distressed children, so many ruined families, and so much litigation with the shopkeepers, in consequence of the bad management of the wives, whose maiden years had been spent like yours, that I feel strongly impressed with the importance of urging this subject upon your most serious attention. Your opportunities are certainly limited, and in too many cases you are not favoured with the advantages of good example; but still as the *house* where you eat, and sleep, and live, is the *place of practice*, every impediment will vanish before a determined disposition. In addition, I would urge the propriety, during the season of youth, of acquiring a moderate acquaintance with the useful arts of reading and writing. Notwithstanding all the schools which are established, I know that many of you cannot read, and very few indeed are able to write. What a pity you should let the present, the only opportunity you may ever have, pass over, without acquiring these invaluable acquisitions! When I see wives unable to read a single word, and whose best method of keeping accounts is by chalking on a cupboard door, do I not see a clear representation of the degradation which awaits you? At any rate, nothing but your own reflection, good sense, and an early change of conduct, can prevent it.

Your *personal behaviour* next claims my notice, and under this head I am afraid I shall run the risk of offending many of you. Be assured, in exercising faithful reproof I have no object but your own good; and though you may not see it now, a time will come when your own reflections will convince you of the fact. Factories have been called the "hot beds of vice;" but this, I presume, is not because there is any peculiar influence in the buildings of a vicious tendency, but principally because of the *unnatural association* which prevents the happy effects of the people being selected and employed as *families*. Regular associations, exclusively of men or of women, are not often useful; but the associations of *hundreds of thoughtless youth*, unconnected with any moral influence, uncontroled by parental authority, unchecked by the guardianship of virtuous example, and untaught by those who profess to care for souls, are the standing and prolific sources of the vices of the class of people to whom I refer. The long hours of lobour [sic] leaving no opportunities for acquiring useful knowledge, may be connected with the above. It may also be added, that the incessant noise, the working of the machinery, and the manual exercise of numbers in the same apartment, are all against mental improvement, or moral culture, and tend to bear you down within the sphere of the brute. I do not say this to induce you to fall out either with your employment or your employers, but to put you upon your guard against the evils of your situation. We have all our peculiar trials, and whilst it is perhaps necessary it should be so, our duty is to "watch and pray lest we fall into temptation."

The most valuable ornament to the female sex is *modesty:* a retiring disposition, a chastened address, and a humble deportment, give unrivalled charms to a woman, and are the basis of pure affection. But I am sorry to say that these are attainments which many of you have yet to acquire. Your bold and immodest carriage in the streets, and in the presence of men, have long been matter of remark. You grow up under the debasing influence of the indelicate behaviour of your associates, and within the hearing of the most impure and disgusting language; and without extraordinary caution, you are sure to glide into the same practice. Let me beseech you to guard against every habit which robs the female character of the charms of innocency and virtue. I argue not for a morose, sour demeanor: I like to see the smile of cheerful contentment sit upon every cheek, and there is none to which it adds more grace than those of your own sex. Of course, you are not called upon to withhold the exchange of the usual courtesies of life, and especially with those who may have bespoken your special esteem; but all this you may easily distinguish from that bold, immodest behaviour, and those rude disgusting freedoms, with which your names have so long been associated.

Next, your *language*. I do not mean to say much as to its uncouthness and vulgarity, inasmuch as many of you have had no opportunities of learning a superior dialect, though these are generally symptoms of an unrefined mind. But what I allude to particularly is the practice which some of you are addicted to of *swearing, damning*, and indulging in *obscene* expressions. How many there are who begin their sentences with a profane appeal to the sacred name of GOD, and how often have I heard *you*, with the greatest facility, rival the worst of this character! When a number of you are together, especially when just let loose from your employment, it is difficult for a stranger to pass without catching your offensive language. How awful to think that that tongue from which ought to flow the law of kindness, and which ought to be the instrument of adoration, is employed in reviling man and blaspheming God! Do you never reflect upon the language you use? Does conscience never reproach you? Does neither a sense of shame nor the fear of future punishment ever smite you with feelings of remorse? "Out of the abundance of the heart the mouth speaketh," and if we are to judge of the state of your minds from the language which some of you use, I regret to say, you are far gone in the road to infamy. Wanton in your demeanour, licentious in your language, and without shame, but one step further, and you join those who have lost all sense of character, and are become the greatest pests in society. Think, thoughtless girls, think, who it is that created your powers of speech, by whose gracious hand your breath is continued; think of all the mercies which kind heaven bestows upon you; think of all the misery you bring upon yourselves and relatives; above all, think of the hour of death, and of the day of judgment, – and then proceed, if you dare, to pollute the streets with your language, and insult the name of your Maker!

Let me here advert to another evil which I have often regretted, as connected with your class, that is, a *neglect and contempt of your parents*. So soon as you are able to earn what is sufficient for your maintenance, you begin to shew your independency, and to assume a tone of insolent dictation. You cast off parental restraint, and make obedience a mere matter of convenience. In this you are very blameable; for as they are your natural guardians, to them, at *every period* of your lives, you ought to pay respect and submission. "Honour thy father and mother is the first commandment, with promise," and under the Jewish law, the children that cursed father or mother were stoned to death. Forgetting your duty, some of you treat your parents as your equals, and if they interpose their demands, you cherish a rebellious disposition. How many of you leave your father's house, which should be the place of safety to virtue and character, and take lodgings where you can give unbridled license to your wandering desires. As soon as you are able to earn sufficient for your maintenance, instead of considering the poverty and infirmities of your parents, or the inability of your younger brothers and sisters to obtain a livelihood, you claim your whole earnings, while the rest of the family have to suffer many privations. Is this right? Would you like to be treated in this manner yourselves? For nine or ten years your parents supported you by *their* labour, without any return, and is this no debt which it is obligatory upon you to discharge? Do for your parents what they have done for you, and then you may begin to think of being independent of them. When your parents get aged, you ought to sympathise with them in their sufferings, to bear with their infirmities, and to endeavour to make the end of their journey as easy as possible. What! can you behold the knees that bore you bending beneath the feebleness of age; the cheek that once beamed with pleasure upon your infant play, furrowed with anxious care; and the index of time pointing the once nimble step towards the place for all living, – without surrendering your earnings, and performing all those filial duties which nature itself enjoins? It is a fiend-like ingratitude to teach or to practice *any thing* that leads to the neglect of parents. You ought to honour the hoary head in every case, but nature claims your special homage to those who gave you birth. Hitherto, I know, this duty has been awfully neglected, but I sincerely hope that enough has been said to induce you to act like good children – like virtuous daughters.

In addressing persons of your age and situation, it would be considered an omission not to touch on that interesting topic, *the choice of a husband.* Parents and friends often act with an unjustifiable delicacy upon this particular. They avoid mentioning it, as if *their silence* would tie down the desires and anticipations of youth. Instead of acting in so reserved a manner, perhaps followed by a violent interference, parents, I conceive, ought, at a proper age, to make marriage the subject of plain and open instruction. In the first place, then, being an undertaking of so great a magnitude, and pregnant with consequences so vastly important, it ought always to be contemplated with *serious reflection.* The thoughtlessness and precipitancy of youth lead many to take steps which they have reason to regret to the last day of their lives. No young women in the world are in situations more calculated to lead them to err than yourselves. Frequently, and almost necessarily, in the company of young men, and accustomed to no forethought, many marry early and precipitately, or are forced to do so to prevent disgrace. You ought to think seriously of the consequences, and at your age, no caution can be too great against the snares which are laid to entrap you. If you reflect as you ought, you will perceive that there are reasons, both natural and circumstantial, which should lead some of you never to think of marrying. A reasonable prospect of being able to provide for a family ought, certainly, in every case, to precede the matrimonial tie. But supposing all impediments apart, "to *whom* shall I consent to be *tied*, for better or for worse, for richer for poorer, till *death us do part?*" is a question which demands great deliberation. Do not be led away with appearances; think of this great truth, that *virtue* alone is the basis of real happiness, and that without this all meretricious qualities are empty as the wind. Never give your hand to the drunkard, the idle, or the profligate: why should you yoke yourselves to a being sunk lower than the brute? Never salute those lips whence revenge, violence, and profanity constantly proceed, for upon *yourselves* the evil will fall. "Oh! silly girl," have I often said to myself, when passing young couples where the man has been reeling drunk, "little do you think that the joy of the moment will be changed into months and years of misery and pain!" There are thousands just now who are ready to say, "Had we been favoured with timely caution, and possessed prudence enough to have acted upon it, we should not now have been the living spectacles of wretchedness in a world of trouble through which we have to fight." Do act, I beseech you, with suitable caution, and try to benefit by the melancholy examples which surround you. But where, it may be asked, amid so much profligacy, are the chances of obtaining a husband of *good* character? I answer, rather than marry a man notorious only for his vices, never marry at all; for under the whole heavens, in my estimation, there is not so miserable a being as the woman who, disappointed of all her hopes, and surrounded with an impoverished family, lives the wretched vassal of a drunken, senseless, infuriated husband. But, further, if women were more particular as to *good character* in their suitors, *men* would be more anxious to possess it. If all the young girls were to make a declaration against drunkards, is it not to be hoped that many of the young men would pay deference to their sentiments? I know no department in our social economy where the women have not *great influence*, and I cannot but think that lessons of morality, supported by their example, and delivered with earnestness and with the insinuations of female talents, would be productive of the happiest results.

But why should I expect *you* to make a virtuous choice? Alas! you have yourselves this lesson yet to learn. And I really cannot conclude without urging again upon you the necessity of *personal* reformation. I ask not to what party you belong, but I urge upon you what they will all approve, the necessity of a *new heart* and a *change of conduct*. Your years, instead of being an excuse for indifference, afford the strongest reason why you should "repent and turn to God."

> "Youth is the time to serve the Lord,
> The time to gain the sure reward."

Flee, then, from bad company; shut your ears against the profane and impious language of your workfellows; shun every place of temptation; attend to every filial duty; listen to your instructors, and love to get wisdom; associate with those who are piously inclined; make the bible your constant study, and shape your whole lives by its holy precepts; give your hearts to the Lord, and seek his blessing night and day. Go on, my young friends, in this holy course: your pleasure and your happiness will exceed all that the world can give. You will diffuse, by your example and influence, goodness and virtue around you, and your latter end shall be peace. If, through the blessing of heaven, this hasty appeal should, in a few instances, be made the means of effecting so important a result, no other reward is expected by your faithful friend,

J. LIVESEY.

Editorial Endnotes

1 S. S. Ellis, *The Women of England, Their Social Duties, and Domestic Habits*, 15th ed. (London: Fisher, Son, & Co, 1839), p. 25.

2 See, for example, R. Fuchs, *Gender and Poverty in Nineteenth-Century Europe* (New York: Cambridge University Press, 2005), p. 111.

3 J. Livesey, 'To the Females Employed in Factories and All Our Large Manufacturing Establishments', *Moral Reformer* 2 (1 February 1832), pp. 37–46, Google Books on p. 38.

4 See, for example, N. Cott, 'Passionlessness: An Interpretation of Victorian Sexual Ideology, 1790–1850', *Signs* 4:2 (1978), pp. 219–236; C. Hall, 'The Early Formation of Victorian Domestic Ideology', in *White, Male, and Middle Class: Explorations in Feminism and History* (Cambridge: Polity Press, 2007), pp. 75–93.

5 See, for example, D. W. Elliott, 'Servants and Hands: Representing the Working Classes in Victorian Factory Novels', *Victorian Literature and Culture* 28:2 (2000), pp. 377–390; M. Levine-Clark, *Beyond the Reproductive Body: The Politics of Women's Health and Work in Early Victorian England* (Columbus: Ohio State University Press, 2004), chap. 2.

Source Endnote

1 I hope that many parts of this Address will be found useful to females of every class.

22

CHARTIST WOMEN

While men dominated Chartist politics (see Volume I Introduction on Chartism), women's presence at Chartist meetings was common.[1] Yet it was unusual to find women as featured speakers at men's meetings. In the first selection (22.1), the Chartist newspaper the *Northern Star* reports on Mary Anne Walker's first speech before a men's meeting, which took place in High Holborn, London. She soon became a regular lecturer on the Chartist circuit.[2] The long introduction is worth reproducing for the gendered rhetoric emphasizing the setting and Walker's femininity in the context of her political speech. The journalist notes that while the room was 'crowded', it was also 'respectably composed', including 'a large proportion of very elegantly dressed ladies, many of whom were of the superior classes of society', which suggests a curiosity about Walker beyond Chartism. When Walker entered the room, she was accompanied by many 'ladies'. About fifteen lines of text were allotted to her appearance and demeanour. Walker describes her presence as 'bold' for a woman but necessary, because it was for the good of her country. She relates the bleak conditions of women's employment that were leading women to commit suicide. As in Volume 1, Part 3, Chapter 21, Walker's speech assumes that women needed to work, but unlike Livesey's judgment about women's immorality (Volume 1, Part 3, Source 1), Walker focuses on the connections between economic and political injustice. Walker presents the case of seamstresses, pieceworkers whose conditions of labour and wages were completely unregulated.[3] Workers got hurt by 'class-legislation', a term Chartists and others used to condemn laws enacted by a Parliament that did not represent them. Women could be paid one penny for a shirt, while royalty and the aristocracy had incomes of tens and hundreds of thousands of pounds a year. Only the Charter, which would allow labouring men to become members of Parliament, would be able to change this striking income inequality.[4]

The second selection (22.2) is a letter printed in the *Northern Star* from Sarah Price, the chairwoman of the Female National Charter Association of Upper Honley and Smallthorn. In this letter, Price appeals to men and women to stop being 'apathetic' and to understand that their 'redemption' from the misery in which they were living lay with the People's Charter. She particularly calls on men and their supposedly 'superior intellect, strength and courage' to become politically

DOI: 10.4324/9780429320323-27

involved in order to protect their wives and children from starvation. Emphasizing a male breadwinner norm, Price envisions households where the husband/father of the family provided for his wife and children. Under current conditions, however, men were unemployed, so women had been forced into factories to support their families; Price describes this as an 'inverted' state, with men dependent on their wives.[5] Women, meanwhile, were being degraded by factory labour, which Price equates with slave labour. She calls on women to join the movement so they can restore their households and stop the 'slavery' of having their children forced to work.[6] It was class legislation, Price argues, that had brought about this world turned upside down, and only the Charter would produce change.[7] Both Walker and Price linked the economic and the political, stressing the need for working-class representation in order to achieve economic improvement. Price, however, tells her readers that they must get involved in the Chartist cause, to become agents in their own experiences of change.

22.1 'Miss Mary Ann Walker on the People's Charter'

A crowded and most respectably composed meeting, convened by public advertisement, was held last Monday evening, in the spacious and elegant hall of the National or Complete Suffrage Association, High Holborn, for the purpose of hearing Miss Mary Ann Walker deliver a lecture on the social evils which afflict the State, and on the People's Charter, as the remedy, and the *only* remedy, for the removal of those evils, and restoration of the happiness and independance of Great Britain and her dependencies.

The meeting was convened for eight o'clock, and soon after that hour the hall began to fill rapidly in all parts. The meeting at this time began to manifest impatience to hear Miss Walker, by loudly stamping on the floor, as a signal to have the chair taken. Among the mass of persons present, was a large proportion of very elegantly dressed ladies, many of whom were of the superior classes of society.

At about ten minutes past eight o'clock, a simultaneous burst of applause from all parts of the meeting, announced the presence in the hall of Miss Walker. She was attended by numerous friends, amongst whom we were glad to see the encouraging and supporting presence of many ladies; and as she advanced up the body towards the platform, the applause consisting of cheering, clapping of hands, waving of handkerchiefs, mingled with the loud "Huzzs," and other demonstrations of welcome, became marked and enthusiastic, almost beyond description. There were a few bad spirits in that part of the gallery to the right of the platform; but their dissentient voices or rather, and the more to their disgrace – *hisses!* – were overwhelmed in the reverberating din of acclamation. On reaching the platform, Miss Walker was again and again loudly cheered, a compliment which she acknowledged by inclining repeatedly to the audience. She was dressed in mourning, a habit which it is her calamity to wear for the death of her father, of whom she has not been very many months bereaved. The body of her dress was partially and becomingly low, displaying a very graceful bust, and tending to set off to greater interest a figure and form of interesting proportions. She appeared more than usually wan in countenance, the effect, doubtless, of her anxiety to do justice to her subject, and convey instruction and satisfaction to her audience. She wore a light sort of crape scarf, or *negligèe* attached gracefully to, and hanging drapery-like from, her arms, the effect tending to set off her costume, enlivening and contrasting with the black material. A jet neklace, suspending a "Cross,"

> "Which Jews might kiss, and Infidels adore."

adorned her bosom, giving a finish to her contour.

The anxiety and excitement of the audience was now wound up to the highest pitch to have the proceedings commence; and, on the motion of Mr. Overton, seconded by Mr. Cuffay, Mr. Balls was unanimously called to the chair.

He could not, he observed, but feel honoured at having been called upon to take the chair on this interesting occasion; interesting, because they were assembled that night to hear the great, the fundamental principles of "The People's Charter" defined and advocated by one of the softer and better sex. (Applause.) He considered, as "The People's Charter" was to remove the misery which afflicted and bore down the people of this country, that the female class ought to be hailed in the cause as the best of "propagators." (Much laughter.) He considered, also, that great praise was due to Miss Walker and Miss Inge, for having come forward in the cause of their country, and of humanity. (Hear, hear, and applause.) Miss Walker had seen the misery, and it was creditable to her to come forward in aid of its alleviation, and to show that it was solely the effects of corrupt "Class Legislation." (Hear, hear, and cheers.) She had come forward to assist the People in advancing "The People's Charter" (Cheers.) He therefore claimed their indulgence in her favour. (Hear, hear.) It was her first time – he might almost say her first – of addressing a great public assembly, and he, therefore, hoped they would hear her without interruption. At the conclusion of the address, Miss Walker would answer any questions which might be put to her. He would not longer detain them than to express the very great pleasure which he felt in introducing to their notice, Miss Mary Ann Walker, (Loud and long continued cheers), amidst which Miss WALKER rose and said, she deeply felt the difficulty of her situation on that evening, but feeling, at the same time, most deeply on the subject of her great and lovely country's wrongs, and of her fellow-countrymen's and women's sufferings, she had no apology to make for presenting herself before the meeting that evening. It was a bold thing, she admitted, for woman to step out of her retirement; and of course there would be always found persons who would put foul constructions on her motives in order to deter and throw her back. (Hear, hear.) And if there were any in that assembly who asked why she (Miss Walker) came out, to him she answered, "She came there at her country's call." If the human misery which afflicted the people of this great country was beyond the power of man to control – if it was the ordination of Providence, then would it be man's duty to submit; but when such was not the case, it was time, she would say, that man aroused himself, and ought to resist its cause. (Hear, hear, and loud cheers.) There never was a time when England possessed such abundance as at present. (Hear.) How was it, then, she would ask, that two-thirds of the population were, in the face of such a fact, without food? (Hear, hear, hear.) How was it that they could not take up a paper, but they were shocked and startled to read some frightful and affecting suicide? (Hear, hear.) How was it that but a few days ago, a young girl, of about fourteen years of age, committed suicide? And, be it remembered, she was of a respectable family, but had disobliged her father – how, but because she could not get employment. How was it that the women of England were reduced to make shirts for one penny each, and had to find thread out of that! (Indignant cries of "Shame!" from all parts of the hall.) How was it that Mr. Comyn, a surgeon, for whose character she (Miss Walker) entertained the highest respect, had recently called a meeting on behalf of those poor shirt makers? How came he to know of their circumstances and most deplorable condition? Alas! through having been called in to one of them, who to put an end to her miseries, had taken vitriol. (Deep sensation.) That poor creature had worked for *sixteen hours a day for sixpence!* (Horror, accompanied by cries of "Shame, Shame!" pervaded and ran through the meeting.) This had led to that gentleman saying, those poor shirt-makers, "would be satisfied with one penny more." In that, she (Miss Walker) did not agree with him. Those poor creatures should have a fair remunerative price for their labour. (Hear, hear, and applause.) She inquired at a shop-keeper's, an employer in this way, on the subject of the "penny a shirt" remuneration, and was informed by him that the taxes obliged him to give thus little, and she then set herself to work to learn who gained by those taxes. "*The Black List*," which she held in her hand, would answer. (Hear, hear.) And she would advise every poor, every working-man to possess himself of that list. First, then, let them take the income of £470,000 a-year, or £1287 12s. a day. Then there was the Duke of Cumberland, now King of Hanover, with Kew Palace. (Groans.) She (Miss Walker) would ask, why should they keep HIM. and give him one and twenty thousand a-year, or £57 10s per day. (Hear, hear, groans for his "Hanoverian" Majesty, and cheers for Miss Walker.) Then, there was another King pensioned on them, Leopold of Saxe Cobourg, (now King of the Belgians,) with Claremont Palace; why was he receiving £50,000 a year from this oppressed country. (Hear, hear.) Why, she would further ask, were the people of this country ground down as they were, taxed to keep a Queen Dowager – Queen Adelaide! who, besides the Royal Manor and Palace of Hampton Court, the park and domains of Busby, also Marlborough House, in Pall Mall, two parks, and three Royal Palaces, drew from the taxes of England £100,000 a-year, or £274 per day. (Shame, shame.) Why was that? And she (Miss Walker) would ask how "an old lady" could spend it. (Hear, and cheers.) – [A voice – She gives it in charity! (Commotion.) She (Miss Walker) very much questioned that. How, then, she would ask, could that "old lady" spend £274 a day, from the time she gets up till the time she goes to bed! (Laughter in the meeting, and much commotion among a section of Tories in the gallery on the right.) She (Miss Walker) did not quarrel with the Queen Dowager for what she got, but she thought that a yearly salary to keep her comfortable would be sufficient, and that before this much was given her, the women of England ought to be paid better for their labour. (Hear, hear, and cheers.) But the gentleman in the gallery had said that the Queen Dowager had given away her income in charity. (Laughter.) It was characteristic of Englishmen to be generous; but then they wished, nevertheless, to see the money they give for particular purposes earned. (Hear, hear.) She (Miss Walker) came there to explain national abuses and social grievances, and she was resolved to explain and expose them, in public and private, and on all occasions. (Cries of "Bravo! Miss Walker!" "Hear," and cheers.)

22.2 'Address of the Female National Charter Association of Upper Honley and Smallthorn'

FELLOW-COUNTRYWOMEN AND COUNTRYMEN, – That the present time is one of great distress, privation, and sorrow no one can deny, for never in our nation's history was ever such deep and universal destitution as at present.

To remedy these evils is the duty of all and every one, both male and female; no one ought to be backward in striving to put an end to the sufferings of the working classes, and yet what apathy, what criminal indifference is there manifested by far the majority of the men and women, who bear the heaviest part of the burden, and have to endure the greatest amount of sorrow.

Men, (we appeal to you,) should this be so? you who pride yourselves on your superior intellect, strength and courage; should you be apathetic; you with all your boasted advantages, should you be indifferent to the suffering privations and destitution of your wives, your children, and yourselves? Surely not. It cannot be, that the father of a family can endure to see the wife of his bosom, the children of his love, pine and die for want, when a remedy lies open before his eyes, a remedy easy to be obtained and only wanting the united energies of labour's sons to obtain that which would at once and for ever arrest the downward march of labour's children, and put an end to all these evils now so severely felt by all.

We fearlessly tell you, that all evils of a national nature centre in class-legislation, and we say that unless the monster be scotched, more and greater evils, deeper and more pungent sorrows await you; and as sure as you now suffer your present load, so sure will you have to suffer deeper and more heartfelt sorrow. We tell you that unless class-legislation is destroyed, you can have no hope of being any better, or of obtaining any real benefit for yourselves, your wives, or your children.

We therefore intreat you no longer to be apathetic, indifferent, or careless, but at once set about the work of your own, your wives, and your children's redemption, and let one determined, one united effort put an end to class-legislation, and on the ruins of party, plant the tree of liberty – the People's Charter.

Women, (we appeal to you,) has not the cold iron of poverty entered deep enough into your souls, but you must by your apathy invite heavier strokes and deeper wounds? You who have seen the order of nature inverted, the female driven to the factory to labour for her offspring, and her husband unwillingly idle at home, dependant alike on female and infantile labour for his own existence; will you, can you longer be in love with a base cruel system that makes you and your infants slaves, that factory lords may amass more gold than would purchase the whole land? Can you, mothers, bear longer the soul-degrading burden; must you still be the mothers of more slaves? You, who possess the finest sympathies of our nature, will you refuse your aid, when the object sought in your's and your children's happiness, and the complete emancipation of your country? No, no; we will not insult you by supposing that you are so besottedly in love with the present soul-grinding body-starving system, as longer to wish its continuance.

Come then, men, women; come all; unite, unite, and by one determined effort, abolish class-legislation, and again we say on its ruins plant universal justice and equality, based on the People's Charter.

In behalf of the Association,
SARAH PRICE, Chairwoman.

Notes

1 See, for example, A. Clark, *The Struggle for the Breeches: Gender and the Making of the British Working Class* (Berkeley: University of California Press, 1995), p. 229.
2 From 1842 to 1843, the *Northern Star* regularly printed transcripts of her lectures.
3 See B. Harris (ed), *Famine and Fashion: Needlewomen in the Nineteenth Century* (London: Routledge, 2016).
4 'Miss Mary Anne Walker on the People's Charter', *Northern Star*, 10 December 1842, p. 7.
5 Frederick Engels famously critiqued industrialization for inverting gender roles in *The Condition of the Working Class in England* (London: Lawrence and Wishart, 1984, orig. 1844), pp. 222–231. On the male breadwinner norm, see, for example, Clark, *The Struggle for the Breeches*; S. O. Rose, *Limited Livelihoods: Gender and Class in Nineteenth-Century England* (Berkeley: University of California Press, 1992). E. Griffin uses working-class autobiographies to examine the struggles of families trying to live in the context of this norm, in *Bread Winner: An Intimate History of the Victorian Economy* (New Haven, CT: Yale University Press, 2020).
6 On the use of the slavery metaphor in nineteenth-century critiques of capitalism, see M. Cunliffe, *Chattel Slavery and Wage Slavery: The Anglo-American Context, 1830–1860* (Athens: University of Georgia Press, 1979).
7 S. Price, 'Address of the Female National Charter Association of Upper Honley and Smallthorn', *Northern Star*, 29 January 1842, p. 17.

23

REPORTS OF SPECIAL ASSISTANT POOR LAW COMMISSIONERS ON THE EMPLOYMENT OF WOMEN AND CHILDREN IN AGRICULTURE

(London: Clowes and Sons, 1843), pp. 3–6, 9–13, 17–19, 22–28

In the 1830s and 1840s, Parliament was busy seating Select Committees and appointing Royal Commissions to investigate the conditions of the labouring classes. These investigations included inquiries into children's work in factories, women's and children's work in mines, and the sanitary conditions of the working classes more broadly. They produced thousands of pages of reports and appendices with evidence collected on-site, as appointed commissioners interviewed local leaders, medical men, employers, religious leaders, and workers themselves.[1] The selection here is from an assistant commissioner's report from an investigation into the work of women and children in rural areas. This inquiry was undertaken by the Poor Law Commission (see Volume 2 Introduction), which was instructed by the home secretary to appoint commissioners to examine 'the sorts of labour at which [women and children] are respectively employed, the wages they receive, the hours they work, and any other similar facts which may tend to throw light on upon their physical and moral condition'.[2] All four appointed assistant commissioners were barristers. This source is from Alfred Austin, who visited Wiltshire, Dorsetshire, Devonshire, and Somersetshire. Austin presents a picture of women undertaking a wide variety of agricultural employments, some requiring heavy labour.[3] He finds it important to note that some of the women's favourite occupations were those which required a lot of effort and that they found jobs that took a lot of strength to be good for their health and well-being. Austin comments that strong women were paid more, suggesting a value placed on the ability of women's bodies, which was not there for middle-class women, who were seen as delicate and fragile, or even factory women, who were regarded as worn out from work.[4] Women did, however, find themselves overworked in certain occupations, such as dairies, and visited doctors for advice. The doctors Austin interviewed generally agreed with working women that outdoor work was good for them,

DOI: 10.4324/9780429320323-28

although they did not think that work should happen before puberty, which was considered a risky time for women's bodies.[5] Austin comments on the generally inadequate state of women's food and housing but indicates that this was due to the condition of their families' incomes. While female factory workers were constantly condemned for their immorality, Austin states that there was very little immoral behaviour among agricultural women.[6] He believed that women in general should not be working, but because these female rural labourers were working to improve the income of their families, he concludes that their work was justified. He recommends that there should be no legislative interference into women's agricultural work by the government.

Women and Children in Agriculture

Women.

The practice of employing women in farm-labour exists in the several districts of the country I visited, and, I believe, prevails throughout the four counties mentioned in my instructions; but the number of women so employed, and the kinds of work which they perform, are not always the same. A difference is sometimes found in their occupations on two adjoining farms. The women of one village have always been accustomed to reap, whilst to those of another in the immediate neighbourhood the practice is unknown. Turnip hoeing is by no means an uncommon occupation for women, yet in many villages they never undertake it. The kinds of agricultural labour in which women are engaged appear to depend upon the habits of narrow localities; and though in a few respects perhaps their occupations may vary with the larger divisions of counties, it is nevertheless impossible to point out any very marked or essential difference between their employments in general in one county and in another. Thus working in the hay and corn harvests, or in the dairy; hoeing turnips; weeding and picking stones; planting and digging potatoes; pulling, digging, and hacking turnips; attending the threshing machine, and winnowing corn; beating manure; filling dung-carts; planting beans, &c., are common to all the counties, though by no means uniformly practised in every part of them; picking apples is confined to the cider counties; and leading horses at plough appears to be a practice of only a few and perhaps remote parts of Devonshire and Somersetshire.

But although the occupations of women do not materially differ with different counties, I have reason to believe, as far as my opportunities of inquiry permitted me to observe, that women are more regularly and constantly employed, although not in greater numbers, in Devonshire than in the other countries. In Wiltshire, Dorsetshire, and Somersetshire, some of the employments already enumerated, viz., those proper to the spring, summer, and earlier part of autumn, are much more followed than the others; but in Devonshire this is not so much the case; for in that county it would appear that the occupations belonging to the winter months are pursued with nearly the same regularity as those of the other parts of the year. In those districts where the women do not work through the winter, the work elsewhere performed by them is done by men or boys.

On arable and grazing farms women are chiefly employed in the hay and corn harvests, in hoeing turnips, weeding corn, picking stones, beating manure, in planting and digging potatoes, pulling and digging turnips, and occasionally in hacking them for cattle. They are also employed in winnowing corn, and occasionally about the threshing machine. In some few cases they are employed in leading horses at plough, filling dung-carts, &c.

Of the more common occupations above enumerated, the most laborious are represented by the women who pursue them to be hay-making, hoeing turnips, and digging potatoes; and when women reap, the work in the harvest-field must be classed amongst their most laborious occupations. Of these four kinds of work, hay-making would appear to be the most fatiguing, owing to the extent of ground walked over in the course of the day in addition to the work done with the arms. Nevertheless it appears to be the favourite employment of women. It is a time of enjoyment, though one of hard labour. With respect to these particular occupations it is also to be observed, that their laboriousness arises more from their being continued through a greater number of hours, than from their requiring a greater exertion of strength. On the other hand, the same kinds of work, except hay-making, being generally job-work, the reward is in direct proportion to the quantity of work done. Not one of the many women accustomed to work in the fields with whom I conversed on the subject of their labour, considered it as generally too severe; they spoke of working out of doors, even of the more fatiguing occupations, when they had become accustomed to it, as desirable for their health and spirits.

The severest labour performed by women, connected with agriculture, is in the dairy-farms. The work lasts during the principal part of the year, and for many months occupies the greater part of the day. Milking and making cheese twice a-day, and at the same time looking after the cheese already made, are described to be "work that is never finished." The work is not only continuous, but very fatiguing. Looking after, cleaning or wiping cheeses weighing frequently a quarter of a cwt., and which have to be turned and moved from place to place, is work that is occasionally followed by consequences to the health of women employed in it which show that it is too severe. Dr. Greenup, of Calne, states, that he is not unfrequently applied to for advice by women suffering from symptoms of over-work, generally attributable to their being employed in the dairy, and that such symptoms are – pains in the back and limbs, overpowering sense of fatigue most painful in the morning, want of appetite, feverishness, &c.

But with respect to the dairy-farms, it is to be observed that where they are small, as is nearly universally the case in these counties, the most laborious part of the work is not performed by servants, but by the mistress herself. The prosperity of such a farm depends entirely on the quality of the cheese, or, in other words, upon the skill and attention bestowed on its making and subsequent management. The entire management of the dairy rests with the farmer's wife, and cannot be left to servants; and where the farmer is not married, he is obliged to keep a dairy-woman to conduct the dairy, upon whom is thrown the whole responsibility, and who consequently is a person of corresponding importance in his household. As on the wife or the dairy-woman is cast not only the responsibility but also the actual labour attending the dairy, more particularly that of attending to and cleaning the cheeses, she performs the most laborious part of the work. The servants kept in the house are not wholly employed in the dairy, where they only assist their mistress or the dairy-woman, but they also do the household work. And the bad effects from excessive labour, observed in women working in the dairies, are consequently observable only in the mistresses or dairy-women, and very rarely in the female servants, their work being by no means so hard as that of their mistresses. [. . .]

The ages at which women are employed vary from 15 to 70, or even older. But there are few employed so early as 15, and they do not often work regularly in farm-labour till they have reached the age of 20: the desire of their parents to get them out to service prevents their being much employed before that age in agricultural labour. But I am inclined to believe, though it is difficult to procure any very decisive evidence upon such a point, that the majority of women who work in the fields are above the age of 30; and perhaps I may add, that they are generally married, and sometimes are widows with children.

The wages received by women do not vary in different counties more than in adjoining parishes: even in the same parish it occasionally happens that one woman is paid 1*d.* or 2*d.* a-day more than another. A woman situated, with regard to her family, so as to be always at liberty to go out to work when wanted by the farmer, and upon whose services he can always depend, gets higher wages than one who can only now and then manage to get out to work, on account of young children, or other circumstances. There is also a great difference in the strength and capacity of women for working in the fields; and a woman who is strong and active, and a good work-woman, is paid higher than one of inferior strength, or who is slow at her work. In piece-work, especially, this difference in the strength and capacity of women for work influences their earnings.

The wages of women also depend a great deal on the farmer himself, and the way in which he likes the work on his farm to be done. It is no uncommon thing to see one farmer paying 1*d.* or 2*d.* a-day more to women than his neighbour. The common explanation given by women, when questioned as to the cause of difference of wages, is, that "Mr. A. is a good master, – he always gives 10*d.*;" or, "Mr. B. is not like Mr. A., – he never pays more than 8*d.* or 9*d.*" Upon further inquiry respecting this difference, however, I found that some farmers always select the best and most regular workers amongst the women, and pay them high wages; whilst the farmers who pay a low rate of wages are satisfied with the inferior workers. Occasionally, also, I found a feeling of kindness on the part of a farmer towards the women who worked for him regularly, prompting him to give a little more than the common rate of wages around him.

The average rate of wages or earnings of women may be seen in the following statements made to me by various persons conversant in the matter.

In Wiltshire

[. . .] The hours during which women work are, in winter from eight o'clock in the morning till four o'clock in the afternoon; at other times, when engaged in weeding corn or stone-picking, or in other work for which they are not paid by the job, or at which they do not work at over-hours, they are generally engaged from eight o'clock in the morning till six in the evening, or from half-past seven till half-past five. But eight o'clock appears the common time for women beginning work, as it allows them to put their cottage into order after the breakfast of the family, and to make arrangements for themselves being absent all day.

In the hay-harvest the regular hours for women are generally considered to be from six in the morning till six in the evening, but these hours are often prolonged by the accident of weather, &c. In the corn-harvest the hours are irregular, the work generally being piece-work, and the object of the women employed is to get through it as quickly as possible. In some cases I heard of women working from four o'clock in the morning till eight at night; but these were exceptions to the ordinary practice, and by no means common.

In the middle of the day an hour is taken for dinner, and in the hay and corn harvest twice or thrice during the day some minutes are taken for rest or refreshment.

With respect to the physical condition of women employed in agriculture, my observations will be comprised under the heads of health, food, clothing, and lodging.

The first question as to their health relates to the effects produced upon it by the employment in question.

The effects of out-door farm-labour upon grown-up women appears on the whole to be beneficial. Women accustomed to it nearly without exception represent it as good for their health and spirits. I did not meet with an instance of a woman complaining of the effects of working in the fields upon her health. Sometimes such work, particularly in the hay and corn harvests, was represented by women who performed it as being laborious, as making them stiff at first, or even as straining them; but I did not find that any woman, from her own statement, had become subject to any permanent disease or infirmity from the employment in question.

As far, therefore, as the testimony of the women themselves is concerned, and which is not to be disregarded, it appears that out-door labour is not injurious to their health. But the experience and testimony of medical men is nearly as uniform. The opinion of Dr. Greenup, of Calne, which was not given without mature consideration, and upon which much reliance may be placed, is to the effect that *t*he [sic] employment in question is healthy. Mr. King, a surgeon and apothecary of the same place, and possessing great knowledge of the labouring poor, says that married women bear the labour in the fields extremely well; that he has never observed any other effects upon their general health than colds, from which they suffer occasionally, caught from wet and exposure to the weather; he was not sure that they were even peculiarly subject to colds; women in the family-way, or suckling children, are certainly not hurt. He does not think that their work is too hard for them, or injurious, even taking into account the fact of their generally having insufficient food. The out-door work is rather healthy than otherwise.

Mr. Henry King, of Blandford, in Dorsetshire, a surgeon, and for many years practising in an agricultural population, thinks that women ought not to be employed in agricultural labour in the winter, for they must be necessarily exposed to the vicissitudes of the weather, and, from the nature of their employment, must be very frequently wet about the feet and legs, which often proves very injurious to the general health. In the summer the work is of a different sort, and he does not consider that much (if any) mischief would result from it. He also adds, that women, when they are employed in out-door labour, do not often work on wet days, as the farmers well know that on those days they cannot get their *quid pro quo*.

Mr. Spooner, another surgeon of Blandford, is of opinion that if women avoid exposure to wet, especially at certain critical times, employment in agricultural labour of the light kind, performed in spring and at the harvest, is not injurious. He has found much more disease in women of sedentary habits of the same class, such as those employed in button making and household service. Where women have no out-door exercise, chlorosis, constipation, and indigestion occur, which are very uncommon with women who labour in the fields. Women who labour in the fields, like men, are, if exposed to too much wet and cold, subject to rheumatism and catarrhs. Women in particular should, especially at certain times, avoid such exposure. Exercise in the open air, under proper limitations, renders people less susceptible of the morbid effects of atmospheric changes.

Mr. Lyddon, of St. Thomas's, Exeter, a surgeon and general practitioner, and attending the poor of a very large agricultural district, says – that women are not so much exposed to weather altogether as men; their work is not so various, and it requires finer weather. He has observed no ill effects from any of the kinds of labour he mentioned, either to girls or grown-up women; no ill effects to young women at the critical age of 15 or 16. He does not think that rheumatism is produced more by such work than by other occupations; he has seen quite as much of that complaint in women who never leave their cottages. Washerwomen are much more exposed to rheumatism than women working out of doors. Pregnant women work as well as others, and the work is not injurious to them. Sometimes an accident may happen to a woman in that state during her work, such as slipping or falling down, perhaps. He has known four or five such cases, which were followed by pains about the sides until labour took place, but without further ill consequences. He has also known women during certain critical periods going out to work in bad weather, insufficiently clad, who have been hurt more than if their work had been in-doors; but generally out-door employment is extremely conducive to regular habits of body in women; and from the want of such regularity, women in the same class of life in towns, or at service, and who do not work out of doors, suffer a great deal. He has not observed that women employed in out-door labour are at all more subject to colds, and in general he should say that such labour is healthy than otherwise.

Mr. Cutliffe, of Southmolton, Devonshire, surgeon and apothecary, and who has attended the poor of an extensive agricultural district for thirty years, says – that women are seldom employed in agricultural labour so as to injure their health; on the contrary, they are, generally speaking, the most robust and healthy females we meet with.

Mr. Tanner, of the same place, surgeon and apothecary, says that women do not suffer in their health from the employment in question.

Mr. Poole, of Bridgwater, surgeon and apothecary, has had no reason to suppose that the employment of women is injurious to their health. And Mr. Tilsey, of North Petherton, a village near Bridgwater, a surgeon and one of the medical officers of that Union, says – that on referring to his books he cannot find that there is any disease peculiar to (boys or) women engaged in agriculture, but on the contrary they (both) seem to be remarkably exempt from illness; for the most part they possess a ruddiness of countenance and a firmness of fibre which he believes to be wholly attributable to the exercise and the exposure consequent to their occupation.

But from the age of 14 or 15, that of puberty in women, to 18 or 20, when they are full grown, the employment out of doors would perhaps appear to be objectionable. Mr. King, of Calne says he does not think that young girls should work in the fields from 12 to 17, or indeed under 20. It is not the severity of the labour that he thinks injurious to them, for it is by no means excessive; but the exposure to wet and cold, which, of course, is inevitable, has a tendency to engender affections of the chest. He was not able to recall any particular instance of such disease being distinctly the result of exposure to cold and wet in the way mentioned, but he thinks that much of the ill health amongst women in that class in after-life, especially consumption, arises from early exposure to weather.

Mr. Spooner says he thinks girls under the age of puberty ought not to be subjected to labour, and that they should not be exposed to cold and wet. Girls, before they arrive at the age in question, are much more liable to contract disease from the same causes than afterwards, when they are full grown and functionally perfect.

Mr. King, of Blandford, says, in regard to the employment of young females in out-door work, it is in his opinion improper that, at any rate during the winter season, they should be exposed to the vicissitudes of weather, and most probably just at the age of puberty, when the general health is of the greatest importance, the work during this season being hoeing of turnips, &c. &c., in which employment they must necessarily be much exposed to cold and wet.

Women employed in dairies as servants are not subject to any permanent complaints caused by their work, though they appear to suffer more from fatigue at certain seasons than women engaged in out-door labour. It would appear that the servants in dairies are perhaps sometimes over-worked, but, generally speaking, certainly not so as materially to damage their health. It is the mistresses or dairy-women who appear to suffer most in their health from the dairy-work, but even in their case no permanent ill effects are produced.

There is, however, a second question respecting the health of women employed in agriculture, and which relates to the effects arising from the physical circumstances in which they are placed, particularly as regards food, clothing, and lodging. It is clear that whilst farm-labour itself may be beneficial to their health, yet that their general condition may be unfavourable to it. How far this is the case will appear from the following observations.

Women employed in dairies are single women, and for the most part, if not entirely, live in the farm-house, and are lodged and fed in a manner not much inferior to that of their employers. Their wages are also amply sufficient to supply them with proper clothing. But with respect to the women who work in the fields, and otherwise about the farm, the case is widely different; their food, clothing, and lodging, being that of the agricultural labouring class in general. Of the women employed in such labour, the greater number are married; and those who are unmarried are sometimes grown-up daughters living with their parents. There are cases of widows, and rarer ones of single women, with or without children, living by themselves, and wholly or partly dependent on their own earnings for support. But generally speaking the wages of women must not be considered as earned for, or applied in, their own separate support, but as a part of the aggregate earnings of a family, and accordingly part of the common fund for its maintenance. The condition of a woman employed in agriculture, therefore, does not depend directly on the amount of her own earnings, but of those of the entire family. She is not well or badly off, well or badly fed, clothed, and lodged according to her earnings, except in the rare case of her being entirely independent of any other means of support than her own labour. The condition of women working at agricultural labour, therefore, depends upon the general means of living of the labourer; and without an inquiry into this extensive and difficult subject, it is clear that their physical condition cannot be properly understood. [. . .]

In conversing with women accustomed to work in the fields, I found, nearly generally, that there was no complaint of a deficiency of food; in some cases the appearance of the cottages, of the women themselves, and of the children, proved that there could be no such deficiency. But there are women occupied in the same employment who cannot be said to have adequate food; for there are maladies amongst them ascribed by medical men to that cause. Such instances, however, which are by no means common, occur principally in Wiltshire and Somersetshire, for I heard of no complaints that women employed in the manner in question had not sufficient food in other counties; and I am inclined to think that where women so employed suffer from a want of food in any case, it is where the means of subsistence of the family is at the lowest ebb, either from a temporary want of work by the husband, the absence of the advantages frequently possessed by the labourer, bad habits, such as drinking, &c., or from, perhaps, the commonest cause, a numerous family of young children. It certainly did not appear to me that a want of food is by any means common amongst the women who work in the fields. But I should observe, that the districts in which I did not hear of it, were (with the exception of the neighbourhood of St. Thomas's, Exeter) those in which there is employment for the agricultural population besides that of farm-labour; viz., in Dorsetshire the button-making, and in Devonshire the lace-making; although on the other hand there are quite as many women on the whole (though, perhaps, they are of a more advanced age) employed in agriculture in the two last-mentioned counties as in Wiltshire or Somersetshire.

The testimony of the medical men whom I consulted induces me to believe that the quality of the food of the agricultural labourers is not too low where the general state of their health is good; but that if there is a disposition to disease, or any deficiency in the quantity of the food, then the quality is found to be defective. Generally speaking the labouring population is healthy; but it appears that when grown-up women are attacked by diseases of certain descriptions, the low quality of their food is unfavourable to their recovery. It would appear, also, that when the quantity of food is sufficient, any effects from its quality are less felt by women accustomed to out-door labour than by those who keep at home. In Wiltshire the food of the labourer and his family is wheaten[1] bread, potatoes, a small quantity of beer, but only as a luxury, and a little butter and tea. To this may sometimes be added (but it is difficult to say how often or in what quantities), cheese, bacon, and in the neighbourhood of Calne, a portion of the entrails of the pig, – a considerable trade being carried on at Calne in curing bacon. I am inclined to think that the use of bacon and those parts of the pig only occurs where the earnings of the family are not limited to those of the husband; or, if his wages form their sole means of support, then it depends upon the number of his family. In more than one cottage, where the mother went out to work, or two of the boys were earning perhaps 3*s*. or 3*s*. 6*d*. a-week between them, I saw a side of bacon hanging against the wall; but nothing of the kind was visible when the only earnings were those of the husband, or the family was numerous and young. Where, from poverty, bacon cannot be obtained, a little fat is used to give a flavour to the potatoes. In Dorsetshire and Devonshire, in cases where the labourer is in constant employ, and possesses the advantages he frequently enjoys in those counties, the consumption of bacon would appear to be more constant, with now and then a little fresh meat. I believe that in these two counties the labourer not uncommonly is in a position to keep for his own use a part, and sometimes not an inconsiderable share, of his pig when it is killed. But in Somersetshire the food appears to be much the same as in Wiltshire, – bread and potatoes, with bacon and cheese at times. In the generality of cases the beer that is consumed is drunk by the husband, the universally favourite drink of the women being tea. At harvest the women drink beer, when given by the master; and not unfrequently, in the cider counties, a portion of the cider which is allowed them as part of their wages, though generally the greater part of it is kept for their husbands.

With regard to lodging, there is no difference between that of the women who labour in the fields and the women of the same class who do not. The want of sufficient accommodation seems universal. Cottages generally have only two bedrooms (with very rare exceptions); a great many have only one. The consequence is, that it is very often extremely difficult, if not impossible, to divide a family so that grown-up persons of different sexes, brothers and sisters, fathers and daughters, do not sleep in the same room. Three or four persons not unfrequently sleep in the same bed. In a few instances I found that two families, neighbours, arranged so that the females of both families slept together in one cottage and the males in the other; but such an arrangement is very rare, and in the generality of cottages I believe that the only attempt that is or that can be made to separate beds, with occupants of different sexes, and necessarily placed close together from the smallness of the rooms, is an old shawl or some article of dress suspended as a curtain between them. At Stourpain, a village near Blandford, I measured a bed-room in a cottage consisting of two rooms, the bed-room in question upstairs, and a room on the ground-floor in which the family lived during the day. There were eleven in the family: and the aggregate earnings in money were 16*s*. 6*d*. weekly (Dec. 1842), with certain advantages, the principal being the father's title to a grist of a bushel of corn a-week, at 1*s*. below the market price, his fuel carted for him, &c. They had also an allotment of a quarter of an acre, for which they paid a rent of 7*s*. 7*d*. a-year. [. . .]

The clothing of women employed in field-labour would appear to be inadequate for their work, but the deficiency is not complained of by them. A change of clothes seems to be out of the question, although necessary not only for cleanliness but for convenience and saving of time. The upper parts of the underclothes of women at work, even their stays, quickly become wet through with perspiration, whilst the lower parts cannot escape getting equally wet in nearly every kind of work they are engaged in, except in the driest weather. It not unfrequently happens that a woman, on returning home from work, is obliged to go to bed for an hour or two to allow her clothes to be dried. It is also by no means uncommon for her, if she does not do this, to put them on again the next morning nearly as wet as when she took them off. It does not appear that any ill consequences to the health have been observed by medical men to arise from this cause, unless rheumatism be partly attributable to it. The want of a change of working clothes, however, does not prevent the generality of working women having a better gown and other articles of dress for Sundays or holidays. [. . .]

The general conclusion as to the physical condition of women engaged in agriculture is, that it is better generally than those of the same class not so employed. The reason is evident; the means of the family are increased by her earnings; she has more food, if she be not better clothed and lodged. Her health is also better. I am now speaking of her own physical condition; the effects of her working at farm-labour upon her domestic economy, her husband and children, will be considered presently.

There are no very apparent effects upon the morality of women from their working in the fields; very frequently they are active, energetic, and well-disposed women, working from the sole desire of increasing the means of subsistence of the family, and personally undergoing the labour of their employment for that object. Their motive, being thus meritorious, is hardly consistent with any great degree of immorality. Instances of a want of chastity on the part of married as well as single women thus employed occur, but not more frequently, as far as I could ascertain, amongst them than amongst women of the same class who do not work at the same labour.

There is no doubt that the mixed employment of men and women in hay-making, and perhaps in the corn-harvest, tends to immorality. Hay-making is a season of comparative license; hard work is expected by the master; but if it is performed, he overlooks conduct on the part of the work-people which he might not suffer to pass unnoticed at other times. Drink, and frequently food, is plentifully supplied to stimulate to work, and gaiety is promoted by every means. The topics of conversation and the language that is used amongst men and women, young and old, is described as coarse and filthy. That breaches of morality occur cannot be doubted; indeed there is plenty of evidence that they actually take place.

But one-half of the women and girls employed in the hay-field are never engaged in any other kind of farm-work, and the licentiousness of that season, as far as the women are concerned, would appear rather to proceed from those occasionally employed. Women who work the whole or the greater part of the year are too much accustomed to work in the company of men, and moreover are too much inclined to look upon their work in the serious light of an important part of their means of subsistence, to conduct themselves in a reckless manner at any particular season; and generally the testimony in favour of such women's good conduct is abundant. At other times of the year than the hay and corn harvests, no extraordinary licentiousness is generally imputed to women employed in farm-labour. [. . .]

A great many women accustomed to work in the fields, like other women of the same class, are unable to read and write, or if to do either, it is very imperfectly. This is more particularly the case with the women above 30; but generally, even where they have been taught to read and write, the women of the agricultural labouring class are in a state of ignorance affecting the daily welfare and comforts of their families. Ignorance of the commonest things, needle-work, cooking, and other matters of domestic economy, is described as nearly universally prevalent; and when any knowledge of such things is possessed by the wife of a labourer, it is generally to be traced to the circumstance of her having, before marriage, lived as a servant in a farmhouse, or elsewhere. A girl brought up in a cottage until she marries is generally ignorant of nearly everything she ought to be acquainted with for the comfortable and economical management of a cottage. The effects of such ignorance are seen in many ways, but in no one more striking than its hindering girls from getting out to service, as they are not capable of doing anything that is required in a family of a better description. The further effect of this is, that not being able to find a place, a young woman goes into the fields to labour, with which ends all chance of improving her position; she marries, and brings up her daughters in the same ignorance, and their lives are a repetition of her own.

There are other consequences, however, resulting from the women working in the fields, besides those affecting their own physical or moral condition, and these consist in certain disadvantages to her family.

When the mother of young children is absent from home the whole or the greater part of the day, the mischief to them is very great. They are neglected in every way, morally and physically. Under the most favourable circumstances, they may be left in the care of a grandmother or aunt; but the more common way is to leave them in the custody of the eldest boy or girl, of 8 or 9 years old, or in that of a girl of the same age, or a little older, hired for the purpose. Sometimes, however, her children are locked up in the cottage, without anybody to take charge of them at all. Where a girl is hired to take care of children, she is paid about 9*d.* a-week, and has her food besides, which is a serious deduction from the wages of the woman at work.

When children are locked up by themselves, sometimes the most fatal accidents happen, those from fire amongst others. One woman, accustomed all her life to work in the fields, and a most excellent specimen of her class, industrious, careful, and thriving, and having moreover a large family, told me – "I have always left my children to themselves, and, God be praised! nothing has ever happened to them, though I have thought it dangerous. I have many a time come home and have thought it a mercy to find nothing has happened to them."

In addition to the dangers of leaving children to themselves, there is the further evil, that they are not taken care of as young children should be. They are left without any control over their conduct the whole day, and without instruction or example of any kind. When left in the care of a child older than themselves, the case is hardly better. No child of 8 or 10 years can feel the responsibility of such a charge, or be able to attend to children, as far as forming their minds, or keeping them from indulging in mischievous propensities. In more than one case it was represented to me, by women working out of doors, that leaving their children without anybody to attend properly to them was the worst part of their employment: the children, they said, were always in a state of dirt; they destroyed more victuals than they ate; they tore their clothes; and there were no means of their learning anything. When the child is old enough, and it can be afforded, it is sent to school for the day, which is a great relief to the mother; but this cannot be the case with very young children. Sometimes, a mother will take her children, who are strong enough to walk so far, with her to her work, and they are kept in her sight all day long, but this is very rarely the case.

To a certain extent, also, the husband is a sufferer from his wife's absence from home. There is not the same order in the cottage, nor the same attention paid to his comforts as when his wife remains at home all day. On returning from her labour she has to look after her children, and her husband may have to wait for his supper. He may come home tired and wet; he finds his wife has arrived just before him; she must give her attention to the children; there is no fire, no supper, no comfort, and he goes to the beer-shop.

When a woman is much employed out of doors, many things in the domestic economy are neglected; particularly such things as require frequent attention. Her own clothes, and those of her husband and family, are rarely in such cases properly attended to.

The number of women employed in agriculture, either absolutely or compared with that of men so employed, must be to a great extent matter of mere conjecture, until a more minute and accurate inquiry than I had the means of executing, be made. From the information which I was inclined to pay attention to, and from the looser statements of the farmers and other persons with whom I conversed, it would appear perhaps that in the hay-harvest about as many women and girls are employed as men and boys, and that at other times of the year during which women are employed their number does not exceed one-third or one-fourth that of the men, except at the corn-harvest, when their number may be nearly equal.

With a slight exception, the work performed by women in farm-labour is not the kind of work which it would answer to employ men upon; the employment of women, therefore, has not superseded that of men in any degree that I could discover. During the war, women were employed in greater numbers than at present in some districts, but they made way for men immediately at the peace. The strength required for the work performed by men effectually prevents women from being employed in it; and the lower rate of wages for which they work has not had any tendency, therefore, to make them more generally employed.

Employment in field-labour is beneficial to the physical condition of women; and when it is regular and tolerably constant, I do not think it is materially injurious to their moral character. The immorality observable amongst women so employed is not a consequence of their occupation, but is the necessary result of the ignorance and poverty of the agricultural labouring population generally. I believe it would be much better for their husbands and children, if women were not engaged in such employment, in certain respects; but the observation repeatedly made to me on the other hand was, that their earnings are a benefit to their families which cannot be dispensed with without creating a great deal of suffering. And, upon the fullest consideration, I believe that the earnings of a woman employed in the fields are an advantage which, in the present state of the agricultural population, outweighs any of the mischiefs arising from such employment. All direct interference in the employment of women in agriculture must be deprecated at present. The evils that attend it can only be relieved by generally bettering the position of the agricultural labouring class; but before any step towards effecting such an object is attempted, the real condition of that class should be accurately ascertained.

Editorial Endnotes

1 O. Frankel, 'Blue Books and the Victorian Reader', *Victorian Studies* 46:2 (Winter 2004), pp. 308–318; M. Levine-Clark, *Beyond the Reproductive Body: The Politics of Women's Health and Work in Early Victorian England* (Columbus: Ohio State University Press, 2004), chap. 1 and 2.

2 *Reports of Special Assistant Poor Law Commissioners on the Employment of Women and Children in Agriculture* (London: Clowes and Sons, 1843), Google Books, p. xv. On the Poor Law Commission, see A. Brundage, *The English Poor Laws, 1700–1930* (New York: Palgrave Macmillan, 2001), pp. 69–71.

3 On women's agricultural labour, see K. Sayer, *Women of the Fields: Representations of Rural Women in the Nineteenth Century* (Manchester, UK: Manchester University Press, 1995).

4 Levine-Clark, *Beyond the Reproductive Body*, chap.1.

5 Levine-Clark, *Beyond the Reproductive Body*, pp. 29–30.

6 On the perception of factory women's morality, see F. Mort, *Dangerous Sexualities: Medico-Moral Politics in England since 1830*, 2nd ed. (New York: Routledge, 2000), pp. 37–39.

Source Endnote

1 Barley bread, universally eaten by the labourer at the close of last century, in the greater part of these counties, as I was told, has everywhere given place to wheaten bread.

24

E. COPLEY, 'INTRODUCTION' TO *THE YOUNG WOMEN OF THE FACTORY, OR FRIENDLY HINTS ON THEIR DUTIES AND DANGERS*

(London: The Religious Tract Society, c. 1840), pp. 1–4

Esther Copley (1786–1851) was the author of many works for adults and children, which, as her obituary in the *Oxford Chronicle* noted, were 'designed and adapted to enlighten and elevate the minds of the humbler classes, and to improve their moral, social, and domestic condition'.[1] Her 1825 book *Cottage Comforts* reached twenty-four editions by 1864, providing instruction on domestic economy, but she also published such titles as *A History of Slavery and Its Abolition* and *Cholera Preventible*, indicating her desire to translate the issues of the day into readable texts for the working classes.[2] This selection, the introduction to her advice book for young women factory workers, is a good example of the religiosity that infused her publications. It is also an unusual text in that it praises factory work as a worthy industry for young women. While Copley clearly sees a woman's ultimate social role as motherhood, she believes that young women of the working classes needed to be occupied until they were ready to take up that role. According to Copley, working in a factory kept young women from idleness, provided them with wages to support themselves and their families, and gave them useful skills. She identifies women's factory work as important to the larger economy, contributing to employers' profits and to domestic and foreign trade. Young women who grew up in factories learned how to live independently, which Copley regards positively. Copley points out the potential dangers of working in a factory, such as 'extravagant spending' and 'the snares of bad company', but she clearly believes that women's work was of value and that being in a factory would not hurt women's future roles.[3] Her book was intended to help women navigate the life of factory work in order to develop the right traits for their ultimate position as wives and mothers. So, while Copley is encouraging about women's factory work, she sees it as a temporary phase of life, until women got married. Copley's view of women's factory work is significantly different from that of Joseph Livesey (see Volume 1,

DOI: 10.4324/9780429320323-29

Part 3, Chapter 21), who saw no value in factory work for women because it conflicted with their roles as wives and mothers and damaged their morals. Copley held that women could overcome the challenges factory work posed to their morality. In many ways, Copley's text looks at women's work in factories pragmatically, accepting that it was happening and would continue to happen, that for most young women it constituted a phase between childhood and marriage, and that the best way to approach it was not to condemn women workers but to instruct them.[4]

The Young Women of the Factory.

'Introduction'

THIS little book is intended for the use of a numerous and interesting class of society. It is calculated that about a million of females, under twenty years of age, are engaged in factory work. In a few years, most of these young people will become the mothers of another generation. We look at them with lively and affectionate interest. We feel an earnest desire for their welfare and happiness; that they may be fitted for the discharge of the various duties at present devolving on them, and those that await them in future life. Gladly should we suggest any thing that might have a tendency to direct them in the good and right way. We should like to make them sensible of the advantages by which they are surrounded, in order that they may improve them: we would also point out to them how they might make the best of any thing which is undesirable in their condition. We would tenderly and faithfully warn them of their dangers, and suggest the means of avoiding or escaping them; and our hearts would rise in fervent prayers to the Father of mercies on their behalf.

Your situation, dear young friends, possesses many advantages. It is a great honour and pleasure to be usefully employed, and a great disgrace to be idle and useless. Some young people may be seen, day after day, idly strolling about the streets, doing no good to any body, but learning every kind of mischief and wickedness. How much better is it to be at work in the factory, moving about the nimble fingers in winding, spinning, or weaving the cotton, silk, wool, or other goods which so greatly promote the comfort of the wearers, the profit of the master, and the honour and traffic of our native country, even to the very ends of the earth.

Suppose all the idle people were sent out of the country; who would miss them for any good they do? But if all the industrious young people who work in the factories, potteries, etc., were sent out of the country, it would be a real loss. All who make, or sell, or use manufactured articles would be put to great inconvenience; and, most likely, the loss would not be made up till another race of young ones were grown old enough to be trained to the same employment.

Besides being useful to society, it is one of your advantages that you earn something towards your own support – perhaps enough to maintain yourselves altogether. In places where there is no profitable employment for children, both parents and children are very much straitened and distressed; and large families are considered a burden. There are many mouths to feed, and but scanty means of support; and thus they have suffered great hardships. They have been poorly fed and clothed, and have suffered from want and sickness, without the means of getting relief. This is not the case with you young people in the manufacturing districts. At an early age you can contribute something towards the support of the family, and be a help to your parents instead of a burden. This is an honour and advantage which a dutiful and grateful child will highly value. Then, too, you are learning a business, by which you may hope to get your living at a future day. If you should be left orphans, how different will be your lot from that of children of your own age, who have never been taught any kind of useful labour! Or, if your parents should be spared, as you advance in skill, knowledge, and ability, what a pleasure may you enjoy, in helping to make their old age comfortable! It is not intended to say that young people in other situations cannot enjoy this pleasure; but perhaps few possess the means to an equal degree with those who, being employed in extensive manufactories – if they are diligent, faithful, and well-behaved – may expect constant work and advancing wages, in proportion to their ability.

But, then, you are exposed to some peculiar evils, or dangers, which, if not confined to your situation, are more prevalent there than in some others. There is the danger of having your attention confined to one object, and of neglecting to acquire other kinds of valuable and necessary knowledge. There is danger connected with your being able early to earn money, lest you should be set free from control before you have acquired wisdom and knowledge enough for your own guidance; lest you should acquire a habit of extravagantly spending that which is easily earned, and of which you may know the want at a future day. You are in danger of a spirit of vanity, emulation, and display; and you are in danger from the snares of bad company, lest from among your numerous workfellows you should be led to form acquaintance with, and copy the practices of those who would do you harm, and not good. It will be one object of this book to point out these dangers to you, and to show you how you may escape them. You will generally be instructed by the example of others, because that mode of instruction has been found most acceptable to young people; and though you will not find in this little book any wonderful stories, it is hoped that you will find enough to interest you, and to show you that, all things considered, the way of duty, the way of obedience to the commandments of God, is not only the right and safe, but the pleasant and happy way; whereas "the way of transgressors is hard," and "the end thereof is death."

Notes

1 'City and County Intelligence', *Oxford Chronicle and Reading Gazette*, 2 August 1851, p. 2.

2 R. Mitchell, 'Copley [*née* Beuzeville; *other married name* Hewlett], Esther', *Oxford Dictionary of National Biography*, 23 September 2004, at https://doi-org.du.idm.oclc.org/10.1093/ref:odnb/55930 [accessed 14 June 2021].

3 E. Copley, *The Young Women of the Factory, or Friendly Hints on Their Duties and Dangers* (London: The Religious Tract Society, c. 1840), Google Books, p. 4.

4 While working-class men benefited from working women's income, they were opposed to the competition of women's cheaper wages. For the ways men responded to women's labour, see, for example, A. Clark, *The Struggle for the Breeches: Gender and the Making of the British Working Class* (Berkeley: University of California Press, 1995), pp. 197–219.

25

ANON., 'FEMALE EDUCATION AND FEMALE LABOUR'

Artizan, A Monthly Journal of the Operative Arts 1 (1845), p. 147

This article, published in the *Artizan*, argues, in a way unusual for its time, that all women should have education suited to their class and that poor women especially should have expanded occupations open to them. The *Artizan* was published between 1843 and 1872, but we have little information about the periodical, other than the main focus reflected in the subtitle it had taken on by the 1850s: *A Monthly Record of the Progress of Civil and Mechanical Engineering*. This essay was one of two in the 1845 volume to focus on female labour. The author condemns current practice, which trained women not to focus on domestic and occupational skills but rather on their appearance and useless trivialities, which caused them to be burdens on their husbands.[1] Because working-class women had so few skills, the types of jobs for which single women could compete were extremely limited, which created an especially glutted market for unskilled female labour.[2] The writer argues against those who believed that education and work outside the home made women unfeminine. Rather, proper education and appropriate occupations would make women more rational and competent. Women who remained single for their entire lives would be able to take care of their own affairs, and married women would be able to help their husbands rather than weighing them down. The author worries about the numbers of poor women who had been committing suicide because of their miserable circumstances. He claims that women needed more employment options with better wages. Tracing the position of women in various historical eras, the writer admits that in earlier periods, women's subordination could be justified, but it no longer made sense in modern society. The definition of femininity should include, he insists, rationality, which for so long was associated only with men.[3] He mocks the equation of femininity with idleness by stating the parallel for manliness would be to equate it with brawling. Perhaps most daring, the author proposes that men should leave occupations for which women were suited, such as tailoring and printing, to women. Instead of worrying about how women's work in these trades brought down wages, men should step aside and allow women's work to establish its own wage scale, while

DOI: 10.4324/9780429320323-30

men adhered to professions in which women could not work, such as engineering. While still adhering to a gendered division of labour, this plan was radical for its time. These changes, the author contends, could only happen along with colonization (emigration) (see Volume 4 Introduction), which, he believes, would help the condition of the labouring classes. Yet, interestingly, he also notes that in a colony where work was plentiful, men would be able to support their wives, who would then have less need to work, which somewhat subverts his radical argument.[4] He still says single women and widows would need jobs, so his overall plan for women's education and employment would be relevant to the colonial context as well.

'Female Education, and Female Labour'

THERE appears to be something radically vicious in the existing state of female education, to which it is high time that mankind should apply a remedy. Instead of woman being trained up to be the helpmate of man, and fitted for assisting him in the occupations in which he is habitually engaged, the tendency of her education is to make her an expensive accessory, which thriving men only can afford to possess. Fathers, instead of training up their daughters to some reasonable occupation by which they may win their bread, are anxious only that they be distinguished by fine persons and showy accomplishments, by which they may hope to captivate some roving fancy; and think their parts well performed when they have succeeded in transferring to the shoulders of a husband the expense of their daughter's maintenance. Many men are prevented from marrying, in consequence of the burden a wife becomes to them; and unmarried females who have their bread to win, are forced, by the narrowness of the circle in which they can look for employment, into a desperate and deadly competition. Every class of the industrial population suffers more or less from surplus labour; but females suffer far more keenly than the other section of the community; and suicide has become fearfully prevalent among them, from a weariness of life occasioned by their innumerable distresses. It may be all very well "to put suicide down," but it would be much more humane, we conceive, and indicate a far higher sagacity, to put down the miseries which lead to so terrible a termination; and we know of no means of accomplishing this but by opening up to woman some of the employments which man at present monopolizes. Educated females should be able to aspire to other situations than that of governess, in which they have outbid one another until the remuneration has become disgracefully low, while it is at the same time a most difficult thing to obtain such a situation: and among the females of the less educated classes some better remuneration for labour should be obtainable than that afforded by the occupation of a seamstress, of which recent revelations have displayed some of the miseries. Woman ought to have the same chance as man: her mind should be strengthened by study and her body by exercise, and she should early be accustomed to habits of business, and be inured to the asperities of the world. This, we shall be told, would be to make her unfeminine; and, in the higher ranks of society, science and all really useful attainments are scoffed at on the same idle plea; yet it is certain that actresses and *prima donnas* lose nothing of their attractions by being female professors; and we certainly think that females would not be less likely to win a husband if they only condescended to deserve one.

It would be curious to trace the causes of the evils we have just indicated, but a full inquiry into them would compel us to exceed the limits to which we are restricted. Among barbarous tribes, women necessarily occupy a subordinate position, on account of their inferiority in physical strength and courage. During the feudal times, when the titles to estates often hung on the condition of military service, women could hardly be expected to stand in the same position as the mailed warriors around them; and as the code upon which our common law is founded had its origin in these times, when the Teutonic race held dominion, it is not surprising that woman has been shut out from the rights of citizenship. If she marry, her individuality is merged in that of her husband; her gains are no longer her own, and in the eye of the law she ceases to be considered an individual agent. In feudal times, however, woman, though she had not attained her just position as a rational being, was cherished by the rude warrior, who pitied her weakness; but the spell thrown around woman by the institution of chivalry was broken by the church. The churchman was doomed by the institutes of his faith to a life of celibacy; and woman was banished from the holiest spots, and her touch esteemed defilement. The degradation consequent on such a state continues even to the present day; and although woman's rights as an immortal being are now widely recognised, a prejudice clings to us, that, in spite of our better reason, resists their practical restitution. The law does not give woman the rights of free citizenship, because she is held incompetent to administer her affairs; and the necessary competency is not sought to be given to her, on account of the state of the law; so that we are running on in a vicious circle without advancing nearer to the goal. Parents should educate their daughters as they educate their sons, and not as if life were an eternal polka, where music and grimace are the only occupations. We would not seek to create a generation of Amazons, or to make woman more like man; but we should desire to see her educated as a rational being, and become more excellent as woman. To be feminine, it is no more necessary that a woman should be idle or listless, or waste her time in frivolous occupations, than that a man, to become manly, should spend his life in perpetual brawls. Every woman should be educated according to her position in life; and, if not independent, should be brought up to some business by which she may earn a livelihood. If married, she will thus become an assistance to her husband; and if left unmarried, there is but little chance that she will be driven by want into vice, and by vice into suicide.

There are some trades into which the admission of females is looked at with much jealousy. Of these, the tailoring trade is one; but we hold this trade to be one of those for which female labour is the best adapted: and it would be a good thing, we think, if female labour were introduced into it more extensively. It is no doubt an evil, that men should be thrown out of work, as their supercession by females must necessarily do; but it is a still greater evil that females, who are more helpless than men, and less able to struggle for a subsistence, should have the price of their labour reduced almost to nothing by the limitations of a trade monopoly. If colonization be largely carried out, the persons engaged in employments that women can practise may obtain other employments, and thus leave a larger field available for them; and the wages of females would then rise rapidly from their present starvation point, and enable them, with moderate labour, to earn a comfortable subsistence. Any scheme of amelioration which does not include female labour in its provisions, is imperfect and unworthy of support. The shoemakers, we see, have lately been taking steps to improve the condition of the females employed in that trade, by inducing them to form a society of their own; and the attempt is worthy of imitation by other trades in which women either are or might be employed. Women cannot be either stonemasons, or engineers, or ship-carpeaters, or grinders of knives; but they may be tailors, and engravers, and upholsterers and setters of type. Out of all the trades that women can practice, men should retreat as speedily as they can – not so as to occasion any sudden shock, or transfer to them the privations that female operatives suffer, but to leave those fields open for female labour in which alone it is applicable – the workman's labour being applicable in other fields with equal advantage. These measures, however, are impossible until there be colonization, and to that powerful remedy all the children of industry must look as the relief for their distresses. If that great measure of amelioration were to be carried into effect, any provision for female labour would be less necessary, as artizans would then be able to maintain their wives in comfort at home; yet, as in every large community, there must be widows and unmarried persons who are dependant on their labour for support, arrangements should be made whereby labour suitable for them is always obtainable, and in a new country, where employment was plentiful, this could easily be done.

Notes

1 Mary Wollstonecraft made the same critique about women of the middling classes in *A Vindication of the Rights of Woman*, 3rd ed. (New York: W. W. Norton & Company, 2009, orig. 1792).

2 See, for example, E. Jordan, 'The Exclusion of Women from Industry in Nineteenth-Century Britain', *Comparative Studies in Society and History* 31:2 (April 1989), pp. 273–296; and S. O. Rose, *Limited Livelihoods: Gender and Class in Nineteenth-Century England* (Berkeley: University of California Press, 1992).

3 On this association, see L. Schiebinger, *The Mind Has No Sex? Women and the Origins of Modern Science* (Cambridge, MA: Harvard University Press, 1989).

4 In the end, it seems, he believes in the male breadwinner norm. See, for example, A. Clark, *The Struggle for the Breeches: Gender and the Making of the British Working Classes* (Berkeley: University of California Press, 1995).

26

M. F. TUPPER, 'THE WORKWOMAN', IN *A DOZEN BALLADS FOR THE TIMES ABOUT WHITE SLAVERY*

(London: T. Bosworth, 1854), pp. 16–17

Martin Farquhar Tupper (1810–1889) was the author of many works, the most famous of which was *Proverbial Philosophy*, a book of verse reflecting middle-class morality, which came out in numerous editions throughout the latter nineteenth century.[1] The poem included here comes from his collection *A Dozen Ballads for the Times about White Slavery*. Many social reformers and writers created a rhetorical comparison between Britain's 'white slaves' – miserable, overworked, and destitute workers – and enslaved Black peoples in the British colonies before emancipation in 1833 and in the U.S. before emancipation thirty years later, to argue the need for limited work hours and improved conditions in Britain. While much of the white slavery rhetoric focused on factories, some, as is the case in this source, applied to slop, or sweated, work – manual labour completed at home or in crowded workshops and poorly paid by the piece.[2] Sweated labour was unregulated, and the workers toiled extremely long days in unhealthy conditions.[3] In most cases, sweating was associated with the needle trades, and sewing in its sweated form was a mostly feminine activity; skilled tailors were men, but needleworkers were women. A lot of public attention was drawn to the cause of distressed seamstresses. The Second Report of the Children's Employment Commission of 1843 brought stories of lives of needlewomen to the British public, and from that moment, narratives of distressed needlewomen proliferated in Victorian culture.[4] Tupper's poem, 'The Workwoman', begins by referring to Thomas Hood's 'The Song of the Shirt', published in *Punch* in 1843. 'The Song of the Shirt', which became extremely popular, called attention to the miserable poverty and monotonous lives of seamstresses.[5] With his words, Tupper seeks to emphasize the veracity of Hood's portrait, while also eulogizing Hood as the 'Bard of Humanity',[6] who could so clearly evoke the exploitation of female needleworkers. Sweated seamstresses, Tupper claims, are slaves to the managers of the workshops but also to women's fashion. He writes of the ignorance of the fashionable classes of the cost borne by seamstresses in creating luxury dresses and fancy embroidery. He

DOI: 10.4324/9780429320323-31

also appeals to Queen Victoria to 'find some Imperial balm' to change the systemic problem facing poor needlewomen.[7] The sacrifice of poor seamstresses' health and 'virtue',[8] suggesting their closeness to prostitutes, Tupper concludes, is not worth the vanities their work produces.

'The Workwoman'

"The Song of the Shirt," – O heart-stirring hymn!
How sternly and terribly true
The portrait of misery, ghastly and grim,
That Bard of Humanity drew:
Go, read it once more; none other may paint
So touching a picture as this, –
For he that imagined it now is a saint
At rest in a mansion of bliss!

Yet, precept on precept, and line upon line,
And effort again and again,
This, friends, is a duty of yours and of mine,
If we wouldn't labour in vain;
And he that would combat White-Slavery-sin
Must hit its most hideous blot,
To tell how poor womanhood, sickly and thin,
Is treated the worst of the lot!

This binder of boots, that stitcher of slops,
These knitters by night and by day,
Are slaves to the tyrants that rule in the shops,
Who grind them for pittance of pay;
And often the delicate daughters of taste,
With needle and need for their goads,
Hard-driven by Fashion with murderous haste,
Like packhorses die on the roads!

O Belle of the ball-room, how little you know
Of the *pain* that has made you so fair;
O bride of Belgravia, hunger and woe
Have drest you so charmingly there!
O buyer of bargains, most cruelly cheap,
Consider what sorrow must lurk
In toil without respite, that strangers may reap
The fruit of such profitless work!

Come, Queen of the Fashions, so gracefully calm,
And yet with heart throbbing within,
Vouchsafe, as you can, some Imperial Balm
To cure this old system of sin;
Your ladylike milliners, – leave them awhile,
And seek out their want-stricken slaves;
'Twere better your Majesty wasted a smile
On poor honest girls, than on knaves.

And, gentle Society, bargain-befool'd,
Ah, think what embroideries cost!
Remember, when self-exultation has cool'd,
Your gain by some other is lost!
It is gambling unfairly, – where virtue and health
And labour these workwomen give,
While all that you stake is an atom of wealth,
Too little for "Live, and let live!"

Notes

1 R. Dingley, 'Tupper, Martin Farquhar', *Oxford Dictionary of National Biography*, 23 September 2004, at https://doi-org.du.idm.oclc.org/10.1093/ref:odnb/27822 [accessed 14 June 2021]; 'Martin Farquhar Tupper', *Independent*, 7 December 1889, p. 1.

2 On the rhetoric of white slavery, see G. Peck, 'White Slavery and Whiteness: A Transnational View of the Sources of Working-Class Radicalism and Racism', *Labor* 1:2 (2004), pp. 41–64; R. Oastler, *Slavery in Yorkshire: Monstrous Barbarity* (Bradford: J. Atkinson, 1835); M. Cunliffe, *Chattel Slavery and Wage Slavery: The Anglo-American Context, 1830–1860* (Athens: University of Georgia Press, 1979).

3 See, for example, S. Blackburn, '"No Necessary Connection with Homework": Gender and Sweated Labour, 1840–1909', *Social History* 22:3 (1997), pp. 269–285.

4 B. Harris, (ed), *Famine and Fashion: Needlewomen in the Nineteenth Century* (London: Routledge, 2016).

5 J. Maclure, 'Rehearsing Social Justice: Temporal Ghettos and the Poetic Way Out in "Goblin Market" and "The Song of the Shirt"', *Victorian Poetry* 53:2 (Summer 2015), pp. 151–169, on p. 152.

6 M. F. Tupper, 'The Workwoman', in *A Dozen Ballads for the Times about White Slavery* (London: T. Bosworth, 1854), Google Books, p. 16.

7 Tupper, 'The Workwoman', p. 17.

8 Tupper, 'The Workwoman', p. 17.

27

SENTIMENTAL DEPICTIONS OF WORKING-CLASS WOMEN IN THE *BRITISH WORKMAN*

These two selections from the *British Workman* (see Volume 1, Part 1, Chapter 6) present working-class women's roles through the paper's pious sentimentality. The first item (27.1), 'A Few Words to the Wives of Working Men', printed in the 'Column for Wives', was purportedly by 'the wife of a working man'. It stresses that what makes a good wife was a woman who was happy and pleased her husband. A wife should always be thinking about what she could do for her husband, and, even more importantly, she should be praying for her husband. The writer, most likely the editor Smithies, recognizes that a wife had difficult duties at home, even as the husband had hard days at work. But God gave women 'the ability to bear much suffering', so it was their responsibility to care for men.[1] This vision of home life reproduces for the working classes the middle-class evangelical ideal of separate spheres, where a husband supported the family in the public economic realm and the wife provided moral example in the private domestic sphere.[2] The next selection (27.2), 'Finery and Freedom, or "Lucy's Choice"', is a moral tale, relating the story of two friends working in service in Surrey. While Mary is content to be in service, Lucy decides to leave her secure position to go into London to become a dressmaker, where she does not have to be dependent. Mary cautions her against this choice, telling Lucy of the dangers of London and the instability of dressmaking.[3] Lucy ignores this advice and proceeds to London, where her life becomes increasingly degraded, and she ultimately commits suicide. Smithies's message in this well-illustrated, detailed story is to advise women to appreciate their positions in service and not to seek out the thrills of the city. Additionally, like Tupper (Volume 1, Part 3, Chapter 26), he warns about the difficult lives of seamstresses, but rather than seeking some redress for these women, Smithies is somewhat unsympathetic, emphasizing their desire for 'finery' and irresponsible behaviour.[4] This conservative message warns poor women of their vulnerability in London and the risk of falling into prostitution if they are not careful with their choices.[5] The article places the blame for women's potential suffering on their individual actions, rather than on the lack of available options for women's work.[6]

DOI: 10.4324/9780429320323-32

27.1 'A Few Words to the Wives of Working Men'

BY THE WIFE OF A WORKING MAN.

WHEN your husband leaves you in the morning to go to his work, let him feel that he is leaving the happiest place in the world; and when he comes home in the evening let him feel that he is coming back to the happiest place in the world.

Make it your business to please your husband. Study his wishes in little things. As soon as he is gone away, think what you can do for him; whether he has told you to do any thing, or even expressed a desire to see a thing done. Believe me, a wife's love, and a wife's care, and a wife's attention do much to make her husband a happy man; and what a solemn thought it is to have the happiness of a fellow creature in our keeping. "A prudent wife is from the Lord." "Whoso findeth a wife findeth a good thing;" – the wisest of men says this, and an inspired apostle writes, in one of his two letters, six verses all about wives; verses which a wife can never read and pray over too often. Let us look in our Bibles for 1 Peter iii. 1–6.

When a man leaves his home to go to his work, his wife little knows the trials of various kinds to which he is exposed; trials from his fellow labourers; trials from his employers, perhaps; trials of fatigue and weariness. True, the wife has *her* troubles too, her children's little and great illnesses, continual worries with her domestic duties, often discomfort and pain of body; but yet God has given great strength to woman – the power of endurance, and the ability to bear much suffering. When a woman's heart is full of love, she can do any and bear any thing. But this love must be anchored on One beyond her husband, on One Friend who is nearer to her than any earthly friend. Therefore, I will conclude these few words to my fellow sisters, the wives of the working men, with this important piece of advice. Pray much for your husband. God will be *sure* to answer your prayer. It will be *sure* to bring down a blessing on your husband, and a blessing on yourself too. While you are at home tending your little ones, cleaning your house, cooking your dinner, or sitting at your needle-work, lift up your heart often to God on behalf of your dear husband. Say, "God bless my husband. God keep my husband. God prosper my husband. God preserve my husband."

When your husband comes home, will he not then find a smile of welcome, a happy fire-side? Yes; and when the children are gone to sleep and the evening has passed away, as together you read God's Holy Word and join in prayer to Him, you will know what St. Peter meant when he says in the verses you have already been reading, "Heirs together of the grace of life."

CAROLINE.

27.2 'Finery and Freedom; or, Lucy's Choice'

IT was a rainy spring evening, and two young women were walking home from church under the shelter of one umbrella; they were both about twenty years of age, tall, and fresh coloured, but there was a great difference in their dress. One had a large warm brown cloth cloak, that kept her wrapped comfortably from the cold, and that covered her dark stuff gown from the weather. Her straw bonnet was close, and neatly trimmed, with a very clean quilling round her happy-looking face; and her feet were protected by strong, well-fitting boots and good clogs over them. Altogether her attire looked so warm and good, that a more respectable young woman you would scarcely see than Mary Grey. It was evident that she was the owner of the umbrella which she held with so much care over her companion, whose dress, indeed, needed its shelter. Lucy Ranger wore a little green silk cape, a thin striped silk gown, very much tarnished with wear and weather – a bonnet on the back of her head, with some large pink bows on it – a crumpled cap underneath, with some blue flowers that tangled themselves in the long curls which, now wetted by the rain, fell on her shoulders like a spaniel dog's ears, while her feet, pinched into a pair of thin drab boots, pattered miserably along the wet streets.

"To think I should be out in this wet!" she said, peevishly, as she cowered under Mary's umbrella. "But," she added, "I'm not going to stay much longer in this humdrum place."

"What! do you mean to leave; and such a good place as you have, Lucy?"

"Good! I don't know what you call good. My old mistress is well enough – she never complains about my having a pretty gown or bonnet, though, perhaps she would, only she's so ill. But the married daughter has been to see us lately, and she's been finding fault at a pretty rate. My hair ain't right, and my dress ain't right; and when I do a bit of crochet-work, she asks me if my stockings are mended, and I don't mean to put up with it. I'm tired of service, so I've given notice, and I mean to go to London. I know a young woman there, that earns no end of money at the dressmaking; and then, when I'm a dressmaker, I needn't wear a cap – I hate caps! – and I may dress as I like."

"Oh, but Lucy, think of the long hours you must work, and then you'll only be a day-worker, and pick up a little bit of the trade. It costs a great deal, both of time and money, to learn dressmaking thoroughly, and then some do make a good living. Those that are in business for themselves do well sometimes, but a poor dressmaker or a day-worker is not half so well off as a respectable servant."

"Well off," said Lucy, with a laugh, "why, they're called 'Miss,' and reckoned quite a cut above servants, I can tell you, and as to long hours, and meals not very comfortable, why, one gets used to that. There's no ringing the bell, and telling one about having a bit of a curl in one's hair. I mean to roll mine, and wear it Empress fashion, as soon as I leave Mrs. Morrison – and I advise you, Mary, to leave. I'm quite sorry to see you always in your dark plain gowns, and never a bit of a flower in your cap, it's dreadful hard upon you."

"I don't think it hard at all," replied Mary quickly. "If I spent my wages in ends of ribbon, and flowers, and flimsy gowns, and thin shoes, I should never have a shilling to buy me good useful clothes.

"I've a good stock of under-clothes, Lucy, and plenty of morning gowns and aprons, and I'm not in want of a change of best gowns, suited for summer or winter, and as to wearing a cap, or answering a bell, I never found that a hardship, and I wouldn't change with any sewing girl in England. I'm sorry to see their pale faces, poor things! I know there's bettermost dressmakers, but they are but few, and they have spent money to learn, and have friends to put them in business. I have only my servitude, and I mean, by God's blessing, to do my best in that."

"Ah! you've no spirit," said Lucy, "I mean to *rise* in the world."

"Take care," added Mary, "that you don't fall. You've been used to live in a good house, eat at a good table – have no cares – with a fixed sum of money to buy clothes; you'll find the difference – I'm sure you will; your place has been very easy – just to wait on your old lady, and do a little needlework. I don't want to complain, but my place is much harder than yours."

"Oh! you're a slave, working for all that family," exclaimed Lucy, "but here you are at home, and I must borrow your umbrella, or I shall get wet."

"Take it, and welcome, Lucy; but think well before you do what you say – for the sake of our old schooldays, take my advice: stay in your place, take care of your wages, and be a respectable servant, and not a half-starved needlewoman."

"Oh, I must leave; I've given notice, Mary, and my time is up next week."

And so the two girls, who had been old schoolfellows, parted. Mary fully expected that Lucy would at least come to bid her good-bye, but instead of that, Lucy sent the umbrella back with a message that she would write soon to Mary.

Accordingly, in three weeks the following letter arrived from Lucy: –

"Dear Mary, – I'm in London, and I have got work at a mantle-maker's, near Leicester Square; oh, such lovely silks, and such sweet shapes as we make. I'm not paid much yet, for I have to get my hand in, but I advise you to leave, for next month we shall be very busy, and I could get you work for the spring.

"I have made myself a jacket out of my old mantle, and my hair looks so well in the Eugenie style. When you write, you must direct to 'Miss Ranger' – I'm not very well suited with a lodging; five of the young ladies rent a room with me, but I shall look out for a better. I began this on Monday, but I couldn't finish it till this Sunday, as we are very busy and work extra hours, so no more at present from your affectionate

Lucy.

"P.S. Could you lend me a pound for a few weeks, or get me a pair of boots on credit of our old shoemaker, for I forgot when I bought my blue frock, that I was in want of boots, and my feet are quite on the ground." Then followed her address.

Mary read this letter with many misgivings. Lucy had been one of the cleverest girls in the school, and her parents had kept her there until she was nearly grown up, and then she obtained a superior situation, to attend on and read to an old lady. The death of both her parents, within a few months of each other, had made her thoughtful for a time and anxious to give satisfaction, but as years passed on and the infirmities of her mistress increased, Lucy was left a good deal to her own guidance – she formed some foolish acquaintances with young people who dressed gaily, until she grew discontented with her circumstances as a servant. At first she did not think of giving up her situation, but she resolved to dress as little like a servant as possible, and her mistress's failing eyesight did not readily detect the change. So Lucy's money was spent in finery that soon spoiled, and that never looked well; instead of the three requisites for dress – *comfort, neatness*, and *suitability* – she had boots that pinched her, gowns that would neither wash nor turn, and colours that did not blend. Many sneered at her, and talked about her, but her friend Mary grieved over her, and gave her advice, until Lucy had petulantly said.

"You dress as *you* like, and I shall dress as *I* like."

When Lucy left the beautiful town of Guildford in Surrey, and went up to London to commence her dressmaking plans, she felt bewildered at first with the vastness of the great city; and now and then as she returned, tired out, to the garret in Bedfordbury that she occupied with the companions Ellen Smithson had introduced her to, she heaved an involuntary sigh as she thought of the clean bed and airy bedroom she had so long been used to; and when she rose in the morning and made a hasty meal of musty-tasting bread and sloppy tea, for which the landlady of the house provided hot water, as the girls had no time to make a fire for themselves, and indeed, could not afford the coals. She then had to walk to the street near Leicester Square, – where she had obtained employment – buying, as she went, two ounces of cold boiled beef, which with a loaf of bread, was her best dinner; on days when money ran short, a penny-worth of potatoes or pease-pudding was fetched in the dinner hour from a neighbouring cook-shop; tea was provided for the workers by the mistress, it consisted of two thin slices of bread and butter, and a breakfast cup of warm fluid very comforting to the jaded girls, though it could hardly be called tea. Then they all fell to work, and when not over busy, left at nine o'clock, but if, as it often happened, work was brisk, they worked over-hours, and sometimes the clocks chimed one or two in the morning before Lucy and Ellen and the others, crept, cold and hungry, into their crowded room, and slept the sleep of exhaustion on the squalid beds; but then, Lucy had some sources of satisfaction, she was called "Miss Ranger," and spoken of by the rest as a young lady; she did not wear a cap, and could dress her hair as fine as she liked, only, she was often too tired even to comb it out, and if she had spoken the truth, she would have owned that if her locks were twisted into smarter forms, they were not so neat and clean as she once used to keep them.

She could by sitting up at nights, and alas! working on Sundays, contrive to alter her clothes into more fashionable or fantastic forms. But she was startled, when by chance, she saw herself in the large glass in her mistress's show-room. Six weeks hard work, and hard living, and scanty sleep, had bleached her once blooming face to a sickly white, and the roundness had left her form. She told Ellen she hardly knew her own face, but the reply made by all, was, that now she looked "Genteel, before she was rustic, indeed vulgar, but to be pale was lady-like."

If these had been the only troubles of Lucy, time might have cured them; but under all the hurry and discomfort, the vanity and misery, there was a yet darker scene. She found as the spring advanced, that with all her toils, she could not get the fine clothes she wanted, her stock was wearing out without any prospect of replenishing it. Some of her companions appeared to manage better – they sported smart bonnets and dresses, and sometimes could afford to stay away a day or two from their work, and then come back with presents. They generally said their cousins treated them, or some relation gave them the much prized finery. She had no cousins to give her anything; and as Satan always lies in wait for the moment of discontent, a foreigner, who used sometimes to meet Lucy as she returned home, and who had often frightened her by his looks, spoke to her one evening, and as Ellen was with her, and nothing loath to have some idle chat, being both of them tired and depressed, they did not, as on former occasions, avoid the man. He asked them to take some oysters. The girls were nearly famishing; they saw a well-filled purse in the libertine's hand, and accepted his invitation. Poor Lucy, from that night, was a stranger to peace. Ellen could brave out her shame, but our country girl used to the propriety of a virtuous home, was overwhelmed with grief. Her companions laughed at her, and to raise her spirits brought the ally of female degradation, the Gin-bottle, to complete her ruin. Yes, Lucy began to drink, and when excited, she forgot her misery, and again and again met her destroyer.

Soon even the semblance of industry was given up, she became irregular at her work, the spring was nearly over, her mistress could do without her, and therefore told her, in anger, not to disgrace her workroom by coming there again. Thus as hundreds are ruined, step by step, poor Lucy became an outcast. While the summer lasted, she did not feel all the consequences of her sorrow. What with drinking and dissipation overnight, and drowsiness by day, she was scarcely able to realize her terrible position. She had some fine clothes, and the praises of some worthless men pleased her vanity; but yet, whenever she thought of her old friend Mary, the tears would rush into her eyes, and a sob would rise in her throat. She had quarrelled with Ellen, and cared not for the others, but her old schoolfellow, whom she never dared to think of seeing again, and whose good advice had always been opposed to her vanities, held a firm place in the unhappy girl's heart.

LUCY IN THE DRESSMAKER'S WORKROOM, AT THE WEST-END OF LONDON.

Towards autumn, Lucy began to be in want. The foreign gambler who had first betrayed her to her ruin, had driven her from his haunts with oaths and insult.

She was in the power of a bad woman with whom she lodged, and who forced her, with threats of a prison, upon a course of infamy. How she began to hate the fine clothes in which she was decked – how the look of her own face – even the once delightful task of decorating her much prized hair – was loathsome. Weary of vice; longing for a home and yet an outcast; women turning from her with shame and horror, men leering on her with mingled insult and cruelty; she fled to drink as a resource from the gnawing agony of her remorse, instead of coming as a penitent sinner to Christ. Just as winter set in, and the cold blasts of boisterous nights were piercing to her very bones, it happened that she once again saw her old schoolfellow. Mary's mistress had been summoned suddenly to London by the illness of a son, a student of King's College. She came by a late train to town, and brought Mary with her. As they were alighting at Norfolk Street, in the Strand, the policeman was telling a young woman to go home, and not to hang about there. The poor creature at the word "home," uttered a wild laugh, which struck on Mary's startled ear, as she was helping the driver to carry the luggage into the house. She immediately exclaimed, "Who is that? – O, Lucy, can it be you!"

The poor outcast darted forward a moment to the door-step, and by the light of the lamp over the door, saw the horror-stricken face of Mary, her old schoolfellow. She caught wildly at her hand, wrung it with a strong grasp, and then with a dismal cry, rushed down the street.

The laugh, the grief, the cry, shook Mary like a convulsion; it was with difficulty she could go through her duties of attending to her mistress, and unpacking, and when she retired to bed it was not to sleep. She had drawn up her window-blind and looked out upon the night. The moon and stars were glittering through the frosty air, and Mary gazed at them through her tears, thinking of the houseless wanderer. Never before had she prayed so fervently for her early friend, alas! those prayers returned to benefit her own kind heart, but Lucy was beyond their reach. The moon that shone so brightly into the little room, consecrated by Mary's humble, but fervent prayers – looked upon a very different scene a short distance off. A young girl, with a rapid footstep, and singing with affected gaiety a snatch of a popular song, put down her halfpenny at the toll-gate of Waterloo Bridge. The man as he took the coin looked into her face, but her jaunty air deceived him. Besides, there were several people on the bridge still. Ah, but the young girl lingers, she sits down in the deep shadow cast by the bright moonshine, until the passengers have all gone, and then springing up on the parapet over the centre arch, she gives a desperate leap – a wild cry, rending its way involuntarily from her lips, as her slender form cuts the gleaming waters in the very track of the moonbeam. A waterman, mooring his boat, hears the cry, the plunge! leaps into his skiff, well knowing the tide and the spot where the head of the drowning girl will rise. But the current is strong, it sweeps her away, he pulls a good oar, and nears the place where twice she has risen. There's some bubbles on the water, but Lucy has sunk to rise no more, except as a swollen, disfigured corpse! It was morning before the body was found. During the following day, the policeman who had been on the beat the night before, called in Norfolk Street, to ask Mary if she knew the young woman who had grasped her hand on the door-step. Mary's answer was, of course, in the affirmative, but no words could paint her horror, when she was asked to go and see the body. Her mistress who had known the lost girl from her childhood, hurried Mary off on her dismal errand. Yes! it was too true! There, in the dead-house, on a stretcher – a scanty garb of faded finery clinging wet around her wasted limbs; her hair in a long tangle twisting round her throat, the face swollen and distorted with the last bitter agony, – lay all that was left of the once light-hearted, blooming, and innocent Lucy. A love of fine clothes, and vanity, and a dislike of wholesome restraint, had brought her to a career of shame, and a death of despair.

Notes

1 'A Few Words to the Wives of Working Men', *British Workman* 2 (1856), British Library General Reference Collection, 1856–1861: LOU.LON 71 [1855].
2 L. Davidoff and C. Hall explain and complicate this ideal in *Family Fortunes: Men and Women of the British Middle Classes, 1780–1850*, 3rd ed. (New York: Routledge, 2019).
3 On needlework, see B. Harris (ed), *Famine and Fashion: Needlewomen in the Nineteenth Century* (London: Routledge, 2016).
4 'Finery and Freedom, or "Lucy's Choice"', *British Workman* 45 (1858), British Library General Reference Collection, 1856–1861: LOU.LON 71 [1855].
5 On prostitution as women's work, see the classic J. Walkowitz, 'The Common Prostitute in Victorian England', in *Prostitution and Victorian Society: Women, Class, and the State* (Cambridge: Cambridge University Press, 1980), pp. 13–31.
6 On women's limited work options, see K. Honeyman and J. Goodman, 'Women's Work, Gender Conflict, and Labour Markets in Europe, 1500–1900', *Economic History Review*, new series, 44:4 (November 1991), pp. 608–628; E. Jordan, 'The Exclusion of Women from Industry in Nineteenth-Century Britain', *Comparative Studies in Society and History* 31:2 (April 1989), pp. 273–296.

28

A. MUNRO, 'OUR UNEMPLOYED FEMALES, AND WHAT MAY BEST BE DONE FOR THEM', IN *TRANSACTIONS OF THE MANCHESTER STATISTICAL SOCIETY, SESSION 1862–63*

(Manchester: Cave and Sever, 1863), pp. 26–38

The Reverend Alexander Munro (1796–1869) was minister of St. Peter's Square Church, Manchester, from 1832–1869 and was supportive of charitable causes in the area, including subscribing to the Salford Asylum for Female Patients. He was also a member of the Manchester Statistical Society.[1] As is clear from Munro's speech included here, Manchester and its environs were in a deep economic depression in 1863, as a result of what later became known as the 'cotton famine' caused by the American Civil War (see Volume 2, Part 3, Sources 33 and 34). Lancashire depended on cotton imported from the United States for its textile industry, and these imports were halted during the course of the war.[2] In this time of economic downturn, Munro was concerned that unemployed women would emigrate to the colonies and Lancashire would experience a severe shortage of female labour when the war was over (see Volume 4 Introduction on emigration). He thus discourages emigration as a solution for women's lack of employment. He mentions that women's labour was scarce all over and that the census had shown that men outnumbered women in the British population. Yet the 1851 and 1861 censuses 'revealed a statistical surplus of women', which caused a crisis in the middle class about 'redundant women' who would neither marry or be employed.[3] Rather than emigration, Munro suggests expanding domestic skills training by offering classes in such things as sewing, cooking, and hygiene for unemployed women. His real point in offering these suggestions was to provide a critique of female factory workers, who in usual times 'are mere appendages to our mechanisms';[4] they only knew factory life and had no domestic skills to bring to marriage. If women could learn to be better cooks, Munro insists, they could forestall beatings from their husbands and improve their married lives.[5] The establishment of Poor Man's Kitchens revealed the attraction of good food for working men. Indeed, Munro warns that husbands and sons had been tempted away from

DOI: 10.4324/9780429320323-33

home to these public kitchens. Munro argues that unemployed women should use this time of the cotton depression productively to strengthen the male breadwinner family.[6] Once women learned domestic skills, their homes would be pleasing to husbands, who would be less likely to seek their meals elsewhere.[7] Munro says he will leave to doctors and nurses to decide whether unemployed factory women should be trained in hygiene, suggesting his uncertainty surrounding how much knowledge women should have of the human body. All of the training Munro recommends demonstrates that he did not see women as economic actors. He concludes that men should be the providers and women should 'keep the Eden of the working man's home'.[8] The cotton famine had given the people the opportunity to 'adjust' women's roles so they could stop competing with men in the factory and better tend to the domestic sphere where they truly belonged.[9] This 'solution' to women's lack of work did nothing to indicate how women's lost wages would be replaced once they left the workforce entirely.

'Our Unemployed Females, and What May Best Be Done for Them'

[Read March 18th, 1863.]

[. . .] our present business is to inquire what is to be done with our unemployed females, – what is best for them, and best, in this case, for the general community.

Some would say, and do say, Let them emigrate; and let all hands be opened in liberality to carry them across the seas. They are wanted there; they are not wanted here. To speak thus sounds well, as if it got us rid of the evil summarily. But this is cutting the knot – not loosing it. There are difficulties here which press themselves on reflecting minds. It is true that, like blood-letting, emigration is a good thing for an over-populous country, and is part of the process for replenishing the waste places of the earth; therefore, in the regular ongoings of national affairs and fortunes, it is well that facilities, not stimulants, be given to relieve old countries, and replenish new, as well as to afford scope for the otherwise hampered energies of individuals. A regulated measure of emigrants we can ordinarily spare; but a wholesale deporting of multitudes may be hazardous to themselves, detrimental to the communities at home, and even to the colonies into which they are thrown.

But besides this, – deprecating anything like injustice, or even heedlessness, to the individual interests of these masses, at present unemployed, – we may fairly adduce a special reason which forbids an undue stimulancy to their emigration. It is this: – How, in such case, will their places be seasonably supplied when the Cotton trade revives? And the alternative is that it must revive, else Manchester sinks, – it is no longer Manchester. Their replacement then becomes a question of moment to our Lancashire community, and, perhaps, to the nation at large. A vast capital – millions realised by antecedent industry – is invested; to do aught that would imperil this involves serious responsibility. We cannot afford to let this vast branch of industry die, founded as it is on the natural wants of mankind, – enriching to the neighbourhood in many ways, – serviceable to the empire, – and destined, in all probability, as civilisation advances, to a still mightier extension. Its depression is not to be allowed to become its destruction. Neither can we afford to make a present of it to other nations. British talent and British minerals have, under Providence, given it birth and nurture; why should we risk our fair and full share of its advantages by allowing it, through any false step, to go to others who might not manage it so well for the world?

The argument – or rather the taunt – so often uttered by splenetic persons against the manufacturers, that selfish motives make them wish to detain their unemployed operatives in the country, is too trivial for refutation. Who has a right to blame men for considering their lawful interests? And it so happens that in this case, as in many others, private interest coincides with public advantage, and may be auxiliary to its promotion.

To deport, on a large scale, our hands because of a depression whose causes are evidently temporary, would be unwise. Depend upon it, it is not alone the loss that would thereby accrue to the manufacturers and capitalists, which with the liabilities lying in so many cases on their property, would embarrass and overwhelm a large proportion of them, but, as these men are the thews and sinews of the practical activity of this vast district, the district itself, with the whole state of society, would materially suffer. Foreign competition would in the interval step in, and snatch from us the returning opportunity. It does not follow, as some suppose, that in the event of the Cotton trade resuming, within a moderate time, its wonted vigour, a full supply of fresh female operatives would readily be obtained from the country at large. Throughout Great Britain generally there exists a scarcity of female labour. What with the regular drain of emigration, especially during the last twenty years, – latterly, a quarter of a million annually leaving our shores, – what with the greater demand than ever for domestic services, – the development of new branches of employment suited to their powers, – the surplus that used to exist is greatly reduced, if not absolutely absorbed. Owing to whatever causes, as appears from recent censuses, the proportion between the sexes in our population has been materially altered; in some counties, indeed, the number of females is smaller than that of males, – a thing previously unknown in our history. Owing, also, to the causes specified, it is found, for instance, that in Northumberland and the two contiguous counties – chiefly pastoral and agricultural, with here and there collieries – the difficulty of obtaining female labour, and consequently the price of it, are quite as great as in our large towns and cities.

In whatever way we look at the subject there is, on public economic grounds at least, no call for the public to bestir itself in multiplying incitements to female emigration, beyond the measure which the enterprise of individuals seeking to better their condition, or the enticements of Colonial projects, may naturally prompt. Besides, the expense of transport, outfit, and settling any considerable number would be enormous.

What then is desirable, and what practicable, to be done with those females who choose to remain in the Cotton districts without stated employment?

Well, the question, it may be said, seems to be in part, or substantially, answered by pointing to what has already been done. Sewing classes have risen, originating in personal compassion at the stern exigency. Physical want demands physical supply. Those classes, along with arrangements for instruction, have been extended and sustained by voluntary, systematic benevolence, with enlarged levies of poor rates. And who will doubt that, as a most seasonable expedient, they have, without any perceptible drawback of evil, done a vast amount of good? The scheme is no slender or partial palliative. That the arrangement for a class of two or three dozen girls, in the Working Men's Institute, Hulme, at the end of July last, should have so expanded as to comprise by September, 1,700 girls, and by the end of November, 2,800, working in ten different rooms or halls in that and the two contiguous townships; that similar classes, under local committees, should have been organised in other districts of the city, as well as in the neighbouring borough, with a number of towns and villages besides, covering the field of the Cotton manufacture, till it comes to comprise some 70,000 young females, saved for the time from the perils of idleness, and supplied with food for the body as well as instruction for the mind; – that this has been accomplished, is a subject of astonishment as well as a ground of gratitude.

Now, it must be borne in mind, that this precise form of arrangement for the employment and support of these females cannot be expected always to last. Hand labour here may compete with hand labour elsewhere, but cannot stand competition with other districts and countries as machine labour can. Where there is large capital, with inventive genius, improved machines will prevail over machines in countries where capital is less. The difficulty, too, of finding work for these girls, or of obtaining, gratuitously, materials for work; the gradual glutting of the market for the sale of the articles; as well as the slackening of purchases made hitherto by wealthy and benevolent persons, for distribution among their dependents; these, with other causes, are now operating, and forbid us to regard the sewing classes as anything more than a temporary expedient. As such, however, they are invaluable; the longer they can be kept in operation the better, as an important means of retaining our female operatives, and tiding over the time till trade resumes its course.

But, in the meantime, it may fairly be asked, might there not be certain modifications introduced, with advantage to the females themselves, as well as to the community? As the demand for that kind of sewing on which so many thousands are exclusively employed, may every month be growing less, would it not be well to economise it, by introducing fresh varieties of sedentary work, but especially by intermixing with the labours of the needle, on a larger scale than has yet been done, the operations of domestic management and household service? By thousands of these girls, accustomed only to supplement the functions of the machine, the acquirement of the use of the needle has been felt to be an accomplishment, as it will be found in their after life to be a utility. Is it not, then, possible to endow them with other and kindred accomplishments, during the time they are waiting for the return of trade? Things that might at first appear to be crotchets – fond fancies – have, under the pressure of difficulties, and by the force of resolute wisdom, been more than realised. Why should not a large proportion of those young persons be taught to wash and dress? Why should they not be enabled to cook, in the best and most economic way, the plain staple of victuals? Why should not at least something be done to instruct them in the general laws of health, and put them in a position to obviate some of the most common causes of disease, as well as to prepare and administer some of the simpler and most approved remedies to the sick and suffering?

I am not solicitous to show how this may be perfectly done, nor to reply to every objection that may be raised against attempting it. The main points before us are – These young women must be occupied; and next, that to remain in the ignorance and unskilfulness, as to domestic matters, in which they have been sunk, is degrading to themselves, and, if they marry, pernicious to their husbands, as well as ruinous to their offspring.

Can nothing be done to raise them out of the state of mere appendages to our mechanisms, up to the proper rank of women?

For the first of these branches of instruction, namely, the washing and dressing of linen and of clothes generally, it may fairly be asked whether the establishments belonging to the Public Baths and Wash-houses Society might not, with the coöperation of their committee, be made available. Surely, it is not impossible to devise an arrangement by which a certain number should, in rotation, be drawn weekly from the sewing classes, and practically instructed in these houses by competent persons; families being publicly invited to furnish employment by sending clothes to be so washed and dressed, at a moderate rate. If the number of these established wash-houses should not be found sufficient, others of a temporary sort might be fitted up, – the work to be done, not by machines, but by the hands. Manchester very much requires something of this kind, at any rate; and the acquirement of this art would not only meet the exigency so far, but would prove of incalculable advantage to these young persons, whether, in the appointments of Providence, they should resume their wonted work, become the mothers of families, enter domestic service, or emigrate, of their own accord, to distant lands and new settlements.

For the second of these branches of training, namely, that they be taught to cook and otherwise prepare, in the best and most economic way, the ordinary staple of victuals.

In this art – the art of making food palatable and salubrious, consistently with that frugality which a limited income demands, – it is confessed, on all hands, that the females connected with our manufacturing system are sadly deficient, though deficiency in this respect is by no means confined to them. From this cause, it is to be lamented that in thousands of cases the hard-won earnings of men are largely absorbed in diet which is at once expensive and indigestible. Nay, in this way, there is not only loss and indifferent health, but much of the infelicity of families springs from the same cause. "The poor man," says a writer in the *Cornhill Magazine*, "beats his wife because with his hard-won earnings she can place only bad food before him. He drinks beer, and drowns himself in gin, because no meat that he can get is half so pleasant. People imagine that by introducing the light wines of France into this country, we shall put a stop to drunkenness. It is a great mistake. The French are a sober people, not because they drink wine, but because they are good cooks." There is, perhaps, some truth as well as point in the boast of a French wit, that while the English can scarcely furnish you a palatable mouthful from a stalled ox, the French can make fifteen delicious soups out of a nettle-top, and cook a bit of leather into a morsel fit for a king.

The question is, Can nothing be done in this direction, on an extended scale, for our unemployed factory girls, as well as for others of the same rank in life? I am aware that something has been attempted; but hitherto the amount effected is but limited. Now, it is hardly to be expected that individual ladies, however benevolent or public-spirited, can take any appreciable number of these girls into their own households, to train them in the culinary art. The task of dealing with even a few, would baffle their powers, and soon they would be discouraged.

But may we not find something suitable for a purpose of this sort in the Poor Man's Kitchens recently established? The number and extent of them is now considerable. Scores of young women are already selected from the multitudes of unemployed, and engaged in these establishments, preparing and serving the victuals. I am aware that at present one condition of this system of kitchens is, that they be self-sustaining; and therefore those who rent or farm the places could not be expected, as things are now arranged, to change their servants, say, every month, in order to admit of a rotation of novices and learners. But still the problem might be fairly set before the kind and capable persons who have done so much in originating these establishments, whether they could not be so modified as that they should each admit a number in rotation, who, under the direction of experienced instructors paid as the mistresses in the sewing schools are paid, might look on, and so far practise the art of preparing and serving food.

The popularity of these kitchens has been immense; and the multitudes that throng to their tables are, I am assured, weekly increasing. They had become a desideratum of the age. Their vast popularity is not the result merely of the depression of trade; wholesome viands, well prepared and at moderate cost, attract daily these thousands. They resort to them not merely in Manchester, where the trade pressure is no doubt severe, but in London, where it is unfelt, and in Glasgow, where it is but slight.

The growth and dimensions of the system in this last place deserve record, as they awaken surprise. Mr. Corbet, of Glasgow, may justly claim a niche among the demi-gods and great inventors who have taught mankind the arts of producing, cooking, and appreciating the good things of this life. The first of his Poor Man's Kitchens was begun in apartments belonging to the Sailors' Home, at the Broomie-law or harbour of Glasgow. Two halls, rented at £100. a-year, accommodated 100 persons at a time. It proved a success. This was in September, 1860. The rooms were warm, clean, and well ventilated; newspapers, periodicals, &c., were supplied. In a few weeks a new branch was opened, with a fresh one every two months, till there are now throughout the working districts of the city 15 in full operation, accomodating 4,000 guests, – employing a staff of nearly 200 persons, – paying in rent, £1,250. per annum, – disposing of nearly 20,000 penny rations a day, – having an income of £45,000., – and frequented by about 9,000 persons on every working day of the week. But the enterprise stops not here; a great central establishment in Pitt-street is projected.

Now, this great system of public kitchens that is fast spreading in our great cities and towns, was a desideratum arising mainly, no doubt, from the dearness and defective cookery of domestic meals. Of course, the comparative dearness of the material purchased on a small scale, as contrasted with the great scale on which caterers for the million purchase, is in some degree unavoidable; but we may fairly infer that want of skill, with slatternly carelessness in preparing as well as serving the food, has exerted no small influence in sending multitudes from the private household repast to eat their meals at public tables.

These kitchens, while they must at the present time be accounted a great public benefit, are yet, so far as this last cause is concerned, to be rated as nothing better than an expedient forced on many by a felt home discomfort, an escape from a domestic evil. It may, with a large measure of truth, be said that this new form in the associative habits of the people, when once developed, will alter the character, by diminishing the attractions of home, – that like the Parisian *café*, and perhaps to a still greater extent, it will interfere with the salutary moral influences which are fostered mainly by the reciprocation of kind thoughts, and the sight of dear familiar faces, at the daily, family meals, – not to speak of its tendency to form the sexes of neighbourhoods into distinctive coteries, an evil which even now is not unknown in our city, and the increase of which cannot be too much deprecated. But, after all, it may be that we cannot stem this course of things, – that the force and form which the associative principle is acquiring in our great towns, in this as well as in other things – in amusements, in excursions, in trade, in building and in coöperative societies – are such that reflective wisdom and philanthropy have, in cases where there happens to be error fraught with ultimate harm, no power to arrest or modify them. Still it is well that the intelligence of society should be constantly awake, watching the progress, and descrying the possible dangers.

Yet if, while they confessedly confer a benefit, there is danger lest the public cooking kitchens may alienate fathers and sons from their proper homes, may it not be possible to extract from them a remedy against the probable evil? Mr. Corbet, their originator, says that –

> "Any really thrifty, managing housewife can provide her husband and family with meals quite as good as those at the kitchens, and at even less money. What they can do at the depôt, she can do at home. To lads in lodgings, and others working at a distance, the kitchen is a boon; but to those living in family, the thing can be done as well at home. Of course, if a married man has to choose between a tough tasteless bit of meat in a dirty house, and a nice plate of beef and potatoes in a comfortable room, he may prefer the latter. But the effect of this will be good. It will stimulate careless and slatternly women to keep their houses neat and clean, and to prepare their meals with more regard to the human palate, and human powers of mastication and digestion."

Well, then, can these cooking establishments, as they exist at this present crisis, be, by any means, made available towards the removal of the unskilfulness and want of care in preparing and presenting the daily food in a working man's home? Can these public depôts be made instrumental in rendering their own existence, by and bye, in a great measure unnecessary?

It is, unfortunately, a fact too well substantiated, that the great majority of the young women in our factories, as well as those in kindred employments, have little or no skill in cooking, or in household management of any sort, having no opportunities of acquiring it. They marry, and, if they continue at factory work, they leave the house and its concerns to some inept old woman, who makes sad work of it. If they remain at home, their cookery and management are wasteful, unorderly and ruinous. They are shiftless and thriftless. This does not, indeed, hold in all cases, but it holds so generally as to produce a vast amount of misery among our manufacturing population – keeping families of good earnings, when trade is good, in poverty and debt, as well as driving, by dirt and discomfort, their male members to seek their solace in places of doubtful resort.

Now, these young women, we know, are all capable of being trained to better things, and if once they acquired the knowledge we desiderate, they would be proud of it, prize it, and practise it. Is it not, then, possible for benevolence, acting in concert with the conductors of those places, and aided by the Poor-law and Relief-fund authorities, to bring, in rotation, considerable numbers of these females to witness and assist in preparing the meals of the thousands that daily throng these public tables? In this way, as well as by frequenting the wash-houses, and by being brought into contact with other domestic processes, they would soon become qualified as occasional helps, in menial offices, or as regular household servants, of whom good ones, at least, are much in demand; so that, when our factories resume their accustomed activity, our female operatives will be there to resume, if they choose, their work; better fitted than before for the duties of their station and their homes.

We are all aware that benevolent ladies, – a class of whom, during the past winter especially, Manchester may well be proud, – have been most assiduous in instructing these females, in their schools and sewing classes. They have done good service, and there has been a marked improvement in the objects of their attention and sisterly care. But this cannot always continue. And, in truth, by far the greater number of these girls can read very well. Yet, though they can read, they are still very ignorant. They greatly need, however, *oral* instruction in practical matters, – in self-government, in the cardinal virtues, with the minor morals; and if kind, matronly ladies would vary and extend conversational instruction in this direction, the best results might be anticipated.

I spoke of their being brought acquainted, in some measure at least, with the laws of health. It would be presumption in me to do more than simply suggest this. The members of the most practically humane and self-denying avocation in Manchester – I mean the Physicians and Surgeons – as they alone can do the thing, are the best fitted to give an opinion as to how far it is competent to impart to these females such a measure of acquaintance with the structure of the human frame, – with the ordinary causes which generate disease, or tend to health, – the diagnosis of incipient disorders, and the methods to be adopted in emergencies, – as well as with the symptoms which demand that they should instantly send for the doctor; – these professional men are best qualified to say how far this can be done, in a plain way, and how such a matter could be arranged with the least trouble to the gentlemen who might give, and with the best effect to those who might receive, this valuable sort of instruction. Who is not aware of the scarcity of good and trustworthy nurses to discharge the momentous duties of the sick room? It is needless to say that such among the girls as may have a turn that way, might prove a signal blessing in private households, as well as in public hospitals and certain other institutions; and all of them might so profit as that these delicate duties would be satisfactorily performed by them, as future wives and mothers, in their own families.

It is neither wise nor safe for us to be hasty or positive in interpreting the final causes of certain uncommon calamities which a sovereign Providence may appoint or permit. We occupy our proper place when we bow in reverence, and say – "He doeth all things well," – out of evil still educing good, – and when we prepare ourselves to coöperate with Him in this Godlike work. But what if, among the important ends He wishes to bring out of this calamity pressing on our trade and district, this be one, namely – the elevation of the character, nature, and functions of our sunken females belonging to the lower manufacturing classes?

It has been said that manufactures, on their first entrance into a district, quicken the minds and improve the condition of the inhabitants, but that in the long run their influence is the reverse. There may be truth in this; but it is not necessary that manufactures should produce deterioration. On the contrary, the conditions of this mode of occupation are, in many respects, more favourable to mind and body than many other forms of labour. The exercise of intelligence is promoted by attention to the processes and movements going on. "There is," as Dr. Ure has said, "the dry and warm atmosphere, with the large and ventilated rooms, – there is protection from inclement weather, – there is no undue physical exertion, – and there are frequent rests." The particles of oily substance afloat, instead of being deleterious, are, it is affirmed, conducive to health, and specific against certain forms of disease, while the wages earned in ordinary times are such as to secure comfortable maintenance.

But still the question is this – Are we not bound to strive and to hope for a state of things in which men shall be *more* and females *less* employed in the mill, – when men shall be the bread-winners, and women be the faithful, skilful and intelligent stewards of their earnings, – when, as wives and mothers, daughters and sisters, they shall mainly live to promote the felicities and assuage the sorrows of the household, and give themselves, with a cheerful industry, to dress and to keep the Eden of the working man's home? That it should be so, is simply in accordance with the nature and the peculiar powers given to the sexes. Men have powers that fit them for permanent toils; women, for slighter and briefer efforts. These are framed for maternal mildness and the watchful offices of affection. All their organs are tender, yielding, and sensitive. Out of home, they are, in a great measure, out of their sphere; and though nature may be overborne by usage, yet, if long thwarted, nature will have its revenge. Society can never be rightly adjusted so as to possess all the virtue and happiness of which it is capable, while the sexes in its various ranks are misplaced as to their respective occupations.

We know that the progress of mechanical inventions, as applicable to the arts of life, has hitherto tended to bring in the labour of females, and to throw out the labour of males. Competition sets its seal to this. It is not well that it should always be so. And though, for a long time to come, the tendency and the practice may prevail, yet the hope and aim of Philanthropy must ever be, that our present depression being past away, – our trade restored, and all our people, male and female, duly and industriously employed, – a course of prosperity will enable us, without detriment to masters or operatives, to ameliorate the evils of which we are becoming more and more sensible; and that we shall accept our present privations in business, and the enforced idleness of our people, as a call gradually to adjust the relations, to ameliorate the domestic conditions of our people, and to raise woman to the intelligence and the moral rank for which both nature and Christianity have designed her.

Notes

1 D. Bebbington and T. Larsen (eds), *Modern Christianity and Cultural Aspirations* (London: Sheffield Academic Press, 2003), p. 290; 'The Rev. Alexander Munro, D.D.', *Manchester Courier and Lancashire General Advertiser*, 6 November 1869, p. 6; 'Manchester and Salford Asylum for Female Patients', *Manchester Courier and Lancashire General Advertiser*, 23 December 1848, p. 6.

2 W. O. Henderson, *The Lancashire Cotton Famine, 1861–1865* (Manchester, UK: Manchester University Press, 1934).

3 See, for example, N. H. Dreher, 'Redundancy and Emigration: The "Woman Question" in Mid-Victorian Britain', *Victorian Periodicals Review* (Spring 1993), pp. 3–7, on p. 3.

4 A. Munro, *Our Unemployed Females and What May Best Be Done for Them* (1863), London School of Economics Library: 331.4137941 MUN, p. 30.

5 On domestic violence in working-class marriages, see A. J. Hammerton, *Cruelty and Companionship: Conflict in Nineteenth-Century Married Life* (New York: Routledge, 2002), part 1, 'Working-Class Marriage', pp. 10–55.

6 On the growth of the male breadwinner norm and domestic ideals for women, see A. Clark, *The Struggle for the Breeches: Gender and the Making of the British Working Class* (Berkeley: University of California Press, 1995).

7 Blaming women for domestic discomforts which resulted in spousal violence or unhappy marriages was typical. See for example, Clark, *Struggle for the Breeches*, p. 262.

8 Munro, *Our Unemployed Females*, p. 37.

9 Munro, *Our Unemployed Females*, p. 38.

29

T. WRIGHT, 'WORKING MEN'S HOMES AND WIVES', IN *THE GREAT UNWASHED*

(London: Tinsley Brothers, 1868), pp. 30–41

Thomas Wright (1839–1909) apprenticed to be an engineer and found work as a blacksmith in Gravesend. He was interested in improving his lot through education and frequented the local Mechanics' Institute, which provided adult education for working-class men.[1] In the early 1870s, he passed the examination to become a local school board visitor, which brought him into the lower middle class. Wright wrote frequently about the working classes from his insider position and published in important venues such as the *Contemporary Review*. His essays led to three volumes about working-class life, including *The Great Unwashed*, a chapter of which is included here.[2] In this chapter on 'Working Men's Wives and Homes', Wright's overall argument is that no matter the condition of the physical space in which a family lived, the wife made the space a home.[3] It was her responsibility to create comfort. Yet, Wright points out, women received no training for domestic skills: they did not learn how to cook, undertake child care, or maintain hygienic practices. Education in these areas, he believes, was essential, and it needed to happen before marriage. Like Munro (see Volume 1, Part 3, Chapter 28), Wright's emphasis on education in these realms challenged the prevailing middle-class ideology that domestic tasks, especially child care, were natural to women. We see this tension increasingly throughout the century, as middle-class women took on the task of visiting poor women to teach them proper child care and sanitary practices.[4] Wright indicates that working-class men usually chose their wives between the ranks of servants and dressmakers, but he finds faults at both ends of the spectrum. Servants as wives were either too focused on their particular area of training (cooking, dusting, etc.) or acted as 'slaveys'.[5] Dressmakers or shopgirls, on the other hand, always saw themselves above their station, acted frivolously, and regarded housework as degrading. This is the same portrait drawn of 'Lucy', in the *British Workman* (see Volume 1, Part 3, Chapter 27), who left domestic service to become a dressmaker. Wright, like Munro, notes that women who were unsuccessful housewives could bring down 'harsh treatment' upon themselves.[6] Still, Wright pulls back his criticism enough to say that these 'dressy and vain'

DOI: 10.4324/9780429320323-34

women were 'emphatically good girls'.[7] The problem was that they were not suited to be working men's wives. The ideal wife for a working man, Wright concludes, was a woman who has had the good fortune to be able to stay at home with her family and therefore had learned domestic skills organically. Like Munro, he believes that the best arrangement for working-class families was to have a wife with domestic skills, whose life had not been disrupted by the need to work in service, factory, or workshop. And, like Munro, he does not blame poverty for the unhappiness and frustrations of the working class; he blames working women.

'Working Men's Homes and Wives'

Comfort is the one great essential to home; without it there can be no home in the best sense of the word: and yet in numberless humble dwellings it has no place – mess and muddle reigning in its stead. That the houses of the working classes are not what they ought to be and might be, has long been notorious; and we have at length had some practical legislation with a view to their improvement. The general opinion seems to be, that the class of houses in which labouring men are compelled to live is solely to blame in this matter; and to this point – the only one indeed on which it could be brought to bear – legislative action has been directed. But the style of a house, though an important, is still a secondary element in the constitution of a home. As

> "Stone walls do not a prison make,
> Nor iron bars a cage;"

so a house alone does not make a home. Among the working classes the *wife* makes the home. In no other rank of life are the home-influences so powerfully and directly felt. The working man's wife is also his housekeeper, cook, and several other single domestics rolled into one; and on her being a managing or mismanaging woman depends whether a dwelling will be a home proper, or house which is not a home. Whatever sanatory or architectural improvements may be made in artisans' dwellings, it will still be found, while wives remain as they are, that of homes supported upon like incomes, one will be a veritable "little palace" in point of comfort, while another will be a domestic slough of despond. It may be said that all this implies that working men's wives are a bad, mismanaging lot; but such is not my meaning. Relatively – considering their strictly-limited means, the want of special training, and the style of management seen among other classes – they may be said to be good housekeepers. The domestic faults, or perhaps it should be said misfortunes, of the average working man's wife are for the most part negative or non-conscious, or at the worst arise from her being to a certain extent imbued with the pernicious idea so prevalent in other grades of society, that the performance of housework is degrading. Her shortcomings are all summed up in saying that, though she is perhaps as good as could reasonably be expected from her surroundings and opportunities, she is not what for the sake of all concerned it is desirable she should be, and could easily be made. There are many wives who in these respects are all that could be wished; and nothing more strongly shows the necessity and possibility of improvement among the general body than a comparison of the household of one of these women with that of even an average housekeeper.

The necessity for, and advantages to be derived from, a technical education among working men are now being urged upon all hands; but there is a still greater need for such education among their wives. Women in the working classes have no organised educational means of qualifying themselves for the position of wives, plain sewing taught in charity or semi-charity schools being the nearest approach to anything of the kind. There are no schools of cookery in which young women might be taught something of the nature of our chief foods, and initiated into the principles and practices of economical cookery. No place where they could be shown that many savoury and nourishing dishes can be made out of what are generally looked upon as unpalatable, unmanageable odds and ends; and that consequently a family could occasionally have the luxury of butcher's meat even when they cannot purchase joints or steaks – beyond the cooking of which the culinary capabilities of many wives extend not. There is no existing means by which they can be systematically taught the care of children, or the application of broad, easily-understood sanatory laws to household health and comfort. And, looking at this state of affairs, the wonder is that the housekeeping of the working classes is as good as it is, and not that it is rarely as profitable as it might be. A woman in this rank of life has to pick up her knowledge of housekeeping *after* marriage, thus paying for experience at a time when she ought to be turning previously-acquired knowledge to good account. This picking up of housewifely acquirements is at all times a problematical affair, and at present the spirit of the age seems to be specially against it.

A working man's choice of a wife usually lies between the domestic-servant class, and the "young ladies" more or less directly attached to the dress-making and millinery businesses, and unfortunately both of these classes are not merely untrained in domestic matters, but labour under the still worse drawback of being, so to speak, mis-educated; so that they have to unlearn as well as learn on becoming wives. The shortcomings of female servants are so well known, and are so frequently and prominently before the public, that there is no need to dwell upon them here. It may be that it is to a great extent a case of like mistress like maid; but still when servants are either "above their business" or ignorant of it to an extent that makes them "the greatest plague of life" to their employers, it is evident that their failings must tend to have a most injurious effect upon the class in which they become wives and mothers, and whose physical and social well-being lies in a great measure in their hands. Domestic service, though perhaps the best means largely available, is still a wofully [sic] deficient one for the training of working men's wives. A general servant in a small family that can really afford to keep a domestic, and in which there is a kind, active, capable mistress, will generally turn out well, and make a capital wife. But, as ill luck will have it, the general servant in most cases has not a mistress of this desirable stamp. She is usually the retainer of some poor housekeeper of the let-us-be-genteel-or-die class, who, herself regarding household work as a degradation, and not being able to employ an adequate number of servants, makes an utter drudge, a much-contemned "slavey," of the one she has got. Under such circumstances as these the general servant becomes a mere muddler, patient and willing, but slow and methodless; always working, yet never seeming to get through her work, and dirtying herself far more than she cleans anything else; and the working man who gets a woman of this kind for a wife is, to say the least of it, not specially blessed in his helpmate.

The subdivision of labour in those establishments in which a staff of servants are kept, though necessary, and an advantage to the employers, has not a good effect when viewed in relation to working men's wives, as it tends to make them women of one domestic idea. If they are cooks, they are most likely to be cooks and nothing more, and then not working men's, but gentlemen's cooks – cooks who require expensive materials to work upon, and who are not up to the only "made dishes" suitable to their married rank in life; those, namely, in which the cheaper and coarser kinds of food are made into dainty dishes by strokes of culinary art to which gentlemen's cooks are strangers. A wife of this class looks upon cooking as the be-all and end-all of domestic management, and speaks with pity or contempt of all other kinds of wives as poor creatures who do not know how to peel a potato properly. The "poor creatures" of course return the compliment, speaking of the cook-wife as one of whom, when you have said she can cook a bit, you have said all the good it is possible to say. The housemaid will tell you that she (the cook) cannot make a bed or dust a room as it ought to be done, while the nurse will "be sorry for her children, if she has any." Thus think and speak the wives, each one regarding her special accomplishment as the one thing needful to complete housekeeping, but few of them being clever all round; and among them the working man but too often comes to the ground.

Bad as is the general run of domestic servants, the "young-lady" class is still worse. It is nothing if not genteel. Commonplace people may call its members shop- or work-girls, and slangy ones style them needle-drivers; but to themselves they are ever young ladies, and their business is "a genteel occupation." What counter-skippers are to the male creation, the young ladies of the needle-driving and cognate businesses are to the female. They are a class by themselves, are dressy, uneducated, frivolous, and affected, and are noticeable for trying to ape their betters even in the present age, when all classes do so more or less. They look with contempt upon domestic servants and service, and even when married regard household work as degrading, and are ashamed to be seen in its performance. On this latter point it might be observed, "And well they may!" Wives of this class say of themselves that they "are not fit to be seen" when they are at work; and they are right – they are not. They go about their housework in a mincing, muddling manner, and clad in some dirty, tawdry, half-worn finery, manner and dress combining to give them a thoroughly slovenly appearance, which contrasts very unfavourably with that of the really clever housewife, who goes actively about her work, and in her clean cotton working-gown looks to the full as comely and attractive as she does when "cleaned up" after her work is done, and is thus in a certain sense "beautiful for ever."

The young ladies are generally as romantic as they are genteel; and it is not until love's young dream of a noble suitor has been dispelled that they begin to realise the fact that they are probably destined to become wives in their own rank of life; and it is at the still later stage, when they have become worldly-wise enough to compare the income of the mechanic with that of the clerk or shopman, that they so far overcome their gentility as to think favourably – not to say designingly – of men who work at what in their romantic period they were wont to style "nasty black trades."

Unfortunately, however, for all parties concerned, the working men who would be the likeliest to make good wives out of young ladies who have come thus far on the road to a better state of things, the men who understand them best, and could let down their young-ladyism gently, are the ones who most avoid them when it comes to a question of matrimony. The go-ahead young fellows, who when single knock about, meeting the young ladies at the cheap dancing-academies of which they are the belles, "doing the grand" with them on Sundays, and generally fooling them to the top of their bent, see so much of the frivolous side of their character that they are afraid to risk marriage, being doubtful as to the good qualities which in many instances really underlie all their frivolity, and which they, knowing the girls, would be more likely than any other men to draw out. It is usually home-keeping youths, of homely wit, who fall victims to the superficial charms of the young ladies, and while "under the spell" plunge upon matrimony with them.

Sometimes the young lady who has come to the pass of marrying a man who is only steady and industrious, without being dashing or swellish, will be sufficiently strong-minded to altogether put away young-ladyish things; but generally they strive to combine the young lady with the housewife, and produce a trollop – a slovenly, muddling, unlovely woman, who makes her home miserable and uncomfortable, and is often harshly treated in consequence.

A favourite idea with the young-lady class is to continue to work at their business on their own account after they are married, with a view to adding to the family income; and in some cases, where they are clever and energetic beyond the average, they do so; but in most cases the idea is soon exploded. The ordinary working dressmaker or milliner, if married, can rarely earn sufficient by her needle to justify her husband in keeping a servant for the household work; and if she has to attend to that work herself it leaves no time for any sewing save that required by the family.

In speaking as I have done of a large class of work-girls, I have had no wish to dwell unkindly upon their faults, or in any way disparage their general character. Speaking from a very considerable knowledge of the class, I have no hesitation in saying that a very common idea that their morality is of a lax order is substantially unjust. They are dressy and vain, and often pretty and much tempted: but as a rule they are virtuous in thought, word, and deed, while many of those who by vicious courses have brought discredit upon the body have really no claim to the sisterhood. And there are numbers of them who, with a self-sacrifice the nobleness of which, owing to the commonplace circumstances under which it is shown, is but little appreciated, work hard day and night to support parents or other relatives, and are emphatically good girls. All that I wish to do is to point out that at present their education, mode of life, and tone of thought tend in a special degree to unfit them for the position of working men's wives – the position to which, if they become wives at all, they are mostly destined.

Perhaps the best wife that a working man can get is one who is the daughter of a family which from its numbers or some other cause has necessitated her being kept at home to assist in its management. In this case the art of domestic management has grown with her growth, and she almost invariably makes a good wife.

Notes

1 See, for example, M. Walker, '"Encouragement of Sound Education amongst the Industrial Classes": Mechanics' Institutes and Working-Class Membership, 1838–1881', *Educational Studies* 39:2 (2013), pp. 142–155.
2 A. J. Reid, 'Wright, Thomas', *Oxford Dictionary of National Biography*, 28 September 2006, at https://doi-org.du.idm.oclc.org/10.1093/ref:odnb/47426 [accessed 14 June 2021].
3 In a much different context, the art critic John Ruskin famously made this argument for middle-class women in *Sesame and Lilies*: 'And wherever a true wife comes, this home is always round her. The stars only may be over her head; the glowworm in the night cold grass may be the only fire at her foot: but home is yet wherever she is'. Lecture 2, 'Lilies. Of Queen's Gardens', August 5, 2019, orig. 1865 (Project Gutenberg ebook), at www.gutenberg.org/files/1293/1293-h/1293-h.htm [accessed 20 June 2021].
4 A. Kidd, *State, Society and the Poor in Nineteenth Century England* (Basingstoke and London: Macmillan, 1999), pp. 83–84.
5 T. Wright, 'Working Men's Homes and Wives', in *The Great Unwashed* (London: Tinsley Brothers, 1868), pp. 30–41, Google Books, on p. 35.
6 Wright, 'Working Men's Homes', p. 40. See Volume 1, Part 3, Chapter 28, n. 5 and n. 7.
7 Wright, 'Working Men's Homes', pp. 40, 41.

30

J. B. KINNEAR, 'THE SOCIAL POSITION OF WOMEN IN THE PRESENT AGE', IN *THE RIGHT OF WOMEN TO LABOUR*

(London: Frederick Bell & Co., 1873), pp. 3–14

John Boyd Kinnear (1828–1920) was a landowner in Fife, Scotland. He ran three times for Parliament as a Liberal, winning once but eventually losing his seat to H. H. Asquith, the future prime minister. He was more successful as a journalist, serving as the lead writer for some of the key publications of the day, such as the *Daily News*, the *London Review*, and the *Pall Mall Gazette*. In an 1884 pamphlet, he came out in favour of women's suffrage.[1] Kinnear's essay, published by the Vigilance Association for the Defence of Personal Rights, a libertarian organization, argues strongly in favour of women's right to work. Like the 1845 *Artizan* article (Volume 1, Part 3, Chapter 25), Kinnear focuses on women 'who have no male relatives to work for them',[2] who had to support themselves and often had dependents (including husbands) to maintain. Women, Kinnear contends, historically had always had occupations that belonged to them, most frequently in spinning and weaving. In industrial society, however, both machines and men had displaced women from these occupations.[3] Because women had emigrated at a lower rate than men, women at all ranks had to find their own means of survival. However, women could not compete with men, and they were forced to take meagre wages, having difficulty finding any jobs at all. The market for female labour was seriously overstocked because so few occupations were open to women.[4] Similarly to the article in the *Artizan*, Kinnear argues that men should leave to women the occupations that women were able to perform – those that focused on domestic tasks and required little strength, as well as jobs such as printing and watchmaking – because men would always find other jobs open to them but closed to women because of the nature of the work. Men, additionally, could emigrate and find the many positions offered in the colonies (see Volume 4 Introduction on emigration). Kinnear dismisses the supposed conflict between work in the public sphere and women's lack of domestic abilities, arguing that women would naturally avoid rough and unwomanly work, which would organically fall to men. Unlike Munro and Wright (Volume 1, Part 3, Chapters 28 and

DOI: 10.4324/9780429320323-35

29), Kinnear believes that women innately possessed domestic skills and therefore did not need outside training. Interestingly, he also points out that trades which people once thought unwomanly were now regarded as acceptable for women, a position which suggests that gender is socially constructed. Kinnear claims that the majority of men in trades unions were in favour of women's right to work and all that was left was to convince the 'waverers' and silence men who held to the idea that women only belonged in the private sphere.[5] In the end, he trusts that enough jobs existed for both men and women, but the occupations were currently wrongly distributed. Some occupations, in his mind, were gendered masculine and some feminine, but there was a range in the middle that was neutral, which men controlled and should relinquish in favour of women's right to work.

'The Social Position of Women in the Present Age'

In what I am about to say I speak to men and women alike, for it is important to both alike that the true position, the true rights and duties of women in this nineteenth century should be ascertained and acknowledged. The question for which I ask consideration, is that of which at present we hear so much – the question of Women's Work. In discussing it I shall not enter into any arguments on questions of intellectual equality, nor will I, on the other hand, invoke sentiments of chivalry or compassion. I appeal solely to plain principles of justice, of common interest, and of common sense.

It is a very moderate and incontrovertible proposition to start from, that at all events women must live. To live they must be fed; and to be fed involves the labour of some one. Whose labour, then, shall it be? There are many women so circumstanced that they have no need to think of this. They have fathers, brothers, or husbands, who provide for them. But we also know too well that there are many women who have no male relatives to work for them; none even whom the law could compel to work for them. These must work for their own support, or be supported by general charity. Nay, there are, as is known to every one of us, many thousands of women who have not only to work for themselves, but who have to work for the maintenance of others dependent on them – daughters who have to support father or mother; sisters who have to support brothers or sisters; wives who have to support husbands; widows who have to support children – or who, if they failed so to work, would fling the maintenance of these loved ones on the poor-rate. Now it is needless here to enter into an inquiry whether women who have not male protectors should be driven to the workhouse, or whether they should abandon the care of those for whom they struggle to the Guardians of the Poor. There are some who argue that the country ought to take both charges on itself. Grave objections exist to that theory, but I will not even state them, because the fact is that the country rejects it. The public approves of the proposition that women should work rather than beg, and the public therefore acknowledges that work of some sort must be allowed to women.

But then we are told, that of course this is the case, but that it is nothing new. Women have always had to work, but they worked, say the objectors, "quietly, and in their proper places: and it is only in this generation that they have grown querulous and discontented, and demand new spheres, and want to enter into competition with men in every trade and profession." There is some measure of truth in the allegation, but it may be met with a very simple preliminary answer. The fact is that men have taken away from women the employments which formerly were appropriated to them, and that therefore it is men who force women to claim the right to new openings for their labour. Let us look at any of the older social organizations, even the most rudimentary, and we find in them, it may be a high or a low, but at all events a distinct, place for women. They are, according to the habits of the respective races and the degrees of civilization and wealth, the tillers of the ground, the tenders of the flock, the grinders of corn, the bakers, the cooks, the spinners, the weavers, the tailors, the leather-tanners and embroiderers for the household, over and above all their maternal and domestic duties. In such functions there was room for more than the wives, or there was place for all as wives. Where the rude life of barbarism prevails, every man needs a wife, and so all women are married as soon as grown up. Where polygamy exists wives are in demand above the supply, and they at least are provided for, whether it be the custom for the wives to work or not. When civilization or Christianity abolished polygamy, there were still female occupations for the mistress of the house and the women whom she gathered round her. In Rome, as in old England, the lady sat surrounded by her maids spinning wool and flax, or plying the needle, for use or ornament; or she superintended and directed the heavier domestic labours, in which the strength of men was needed. Within the present century, the women in humble life had always (in some districts they have even still) the spinning-wheel at hand, as a means of support if single, of filling up empty time if married. And when these and such-like avocations were available to women of every rank, they were not only provided with subsistence, but they held that definite place in society, and filled those recognized duties which placed them on a footing of substantial dignity, and forbade the raising of any question whether their capacities were equal with those of men or not.

Not intentionally, but actually, by the progress of science and the new forms of social existence, that position has been taken from women. Machinery spins, weaves, grinds, and even where women can gain employment in connexion with machine-labour, it is no longer exclusively their own, no longer domestic, but it exposes them to competition and forces them to compete. Other vocations, such as baking and brewing, once the toil of separate households, are now carried on upon a large scale in manufactories, and men have wholly displaced women from them. Meantime emigration, the source of infinite benefit and the relief from infinite suffering, carries off far more men than women; and while it increases the proportion of women left at home, it diminishes the number of the households in which women can find work. The higher standard of comfort now prevalent disinclines men to marry so early as they used in olden times, and the spread of luxury in an equal degree withholds women of the upper ranks from marriage till suitable establishments are offered them. But every such restraint of marriages diminishes the field open to women of the humbler classes in domestic service. Gradually also some of the coarser and rougher trades in which women have heretofore worked along with men are, either by direct legislation (as in mines, etc.,) or by the influence of public opinion, closed against them. Such a fact is in some cases not to be regretted, but it inevitably swells the number of those who must seek a livelihood in other ways. Again, competition in all trades is so sharp that masters are forced, or at least many think themselves forced, both to cut down the wages of women in their employment to the minimum which the supply of labour makes possible, and to dismiss their surplus female hands whenever the season of the year brings slackness of business. While such causes spread destitution through the lower and middle ranks, the higher do not escape the consequences of the peculiar tendencies of the age. The enhanced competition in display, the recklessness of speculation, the temptation to invest in doubtful securities, bring many a family to ruin. The daughters are thrown upon the world, only to find the market for their superficial accomplishments sadly overstocked; and by increasing the supply, they add to the distress of others while hardly alleviating their own. Thus from every rank and class of women there rises up the cry that work is wanted and no work is to be had.

These considerations must satisfy every candid mind that the movement and stir among women is not gratuitous, but is urged by the iron law of necessity. And it will be observed that in thus stating the case I am purposely, in the first instance, confining it to the question of physical necessity, and therefore placing it, if on the most incontrovertible, yet also on the lowest ground. But this simple and elementary view will serve to show clearly the true answer to be made to the objection taken to the competition of women with men. In a sense, such competition is inevitable, unless men will undertake, which they now do not, to support all women without their working at all. Since this is not proposed it is rather for women to complain that men compete with them. What right, they might well ask, have men to become spinners, bakers, sellers of lace and silks, and of all the nicknacks of women's own attire? Why do they encroach, with the help of machinery, upon the avocations that are purely domestic, and, under the name of free trade, upon the employments in which no strength of muscle is required? Their answer is, that they have a right to do anything in any way by which they can make a profit. Well, so they have, but they can clearly have no right to grumble at others doing the same. If men are entitled to sell pins and tapes because they can do it to profit, how can they object to women setting types, painting porcelain, or copying law-papers, if they can do such things to profit? Obviously, when men appeal to public support, demonstrated by public patronage, as their justification in invading the women's kingdom, they appeal to a principle which is a sufficient defence of women, if in any instance they undertake duties hitherto confined to male hands. The public, if it is ready to buy of either, settles the question of the right of either to sell.

The truth is that there is no middle course between a system which shall map out precise duties, not only to each sex, but to every class and to every individual constituting the State, and the system which leaves to all equal freedom to work at what they choose and what they are fit for. And the principles on which modern society is based, forbid that any system should live save that of freedom of labour, a freedom which, from its nature, must be complete and universal.

Nor is the result to be regretted, even by the sentimental. It is often, indeed, hard and pitiless in its processes. Men and women may starve when doing their very best, because they have taken a wrong line, in which somebody else can do better. But the cruel teaching saves more suffering than it causes. It points out the departments for which special qualifications are required, and, drawing to them those who are best qualified, it relieves other departments of the competition that would cut down the returns which these afford. It divides the workers into groups, not by accident of birth, but by the test of fitness. So it gives to the world the best service at the lowest rates, and all in turn benefit by obtaining cheaply what is good. But at the same time it gives to each the best remuneration, because each must gain most at the work for which he has most aptitude. Labour is thus employed in the manner in which it can produce the most, and we are all the richer for it. Consider only the difference which would be seen between the nation which lets strong men do rough work, clever men do skilled work, and weak men do delicate work, and the nation which would set the muscle of porters and draymen to weave straw hats, utilize its fools as schoolmasters, and benevolently encourage cripples to make earthworks on a railway; and we shall recognize at once the true principle and the true merit of the doctrine of free competition.

Now, if we recognize this truth in the case of men as between themselves, how can we refuse assent to it as between men and women? Our assent to it is indeed already given. We do not hire men as nursemaids even for a family of boys; nor have men yet complained because we do not turn female cooks out of our kitchens in order to instal substitutes of the male sex. Some employments, in point of fact, are virtually confined to women; in others, men and women compete on equal terms. The question then is narrowed to the single point, Why should there be enforced exclusion from *any* trade? There are two social reasons for this exclusion commonly given. The one is, that the competition of women, if it were allowed, would lower the rate of wages. The other is, that women ought not to be encouraged to renounce domestic duties, and throw off feminine reserve, by mixing with men in what are called the occupations of men.

The former of these arguments may be true, if we confine our view to only a limited range of employments and of time. Suppose that in a given trade the workers at present are only men, and that there is work only for so many as are at present employed; it is then obvious that women can only gain admission (apart from any chance individual sympathies) by underbidding and displacing the men. And if such were the case in all the employments in the world, so that there was really no more work to do than what men could do, the argument would be a strong one in favour of letting men continue to be the workers, and imposing upon them the necessary duty of earning all that could be earned, and out of it supporting all women as well as all of themselves. But no one can assert for a moment that the world's work is thus restricted. If men are displaced in one trade by women, there are other trades open. If in this country there were no trades open, there are the Colonies and foreign countries in which men's labour will be remunerated – not only in trades, but even in cultivating the soil – much more highly than in most trades with us. Far from the world being over-populated, it is still infinitely under-populated. Nature offers room for a thousand times more labour than has yet been bestowed upon her. The beginning of all wealth is in her gifts, and human labour is, in the first instance only spent in appropriating them in a useful form. But her unappropriated gifts are still boundless. In Asia, in America, in the islands of the East and South, there are tracts far larger than Europe, capable of supporting a population denser than that of Europe, and which yet are all but unexplored. Even within Europe there are vast regions only half cultivated, and mineral treasures known to exist, but as yet unused. The labour that might be bestowed in acquiring these riches would do more than make the labourers rich, it would make the whole of mankind richer; for each labourer would in some shape redeem more than he could consume, and the surplus would in some shape be available for the consumption of others. When, therefore, we speak of there being a surplus of labour, we may be quite sure that there is only a surplus in some employments, because the labour is wrongly distributed and wrongly divided. There is not, and there cannot be, for more years than the world has yet lived, a real surplus of labour in the world. On the contrary, there is a huge unsupplied demand for labour; and our blunder is in forcing too much labour artificially into certain channels, and thus artificially depriving ourselves of the benefit it would yield us did it flow in natural channels.

Now, competition of men with men, and of women with men, is precisely the teaching of Nature as to what channels are the most profitable for the work of all to flow in. There are some things that men can do and women cannot. Of course in these men will beat women out of the field. But there are other things that women can do at least as well as men. Whatever needs delicacy, taste, accuracy, what can be done indoors, by the fireside, or in suitable workshops, and what does not need a great deal of manual strength, can, as we all know, be done as well by women as by men. Then why should women not do it? Because some of the men will need to resort to other employments? Then let them. There are employments in which, besides skill, strength is needed, and in which they will have no rivalry. What folly in them to reject such employments in order that they may do a woman's work, and drive a woman out of work! In some things they see this. There are, doubtless, men who could make as good milliners as any woman: there is said to be one in Paris now who is superior in taste as a lady's dressmaker to any woman. But if men were generally to take the making of ladies' bonnets and dresses into their own hands, they can see that they would force just so many women to stand idle, and that they would be fools to do it. The women would have to stand idle because the range of their employments is limited by their strength and their sex. But if women were to take to printing, or watchmaking, or wigmaking, the men displaced from these trades would find countless other trades or occupations open to them. Are they not then as unwise if they try to prevent women from being printers, or watchmakers, or wigmakers, as if they tried to drive them out of the business of making dresses and bonnets?

I have conceded, for the purpose of illustrating the argument, that in each special trade the admission of female competition might for the moment cause some distress. But let us not be frightened by that apprehension till we have examined its basis. Distress, in any special trade, is caused either by a cessation of demand; or by some sudden modification of labour, such as the introduction of machinery; or by a want of intelligence in the operatives, in not recognizing that other fields of labour afford better remuneration. The first cause cannot operate from the admission of women to work. As little can the second; for they must of course pass through apprenticeships, and only a few at a time will become fit for the trade. Besides, it is not the opening of any one trade we are considering, but the opening of many, among which women-workers would be distributed in comparatively limited numbers. And the third cause of a fall of wages ought not, and with a higher education cannot, occur in any special trade. If it is recognized that girls are being apprenticed in some trades, the obvious effect will be to lead parents to apprentice a corresponding proportion of their sons to some other trade where wages are likely to be better; or to lead a certain number of young men, married or unmarried, to emigrate instead of entering any occupation at home. Both male and female work will in fact, when dealt with alike, form one fund, which will be apportioned, according to the irresistible laws of political economy, in such a way as to equalize the rate of wages in proportion to skill, trouble, and risk. Only let there be no artificial favour or compulsion, and labour will leave the avocations that are poorly remunerated, and betake itself to those that are better. Nor can there be any general fall of wages so long as emigration offers still better returns, and while there is intelligence in the country to understand their existence. The addition then, of female labour to male, in all suitable avocations, would be so much addition to the wealth of the world; and being both gradual and widely diffused, it could not exercise any appreciable influence in diminishing wages in any trade to which it might be admitted.

If therefore, these words should reach any members of a Trades' Union which at present resists the introduction of female labour, this is the suggestion I should wish to make to them: Is it better for you, as fathers and brothers, that your girls and sisters should grow up in idleness, or that they should be allowed to be apprenticed in your trade, or in some other trade? If you cannot support them, and make sure of there being some one else to support them when you are dead or disabled, what are they to do? Become servants, or milliners, or dressmakers, or ballet girls, or go on the streets? You know that every one of these employments, down to the miserable last, is so overstocked, because there is scarcely any other calling open to women, that they can but make a poor livelihood in their youth, and can save nothing for their old age. Now, suppose you let them work at your own trade, what will happen? Why, you and your mates will have to look round you for some other employment for your boys; that will be all. And you know that there are plenty of trades your boys can enter, quite as good as your own: and that there is the best trade of all, that of going to foreign parts, where they will secure a competence, possibly a fortune, before you yourselves are greyheaded. Meantime your girls will be provided for honestly, each becoming able to make for herself as good wages as you are now making for all your family. Put this to your own minds, and you cannot doubt which course is the best. Then put the case, as frankly and fairly, to those of your fellows who do not happen to have girls of their own to provide for, and do not doubt that they will see as well as you that what is best for women in general must be, in the long run, best for men too.

And this that is said to Trades' Unions, and will, sooner or later, be acted upon by them, is not, in anything but detail, different from what ought to be accepted and recognized by the upper professions.

As to the argument that if women were admitted to trades or professions it would take them from domestic duties and make them unwomanly, little need be said; for both points, I think, we can pretty safely leave them to themselves. Their own instincts in these matters are too strong to need any guardianship from us. Whatever business is essentially unwomanly they will of themselves avoid; and whatever is only unwomanly because at present coarse men make it so, they will by their mere presence refine. It is possible also that fashion may err in thinking some things unwomanly which are really not so, just as fifty years ago it was thought hardly womanly to write a book! Public opinion varies; but, except in some very depraved states of society, it never errs on the side of too great laxity as regards women's public conduct. Nor do women go against public opinion, unless they feel that they can ultimately carry it with them. We may leave, then, the question whether any employment is womanly, to be settled by the women who may wish to adopt it, and by the public which may judge them.

Far then from trembling at the possibility of evils to follow from the admission of women to a share in fields of honest labour, we may rest assured that women and men will be drawn the closer in the bonds of mutual service, and love, and comfort, when we seek women's aid, and train them to give their aid, no longer only in our idleness and amusements, but in the daily round of duties which makes the noblest portion of our lives.

Since the paper from which the following arguments are extracted was printed, the simultaneous rise in wages and reduction in hours of labour, which forms one of the most beneficial events of the present age, has been in rapid progress. Combined with this change in the cost of labour, machinery has been brought into very extended employment. But while nearly all classes of men have experienced advantage from these modifications, women have in general shared in it to a very inadequate extent. They cannot, from domestic and social reasons, form effective trades unions to secure their rights in the labour market, and the manual work that machinery displaces is in many important branches peculiarly that of women.

At the same time it has been shown, by the action of the Medical Trades-Unions, that a superior education is not sufficient of itself to deter men who are either purely selfish, or who are secretly conscious of their own inferiority, from seeking to drive away the competition of women by means which do not differ in principle and hardly in practice from rattening. And I can therefore have no strong hope that any progress of education will induce bad or lazy workmen, either in trades or professions, to abandon the vantage ground in which they feel themselves safe. But it becomes the more necessary that those who do recognize the justice of the claims of women should be energetic in supporting the efforts that are being made in their vindication. In every social grade, and in every Trades-Union, there are many, if not in truth a majority, who feel strongly that women ought to have a fair and equal chance in the race for existence. I would then urge all who think so to be no longer content with an abstract acknowledgement of that right, but energetically to proclaim their opinions, to combine together to enforce them, to gain converts among the waverers, and by force of shame, if neither of reason nor of generosity, to put to silence that class of men who declare that they are so superior to women that women must be kept to their firesides, or, if they have none, driven to the streets, sooner than men should have to meet them in fair rivalry for honest employment.

Notes

1 G. F. Millar, 'Kinnear, John Boyd', *Oxford Dictionary of National Biography*, 23 September 2004, at https://doi-org.du.idm.oclc.org/10.1093/ref:odnb/40269 [accessed 14 June 2021]; 'Mr. John Boyd Kinnear', *Aberdeen Press and Journal*, 11 November 1920, p. 3.
2 J. B. Kinnear, *The Right of Women to Labour* (London: Frederick Bell & Co., 1873), London School of Economics Library: HD6/D342, p. 3.
3 This is an interesting twist on the usual argument made by working men that machines had allowed women to displace them from what had been skilled jobs. See Volume 1 Introduction. Also see A. Clark, *The Struggle for the Breeches: Gender and the Making of the British Working Class* (Berkeley: University of California Press, 1995).
4 See, for example, E. Jordan, 'The Exclusion of Women from Industry in Nineteenth-Century Britain', *Comparative Studies in Society and History* 31:2 (April 1989), pp. 273–296.
5 Kinnear, *The Right of Women*, p. 14.

31

M. HARKNESS, 'PALM-WORKERS', IN *TOILERS IN LONDON; OR INQUIRIES CONCERNING FEMALE LABOUR IN THE METROPOLIS*

(London: Hodder and Stoughton, 1889), pp. 47–57

Margaret Harkness (1854–1923), born in Worcestershire, moved to London and trained as a nurse. In the early 1880s, she gave up nursing and became a writer, supported financially in part by her cousin Beatrice Webb (then Potter) (see Volume 3, Part 2, Chapter 13), who introduced Harkness into London's radical circles. Harkness moved into working-class housing in London's East End in 1886, right in the middle of a deep trade depression, in order to observe the lives of the poor. She was increasingly drawn to socialism and the Social Democratic Federation (see Volume 3, Part 3, Chapter 23), where she met John Burns (see Volume 3, Part 3, Chapter 26), among others. From 1887, most of her writing was published under the pseudonym John Law, most likely in an effort to distance her from her conservative family and to provide her more authority for the radical stances she advanced. Her novels, *A City Girl* (1887) and *Out of Work* (1888), address from working-class perspectives the issues with which she became familiar while living in London, such as women's casual labour and clashes between the unemployed and police. The *British Weekly: A Journal of Social and Christian Progress*, a nonconformist journal founded in 1886, employed Harkness in 1887 and 1888. During this time she produced two edited series, 'Tempted London: Young Men' and 'Tempted London: Young Women', the latter of which Harkness was the primary author.[1] According to its title page, *Toilers in London* was the second part of this series, although it was published independently of the journal. It is similar in form to the earlier, more voluminous, and well-known investigative journalism *London Labour and the London Poor*, by Henry Mayhew.[2] Both describe different groups of workers and their circumstances in order to expose the misery and want in which they lived. Unlike Mayhew, Harkness focused specifically on

 DOI: 10.4324/9780429320323-36

female labour. *Toilers in London* presents Harkness as the editor of evidence that was collected by the *British Weekly* 'commissioners', who were sent to investigate conditions among the poor. This selection looks at home industries, also referred to as sweated labour.[3] Harkness uses the commissioners' reports to paint a picture of extreme poverty among a class of people struggling for work and respectability. She challenges the public for not taking seriously the horrible conditions described in such exposés as Andrew Mearns's *The Bitter Cry of Outcast London*.[4] She argues that the poor themselves did not complain because of hunger; the people were starving and therefore did not have the strength to voice their grievances, so other people needed to tell their stories. Harkness writes briefly of women who mended damaged nutmegs, who strung beaded necklaces, and who relined fur jackets, providing a taste of the types of work that women took in at home. Then she focuses on what were called palm needlewomen, who worked with heavy fabrics that necessitated protection of their hands with a 'palm thimble' so the needle did not go into the flesh of their palms.[5] Harkness relates how the commissioners found that all these women had scars and wounds from their work and that the good thimbles cost money they could not afford. The injuries they suffered kept the women from their work and, according to a commissioner, healed slowly. Much of the palm-workers' labour apparently was for government projects, such as tarps for ships. The women blamed the government for their lack of work and their poor pay and worried that machinery was replacing their handwork, brutal though that work was.[6] The workers' references to 'Jews' and 'Jewesses' and appeals to English nationalism reflect their fears and biases concerning Jewish immigration in London's East End.[7] Harkness wrote that the palm-workers asked why the commissioners were interested in their condition. She explained to her readers that by providing publicity about these 'unfortunate women' in home industries, hopefully some change could occur. But, she remarked, 'we are not very sanguine'.[8]

'Palm-Workers'

OUR Commissioners give a deplorable account of the poverty and distress which they have witnessed during their inquiry into home industries. House after house, street after street, has shown men out of work, wives and daughters supporting the whole family.

They say that they wish readers could accompany them in their visits to the homes of the girls and women they have been obliged to see lately. The hardest part of their work consists of visits paid to starving people. The women flock out of their houses when they hear that an inquiry is being made into home industries and mob our Commissioners to ask, "Have you got work for us?" Girls run after them down the streets, and men follow them to the railway-station. They have not once been asked for money, only for work; and all they can do is to show their empty pockets.

A Commissioner reports a poor woman visited near Shoreditch, whose husband is out of work, and who has not had work herself lately. She weaves fringes for toilet-covers, and is paid two shillings for a piece thirty-six yards in length. Her husband puts the cotton on the loom for her over-night, and if she gets up at 4 a.m. and works until 11 p.m., she can make a piece in one day. But lately she has not had any work. When our Commissioner went into her room it presented a strange picture of cleanliness. The floor was white, and the furniture had not a speck of dust upon it. A clean patchwork-quilt covered the bed, and the empty grate was spotless. By the table stood two little children, without shoes or stockings, but as clean as the furniture; and the mother was clean herself, although her apron consisted of an old sack, and she wore a piece of sacking over her shoulders. The poor thing burst out crying when our Commissioner spoke about the fringe for toilet-covers, and said that she had had no work lately. No food had touched her lips that day, and the children had been to school without any breakfast.

People often say, "If things were really as bad as this we should hear more about it." Only those who go amongst the London poor can interpret their silence. They are still because they are starving. Nothing saps a man's strength like being hungry. Hunger takes all the spirit out of the unemployed, and so the public are inclined to think "Outcast London" a myth, and "Bitter cries" sensational stories. An intelligent working-man said to one of our Commissioners, "If we broke the heads of fifty Jews down here in Whitechapel something would be done to prevent this immigration. While we content ourselves with singing 'England for the English,' Government will say that these foreigners are a blessing to us."

It would be impossible to notice all the home industries, for their name is legion. Thus a little colony of women near Hackney are engaged in mending bad nutmegs. They fetch the worm-eaten nutmegs from factories, and mend them with nutmeg dust. A good nutmeg is ground very fine, and the dust is mixed with glue or gum. The mixture is then used to fill in the holes, and the mended nutmegs are returned to the manufactory. They are paid by the gross; but our Commissioner could not find out how much the women receive for their work. The women visited by our Commissioners are sometimes afraid of being "told upon;" and although they are generally willing to give any amount of information about the work of their neighbours, they often keep a discreet silence with regard to their own particular industry. But owing to the fact that most of the workers possess the same failing, it is not difficult to arrive at a general idea of what the pay is all round in most of the home industries. So far as our Commissioners could gather, the gum and the good nutmegs are supplied to mend the worm-eaten wares, and twopence per gross is paid for the mended nutmegs.

Another small industry is that of making necklaces for China and Japan. This is practised in several parts of the Tower Hamlets. Beads and clasps are supplied; but the workers must provide the cotton on which the beads are strung. The usual pay for these necklaces is 2*s*. 3*d*. per gross, and a worker can make half a gross in the day, if she "sits at it." These necklaces consist of four rows of beads, twisted, and fastened with a metal clasp. They are made up into packets of a dozen, or half-a-dozen, and are returned to the manufactories. Fetching and taking back form an important part of the work, as the manufactories often lie far away from the homes of the workers. A Commissioner visited two girls who earn their living by stringing beads, and found them busy at work. Both girls were dirty, untidy, and badly fed. They gave a sad account of their life when "slack" times prevent them from having enough to eat and drink. The room they live in is small, and at the top of a lodging-house. They pay for it 3*s*. 6*d*. per week, and are in arrears for rent. It is a "furnished" apartment, and the furniture consists of a bedstead, a table, and two chairs. "The boxes are ours," they said. "But there's not much in 'em, for we've pawned all our clothes, mostly." The bed was covered with old newspapers, and on these were strewn white china beads in large quantities. One girl stood up stringing the beads, the other sat by the table fastening the clasps to the readymade necklaces. A tin teapot was on the hob, and some slices of bread-and-butter were ready for "dinner." When asked if their usual fare consisted of tea and bread-and-butter, they answered "Yes."

"Do you ever get meat?"

"Well," said the eldest, who looked delicate, "I just *longs* for it."

These girls make a variety of cheap necklaces, but their chief work consists in stringing coloured beads for "foreign parts."

"I've seen necklaces like those we make in a shop near Bishopsgate," one girl said. "I don't think English girls wear them, but perhaps they are sold to the Jewesses."

In the neighbourhood of Holborn a great deal of work is done by girls and women for the fashionable shops, especially the re-lining of fur muffs and jackets. A Commissioner visited a poor woman near Red Lion Square the other day who had been out of work for some time, but who had just received an order from a well-known shop. When our Commissioner called, the woman was discovered sweeping the floor of her dirty little room, and emptying the contents of her dust-pan into a basket.

"What are you going to do with that dust?" our Commissioner asked.

"Well, you see, I'm short of wadding," the woman said. "They won't pay me till I take the work back, and I've not got any more wadding. If I go to the shop they'll say I was careless, so I'm just filling in with these sweepings."

On the table lay a magnificent seal-skin jacket, which had been sent by its owner to the shop for repair. Little does the owner of that jacket think that she will wear next winter the sweepings of a filthy little den in the neighbourhood of Red Lion Square!

So far as we are aware, no one has yet written "the history of a palm-thimble;" but when this is done, it will be so pathetic that readers will say, "It is not a true story." Directly a thing is told that pricks the conscience of the reader, we hear, "You are sensational," and when against the will tears come to the eyes of readers, they tell us, "It is not a true story."

A palm-thimble can be bought for 2*s*. 6*d*. This is made of lead. Steel palm-thimbles are very expensive. But the latter wear a long time; and it is the ambition of every palm-worker to possess one. Those made of lead wear out very fast, and the needle is apt to slip off them into the hand of the worker. Palm needlewomen have shown their right hands to our Commissioners, scarred with wounds made by the needles that have slipped off the lead and gone deeply into their flesh. Such wounds take a long time to heal, and prevent women from working. The lead or steel is rather larger than the top of an ordinary thimble, flat, round, and placed in the centre of a broad piece of leather. This leather is fastened with a buckle and strap round the palm of the worker's hand, so that the piece of steel or lead comes exactly in the middle of the palm, and the needle can be pressed with all the manual force of which the worker is possessed into the canvas.

A Commissioner reports a palm-worker visited in Aldgate, a widow with two children. The eldest girl helps her mother, and some of the work is done by the grandmother. The three work in the same small room; one stands by the bed, the second stands by the table, the third stands by the fireplace. Palm-workers do all their work standing up; sitting down they would not have enough force to pass the long needles through the stiff canvas. These three women do "Government work." They think that the Government is responsible for their hardships, and speak as if Government were a Pharaoh in Egypt.

"I suffers murder from pins and needles in my hands at night, all along of Government," says the mother.

"The work tears my clothes to bits; I wish Government had to pay for them," says the daughter.

"Men used to get 7*s*. for ten sacks, and Government only gives 4*s*. for ten to us poor women," says the grandmother.

At the present time they are making coal sacks for ships. Each sack has four splices, eight holes, two patches. Each sack is sewn and roped. Each sack has a broad R worked on it for Government.

By working hard the mother can make such a sack in two hours; and she receives 4¾*d*. for it. How hard the work is our readers can guess when they hear that she has sprained both of her wrists over Government work. Yet her only complaint is, "I can't get enough of it." She says, "Such a lot flies to the work that it's eaten up quick, and if Government liked it could get the work done for next to nothing. I work from five in the morning till late at night, and I'd work all night long if I could get more to do. I want to bring my girl up to something better than Government work. But work's difficult to get anywhere, and she set herself against going into service."

"They *do* say about here as the men will have to stay at home and mind the children, because the women are getting the work," said the grandmother. "She was a wicked woman who made the first sack for Government. Government was obliged to pay the men, but it can get women for next to nothing."

Another woman, visited in the far East, works for a well-known manufacturer. She makes tarpaulins for barges, break covers, blinds for shops, tents, sacks, etc. When our Commissioner called, she was sitting at her door. "School Board" (the School Board visitor) "told me you were coming," she said. "I thought maybe you wanted a charwoman."

"Then you are slack just now?"

"Yes, nothing's going on in our trade; it's all getting done by machinery; there'll be nothing left soon for us poor women. I used to make hammocks for Government, but Government's getting them done now in the prisons."

"How much did you get for the hammocks?"

"Five-and-sixpence for ten."

"How much are you paid for your coal sacks?"

"Two shillings for twelve."

"What are you doing now?"

"Nothing in the canvas line. Maybe you'll come in."

The Commissioner complimented her on the neatness of the kitchen; and she said, "I like to keep a bit near the mark if I can; but I don't know what will become of us if I can't get a job. I was sitting at the door, hoping a neighbour would call me in to do a bit of washing. I've a little girl in there" (pointing to a door) "light-headed with scarlet fever, and I thought if the neighbours came in and heard her, they'd be afraid to give me any washing."

The Commissioner pointed out the doubtful morality of this conduct; but the answer was, "One's own come first, and my little girl wants what I can't give her. So don't you tell of me to School Board; I thought from what he said you'd a job to give me."

She looked very much disappointed when our Commissioner went away. Like many other women, she was anxious to know *why* we are making this inquiry. Of course our Commissioners can only say the truth, which is that we hope, if public opinion is directed towards home industries, something may be done for these unfortunate women.

But we are not very sanguine.

One of the greatest hardships of palm-workers consists in carrying loads backwards and forwards. Some carry on the head, some on the hip. The tarpaulins are especially heavy, and women may be seen staggering beneath them in some districts. They say that the loads make them feel "lightheaded;" but as the tar is healthy it has "no fevers attached to it."

Mending old sacks is better paid, because the work is so very unpleasant. This is done at home, and also in the markets. Canvas work is much better paid in manufactories than at home. Women can make 12*s*. a week, or 2*s*. 6*d*. a day as palm-workers in manufactories.

Notes

1 T. Elkiss, 'A Law unto Herself: The Solitary Odyssey of M.E. Harkness', in F. Janssen and L. C. Robertson (eds), *Margaret Harkness: Writing Social Engagement 1880–1921* (Manchester, UK: Manchester University Press), pp. 17–38; J. Lucas, 'Harkness, Margaret Elise', *Oxford Dictionary of National Biography*, 26 May 2005, at https://doi-org.du.idm.oclc.org/10.1093/ref:odnb/56894 [accessed 14 June 2021].

2 H. Mayhew, *London Labour and the London Poor* (London: Griffin, Bohn, and Company, 1861).

3 On sweated labour, see S. Blackburn, *A Fair Day's Wage for a Fair Day's Work? Sweated Labour and the Origins of Minimum Wage Legislation in Britain* (Burlington, VT: Ashgate, 2006), part 1.

4 A. Mearns, *The Bitter Cry of Outcast London* (London: J. Clarke, 1883).

5 M. Harkness, *Toilers in London; or Inquiries Concerning Female Labour in the Metropolis* (London: Hodder and Stoughton, 1889), Archive.org, p. 52.

6 See Volume 1 Introduction and Volume 1, Part 2 on mechanization displacing men's manual labour.

7 See D. Feldman, *Immigrants and Workers, Englishmen and Jews: Jewish Immigration to the East End of London, 1880–1906* (Cambridge: Cambridge University Press, 1985).

8 Harkness, *Toilers in London*, p. 57.

32

G. REID ET AL., 'LEGAL RESTRAINT UPON THE EMPLOYMENT OF WOMEN IN FACTORIES BEFORE AND AFTER CHILDBIRTH'

British Medical Journal II (30 July 1892), pp. 275–278

The piece selected here offered *British Medical Journal* (*BMJ*) readers a view of the medical debates regarding married women's work and protective legislation. Throughout the nineteenth century, various legislative acts for the 'protection' of women limited women's hours and conditions of work in a variety of industries and trades. Medical men played an important role in providing evidence about the impact of different types of labour on women's bodies.[1] This source is a *BMJ* transcription of Dr George Reid's presentation on the relationship between married women's work and infant mortality to the British Medical Association's Section on Public Medicine in July 1892 and the discussion that followed. Dr George Reid (1854–1925) was the Medical Officer of Health for Staffordshire, a position he held for over thirty years. According to his obituary, 'Dr. Reid was responsible for the inauguration of a combined scheme of medical inspection, health visiting, and school nursing, and also of infant welfare centres' in Stafford. He also wrote a popular public health textbook, *Practical Sanitation: A Handbook for Sanitary Inspectors and Others Interested in Sanitation* (1892).[2] In this address, Reid compared the north and south industrial areas of Staffordshire for evidence of infant mortality. The industries in the North of the county focused on the potteries, where married women regularly worked. In the South were coal mines and iron works, forms of labour in which married women did not participate. Medical officers' reports showed that in the North where women worked, infant death rates were significantly higher. Reid then presented more detailed studies of Staffordshire and comparative studies with other counties that led to the same conclusion: where married women worked in large numbers, infant mortality rates went up. Although he recognized that mothers could not be banned from working outside the home altogether, Reid recommended legislation that would keep mothers home for three months after giving birth so they could breastfeed early in their

DOI: 10.4324/9780429320323-37

infants' lives. He thought Parliament should have a commission explore the issue. In the discussion, Dr Tatham of Manchester indicated that he had earlier provided testimony to a Royal Commission, presumably on factory work, encouraging legislation of the type Reid was promoting, but he was 'taken to task' for advocating government interference in the private worlds of industry and family.[3] He still believed mothers' work was causing infant mortality and legislation was needed. Other medical men commented on the quality of milk, the use of opiates, and poor child care as factors contributing to the death of infants in factory towns. The vast majority agreed that as things stood, the work of mothers with infants (or young children more generally) was damaging to the children's health. Some doctors thought the establishment of crèches could help women return to work, with suitable child care. The president of the section, however, was opposed to any kind of central government action, preferring local authorities to take up the issue. He, like the legislators who took Dr Tatham to task, worried about competition, seeing protective legislation of women's work as a hindrance to free markets. Reid desired very strongly that the group pass a resolution asking Parliament to undertake an inquiry to 'produce statistics' with the goal of legislative action to keep new mothers out of factories for three months.[4] The president, however, moved the group to resolve that the Parliamentary Bills Committee of the British Medical Association look into the findings of Reid's paper to see if they should petition Parliament for an inquiry on the subject. The 1891 Factory Act had already prevented the employment of any woman in a factory 'within four weeks after her confinement', and the 1895 Factory and Workshop Act extended this to 'laundries'. It also regulated women's work in terms of hours, meals, and holidays.[5]

'Legal Restraint upon the Employment of Women in Factories Before and After Childbirth'

Dr. George Reid, M.O.H. Staffordshire County Council, said that it was not his intention to attempt to gauge the proportional responsibility that should be attached to the various admitted causes of infant mortality; it was generally admitted that, among these, injudicious feeding took a prominent place, not so much, probably, as a direct cause, but by reason of its predisposing influence on ailments for which insanitary conditions were mainly responsible. It would, therefore, be reasonable to expect to find a marked difference in the infant death-rate among communities differing in no appreciable degree as regards their material surroundings, but presenting prominent distinctions in the sense of hindrances to providing infants with the food which nature intended they should have; any cause which took the mother away from home at a time when she should be suckling her child must prejudicially affect the health of that child, and thus predispose it to fatal diseases, which, under more favourable dietetic conditions, it might have resisted or overcome. Now the administrative county of Stafford was, he observed, divided into two populous areas, one in the north and the other in the south, each composed of abutting urban districts (central Staffordshire being mainly rural). As regarded the general sanitary conditions, no apparent distinction could be drawn between the northern and southern towns, but in one respect – namely, occupation – the two populations differed considerably. In the south of the county the people were mostly engaged in coal mines and iron works, in which the element of female labour must be disregarded; while in the north the chief industry was potting, in which large numbers of married women were engaged. Collation of the reports of the various medical officers of health, for the information of the Staffordshire County Council, showed that the infant death-rate was much higher in the north than in the south of the county, a circumstance which had been proved by figures covering, in most cases, a period of ten years, and which showed a rate of 182, as compared with 158. This difference was not to be attributed to any appreciable difference in local conditions. An inquiry had been instituted with the view of determining, if possible, whether and to what extent female labour would account for the marked difference in the rates. In order to substantiate the conclusions drawn from the figures I am about to give (Dr. Reid continued), it is necessary to explain shortly the nature and scope of the inquiry. In the first place, the population included in it amounts to 529,501, and it covers a period of ten years; the element of chance, therefore, is not likely to invalidate the conclusions. In dividing the towns into groups for the purpose of comparison, those which are distinctly rural as regards density of population, as well as others which are largely residential, have been excluded, the only towns included being those having distinctly artisan populations. Of these there are 26, with populations varying from 32,121 to 2,454, and a total population of 438,712. These towns have further been subdivided into three groups, according to the relative proportion of married women engaged in work. I should like to have arrived at this classification on the actual figures of the census, but this was impossible, as, in the case of towns under 50,000 inhabitants the returns are not published, and although I applied to the Census Office authorities for permission to extract the figures, my application was refused. It became necessary, therefore, to adopt another plan of classification, and this, with the kind assistance of the medical officers of health, I was enabled to do. In addition to blank forms for decennial returns of infant deaths, etc., a circular letter was sent to each medical officer of health, explaining fully the object of the inquiry, indicating the general basis of the classification, and inviting qualifying comments where such were considered necessary. From this information, amplified in certain cases by further details from various employers of labour, the industrial towns have been subdivided into three broad classes as follows: (1) towns in which married women are largely employed in work; (2) towns in which married women are engaged to a less extent in work; and (3) towns in which few married women are engaged in work. In the first group are placed those towns where one chief industry is in operation in which married women are largely engaged; the second group comprises those towns in which different industries are carried on, in some of which married women are employed in considerable numbers; in the third group are those towns where the industry or industries do not admit of the employment of married women. From the returns obtained I am able to give the averages of the general death-rate, the zymotic death-rate, and the death-rate from diarrhœa during the decennial period:

STAFFORDSHIRE.

Average Rates in Groups of Towns for 10 years – 1881–90.

–	*Mean Population.*	*Deaths in Children under one year per 1,000 Births.*	*General Death-rate per 1,000 of Population.*		*Zymotic Death-rate per 1,000 of Population.*	*Deaths from Diarrhœa per 1,000 Births.*
			Actual.	*Hypothetical.*		
Class I. – Many Women engaged in Work.	112,078	195	22.8	19.8	3.17	28
Class II. – Fewer Women engaged in Work.	161,580	166	19.4	18.9	2.45	20
Class III. – Practically no Women engaged in Work.	165,074	152	18.1	18.1	2.46	19

As regards the infant death-rate, in the first group of towns, namely, where married women are largely engaged in factories, etc., 195 children die during the first year of life in every thousand born, as compared with 152 in the third group which embraces towns where practically no married women are engaged. In other words, 28 per cent. more infants die in the former than in the latter. Again, in the second group consisting of those towns intermediate between the other two as regards the number of married women engaged in work, the figures are 166, a decrease of 15 per cent., as compared with the first group, and an increase of 9 per cent. as compared with the third. Bearing in mind that the only apparent dissimilarity as regards conditions in the three groups of towns which are likely to influence infant life, is the relative proportion of married women in each, who, through being engaged in trade, are prevented from suckling their children, to say the least of it, it is extremely probable that to this circumstance the unfavourable infant death-rate is to be attributed. Granting that this is the case one would expect to find that the death-rates from diarrhœa would show a proportionate decrease in the three groups. The figures show that this is the case, although not to the extent one would have anticipated. In the table the general death-rate is given as well as the zymotic rate. As regards the former, it is interesting to notice that the high rates in Groups I and II are almost entirely owing to the excess of deaths among infants, for, if we take a hypothetical infant mortality, corresponding with that of the third group of towns, and work out the rates on that basis, the result is that the actual death-rates in the first two groups are reduced from 22.8 and 19.4 to 19.8 and 18.9 respectively. This fact may be taken for what it is worth, in support of the statement that the general local conditions in each group of towns are fairly identical. It may be said that in attributing the excessive infant mortality entirely to female labour, the effect of the probable excess of illegitimate births in towns where men and women work together has been disregarded. Allowing for this, however, and supposing that the illegitimate births in the one case amount to 10, and in the other to 5 per cent., reckoning the infant death-date [sic] among illegitimate children at 350 per 1,000 births, this would only have the effect of increasing the rate in the first group of towns about ½ per cent., an amount which is not worth considering. So much for Staffordshire. Let us now see how the figures for other towns in England compare with those just given. Here, in one sense, our information is more accurate, for in the case of towns whose populations exceed 50,000, the exact number of women engaged in work is given; on the other hand, not knowing the precise nature of the work carried on in different towns, it is impossible to say what proportion of the female workers are married, and also, as outsiders, we cannot estimate the possible influence that local conditions may have in causing infant ailments. Another source of error exists in the fact, that while the census figures refer to sanitary districts, the Registrar-General's figures embrace the registration districts, although, in [sic] is true, the town populations of these constitute the greater part in each case. Among the large towns, the proportion of women engaged in work varies from 25 to 6 per cent. of the respective populations. By dividing these towns into three groups, in accordance with the preponderance of female workers, the following are found to be the infant death-rates and diarrhœa death-rates per 1,000 children born under each group, as derived from the Registrar-General's returns for the years 1871–80, the last that are published in the form of a summary: –

ENGLAND.

Rates in Groups of Towns, excluding London, whose Populations amount to 50,000 and upwards, 1871–80.

	Group I. Over 15 per cent. of Female Workers.	*Group II. Under 15 and over 10 per cent. of Female Workers.*	*Group III. Under 10 per cent. of Female Workers.*
Population	2,645,357	1,500,954	1,127,010
Deaths in infants under one year per 1,000 births	175	171	154
Total diarrhœa deaths per 1,000 births	36	37	32

As these figures are for a different decennial period to those given in the case of Staffordshire, even if in other respects they were comparative, which they are not, they cannot be used for the purposes of comparison. I give them for what they are worth, without any comment, except that they support rather than otherwise the conclusions I have drawn from the figures for Staffordshire. In conclusion, Dr. Reid asked whether legislative interference was not called for? It might not be reasonable to require women who had children entirely to give up work which took them away from their homes, but if a compulsory period – say of three months at home after their confinements – was established by law, it could not be looked upon as a hardship, and its influence for good would be great; infants would then have the chance of getting a good start in life, and would thus be better able to contend against illness. The month's absence from work which was imposed by Section 17 of the Factory and Workshops Act, 1891, is of little practical utility so far as infants are concerned. He thought that a special Commission ought to be appointed by the Legislature to inquire into the whole matter.

The PRESIDENT said that the carefully prepared paper which had been read by Dr. Reid must commend itself to the close attention of all who were interested in this most important subject. The figures which had been presented were particularly valuable, and he did not think they could have a better proof of the useful kind of work which county medical officers of health could carry out than had been afforded by Dr. Reid's paper. If in various districts of the country the same kind of interest was taken in compiling statistics bearing upon great public questions like this, work connected with public health would advance by strides year by year, not only in public estimation, but in public usefulness.

Dr. TATHAM (Manchester) said he should not like his silence to be interpreted as meaning that he had no feeling on the matter or that he did not think it one of great importance. Many years ago, in Salford, the question of the employment of women in factories, as influencing the death-rate among their children appeared to him to be so important that he took very considerable trouble in making investigations in regard to it. He had published some reports on the subject and he had had the honour a little time ago of being invited to give evidence before a Royal Commission. He was afraid that he got into hot water rather because, with the object of restraining the employment of young mothers in factories, he ventured to suggest that a limit should be imposed in regard to the time at which puerperal women might return to the factories. He was considerably taken to task over the matter, it being said that he was going to interfere with trade and ruin working men and their families. He failed to see it himself at the time, and he failed to see it now, after having given the matter long and most anxious consideration. He felt certain that the rate of infant mortality was considerably increased by the practice which obtained in most large manufacturing towns of allowing women to return to work within a week or ten days after their confinement. It meant – and he spoke more especially of Manchester and Salford – the delegation of the duties of the mother to some young member of the family, probably to a girl of 12 or 14 years of age, the mother only seeing the child early in the morning and during the night. To reduce the rate of mortality arising from this particular custom it would be desirable to impose some legislative check on the employment of women in factories within a certain period of their confinement.

Surgeon-Major PRINGLE alluded to the great importance of inquing [sic] into the quality of the milk sold in tins. Milk of bad character was very largely used in the feeding of children, and it was very desirable that steps should be taken to ascertain its real character. Condensed milk, he had found, was often used because it was cheaper, and in relation to the question under discussion, it was of importance to remember that from the occupations they followed in factories, mothers were often prevented from suckling their children.

Dr. ALDRED (Manchester) spoke of the use of narcotics in the case of young children as one of the causes of excessive mortality. He lived in a densely-populated district, and he found that women having their living to earn often put children out to nurse with some old crone who could scarcely nurse herself. The latter took the infant for the small pittance probably of 2s. or 2s. 6d. a week, and in order that she might keep the child quiet in the day-time, she administered some cordial which invariably contained opium. The result was that the child often slept all day, and when the mother came home in the evening she found the child wide awake. Naturally it had had its sleep out and wanted to be playing about. The mother did not quite understand it, and, in order that she might have a night's rest, administered some similar preparation, with the consequence that the child was dosed both night and day. He thought that some legislation should be put in force that might prevent this frequent cause of mortality.

Dr. THRESH (Chelmsford), Medical Officer of Health for Essex, referred to his experience in Manchester, where he said he had seen as many as six children asleep in a large soap box. It was the custom of certain persons to take care of children in the absence of their mothers. They gave the infants a little paregoric in the morning, the result being oftentimes that they had no food for the rest of the day. He thought that in cases where children were taken in to nurse in the manner in which he had described, there should be an adequate system of supervision. In Manchester and Salford the taking of children in this way was made a regular means of gaining a livelihood by many elderly people. In large towns it was not uncommon for mothers to return to their work at the factories within a week of their confinement. This obviously was prejudicial to the health of the women, and prejudicial also to the children. Those who had given the subject serious consideration must recognise that the time had come for some legislative interference.

Dr. Groves (Isle of Wight) advocated the establishment of *crèches* under proper regulations for the care of children whilst the mothers were engaged in the factory. The children were not only under proper care and received proper food, but as they got older care was taken that they were properly amused. As a result of the establishment of the *crèches*, the rate of mortality amongst the children of *employées* in a factory as to which he had information had diminished very largely indeed.

Dr. H. G. H. Monk (Shrewsbury), as an old practitioner in a rural district, spoke of the difficulty experienced oftentimes in obtaining a good and abundant supply of milk in country places. This applied particularly to labouring people who required the milk for their children. At a place only 9 miles from Nottingham, at one farmhouse only out of every eight or nine was it possible for the labourer or any other inhabitant to obtain the necessary supply of milk, the explanation of this being that the milk was despatched to the markets in the large towns.

Dr. Simpson (Manchester) said he presumed the object of the discussion was to suggest some remedy for a state of things which they deplored. The suggestion which had been thrown out for the establishment of *crèches* was an admirable one, and one which would, no doubt, do a great deal towards diminishing the rate of mortality amongst the infants; but he was rather disposed to take exception to the responsibility of the supervision being thrown upon the State. He thought it was far better for people, as far as they could, to help themselves. This was a matter for voluntary action rather than for State interference. The moral responsibility rested upon manufacturers, who brought people together in large numbers.

Dr. Strachan (Dollar), speaking from twenty-five years' experience, expressed the opinion that it was far better that pure milk should be given to children than that milk should be mixed with water.

After some observations from Dr. Mumby (Southsea),

Dr. Butterfield (Sevenoaks) said that when he occupied the position of medical officer of health for Bradford he had considerable experience of the ill effects of the employment of women in the worsted and spinning mills in that town. During several periods when autumnal diarrhœa was particularly rife in Bradford he made special inquiry in regard to the food given to the infants. He generally found that the children, in the absence of the mothers at the factories, were left to the care of some old woman, who fed them on bread and water, in which there was but an infinitesimal proportion of milk. The matter was one, in his opinion, calling for very serious attention.

The PRESIDENT said that one of the great objects he had had in view in Parliament in drawing attention to the question of allotments and the distribution of land among labourers was that the men might be afforded the means of obtaining proper nourishment for their children. He thought that until the policy of "three acres and a cow" was more generally recognised they would not get all that was needed in this direction. In reference to this matter, he did not think that central action was altogether desirable. What they needed rather was that steps should be taken locally to effect a remedy. He deprecated the habit of constantly saying that the State must do this and do that. In relation to legislation on this subject he thought that the trade of the country had also to be considered. Trade competition was now so keen, and foreign competitors had become so skilled, that the greatest caution was necessary so that there should be no undue hampering of trade. Nottingham afforded a notable example of the difficulties connected with the carrying on of one of the most important and one of the most valuable of the artistic industries of the country. If in Nottingham they were to interfere to any large extent with female labour the result must be, as elsewhere, to take away a large amount of trade from the country. Yet whilst recognising this there was the higher question beyond it all, of the well-being of the children. If evils resulted from the present system they ought not to allow trade competition to offer up a hecatomb of victims every year. The remedy seemed to him in the direction of some wise local action. There might with advantage be a system of control instituted with regard to the nursing of young infants, either when established in connection with factories or independently. He was convinced it would be a very valuable arrangement if local authorities would undertake the supervision of places where children were left during the absence of their mothers at work. He was above all anxious that they should not rely too much on the State, but rather that a healthy opinion should be developed in each manufacturing centre, and that local authorities should undertake the necessary work in consonance with the wishes of the inhabitants of the district. This would be much preferable to central action on the part of any department sitting at Whitehall or elsewhere.

Dr. REID, in replying on the discussion, said it had been taken for granted by the speakers that children were largely affected through the engagement of their mothers in factories. That was the main point he wished to establish. It was capable of proof that where women were engaged in factories the infant mortality was much higher than where they were not so employed. Whatever the secondary cause might be, the main cause of the increased mortality was undoubtedly the employment of women in factories. With regard to the quality of tinned milk and the supervision of food of children in general, these were matters which affected all children more or less, irrespective of position; he agreed with the importance of what had been said as to the use of narcotics in contributing to increased mortality. He thought it would be a great advantage if the period within which women, according to the Factory Acts, were allowed to return to work after their confinement was extended from one to three months. It would be possible if the period were extended for children oftentimes to have three months' suckling, whereas at present they had often none at all. One month, as at present provided for by the Act, was useless. The woman knew that at the end of the month she could return to work, and therefore she did not think it worth while to commence to suckle the child at all, whereas if the period were extended to three months very different conditions would obtain. He thought it would be of advantage if a State inquiry were instituted with a view to concentrate the evidence and produce statistics that would lead to legislative action being taken. He suggested that a resolution should be passed to the effect "that in view of the apparent injurious influence on the lives of infants arising from the practice of married women leaving their homes to engage in work this meeting is of opinion that it is desirable that a special commission should be appointed to inquire into the whole question with a view to possible legislation."

The President suggested that the better plan would be to call the attention of the Parliamentary Bills Committee to the matter, so that they might discuss it with a view of considering what steps should be taken to draw Parliamentary attention to it. He suggested a resolution in these terms: "That the attention of the Parliamentary Bills Committee be called to Dr. Reid's paper and the discussion thereon, with a view to taking action for obtaining the attention of Parliament to the cause of infant mortality pointed out in the paper and during the debate."

Dr. Reid said that he would accept the resolution. He was particularly anxious, however, that it should be made quite clear that it referred to the cause of infant mortality arising from the employment of women in factories.

Sir Walter Foster inserted words to indicate this; and Dr. Reid, having withdrawn his proposal, the resolution was carried in the following form: "That the attention of the Parliamentary Bills Committee of the Association be called to Dr. Reid's paper, and the discussion thereon, with a view to taking action for obtaining Parliamentary inquiry into the influence of the employment of women in factories on the mortality of infants."

Notes

1 S. O. Rose, 'Protective Labour Legislation in Nineteenth Century Britain: Gender, Class, and the Liberal State', in L. L. Frader and S. O. Rose (eds), *Gender and Class in Modern Europe* (Ithaca, New York: Cornell University Press, 1996), pp. 193–210.
2 'Death of Dr. George Reid, Stafford', *Tamworth Herald*, 14 November 1925, p. 6.
3 'Legal Restraint upon the Employment of Women in Factories before and after Childbirth', *British Medical Journal* 2:1648 (30 July 1892), pp. 275–278, on p. 277.
4 'Legal Restraint upon the Employment of Women', p. 278.
5 'Factory Legislation for 1895, and the Medical Profession', *British Medical Journal* 1:1838 (21 March 1896), pp. 750–751, on p. 750.

33

ANON., 'HEALTH OF LEAD WORKERS'

Labour Gazette 1 (December 1893), p. 197

The Labour Gazette was the official journal of the Labour Department of the Board of Trade. The Labour Department was tasked with the collection of statistics related to business and industry, and the journal, which was published from 1893 to 1905, provided useful information to working men and others interested in labour questions. In its first issue, the journal declared, 'With mere questions of opinion the Labour Gazette will not be concerned. The aim of the Department in the publication is to provide a sound basis for the formation of opinions and not to supply opinions'.[1] The article included here on the 'Health of Lead Workers' is typical of the journal's presentation of information. It is a summary of a report from a Departmental Committee into White Lead and Allied Industries, which had recently been submitted to the home secretary, H. H. Asquith. Based on the 1891 Factory and Workshop Act, which created a structure for controlling dangerous trades, white lead was declared a dangerous trade in May 1892. In December of 1892, the *Daily Chronicle* published a sensational article titled 'Death in the Workshops: How Women Are poisoned', which cited a doctor, Sir Thomas Oliver, stating that women were more liable to become ill from white lead. This doctor became the Departmental Committee's medical expert. According to historian Carolyn Malone, the committee proceeded with the assumption that the white lead industry was worse for women's health than men's and particularly dangerous to women's future offspring. Women involved in the trade testified to their own good health and the health of their children, but this evidence did not seem to matter. Malone also emphasizes that the women who worked with white lead earned high wages, suggesting a reason why men might want to push them out of the trade.[2] This summary of the report of this Departmental Committee in the *Labour Gazette* shows that, based on the medical evidence, the committee concluded there was general danger to all labourers working with lead but that there was more danger for women and even more danger for girls and young women. The report does not indicate what the evidence said directly, but it was strong enough for the committee to recommend that all females be excluded from working where they would be in 'direct contact' with white lead. The rest of the article is devoted to detailed recommendations for the various facets of white lead

DOI: 10.4324/9780429320323-38

trades and allied industries. Some recommendations applied to both sexes, such as having all employees undergo a medical exam once a month and, in lead smelting, 'the prohibition of anyone working more than two hours in the flue at a time'. Yet many recommendations applied only to women. For example, only females were to have a medical exam before they were employed at all in working with white lead, and no females under twenty years of age could work in a 'brushing room'.[3] These recommendations would form another type of gendered protective legislation, like Reid was advocating for new mothers in the source in Volume 1, Part 3, Chapter 32. However, the prohibition on female labour went much further. The Factory and Workshops Act of 1895 allowed the home secretary to exclude certain categories of people from dangerous trades. This clause, according to Malone, was enacted specifically to enable Asquith to execute the Departmental Committee's recommendation on women's work.[4]

'Health of Lead Workers'

THE Departmental Committee, appointed by the Home Secretary to enquire into the White Lead and Allied Industries, have issued their Report. They have extended their enquiries into England, Scotland and Wales, and visited 46 works and examined 184 witnesses.

The Report first discusses the manufacture of white lead by the old Dutch process and the Chamber process, and the effects of lead upon the health of the operatives. The conclusion is arrived at that the danger attending the old Dutch process is centred in (1) the stripping of the stacks, or "white beds," (2) the rollers, (3) the washbecks, but (4) chiefly in the stoves and the packing. The Committee further conclude that (*a*) women are more susceptible to lead-poisoning than men, and (*b*) young girls than full-grown women. On an analysis of the evidence of the doctors whom they have examined, it will be found that on question (*a*) this is the opinion of eight out of thirteen, and that only four dissent; while on (*b*) fourteen doctors agree, while three disagree.

The proposed recommendation made is the exclusion of females from all direct contact with white-lead; and it is suggested that this provision should not come into force until January 1st 1896.

This and the other recommendations of the Committee are summarised below.

The Report then discusses the substitutes for white-lead, and arrives at the conclusion that at present there is none that could take the place of carbonate of lead made by the old Dutch process, which the Committee consider may by suitable precautions be rendered comparatively free from danger.

The Report also discusses the manufacture of red and orange lead, litharge and colours, the process of lead-smelting, the manufacture of blue and yellow lead, the use of red lead in electric accumulator works, the enamelling of iron plates, and the tinning and enamelling of iron hollow-ware.

The results of an investigation into the death of a girl engaged in enamel working is also given in the report.

The Committee estimate that the number of women who would have to be replaced if the proposed exclusion is carried out would not be more than six hundred, and they point out that each of the reforms proposed is actually in force in some works in the United Kingdom.

The following is a summary of recommendations and suggestions: –

Summary of recommendations.

White Lead –

The institution of a medical examination previous to the employment of females.

The requirement of a medical certificate after absence through illness, before re-employment, for both sexes.

The prohibition of females under 20 years of age from employment.

The requirement of a certificate of birth or baptism, or other proof of age, for females, before employment.

The reduction of the price of such certificate to not more than 6d.

The abolition of female labour in all processes where there is direct contact with white lead, *i.e.*, white beds, rollers, wash-becks, stoves and packing.

The adoption of the overalls and head covering for females in the blue beds and all parts of the works.

The provision of shoes and stockings for all females employed, and the enforced wearing of these during working hours.

The provision of a hood connected with a fan for packing and storing dry white lead.

The provision of a dining-room.

The provision of a stand-pipe or hose in the white beds.

Red and Orange Lead –

The prohibition of the use of the rake in drawing charges of massicot, or of red lead, or of orange lead, from the furnace.

The prohibition of such charges being drawn from the furnace on to the floor of the workshop or factory.

The prohibition of packing massicot, red lead or orange lead, in the same place where its manufacture is carried on; and the provision of a hood, connected with a fan, for packing massicot, or orange or red lead.

The provision of bath and lavatory accommodation, with a plentiful supply of hot and cold water, soap, nail brushes, and towels.

The institution of a weekly medical inspection of all persons employed in such works.

The provision of the prescribed drink.

Colours –

The adoption of respirators and overalls wherever dust is generated.

The provision of bath and lavatory accommodation, with a plentiful supply of hot and cold water, soap, nail brushes and towels.

The prohibition of any male young person or female in such works.

Lead Smelting –

The prohibition of females and young persons from employment in cleaning the flues.

The adoption of respirators and overalls for those employed in cleaning the flues.

The prohibition of anyone working more than two hours in the flue at a time.

The requirement that everyone employed in cleaning the flues must take a bath before leaving the works.

The provision of bath and lavatory accommodation, with a plentiful supply of hot and cold water, soap, nail brushes, and towels.

Yellow Lead –

The provision of fans.

The adoption of respirators and overalls for all those engaged in dry processes; *e.g.*, carding yellow yarn, &c.

The provision of an adequate supply of Epsom salts and the prescribed drink.

The provision of bath and lavatory accommodation, with a plentiful supply of hot and cold water, soap, nail brushes, and towels.

Electric Accumulator Works –

The adoption of the respirators and overalls for mixers.

The provision of gloves and aprons for rubbers.

The provision of bath and lavatory accommodation, with a plentiful supply of hot and cold water, soap, nail brushes and towels.

Enamelling of Iron Plates –

The institution of a medical inspection of all employees at least once a month.

The prohibition of females under 20 years of age from employment in a brushing-room.

The institution of a medical examination previous to the employment of females.

The requirement of a medical certificate after absence through illness, before re-employment, for both sexes.

The provision of half-a-pint of milk and a biscuit for each female employed before beginning work.

The provision of a fan to each perforated table or bench.

The provision of a dining-room and a cloak-room.

The Tinning and Enamelling of Iron Hollow Ware –

The provision of bath and lavatory accommodation, with a plentiful supply of hot and cold water, soap, nail brushes and towels.

The requirement that everyone employed must wash face and hands before meals and before leaving the works.

The prohibition of taking any meal in any part of the works except in an apartment provided for the purpose.

The provision of a dining-room.

To apply generally –

The substitution in all copies of Special Rules, for the words "As to Persons Employed," of the words "Duties of Persons Employed."

The extension to cases of lead poisoning of the same usage as obtains in cases of accidents, namely, a compulsory report to Her Majesty's Inspector of Factories and to the Certifying Surgeon for the district.

Summary of suggestions.

White Lead –

The treatment of the washing water from the first tank below the rollers so as to render it free from acetate of lead in solution; or

The prohibition of the immersion of the workpeople's hands into this liquid.

The provision of food for the operatives.

The postponement of the abolition of female labour in processes where there is contact with white lead until 1st January 1896.

The adoption of mechanical means for stacking, stripping, drying, and packing white lead.

The discontinuance of wearing gloves for manipulating white lead.

The adoption of the cambric, bag-shaped respirator.

The postponement of stripping white beds until they are "mature."

Blue Lead –

The careful observance of all cases of lead poisoning which come to the notice of Her Majesty's Inspectors of Factories, and which have arisen in lead pipe or sheet works, in order to accumulate sufficient data on which to base future recommendations.

The Tinning and Enamelling of Iron Hollow Ware –

The prohibition of the use of lead and arsenic in the enamelling and tinning of hollow ware for kitchen purposes.

Notes

1 'The Labour Department and the Labour Gazette', *Journal of the Royal Statistical Society* 56:2 (1893), pp. 330–333, on p. 331.

2 C. Malone, 'The Gendering of Dangerous Trades: Government Regulation of Women's Work in the White Lead Trade in England, 1892–1899', *Journal of Women's History* 8:1 (Spring 1996), pp. 15–35.

3 'Health of Lead Workers', *Labour Gazette*, 1 (December 1893), Google Books, p. 197.

4 Malone, 'The Gendering of Dangerous Trades', p. 20.

34

E. DILKE, 'PREFACE', IN A. BULLEY AND M. WHITLEY, *WOMEN'S WORK*

(London: Methuen & Co., 1894), pp. v–xiii

Emilia Dilke (1840–1904) devoted much of her life to the cause of women workers. She became president of the Women's Trade Union League in 1886, remaining in that position until her death, and was committed to building women's participation in unions. She campaigned for a number of working women's causes, including the improvement of conditions in the dangerous occupations (see Volume 1, Part 3, Chapter 33).[1] In this selection, Dilke's preface to *Women's Work*, by A. Amy Bulley and Margaret Whitley, Dilke argues that in fighting to improve the conditions of labour for everyone, women and men needed to see their interests in common and not as rivals. She claims that women's assertive stances and 'extreme reaction' fighting for political reform had damaged efforts to help working women.[2] Instead of demanding equality, a demand Dilke calls 'absurd', women should have been focusing on issues such as wages, education, property rights, and the expansion of job opportunities.[3] Dilke believed, as did many late-Victorian feminists, that any reforms needed to consider the natural differences between the sexes and that equal human rights could exist in a society that also recognized the 'divergent' abilities of men and women.[4] In terms of work, Dilke argues that men and women were suited to different occupations. Women of child-bearing age, for example, worked at jobs from which they should be prohibited because of the danger to themselves and their future offspring. Dilke specifically brings up the case of married women working with white lead (see Volume 1, Part 3, Chapter 33), which was damaging not only because of the occupation itself but also because mothers left their children in a 'stranger's care' in order to go to the factory.[5] To stabilize the labour market for male breadwinners, Dilke believed married women's work had to be restricted. She regarded the industrial system as creating a market that forced women to compete with men, which lowered men's wages and caused men's unemployment. In this situation, women had no choice but to work to help feed their families. They 'are no more free to choose to work . . . than were the slaves on a Virginian Plantation'.[6] The unfortunate result of married women's work, according to Dilke, was the destruction of working-class homes and the sacrifice of 'the health of future generations'.[7] Dilke urges a rational organization of labour where men and women were employed in the jobs that were suited to them, which would end men's claims that women were 'unfit'

DOI: 10.4324/9780429320323-39

for the occupations for which they competed with men. While she supported government action to regulate the work of women of child-bearing age, Dilke did not back any other 'artificial barriers' to women's employment.[8] She concludes her preface by stressing the importance of recognizing that questions of women's labour were intimately connected to men's. Trade unionism helped all workers, and women's position should be seen as 'an essential part of the general problem' connected to unemployment, low wages, and excessive hours.[9] Dilke believed that men and women needed to recognize their 'mutual relations' in the world of work.[10] While women would have to make sacrifices for the organization of labour to function, these sacrifices were 'best for the family, best for our society and best for our national life'.[11] The definitive goal of women's trade unionism, then, was the ability of women to remove themselves from the labour market to return home. Implied here is Dilke's desire to see the male breadwinner norm made more of a reality among the working classes.

'Preface' to *Women's Work*

The writers of the present volume have a purely practical object in view. They have no desire to discuss, theoretically, the duties, rights, and responsibilities of women. They consider that it would be unwise to give prominence to considerations affecting the political or social position of women, in a work dealing specially with their industrial situation.

On the other hand, they are fully aware that there is a necessary connection between the views which appear to be in course of formation as to the proper position of women in the labour market, and the change which has taken place in the standpoint from which all questions – even the most abstract – regarding the condition of women are now discussed. Various reforms have been forced on us within the last thirty years through the necessity of recognising, legally and socially, that development in the relations of women to the state and to society which has been brought about by the pressure of the altered circumstances of modern life. Unfortunately, the agitation which has accompanied the carrying of these reforms has been characterized, in some directions, by a deplorable lack of self-control and judgment on the part of certain of those who have put themselves forward as the leaders of their sex. In the past, it must be confessed that our social system has not afforded to the majority of women those opportunities for the acquisition of disciplined habits of mind which are to be found only in bearing the responsibilities of independent action and self-government. When we hear the voices of those who have been called the "shrieking sisterhood" uplifted in frenzied violence against the male oppressor, when we are tempted to repudiate their follies, we may remember that crimes against good sense, good taste, and good feeling are, like other crimes, bred of the bitter resentment of wrong which springs in the breasts of all who awake to consciousness of the suffering inflicted by centuries of unjust rule. This being so, we may see some extenuation even of the ravings of those unhappy "wild women" who appear to hold the most serious national interests as of no importance, in comparison with the fascinating amusement of fostering an unwholesome antagonism of sex.

The clamour raised by those who have taken this line of extreme reaction has retarded the advance of public opinion in the direction of practical and needed reform, and has gravely hampered the efforts of those who have striven to arouse public interest in the attempt to better the position of women in various fields of labour. People have, not unnaturally, been alarmed by what seems to many the absurd suggestion of equality between the sexes, and, shrinking from the assertion of such principles, have adopted an attitude of hostility to the just claims of women for consideration in respect of their labour and wages, their education, the protection of their earnings and property, the removal of such trade and professional restrictions as are of an artificial character, and the opening out to them of wider means of obtaining a livelihood.

In view of the responsibilities and duties which society now imposes on women, changes in the direction of these reforms are not only reasonable but necessary in the common interest. To insist, however, that such reforms shall under no circumstances take account of the differences of sex is to fight against indisputable facts which must, in the end, prove too strong for us. There is no danger to society in the recognition of equal human rights for both sexes, if we are also ready to recognise the divergence of their capabilities, for the relations of men and women to each other, their functions in the family and the state, must ultimately be determined – however ill it may please the more ardent female reformer – by the operation of natural laws.

If we attempt to ignore these laws we are at once landed in a sea of difficulties. Take this very question of "Women's Work." At the outset we are brought face to face with facts that show us that all employments are not equally suitable to men and women. We find that, in the case of mothers at least, there are many occupations for which they are wholly unfit, but in which men may engage with impunity. Day after day we find child-bearing women compelled to labour after a fashion for which they are temporarily unfit, and which is not only the frequent cause of permanent injury to their own health, but entails a heritage of disease, or of that feeble health which falls a ready prey to disease, on all their offspring.

I have seen many married women who were habitually employed in handling white lead, and in but two instances has my question as to the health of their children been satisfactorily answered; whilst in certain branches of the potters' trade the employment of the mother not unfrequently means the death of her children in their early infancy. Even where the employment is not in itself unhealthy, its pursuit, regardless of the claims of the family – as in the case where working mothers leave their little ones at the gate of the factory to a stranger's care – has to be paid for by a high per-centage of infant mortality.

It is impossible to look into facts of this class without realising that natural laws impose severe limitations, and will probably continue to impose much the same restrictions, as to health and strength on women workers; and when these marry there arise ties which conflict, and, as far as one can see, will always conflict, with the efficiency and regularity of the labour of married women. The violation of these restrictions on any large scale not only constitutes a danger to the state by causing the steady deterioration of a large section of the population, but the intermittent character of the supply of labour from the ranks of married women greatly heightens the difficulties with which those who are concerned with the organisation of modern industry have to deal. It is indeed a commonplace now-a-days, that without improved organization and regulation of the labour of women there can be no security for the majority of breadwinners.

The present state of anarchy in the labour world, and the difficulties of our industrial situation, have been appreciably heightened by the course of conduct pursued and advised by those who persist in regarding the interests of women as in themselves separate from the interests of men. Colossal fortunes are built up in large measure by the enforced labour of women and children, who are encouraged in their suicidal rivalry with their husbands and fathers in the labour market by those who do not realise the retribution which follows on the adoption of their counsels. I have used the word "enforced" advisedly; unchecked competition is a force of great power. There are masses of workers in England who are no more free to choose their work, or to make terms for it, than were the slaves on a Virginian plantation. The Newcastle woman in the white lead works of Elswick, who counts seven little ones at her board, whose man is out of work, is tied and bound as with chains. Her man, her children, look to her for food, and at her heels are hundreds of other women in similar distress, whose breadwinners are, perhaps through no fault of their own, also out of work, or in receipt of wages wholly inadequate to the maintenance of the family. Those who encourage our women to treat men as their rivals, to compete with them, and by their competition to persistently reduce the earnings of men, are doing their best to aggravate this state of things. The wages of the husband and father being reduced by the entrance into his trade of the women who undersell him, the wife and mother needs must turn her back upon her home, and give her working day to make up the difference. In this way the homes of our working classes are too often destroyed, and the health of future generations sacrificed.

Apart from the fact that, in most trades, women have made their appearance on the scene in the capacity of "blacklegs," it must be admitted that there has been, on the side of men, something like resentment at the intrusion of women into professions or branches of industry which have been hitherto reserved to themselves. The expression by the men of this natural feeling – in the case of the doctors it was something more – has, as naturally, irritated the friends of those women who are seeking fresh means of employment; it has enabled them to appeal for sympathy and support from the public as against the "injustice" of men, and it has strengthened their determination to treat men, at all costs, as rivals and enemies who must be driven from their occupations by what I once heard one of these ladies describe, with more force than elegance, as "the cheaper animal."

To the onslaught of these shortsighted champions of the working woman's cause, the men, with equal unwisdom, have retorted by raising, on every occasion, possible or impossible, the plea of "unfitness" as a bar to the treacherous encroachments of the opposite sex, and they have thus, in their turn, tried to win popular sympathy with their efforts to prevent the entrance of women into certain coveted employments, or to expel them from others in which they have already gained a footing. "Unfit!" Yes, undoubtedly, much labour at present performed by our women is unfit, if there is any fitness in our old and cherished ideal of home and of the place of the woman in the family; but, if we once enter on the line of restricting their employment by artificial barriers, it seems to me difficult to foresee the number and variety of the complications which would ensue.

We may, however, freely concede that some interference may be necessary where, through the helplessness of the employed and the unscrupulousness of the employer, the health and wellbeing of future generations is jeopardised. In other words, certain restrictions on the labour of children and child-bearing women may be required by the interests of that society of which they are a part; further than this it seems scarcely wise to go in our demand for anything like legislative interference in respect to this matter of "unfitness." The true remedy lies in the direction of the better organisation of the trades themselves. The same too may be said of the disastrous effect on the market of that increasing supply of cheap labour which is ever swelling to larger and larger proportions through the influx of our women. Instead of encouraging them to enter into competition with men, and by so doing to drag wages down to lower and yet lower levels, the task before us is to teach them that the interests of labour are one, and that wherever they enter a trade they must in self-protection refuse to sell their labour for less than a rate proportional to that demanded by their men.

Increased and effectual organisation would do away with the causes which provoke that clamour for prohibitive legislation which, as in the case of the pit-brow women, calls forth angry protest from those who see their livelihood endangered, and intensifies that bitter spirit of rivalry of sex which is a fatal obstacle to the better and harmonious ordering of the world of industry. The only safe course for women, the only safe course for the community at large, is to consider their industrial position as an essential part of the general problem, not to be dissociated without risk from the organisation of the men. The cardinal points of the programme of the leaders of labour – the shortening of hours, the abolition of overtime, the regulation of wages, the limitation of the number of apprentices in the overcrowded trades – these are matters of chief importance to all workers, matters in which the interests of all, whether they be men or women, precisely coincide. Even where, at first sight, their interests appear to diverge, it will on further consideration be found that such sacrifice of personal freedom as the woman may be, on certain points, called upon to make, she makes for the sake ultimately of her own hearth and of her own children. Those who prefer to regard the interests of men and women as opposed must accept a view of their mutual relations which, involving as it does antagonism of sex, pits the woman against the man in an unregulated competition for employment, which, if forced to its extreme, will end by lowering the whole level of English life far more surely than the immigration of any number of "destitute aliens."

The difficulties which meet us therefore in adjusting the relations of the sexes in the great field of labour are not insuperable. Once our women workers see how much depends on their co-operation, on their self-restraint, on their standing firm they will not fail their men, and the difficulties which beset them and their position in the labour movement of the day, once solved in the full light of that which is best for the family, best for our society and best for our national life, we shall assuredly be far on our way towards the settlement of those less pressing grievances which are put forward by the idle classes. The highest interests of women in every sphere of life are indissolubly bound up with those of men, and any attempt to deal with either separately is fraught with danger to the State and to the nation.

This principle lies at the bottom of all reasoned Trades Unionism, which, in so far as it is concerned with the organisation of women's work, has for its ultimate object the restoration of as many as possible to their post of honour as queens of the hearth.

EMILIA F. S. DILKE.

76, SLOANE STREET.
May, 1894.

Notes

1 'Death of Lady Dilke: Sudden End of a Brilliant Career', *London Daily News*, 25 October 1904, p. 12; H. Fraser, 'Dilke [*née* Strong; *other married name* Pattinson], Emilia Francis, Lady Dilke', *Oxford Dictionary of National Biography*, 3 January 2008, at https://doi-org.du.idm.oclc.org/10.1093/ref:odnb/32825 [Accessed 14 June 2021].
2 E. Dilke, 'Preface', in A. Bulley and M. Whitley, *Women's Work* (London: Methuen & Co., 1894), Google Books, p. vi.
3 Dilke, 'Preface', p. vi. On the complicated politics of the women's movement, see B. Caine, *English Feminism, 1780–1980* (Oxford: Oxford University Press, 1997).
4 Dilke, 'Preface', p. vii. See S. K. Kent on 'difference feminism', *Sex and Suffrage in Britain, 1860–1914* (Princeton, NJ: Princeton University Press, 1987).
5 Dilke, 'Preface', p. viii.
6 Dilke, 'Preface', p. ix.
7 Dilke, 'Preface', p. x. Dilke clearly believed in a male breadwinner norm, where men earned enough to support wives at home. See M. Levine-Clark, *Unemployment, Welfare, and Masculine Citizenship: 'So Much Honest Poverty' in Britain, 1870–1930* (New York: Palgrave Macmillan, 2015), especially chap. 3.
8 Dilke, 'Preface', p. xi.
9 Dilke, 'Preface', p. xii.
10 Dilke, 'Preface', p. xii.
11 Dilke, 'Preface', p. xiii.

35

H. BOSANQUET, *ECONOMICS OF WOMEN'S WORK AND WAGES*

(London: P. S. King & Son, 1907), pp. 1–11

After becoming one of the first graduates from Newnham College, Cambridge University in 1889, where she concentrated in political economy, Helen Bosanquet (1860–1925) moved to London and became active in the Charity Organisation Society (COS) (see Volume 2, Part 2, Chapter 20). Her interests were located at the intersection of charity and social work, and she helped develop the COS's school of sociology and trained charitable visitors to use social science casework. She was appointed to the Royal Commission on the Poor Laws and Relief of Distress in 1905 and was influential in putting together the Majority Report (see Volume 2 Introduction).[1] This selection is a reproduction of a talk Bosanquet gave before the National Liberal Club Political and Economic Circle in 1907. Her lecture focused on economic issues that differentiated women's work from men's. She argues that six key factors hurt women in the labour market: the 'persistence of custom', the subsidiary relationship of women's labour to men's labour, the false idea that women had no dependents to support, women's domestic duties, the constant availability of domestic service jobs, and 'the nature of women themselves'.[2] To expand on these: Bonsanquet argues that the 'persistence of custom' influenced the types of jobs for which women were considered suited and parents' prioritization of sons' over daughters' education and training. She indicates that the 'marriage risk' – the custom that women marry and leave the labour force – made parents' support of their daughters' training a poor economic choice, since the money spent would be wasted. Women also suffered from the custom that dictated that they could survive on lower wages than men, since they did not consume as much. Employers tended to pay women 'customary' wages, rather than paying for what their work was worth.[3] Bosanquet states that reliance on custom could exist because women's lower-skilled labour market was always flooded, so employers always had women seeking work. In addition, women's wages were always regarded as secondary to men's, on the assumption that women would be dependent on men's wages. Bosanquet mentions the existence of 'demoralizing'

DOI: 10.4324/9780429320323-40

cases when women were forced to support their families on their own small earnings due to the decline in the husband's industry. Even though women often had to support others besides themselves, Bosanquet argues, this had not caused their wages to rise, most likely because custom did not consider women to be providers.[4] Bosanquet sees the most 'interesting' of all factors particular to women's work in the combination of women's industrial and domestic roles.[5] She critiques the idea that a woman had to stop having to 'earn her living' once she was married; rather, the work of the domestic sphere was indeed earning a living for which women should be trained.[6] She challenges the common opinion that women became unsuited for domestic roles if they had been brought up in industrial occupations. Bosanquet insists that any training was good for women to learn discipline and organization, which helped them manage their families and households. Domestic service, she believes, provided solid wages and respectable training for women's futures. In looking at the traits peculiar to women that influenced their economic lives, Bosanquet notes that women were not as strong as men and therefore would not compete with them in industries requiring strength. However, women were more adaptable than men, so they could more readily find ways to be useful economically. This, unfortunately, Bosanquet points out, could tend to depress their wages, since women took on odd jobs and remained in the labour market into old age. In conclusion, Bosanquet argues that custom was the factor hurting women's economic status that employers could most easily alter. She had no interest in changing the marriage risk, because she thought it was a good thing for women to move between occupations, even if it cost them achieving high positions in industrial or professional life. She was against married women working and criticized the 1906 Education (Provision of Meals) Act, which allowed local authorities to give elementary school children meals at school, for encouraging married women to work. She sets this act in opposition to protective legislation that limited women's hours of work, which, she argues, prevented these freed-up married women from finding jobs. In both cases, Bosanquet sees the interference of the state in a negative light, which is very much in line with COS principles. Overall, while Bosanquet was a clear advocate for improving working-class women's conditions in the labour market, she believed differences between women and men should continue to shape that market.

The Economics of Women's Work and Wages

On Monday, 11th February, 1907, the National Liberal Club Political and Economic Circle held its Sixty-third Dinner in the Committee Room of the Club.

Mrs. Jane Cobden Unwin presided, and Mrs. Helen Bosanquet read a Paper on the above subject as follows: –

In discussing this question it would be absurd to ignore the fact that to a large extent the economic conditions of women's work coincide with those of men's work. But, though in their broad outlines, the problems which offer themselves for discussion are the same, the facts with regard to women are complicated by a number of considerations which are either absent in the case of men, or have a different application; and it is with these that we are more especially concerned in the subject before us. Some of these considerations, such as the marriage risk, or the lesser needs of women, are familiar to everyone, but need more careful statement. Others have hardly received sufficient recognition. In what follows I attempt to present them separately, but it must be remembered that to do so is an effort of abstraction; in real life they will be found mingled in very various combinations.

I. *The persisting influence of custom.* I am inclined to think that even with regard to men's work and wages, the influence of custom has been too completely banished from the text-books of Political Economy. With regard to women, we are now beginning to recognise what a large part it still plays in determining their economic position. It makes itself felt primarily in three directions: –

(*a*) The kind of preparation which a girl will get for her work is largely determined by custom, which not only limits the range of occupations considered suitable for a woman, but also limits the cost which parents are willing to incur in educating their daughters. To a certain small extent it may also limit the choice open to men, but mainly in the direction of excluding low-paid industries. Where large profits or high wages are to be made – as in dress-making or cooking – custom is powerless to exclude men. And when a parent has both sons and daughters to prepare, custom always rules that the most possible shall be expended on the sons, the least possible on the daughters. Even when there is no question of an alternative, custom still rules that it is unnecessary to expend much upon a girl's training. Partly this is due to a business calculation of what I have called the marriage risk; the economic parent does not wish to have been at the cost of an industrial training which may not be needed for more than a few years, and discounts the risk by making the training as inadequate as possible. Of this mistaken calculation I shall speak again upon under another head. In the great majority of cases I am convinced that the marriage risk is only adduced to give a plausible colouring to a convenient custom.

(*b*) Custom also exercises a very adverse influence in determining what is commonly considered to be the necessary expenditure for a woman. I am, of course, speaking here only of the expenditure of women who earn their own living. For women who are spending other people's earnings custom appears to act in an opposite, though, perhaps, equally mischievous way. But there is no rank of industry from the highest to the lowest in which you may not hear the plea put forward for underpaying women, that "a woman needs less than a man." Now in so far as this plea depends upon the cubic-contents theory of the relation of the sexes (a theory which in various forms vitiates a great deal of plausible reasoning), I believe it to be quite incapable of defence. The fact that a woman does not – I will not say cannot – habitually consume so much as a man, in no way proves that it may not be as costly a matter to keep her in a condition of industrial efficiency. Indeed the very fact of her greater physical weakness would seem to suggest the contrary. The argument is far stronger when we take it as meaning that the man's wages are expected to cover the maintenance of others than himself, and I will consider subsequently how far this position is a sound one. It ceases then to be an argument from mere custom, and becomes a genuine calculation based more or less upon the needs of the case.

(*c*) It is, perhaps, in the actual determination of wages that we are most surprised to come upon custom as an important, sometimes, perhaps, the sole factor. I suspect there is no sphere of woman's work where the remuneration is not mainly determined by reference to custom, directly or indirectly. In the higher ranks, especially where women are making their way as pioneers and there is no precedent to go upon, you may constantly hear from employers such arguments as "it would not do to pay them as much as the men," or "that is about what they would get as teachers." There is seldom any reference to the relative value of the work. In low-skilled industries the appeal to custom is even more direct. In fixing his rate of pay the employer will make his wages a first charge, and determine them not by what he can afford to give, but by what it is generally considered that women ought to get. He finds, e.g., that 7s. or 10s. is the customary pay for women in the district, and fixes his piece rate so that an average worker may earn about that amount. (See Cadbury and Matheson on "Women's Work in Birmingham.")

But how is it possible that custom should continue in this age of competition to be so decisive in determining wages? It is only possible because in these low-class trades the competition is all on one side – that of the workers. The employer stands altogether above the reach of it. So far from having to compete for his workers, he need only let his standard fall low enough, and he can have, at an hour's notice, not as many as he wants, but five or six times as many as he wants. And he can treat them as he likes: he can fine them, he can cheat them, he can turn them off at half-a-day's notice, he can leave them unemployed for six months out of the twelve; whatever he does he can always have them back in superabundant numbers as soon as he wants them.

In this entire absence of competition, by what principle are wages to be regulated? That the employer falls back upon custom is probably an advantage to the workers themselves. He would not like it to be said that he was paying *much* less than other people (a little less he can explain away); he fears public opinion and the daily press; else to his short-sighted calculations there is absolutely no reason why he should not pay even less than he does. So that in this particular respect, and as regards the lowest class of workers, custom is probably a safeguard.

Of course, as soon as employers become enlightened enough to recognise that it pays better to employ a higher class of worker, even though it is not more highly skilled, the element of competition enters in again, and in order to attract and keep the steadier, healthier, more disciplined women, they offer better conditions, better wages, more regular work. Thus we get the economic anomaly of different rates of wages in the same industry and in the same district. It is the first step towards breaking down – or, rather, breaking up – the customary rate.

But, as soon as women's work becomes skilled, custom ceases to be a safeguard and becomes a barrier. There is no province of expenditure in which employers are so grudging as in the remuneration of women's work, and in which they so strenuously resist any forward movement. Defoe wrote a long and bitter denunciation of the domestic servant who had the impudence to demand as much as £6 a year, and every generation renews the outcry against the exorbitant demands of the women upon whom so much of its domestic comfort depends. Even in the occupations which approach to the professional, and with the fear of being "undersold" hanging over the men, custom cannot endure that women's earnings should approximate to those of men, and every step forward is felt as a new trespass upon the part of the "new" woman. [. . .]

II. The second great influence affecting the remuneration of women's labour is its relation to men's labour. I am not speaking here of competition between men and women; as a matter of fact they form, for the most part, non-competing groups. But the relation I have in mind is that of which the typical case occurs when the staple industry of a district is carried on by men, and subordinate industries spring up to take advantage of the presence of the women. The women's labour is then a bye-product, and, as such, is not expected to repay its cost of production. In other words, their earnings are merely subsidiary to those of the men upon whom they are dependent. This relation is not invariable – e.g. in the textile trades men and women often stand upon an equal footing. But it is very frequent, and especially so in middle-class families, where the women may work for what is little more than pocket-money. Any trade with a pretence to "gentility," such, e.g., as journalism, typewriting, even teaching, is exposed to the deteriorating influence of women who "do not need to work." The various phenomena described as "working for pocket-money wages," "underselling," the "subsidising of wages" are all different aspects of the fact that to a large extent women's earnings are still regarded as only subsidiary sources of income. This point of view tends to be perpetuated in so far as the first consideration determining the movements of a family must be the man's work. It may often happen that his industrial interests are opposed to those of the women of his family, and it is his industrial interests which must predominate. Sometimes, indeed, the process is reversed, and then we get the most demoralising conditions to be found in modern industry. There are, for instance, several districts in London at the present moment where the original staple industry has been one carried on by men; to take advantage of the unoccupied women attached to them a number of minor industries have sprung up; later on the men's industry has decayed, and from various causes the men employed in it have failed to follow the labour market. Then we get the painful spectacle of whole families endeavouring to subsist upon wages which were originally no more than an addition to the men's earnings. And it is important to note that this additional claim upon the women's wages has not the least tendency to make them rise. This brings me to a third reason which is adduced for the comparative lowness of women's earnings.

III. – Women have only themselves to support. I have already admitted that there is a good deal of truth in this axiom, and if it were stated rather as a postulate – "Let women have only themselves to support," &c. – I would admit the conclusion also. But stated baldly and positively it is a very inaccurate description of the facts. Amongst the lowest industrial class very many women are the principal wage-earners for the family. Amongst all industrial classes there are very many widows who are the sole wage-earners, and amongst single women the proportion of those who contribute to the maintenance of some other than themselves is very large. The truth seems to be that women, speaking generally, are just as eager as men to share their incomes with someone else; but the fact, as I have pointed out, seems to have no tendency to increase them, probably because the burden is not a recognised one.

IV. – I now come to what is to my mind the most interesting of the special conditions attaching to women's work. I refer, of course, to the fact that there is one great industry, combining the duties of housekeeper and mother, in which most women expect to earn their living during a part at least of their lives, and whatever may have been their occupation before. This means that the normal expectation for the industrial or professional woman is, that her life will alternate between or combine two occupations instead of being confined to one. I do not look upon this as necessarily a disadvantage in any important respect; that it sometimes appears to be so is partly due to a perverse way of looking at the facts. For instance, I regard it as misleading, and little short of stupid, to say that when a woman marries she need no longer earn her living. It is then, if ever, that she should begin to earn her living, and earn it, moreover, at one of the most important industries of the world – the industry of home-making and child-rearing. It is owing to the failure to recognise this that so many girls take up the duties of married life without any sense of responsibility, and fail so often to carry them out.

Another mistake arising out of this perverse view of the situation is that which refuses to give girls a good industrial or professional education on the ground that it will unfit them for domestic duties. Those who hold this view ought at least to train them for the domestic duties; but they don't, they simply leave them without any training at all, with a result that is deplorable for all concerned. My own experience, in very various ranks of industry, goes to show that almost any training for orderly work makes a girl more, rather than less, fit for her ultimate duties, provided of course that it does not adversely affect her health. The more completely she can become possessed of a trained intelligence, and a disciplined mind and body, the better qualified she is to undertake the arduous cares of a family. It is notably the rough, undisciplined factory girl, whose work has made no demands upon her intelligence, who proves unequal to the delicate handling of little children and the making of an orderly home. And this is the answer also to those who say that it is not worth while to invest time and money in preparing a girl for work which she may practise for only a short time. So far from risking a loss, they have a twofold chance of a return; indeed, if we look to the following generations it is a return which will multiply itself indefinitely.

V. Another condition which may almost be said to be peculiar to women is the existence of a very large and fairly well-paid industry in which they can be certain of earning a decent livelihood. The ranks of domestic service seem capable of absorbing an unlimited number of almost any age and almost any degree of skill. Certain reservations must be made. It is not true, of course, that any woman can at any moment enter into domestic service; she may be rendered quite unsuited for it by a rough undisciplined life, or she may from the first be unsuited by disposition and capacity, and I wholly disagree with those who find something culpable in a girl's preference for a more independent life than that of service. Still, it must, I think, be the case that this large and, on the whole, well-paid industry has a steadying effect on the field of women's work as a whole.

VI. Finally we must not omit the nature of women themselves as determining the conditions of their work. It is difficult to generalise about this, since women differ amongst themselves almost as much as they differ from men. But it is safe to say that on the whole they have not the same physical strength as men, and cannot therefore compete or co-operate to any purpose in industries requiring merely physical strength. The only other generalisation which I am inclined to make about them is that they are more adaptable, more given to what the Germans call *sich fügen*, readier to turn their hands to anything, and to accept whatever comes along. The economic effects of this are striking. For instance, of the old people in the workhouses by far the larger number are men. In Lancashire they explain this by saying that a woman is worth more all her life than a man. Unhappily for the woman this does not mean that she gets higher wages, only that she never ceases to be useful to someone from the days when she "minds" brothers and sisters almost as big as herself, to the old age in which she is willing to turn her hand to any odd jobs of sewing and washing, or to earn a wretched pittance at some sweated trade. One effect of this is that she lingers on in the labour market, and does her share towards depressing wages. It is, in short, another aspect of the fact that in women's work there is less unemployment and more underpayment than in men's. Here, then, is a complex of conditions more or less peculiar to women's work. How far is it possible or desirable to modify them?

If we take first the persistence of custom, I have little hesitation in saying that women would get on better without it. It is true that it probably prevents bad conditions being still worse in the lowest ranks of industry; like the brake on the wheel, it prevents the cart slipping backwards downhill. But, also like the brake on the wheel, it checks any movement upwards, and if we can gain a forward impetus we can dispense with the brake. And the conditions imposed by custom are of all others those which seem to be most within the power of human volition; when once they are seen to be wrong or unnecessary they vanish as a bad dream vanishes when we wake.

It is very different with the next consideration: the fact that women's industries must follow those of the men, and, as a rule, be more or less secondary to them. I do not see how this difficulty, which is one of localisation, is to be entirely overcome, but I think that its effects may be much reduced when other conditions are modified.

The consideration that women have only themselves to support I may pass over; as far as it is true it is likely to remain true, and I see no reason to think that to add to their responsibilites would improve their position.

With respect to the marriage risk, we may take it that nothing can alter the fact that the majority of women must alternate between two occupations – the industrial and the domestic. Nor do I, for my part, desire to see this altered. There is no particular merit in passing one's life in always doing the same thing; and though the alternation probably militates against the chances of a woman attaining the highest rank in any profession, there are great advantages to be set on the other side. It is worth noting here, that the higher the kind of work engaged in, the less the loss of power incurred in a change. It is the man or woman whose skill lies all in the fingers, and none in the brain, who finds it difficult to take up a new occupation.

But what might be changed, and in the majority of cases needs greatly to be changed, is the attempt made by so many women in the industrial classes to carry on both occupations together – to earn their living in two ways at once. There are various reasons why they do this – partly they are driven to it by sheer necessity, partly by the mistaken estimate of the housewife's duties to which I have referred, and partly because they find work outside the home more interesting than in. The remedies must also be various. Much would be effected by the better domestic training of girls; duties become more interesting in proportion as we learn to carry them out effectively. But also we need a great strengthening of public opinion on the matter of married women's work – or, more precisely, of the mothers of young children going out to work. Had there been any real appreciation of the evils involved in it, the new Act for feeding school children could never have been passed in its present form. Indeed, it might quite appropriately have been entitled an Act for the Promotion of Married Woman's Work. The difficulty of the situation created by it may be made apparent by considering its connection with the proposal sometimes made for prohibiting the employment of married women in factories, &c. The contradiction involved in first legislating to relieve mothers of their home duties, and then legislating to prohibit their seeking duties elsewhere, would be startling. But there is just as great a contradiction operative – though less clearly formulated – between the views of those who deprecate married women's work and of those who advocate school-feeding, though no doubt they are often combined in the same person.

Notes

1 J. Harris, 'Bosanquet [*née* Dendy], Helen', *Oxford Dictionary of National Biography*, 23 September 2004, at https://doi-org.du.idm.oclc.org/10.1093/ref:odnb/37208 [accessed 14 June 2021]. For more on Bosanquet in her context alongside other women developing social work, see J. Lewis, *Women and Social Action in Victorian and Edwardian England* (Palo Alto, CA: Stanford University Press, 1991).

2 H. Bosanquet, *Economics of Women's Work and Wages* (London: P. S. King & Son, 1907), Gale, *Making of the Modern World*: GALE|U0112882010, pp. 2, 9.

3 Bosanquet, *Economics*, p. 4.

4 Each of the issues arose because of the male breadwinner norm. See, for example, M. Levine-Clark, *Unemployment, Welfare, and Masculine Citizenship: 'So Much Honest Poverty' in Britain, 1870–1930* (New York: Palgrave Macmillan, 2015), especially chap. 3.

5 Bosanquet, *Economics*, p. 7.

6 Bosanquet, *Economics*, p. 7.

INDEX

'Address to the Female Chartists of Manchester to Their Sisters of England, Ireland, Scotland, and Wales, An' 176–180
'Address to Working Men, An' 22, 41–47
Adshead, Joseph 22, 58–64
advice literature 4, 28, 41, 43–47, 65, 75, 77–80, 223, 225–232, 254, 256–257
agricultural labourers 2, 7, 28, 35, 38, 148; adjustment to machines 118, 201; census tables 206; destruction of machinery 117, 118, 123; migration of 2; poverty 151, 253; social welfare 144; Tolpuddle Martyrs 181; women in 242–248, 251
agriculture 28, 120, 148, 152; displacement of hand-labour in 205–209; economics of 139–140; objection to machinery in 119; rural ideal and 22, 65; women and children employed in 240–253
Alpert, Daniel 12
Americans with Disabilities Act of 1990 10
anti-Corn law politics 41
Artizan 29, 258–262, 294
Asquith, H. H. 321

Barham Tracts 75
Benbow, William 180n9
Bentham, Jeremy 3, 20
Beveridge, William 3, 9, 13
Bitter Cry of Outcast London, The 305
Booth, Charles 9
Bosanquet, Helen 29, 334–342
Boyer, George 5
Bray, John Francis 21, 22, 48–49, 51
breadwinner norm 4, 6, 15n25, 17n51, 26, 114n6, 234, 328
Brierley, Benjamin 26, 194
British Medical Journal (BMJ) 311
British Periodicals, ProQuest 9
British Weekly: A Journal of Social and Christian Progress, The 304–305
British Workman 1, 22, 23, 100, 287; on the nobility of labour 65–73; sentimental depictions of working-class women in 267–275; on women's labour 28
Bronte, Charlotte 26
Bulley, A. Amy 327–332
Burnett, John 24
Burns, John 304
Burrows, George Crisp 24, 133–142

capitalism: conditions of industrial 23, 100–101; critiques of 3–4; devotion to work and 3; Max Weber on 3; men's identities in 4; Protestantism and 22; unemployment as a structural problem of 12–13
Carlyle, Thomas 3, 9, 14n12, 22, 65
Carpenter, William 24, 181–191
charity 154, 237; classifications of the poor and unemployed and distribution of 8; dependence on 12; efforts to curb indiscriminate 6; individual moral failings and dependence on 3; recommendations for avoiding need for 39, 43; technical schools and 289; women supported by 296
Chartism 25–26, 181; J. F. Bray and 48; women and 27, 28, 176–180, 233–238

Chartist Circular 21, 22; 'The Production and Distribution of Wealth' 51–57; *see also* Chartism
cheapness of goods: increased supply and 126; mechanization and 23, 24, 124, 133, 138, 139, 184
childbirth, women's work before and after 311–320
children, agricultural employment of 252–253
Cholera Preventible 254
Christianity 20; *British Workman* on the working-man and 72–73; Rev. Oxenden on labouring man and 75–80
City Girl, A 304
Clark, Anna 24, 176
class formation: investing capital at home and 41–42; lower middle 106, 287; middle-class separate spheres ideal 28, 267; mid-Victorian fixation on work and 2–6; New Poor Law and 2; upper class idlers and 22; women and 4, 223, 240, 338
Cobbett, William 21, 35–39
Commonweal 23, 100
competition: among labourers 44, 162, 203; emigration and 154; employers embrace of machinery for 202; foreign 152, 194, 198, 215, 279, 319; between machines and human labour 124, 138–139, 142, 190, 209, 218; between men and women workers 285–286, 296, 298–300, 302, 312, 331–332, 338; open markets 20, 135–137; wages and profits reduced by 208, 297–298, 337–338
'condition of England' novels 26, 193
'Condition of the Hand-Loom Weavers' 181–191
Contemporary Review 1
Copley, Esther 27, 254–257
Cottage Comforts 254
cotton famine 276–277
cotton industry 20, 56, 166, 168–169, 306–307; census numbers on labourers in 217; cotton famine and 276–277; dignity of labour and 22, 68; foreign demand and 147, 151, 153; machinery in 124–125, 129–130, 131, 184–187; *The Petition of the Undersigned Operative Spinners and Others Employed in the Spinning of Cotton Wool Into Yarn, in Ashton-Under-Lyne and Its Neighbourhood* 129–132; women working in 256, 278–279, 291
COVID-19 pandemic 10, 11–12, 18n63
Cowle, Sarah 176–180

Daily Chronicle 321
Daily News 294
dangerous trades 321–322, 323–326
degradation of labour 56, 101, 104, 130, 193, 223, 261
deservedness 6, 13
destitution 5–7
Diary of a Nobody 106
Dickens, Charles 26, 35, 193–194, 195–197
'Dignity of Labour, The' 68–71
Dilke, Emilia 29, 327–332
disability studies 10
Disraeli, Benjamin 26
Distress in Manchester 22, 58–64
domestic ideal *see* breadwinner norm, separate spheres
domestic service: as deficient for training of wives 287, 290; increased demand for 279, 334, 340; married women in 27; women advised to pursue 28, 76, 224, 281, 335; women leaving 287; women limited to working in 297
domestic sphere 4
domestic violence 41
Dozen Ballads for the Times About White Slavery, A 263–266

Economics of Women's Work and Wages 334–342
education of women 258–262
Elizabethan assistance from the state 1–2
emigration, as remedy for unemployment 7–8
employment conditions 3, 5, 6, 83; for emigrants 8; harsh 22, 27–28; health of 84–98; investigations of 82; workers' demands for better 35–36
equality of rights 49
Evangelicalism 20, 25, 267

factories 25; division of labour in 23, 259; health dangers of 27–28, 321–326; immortality of 20, 25–26; reform of 25, 130; women and 27–28, 223–232, 254–257, 311–320; work-discipline 20
factory girls 27, 104, 254–255, 256–257, 281
factory reform movement 25, 129, 130
'Female Education and Female Labour' 258–262
'Few Words to the Wives of Working Men, A' 28
fiction, Victorian 26; *Hard Times* 26, 193–197; *Tales and Sketches of Lancashire Life* 26, 194, 197–199
'Finery and Freedom, or Lucy's Choice' 28
Foster, Joseph 117–118, 122, 124
free trade/free markets 20, 24, 43, 46; debates over 135–137; George Poulett Scrope on 144–152; John Maxwell on 161; and trade unions 43–44, 46; women's work and 298; *see also* political economy
Frost, John 177

Gaskell, Elizabeth 26
gender norms 8, 13n7, 17n51, 24, 27, 29; Chartism and 176, 233; domestic sphere 4; social construction of gender and 295; *see also* breadwinner norm; masculinity
'genuine unemployed' 7
gig economy 11–12
Glasier, John Bruce 1, 23, 100–104
gospel of work 1–3, 13n2, 14n12, 22
government/state intervention 7
Great Exhibition of 1851 3, 14n16
Great Unwashed, The 28, 287–292
Grossmith, Weedon 106

Hall, John Charles 23; on health of filers and grinders 82–98
Hall, Newman 65
handloom weavers 24, 117–118, 119, 124–126, 182; Benjamin Brierley 194; George Scrope on 146–148; Hand-loom Weavers' Central Committee 144–145, 148–155; *Manual Labour vs. Machinery* on 157–173; political economy and the condition of 144–155; William Carpenter on 188–191
Hardie, Keir 100
Hard Times 26, 193–197
Harkness, Margaret 28, 304–310
'Health of Lead Workers' 321–326
health of workers 27–28, 31n20, 82–83, 85–88, 93–98, 241–242, 243, 245–247, 250, 321–326
History of Slavery and Its Abolition, A 254
Hobson, J. A. 1, 3, 12–13
'Honest Toil' 1, 23, 100–104
Hood, Thomas 263
Household Words 193
Howitt, Mary 65
'Hungry Forties' 58
Hyndman, Henry 100

idleness 72; Evangelical views of 20; reformers efforts to cure 3, 22, 142; machinery and 139–140; women and 227, 254, 258, 279, 301
idlers 7, 21, 48, 75; costs of 54–55; critiques of upper-class 22, 55; *vs.* producers 49, 51; unwilling 53
Illustrated London News 82
independence 2, 7–8, 12; self-help and 3
industrialization 6, 29; changes brought on by 21; loss of work with 23; social consequences of 26, 193; *see also* machinery; mechanization
industrial revolution, the 20; *see also* industrialization
investigation of character 13
Ireland 8

Jones, William 177

Kinnear, John Boyd 29, 294–303

labour: degradation of 56, 101, 104, 130, 193, 223, 261; productive and unproductive 8, 54, 75; protective legislation for 82–83, 311–312, 322, 335; sweated 263, 305; unskilled 202, 207–208, 217, 334; *see also* manual labour
'Labourer at His Work, The' 75–80
Labour Gazette 321–326

Labouring Man's Book, The 22, 75–80, 100
Labour-Saving Machinery 201–219; on displacement of general labourers by machinery 209–217; on displacement of hand-labour in agriculture 205–209
Labour's Thanksgiving Hymn 67
Labour's Wrongs and Labour's Remedy 21, 48–49
labour theory of value 21, 48, 65
laissez-faire economics 2, 24, 25, 41; *see also* political economy
landowners 1, 120, 161, 294; Chartists on 51; protectionist impulses of 20; revolts against 203
lead workers 321–326
Lees, Lynn Hollen 5
'Legal Restraint Upon the Employment of Women in Factories Before and After Childbirth' 311–320
Leggeth, H. 176–180
liberalism 2, 3, 41; individual property rights and 36; *see also* free trade, laissez-faire economics; political economy
Life through Labour's Eyes 23, 106–113
Livesey, Joseph 22, 27, 254; 'An Address to Working Men' 41–47; 'To the Females Employed in Factories and All Our Large Manufacturing Establishments' 223–232
Lloyd George, David 13
local vs central government 6
Locke, John 35
London Labour and the London Poor 304
London Review 294
Luddite Rebellion 117

MacDonald, Ramsay 100
machinery 23–26; displacement of general labourers by 209–217; displacement of hand-labour in agriculture by 191–192n1, 205–209; labour-saving 203–205; *Machinery as it Affects the Industrial Classes and the Employment of Children in Factories* on 181–191; *A Word to Electors. Letters to the Present Generation on the Unrestrained Use of Modern Machinery Particularly Addressed to My Countrymen and Fellow Citizens* on 133–142; *The Working Man's Companion* on 117–128; *see also* mechanization of work
Machinery as it Affects the Industrial Classes and the Employment of Children in Factories 181–191
'Machinery Creates a Demand for Manual Labour' 181–191
Making of the English Working Class, The 24
Malone, Carolyn 321
Malthus, Thomas 21
Malthusianism 21
'Man and His Work, A' 106, 108–109
manhood *see* masculinity
manual labour 24–25, 108–109; displaced from agriculture by machinery 205–209; as honest toil 100, 103; John Maxwell on 157–173; machinery creating demand for 120, 141, 181–191; pain of transition for 24; respect and moral uplift of 22, 106; value attached to 6, 8, 10, 21, 23, 66; *see also* handloom weavers
Manual Labour vs. Machinery 157–173
married women's work 27, 245, 258, 327, 330, 335, 341–342; medical debates over 311–320; regulation of 29
Marx, Karl 4
Mary Barton 26
masculinity 4, 6–7, 56, 66, 72, 106–108; breadwinner norm and 4, 6, 15n25, 17n51, 26, 114n6, 234, 328; competition between men and women workers and 285–286, 296, 298–300, 302, 312, 331–332, 338; respectability and 107–113
Maxwell, John 24, 157–173, 173n4
Mayhew, Henry 304
McClelland, Keith 4
Mearns, Andrew 305
mechanization 2, 4, 23–26; benefits of 23, 133; disadvantages to workers 11, 26; effects on men *vs.* women 29–30; literary depictions of 193–199; *see also* handloom weavers; machinery

men, breadwinner norm and 4, 6, 15n25, 17n51, 277, 335
men's labour: displacement by machines 29–30; displacement by women 257n4, 285–286, 296, 298–300, 302, 312, 331–332, 338
Mersey Magazine 106
Methodist movement 20
Milligan, George 23, 106–113
moral economy 25, 129
Moral Reformer 22; 'An Address to Working Men' 41–47; 'To the Females Employed in Factories and All Our Large Manufacturing Establishments' 223–232
Morris, William 9, 23, 35, 100
Munro, Alexander 28, 276–286

needleworkers 28, 263, 265–266, 267, 270–275
New Poor Law *see* Poor Law (New Poor Law/Poor Law Amendment Act of 1834)
Nokes, Tom 37–38
North and South 26
Northern Star 176, 180n9, 233

Oastler, Richard 25, 28, 129, 181
O'Brien, Bronterre 180n9
O'Connor, Feargus 180n9
'Only a Working Man' 106–107, 109–111
Our Unemployed Females and What May Best Be Done for Them 276–286
Out of Work 304
Oxenden, Reverend Ashton 22, 75–80
Oxford Chronicle 254

Pall Mall Gazette 294
'Palm-Workers' 304–310
parasitic aristocracy 48; *see also* idlers
Past and Present 65
patriarchy 4
paternalism 21–22, 25, 36, 41, 129
pauperization 6
Pattison, William 51
Petition of the Undersigned Operative Spinners and Others Employed in the Spinning of Cotton Wool into Yarn, in Ashton-Under-Lyne and its Neighbourhood 129–132
political economy 2, 20–22, 26, 203, 218, 301; Charles Dickens on 193; George Poulett Scrope on handloom weavers and 144–155; Helen Bosanquet on women's work and 334–336; John Maxwell on 161; laissez-faire economics 25
Political Register 35
Poor Law (New Poor Law/Poor Law Amendment Act of 1834) 1–5, 11–12; factory movement and 25; 'The Present Condition of British Workmen' on 174–175; *see also* Poor Law Commission
Poor Law Commission 17n47
Poor Man's Guardian 144
poverty/destitution: depictions of 5, 23, 46, 48–64, 175; experiences of 4–5, 164, 166, 193, 223–232, 267–275; of labourers 41–47; in Manchester, Adshead on 22, 58–64; production and distribution of wealth and 51–57
Practical Sanitation: A Handbook for Sanitary Inspectors and Others Interested in Sanitation 311
'Present Condition of British Workmen, The' 174–175
Preston Chronicle 1
Preston Temperance Advocate 41
Price, Sarah 27, 233–234, 237–238
Principles of Political Economy 23–24
'Production and Distribution of Wealth, The' 51–57
productive/unproductive classes 8, 54, 75
progress: Chartist political 176; Great Exhibition of 1851 showcasing Britain's 3; of mechanical inventions 285; resistance to 120, 133; of science 297
property rights 35–39
prostitution 27, 51, 57, 224, 264, 267
protective legislation 82–83, 311–312, 322, 335
Protestant Ethic and the Spirit of Capitalism, The 3
Proverbial Philosophy 263
Punch 263

'Question of Machinery Fairly Stated, The' 181–191

radicalism 21, 24–25, 35–36, 48, 51–52, 133
ragged school movement 58, 64n1
reform movements: anti-Corn law 41
Reid, George 28–29, 311–320
religion 20, 71, 161; honour and 103
Reports of Special Assistant Poor Law Commissioners on the Employment of Women and Children in Agriculture 240–253
Representation of the People Act, 1832 13n2
respectability 2, 5–6; of honest toil 21–23, 41; masculinity and 107–113; women's 27
Ricardian socialism 21, 48
Ricardo, David 21; on machinery effects on employment 23–24
Right of Women to Labour, The 294–303
right to property 35–36, 158, 327; *see also* property rights
Ross, George 51
rural ideal 22, 65, 194
Ruskin, John 9, 23, 35, 100

Samuelson, James 24, 201–219
Scrope, George Poulett 24, 144–155
self-help 3, 41
separate spheres 3, 20, 28–29, 267
Shirley 26
short-time movement *see* factory reform movement
skilled labour, decline of 202, 207–208, 217, 334
slavery, rhetoric of 25, 100, 108, 234; to critique factory 145; *see also* white slavery
Smiles, Samuel 3, 14n12
Smithies, Thomas Bywater 22, 65, 66
Social Democratic Federation (SDF) 100
social hierarchy 36, 48, 66
Socialist League 23
Society for the Diffusion of Useful Knowledge (SDUK) 24, 117–128, 133–134
state intervention *see* protective legislation
Stiles, John 37–38
Struggle for the Breeches: Gender and the Making of the British Working Class 24
surplus labour 3
sweated labour 2, 27, 263, 305, 306–310, 340
Sybil 26

Tales and Sketches of Lancashire Life 26, 194
temperance movement 22, 41, 43
Thompson, Dorothy 25
Thompson, E. P. 20, 21; on handloom weavers 24; on social norms and the poor 25
thrift 2, 22, 283
Toilers in London; or Inquiries Concerning Female Labour in the Metropolis 304–310
'Toiler's Toast, The' 106, 112–113
Tolpuddle Martyrs 181
Tosh, John 4, 26–27
'To the Females Employed in Factories and All Our Large Manufacturing Establishments' 223–232
'To the Labourers of England, on Their Duties and Their Rights' 21, 35–39
Trades of the Sheffield, The 82–98
trade unions 29, 41, 43–44, 46, 295, 327–332
Tupper, Martin Farquhar 263–266

unemployed, attitudes toward the 2, 12
unemployed workers, efficiency of 11
unemployment: as a category 1–9; Chartists on 51–52; cyclical 5; 'discovery of' 2–7; economic meanings of 2–13; emergence of public discourse on 5; middle-class attitudes to 2, 8, 12; moral meanings of 2–4, 6–8, 12; norm of male breadwinners and 4; politics of 7; women and 276–286
Unemployment: A Problem of Industry 9
unskilled labour, growth of 202, 207–208, 217, 334
urbanization 2, 21, 110, 182, 203, 282
urban living: corruption from 22; degeneration from 4, 130
utilitarianism 3, 20, 26

Walker, Mary Anne 28, 233, 235–237
wealth, distribution of 51–57
Weber, Max 3
welfare state 5–6, 13
white slavery 28, 263–266
Whitley, Margaret 327–332
Williams, Zephaniah 177
willingness to work 8
Winding Road to the Welfare State, The 5
Women's Work 327–332
women 12–13, 26–30; in agriculture 242–253; Chartism on 27, 28, 176–180, 233–238; corruption of 26, 194, 224; displacement of men 2, 257n4, 285–286, 296, 298–300, 302, 312, 331–332, 338; domestic role 4, 6–7, 20; in domestic service 27–28, 76, 224, 279, 281, 287, 290, 297, 334–335, 340; education of 258–262; in factories 27–28, 223–232, 254–257, 311–320; factory girls 27, 104, 281; immorality of 233, 241, 250, 253; infant mortality and 28–29; labour market 302, 328, 329–330, 334–335; in prostitution 27, 51, 57, 224, 264, 267; sentimental depictions of working-class 267–275; social position of 294–303; sweated labour of London and other cities 304–310; trade unions and 29, 295, 327–332; unemployed 276–286; value of 27, 254–255; wages of 334–342; and white slavery 263–266; and childbirth 311–320; as working men's wives 287–292
Word to Electors. Letters to the Present Generation on the Unrestrained Use of Modern Machinery Particularly Addressed to My Countrymen and Fellow Citizens, A 133–142
work 1–19; as art 27, 111, 113, 160, 162, 207–208, 219, 313; as a blessing 72–73; classical economics on 21; COVID-19 pandemic and 10, 11–12; dignity of 4, 21–23, 41, 68–71, 103, 107, 112; by disabled persons 10; duties and rights of labourer in 35–39; equality and 49; Evangelicalism and 20; by manual labourers 24–25, 108–109; narratives of dignity of labour and 22–23; nobility of 65–73; pride in 109–111; respectability of honest 21–23, 100–104; spirituality of 22; Victorian values around 2–4, 8, 12, 14n9; as white slavery 263–266; *see also* handloom weavers; machinery; mechanization; women
work-discipline 20
workers *see* agricultural labour; children; competition; domestic service; employment conditions; factories; factory girls; handloom weavers; health of workers; labour; lead workers; machinery; manual labour; married women's work; men's labour; needleworkers; skilled labour; sweated labour; unskilled labour; women; work; work identities
work identities 4, 58
work imperative 2, 6–8, 13, 13n7, 20–21
working-class families: domestic skills of wives in 288; industrialization and destruction of 26, 177; male breadwinner norm and 4, 6, 15n25, 17n51, 234, 285
working hours 25
Working Man's Companion, The 117–128, 134
'Working Men's Homes and Wives' 287–292
work, pride in 109–111
Wright, Thomas 28, 287–292

Young Women of the Factory, or Friendly Hints on Their Duties and Dangers 254–257

For Product Safety Concerns and Information please contact our EU representative GPSR@taylorandfrancis.com
Taylor & Francis Verlag GmbH, Kaufingerstraße 24, 80331 München, Germany

www.ingramcontent.com/pod-product-compliance
Lightning Source LLC
LaVergne TN
LVHW010630300926
849162LV00001B/109

* 9 7 8 0 3 6 7 3 3 5 1 5 1 *